The Keswick Fruit Festoons.

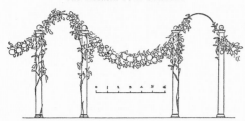

Arches and Festoons.—We can supply and fix these in a variety of designs from the most rustic forms, in peeled larch or oak, to elaborate designs in wrought iron. In the Keswick Fruit Festoons, as illustrated, the posts are turned, but they can be made square, and have double arch bars instead of single as shewn (see page 18). The swag is formed of wrought iron chain. When running for a considerable length on both sides of a walk, a very pretty effect may be obtained by carrying flat arches across the walk from each post to the posts on opposite side. We strongly recommend this form of arch and festoon for positions in which, whilst desiring some form of decoration, it is undesirable to obstruct the view.

Prices may be obtained for arches or swags ready for fixing, or for the work fixed complete. As illustration, would cost 10s. per yard run on rail.

The Broughton Rose Festoons.

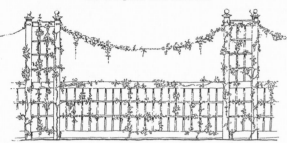

The Broughton Festoons are designed with a view to use in positions where a fence is necessary, but must be such as to be in itself an integral part of the garden scheme. The effect, when placed along either side of a paved walk with archbars across the walk between the posts, and covered with rampant roses and foliage vines, is unsurpassed, especially if the walk have some attractive terminal features, such as one of the arbours on page 22.

Price in deal, painted four coats, 8 feet 6 inches between the standards, hand rail 3 feet high, posts 6 feet 9 inches, extreme height with open link wrought iron chain suspended from ornamental wrought iron brackets, per bay £3 5s. 0d. In oak, per bay £3 15 0. Fixing extra.

The Graythwaite Garden Espalier.

A really effective Garden Espalier is seldom seen, the mistaken attempts to make them as light in appearance as possible having resulted in flimsy unstable Espaliers which in a very short time are out of line and shape. The above design shews an attempt to secure all the requirements of an Espalier, and at the same time a firm and lasting piece of work. As shewn it is only 4 feet 6 inches high, but it can be erected to any height, and with as many strained wires as required. These Espaliers can be made in either Deal or Oak, and fixed on a dwarf wall as in the illustration, or with posts set into drain pipes let into the ground, with the interspaces between pipe and post filled in with cement.

As illustration, in pitchpine, 3/6 per yard (curbing not included). Arches 12/- each extra.

The Applethwaite Trellis.

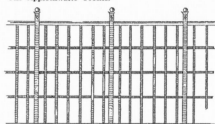

The Applethwaite Trellis, 5 feet high with 3 by 3 square posts, 4 feet 6 inches apart, with sunk design in heads, moulded caps and balls, 3 by 2 top, 4 by 3 bottom rail and 1½ by ⅜ lattices, nail rivetted at each crossing, fixed together at works in bays, and painted three coats, price per yard   10/6

The same design but 6 feet 6 inches high, requiring a middle rail, per yard   13/6

View of the Applethwaite Trellis in the larger size, as shewn above, made by us and fixed to form a climber covered screen near a quaint old-fashioned building in Surrey which is used as a laundry.

Section 9.—Porches.

Porches for the main entrance of small houses, and the garden entrance of larger ones, which are artistic and well adapted to their surroundings, are rarely seen. We give on this page two specimens of porches which are at the same time simple and harmonious in design, but as every situation has its own peculiarities to which the design must be adapted, we shall be pleased to submit designs and estimates suitable to each case on learning full particulars and requirements.

The Avon Garden Table.   The Heathcote Table.

The Avon Garden Table, a strong and simple but nicely proportioned table, made to stand exposure to the weather.

Price in deal, painted, 2 ft. 6 in. in dia. £1 10 0   Price in oak, painted, 2 ft. 6 in. in dia. £1 15 0
do.   do. 3 ft.   do.   1 15 0   do.   do. 3 ft.   do.   2 0 0

The Heathcote Table, a light table for conservatories, verandas, summerhouses, &c.

In deal, painted, 2 feet diameter . £1 5 0   In oak, 2 feet diameter . . . £1 10 0
do.   do. 3 feet do. . 1 10 0   do.   do. 3 feet do. . . . 1 15 0

The Downs Table, originally designed to stand on rough cobble paving. It has two distinct bearing points on each leg. An exceptionally strong table, very suitable for afternoon tea out of doors, having a large shelf below.

In deal, painted, 2ft. 6in. across the top £1 10 0   In oak, 2ft. 6in. across the top . £1 15 0
do.   do. 3ft. 6in.   do.   2 0 0   do.   do. 3ft. 6in.   do. . 2 5 0

The Langdale Table, designed in keeping with the Langdale circular seat, with shelves on all four sides for ...

In ...   , 2 ft. 6 in. . . . £2 15 0
d...   3 ft. . . . 3 0 0

The Langdale Table.

Thomas Mawson

Thomas Mawson
Life, gardens and landscapes

JANET WAYMARK

F

FRANCES LINCOLN LIMITED
PUBLISHERS
www.franceslincoln.com

Dedication
To PETER

Frances Lincoln Ltd
4 Torriano Mews
Torriano Avenue
London NW5 2RZ
www.franceslincoln.com

Thomas Mawson: Life, gardens and landscapes
Copyright © Frances Lincoln 2009
Text copyright © Janet Waymark 2009
Picture credits are listed on page 240

First Frances Lincoln edition published in the UK and the US in 2009

A catalogue record for this book is available from the British Library.

ISBN 13: 978-0-7112-2595-4

Printed and bound in Singapore

9 8 7 6 5 4 3 2 1

Commissioned and edited by Jane Crawley
Designed by Ian Hunt

ENDPAPERS *Mawson Brothers' Catalogue of Garden Furniture*,
published at the beginning of the twentieth century, stressed the need
for the garden designer to know about the crafts which accompanied
garden making such as building walls and providing garden furniture,
as well as horticulture and arboriculture. The catalogue showed
Mawson Brothers could supply everything from dovecotes to sundials
and from summer houses to boats 'for ornamental water'.

TITLE PAGE Graythwaite Hall in the Lake District was Thomas
Mawson's first important commission. The view from the formal
terrace of rhododendrons and azaleas framing green lawns and distant
woodland was to be a typical Mawson landscape.

Contents

Preface

HOW IS IT THAT the most prolific garden, park and civic landscape maker of Edwardian times, Thomas Hayton Mawson, has remained on the fringes of published appraisal? A man who designed parks and gardens for royal families in Europe, and some of the leading industrialists of the day; a man with private and public commissions in nearly every county in England and in Scotland, Wales, Greece, Denmark, Germany, France and Canada? It seemed to me that it was high time that Mawson's story was told. His wide-ranging abilities made him the most sought-after professional of his age, and gave him international status from the beginning of the twentieth century to his death in 1933. Thomas Mawson used his architectural skills to shape gardens which blended into the landscape and used his horticultural knowledge of trees, shrubs and plants to design formally near the house and informally round the perimeter – his composite style. But he was much more than a garden maker. He designed parks with imagination and style, and entered wholeheartedly into shaping the new realms of town planning – which he called civic art – because he felt that the beautification of towns helped people to live better lives.

Working as a gardener as well as a landscape architect, Mawson wanted to give practical advice to those who needed it and five editions of *The Art and Craft of Garden Making*, with illustrations of completed commissions, instructed and delighted many readers. The same approach was adopted for the equally successful *Civic Art* for town planners. Mawson was anxious that there should be professional instruction for landscape architects and he was invited to lecture on the first course of its kind in Britain at Liverpool University.

The Edwardian garden has long been the delight of wanderers round country houses. Harold Peto's architectural skills at Easton Lodge and his sublime water garden at Buscot, and Gertrude Jekyll's horticultural coordination of colour and drifts at Hestercombe and Barrington Court are well known. William Robinson enthused over the natural arrangement of species which enjoyed the same conditions, while Harry Inigo Triggs compiled his *Formal Gardens in England and Scotland* in 1902 in praise of geometry. Edwin Lutyens' cooperation with Jekyll finally ended the war between architects and horticulturists as to who should have territorial rights in the garden.

Mawson offered so much more than this: but how did he achieve it? As I began to research the Mawson trail, travelling through Canada and Greece as well as visiting sites in Europe and Britain, it became obvious that this was to be the history of a family, not just of one man. Thomas Mawson could not have attracted the astonishing breadth of commissions – from country house landscapes to small suburban gardens, from town parks to the great parks on the wildnesses of the Rivington Pikes, from houses in Hest Bank to town plans in Exeter and Northampton, Canada and Greece – without the contribution of his siblings, his children and their families.

He worked on small and large commissions, for the small householder, for aristocrats, for the new industrial rich and for crowned heads in Europe. He was always on the move, cigarette in hand, making friends, surveying sites and working up ideas until illness slowed him down in the late 1920s. There is space for only a selection of sites to illustrate this book from the hundreds he must have worked on. With the help of his family, he pursued a remarkable career, much fuller and with more to contribute to society than those of the country house garden makers of the legendary and short-lived Edwardian 'golden afternoon'.

LEFT Thomas Mawson in early maturity. Aspiring to extend his skills in city planning, he had already begun his successful practice in garden and landscape making before he set out to lecture and design in the United States in the early twentieth century.

Early life 1861–1885

IN 1927 THE MOST IMPORTANT English landscape designer of his day, Thomas Hayton Mawson, published his autobiography. It tells a tale of self-help and determination to rise from poverty to the position of respected landscape designer; of the supportive clannishness of the large family; of the significance to him of nonconformity and Liberalism; of the discovery of the beauty of plants, trees, buildings and landscapes; of international travels, trials and tribulations through the First World War; and of the gathering in of his sons as vital assets to his business. Mawson's autobiography has informed much of the core of this book, including his cheerful account of his early life in Lancashire.

Thomas Hayton Mawson was born at Scorton, a few miles north of Garstang in Lancashire, on 5 May 1861. Scorton remains a small village, now uncomfortably close to the M6 which forges its way northwards nearby. Along one side of the main street, artisans' houses retain the sloping upper windows that allowed greater illumination for skilled hands and reveal the connection with the cotton weaving industry which flourished here in cottages until mechanisation forced it into factories. Thomas' father, John, was born in 1835 into a family of nine (completed by his brother Isaac, born two years later). John Mawson was a cotton warper, weaving threads in a loom to make cloth. He came from Halton, a short distance north of Lancaster. His son Thomas refers to the effects of the cotton famine on Lancaster – when the shortage of imported cotton from the south of the United States during the American Civil War of 1861–65 brought many textile workers to their knees. Without complaint, he explained this as one of the causes of the family's shortage of finance and his own subsequent lack of a suitable education for one destined to work with professionals.

But the main reason for John Mawson's drifting in search of a job to replace his employment in cotton was his lack of aptitude for business. 'He would have made an ideal pastor,' Thomas claimed, remarking on his warm and sympathetic personality. John's lack of direction was balanced by the practicality of his wife, Jane Hayton. Her maiden name appears for the first time in the family in Thomas' own, as the male heir and, all too soon, leader of the family. Thomas also stressed the importance of his father's nonconformity – and Liberalism, qualities which the young man absorbed into his own approach to life.[1] Thomas' early childhood was spent in Scorton, with his older sisters Mary and Sarah, and his younger brothers Robert and Isaac, until his father decided to move away to find other work. This was to be the first of many uprootings, which in the end proved unsatisfactory for both the man and his family.

John Mawson had five brothers who were builders in Lancaster, including his younger sibling, Isaac, who was to prove to be useful to his nephew, Thomas. With his brothers' help in 1866, John built a pair of semi-detached houses – one for his family and one, presumably to let, on the edge of Lancaster. Thomas went to the local church school. But after a few years, he was very sorry to be told that the family had to move to Ingleton in Yorkshire, northwest from Lancaster, where his father had found 'a position' – maybe as a gardener. Thomas saw his childhood in the house in Lancaster as the beginning of his interest in gardening. Lacking in strength and prone to illness, he was given the garden plots to dig to improve his physique. Trenching for vegetable planting and buying penny packets of 'candytuft, mignonette...stocks and clarkias' gave the boy great satisfaction and 'a keen interest in all Nature's handiwork'.[2] Here, on the western side of the Yorkshire Dales, Thomas' restless father built Prospect House in 1875 for his family, overlooking the river Greta,[3] and later bought land at Langber End between Ingleton and Bentham to set up a fruit farm and nursery, presumably having abandoned his earlier 'position'. Thomas and his brother Robert, now aged fourteen and twelve respectively, were required to work on the nursery, which pleased the older boy, even though plans for him to enter the design department of Gillows in Lancaster were abandoned in favour of a life on the land. Robert had to leave school to help the family enterprise. Despite the heavy clay and high altitude of the nursery, the boys dug and turned over sixty square yards of pasture daily to transform it into cultivable land, and also excavated storage cisterns for the water supply for house and nursery.[4] When he had time, Thomas took his sketchbook into the countryside to draw waterfalls spilling over slabs of millstone grit and the grassy moorlands below the flattened, stony outcrop of Ingleborough.

Despite his scanty education in local schools, Thomas at twelve had been employed and housed by his uncle Isaac as an office boy in his firm in Lancaster. He traced contract drawings and kept account of building materials while work was in progress. Here he gained 'the best technical training I could have had' and the beginnings of a knowledge of architecture.[5] Drawing was to emerge strongly as an occupation which he enjoyed and his uncle had the good sense to let him have

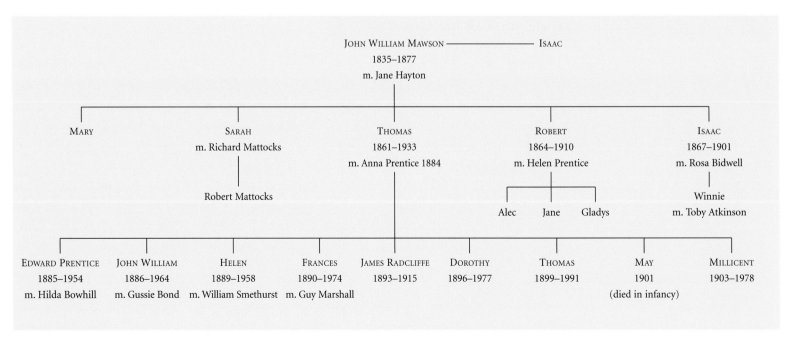

JOHN WILLIAM MAWSON ———————— ISAAC
1835–1877
m. Jane Hayton

MARY	SARAH	THOMAS	ROBERT	ISAAC
	m. Richard Mattocks	1861–1933	1864–1910	1867–1901
		m. Anna Prentice 1884	m. Helen Prentice	m. Rosa Bidwell
	Robert Mattocks		Alec Jane Gladys	Winnie
				m. Toby Atkinson

EDWARD PRENTICE	JOHN WILLIAM	HELEN	FRANCES	JAMES RADCLIFFE	DOROTHY	THOMAS	MAY	MILLICENT
1885–1954	1886–1964	1889–1958	1890–1974	1893–1915	1896–1977	1899–1991	1901	1903–1978
m. Hilda Bowhill	m. Gussie Bond	m. William Smethurst	m. Guy Marshall				(died in infancy)	

LEFT Mawson Brothers
Nursery, later Lakeland
Nursery, was run by Robert,
standing, and Isaac, left,
with their elder brother
Thomas' direction. Later
they carried out contract
work for Thomas' designs.
This early picture of Thomas,
with his gardener's boots and
rumpled appearance, makes
a contrast with the brother
whom he affectionately
called 'Robert the Toff', and
with his more sophisticated
photograph on page 6.

BELOW LEFT A family tree
giving three generations of
the Mawson family.

time off to follow this inclination at an art course at the Lancaster Mechanics' Institute. Not only did Uncle Isaac teach him about building and encourage his drawing but he also shared his amateur knowledge of horticulture, especially British ferns, with his nephew.

Thomas collected books on horticulture from adults who understood his interests and were prepared to pass on volumes on gardening and botany. Two journals – the practical and informative *Gardeners' Chronicle* and the *Journal of Horticulture* – were devoured regularly, and hours were spent in the house of an Ingleton neighbour whose late gardener husband had key works by horticultural and landscape giants such as John Claudius Loudon and Humphry Repton. He discovered the eighteenth-century commentary on the Picturesque by Uvedale Price and *Forest Scenery* by William Gilpin, and the nineteenth-century *How to Lay out a Garden* by Edward Kemp. All this, said Mawson in his autobiography, together with the elements of architecture and drawing, 'set the direction of my thoughts and studies towards Landscape Gardening'.[6]

But, shortly after taking on the fruit farm and nursery, John Mawson became seriously ill. He had made allowance for capital outlay on the property, plants and fruit trees, but not for the period before the trees gave fruit. Nor had he foreseen his own lack of physical strength for such an enterprise. Ever the optimist, he had thought that the annual yield of nursery vegetable crops would give sufficient return to tide the family over the later maturing of the fruit trees. He turned his head to the wall, and died two years later in 1877. Determined to continue, and with food provided by their smallholding's chickens and eggs, the family battled on, but the burden of debt, distance from towns, and a nursery not yet in full production, made Jane Mawson decide that the only solution was to sell up and move south. She accurately foresaw that her sons would prosper as nurserymen and that there was training to be had and a market for such training in the fast-growing suburbs of London. In 1879, at the age of eighteen, Thomas was to be despatched south 'with twenty shillings in addition to my train fare, the intention being that I should obtain a situation and hold on as best I could until I could fix up an opening for my two younger brothers'.[7]

The awfulness of his predicament and his father's death had been sturdily put aside and in March 1879 Thomas set off determined to do his best for the family. It is likely that he had a list of nurserymen who might employ him culled from the *Gardeners' Chronicle* and other journals, and that he may have written in advance

of his visit for an interview, as he needed accommodation in London. Nevertheless, as he stood on the station platform the enormity of his responsibility flooded over him. The 'change from a Yorkshire upland moor with its breezes and wide prospects to the most depressing atmosphere of London back yards was too much for me. At Bethnal Green where I had to change [trains], I sat down and wept.'[8]

The move to London opened the door on manhood and responsibility for Mawson. His sister Sarah had married Richard Mattocks, a Windermere greengrocer, whose son Robert was to become a president of the Landscape Institute, and she was no longer a responsibility to be carried by her brother. But he had to find work for Robert and Isaac and a home for his mother. After selling up in Yorkshire the four Mawsons rented a house near Barnes Common, letting the upper floor in order to afford the £30 rent which they paid annually. The brothers were taken on by William Iceton, a supplier for Covent Garden Market, whose nursery in Putney Park Lane, Roehampton, was a short walk from their new home. Thomas had already found work with John Wills, a man from Somerset who had learned his trade as a gardener to a titled landowner in Cheshire, later moving to set up on his own in Onslow Crescent in

RIGHT Trunch church
in Norfolk, where Thomas
Hayton Mawson and Anna
Prentice were married
in 1884.

South Kensington. He had a flower nursery at Annerley in Fulham, and had made his name as a floral decorator and landscape gardener.[9] Mawson was taken on at eighteen shillings a week.

Wills was an accomplished man; he was decorated by King Leopold of Belgium for services he had carried out for the monarch, and was honoured by the French for his decorative work for the Paris Exhibition of 1875. Mawson was impressed with the way in which Wills had expanded his business into a public company and had prestigious premises in South Kensington and Regent Street. Privately Mawson had misgivings about Wills' ability to lay out his landscapes and the lack of good plans and drawings in the firm. He noticed that Wills relied on verbal instruction – a practice which Mawson himself was to follow, though he insisted on working drawings as well. Although Mawson saw no future for himself in decorative work for balls and receptions, he enjoyed meeting famous men and women in the worlds of politics, art and society and absorbed all he could in the busy atmosphere. He began work at six in the morning and sped off to the South Kensington Museum in his lunch hour to delight, in an unstructured way, in its contents.

Mawson stayed with Wills for two years until the firm suddenly went into liquidation in 1881 and once again he found himself searching for a position. After six weeks' work for Kelways at Langport in Somerset, Mawson decided that invoicing new plants led nowhere, and he could see no future in staying with the firm. But even in this short period he had not wasted his time; he found out all he could about plant propagation, alpines and hardy herbaceous plants. He was determined to become a garden designer and such a store of knowledge would be essential if this was to be his career.

Another search through the garden journals brought Mawson back to London and to a hardy plants specialist delighting in the name of Thomas Softly Ware, at Hale Farm Nurseries in Tottenham. Mawson described Ware as 'a tall, stately old gentleman' who had been a draper for most of his life until he inherited the business from his wife's father. 'He scarcely knew one plant from another, but he had the good sense to recognise his deficiency.'[10] To compensate he employed knowledgeable managers, and Mawson thrived on the company of hardworking men such as Amos Perry and Francis Fell, who were expert in their knowledge of hardy flowering plants.

ABOVE Hartpury in Gloucestershire has walls which Mawson often supplied to his clients, with half-circle terracotta tiles topped by a limestone coping. His first clients would be the owners of country houses, whom Mawson met in his early years of horticultural training, and he realised the significance of attractive stonework in their gardens.

Mawson relished the study he made, notebook in hand, allocating the different plants to their genus or family, as he moved through the 120 acres of the nursery at six in the morning or late in the evening. The long hours led him to move into lodgings shared with a T.S.Ware foreman, rather than stay with his family and disturb them with his coming and going.

Gradually he built up sufficient knowledge and confidence to answer clients' letters. He mentions 'Miss Jekyll writing about daffodils…Reynolds Hole writing about carnations…Dr Ellacombe interested in peonies… Robert Marnock wanted alpine plants…' and 'Mr William Robinson wrote from time to time about nymphaeas and other aquatic plants'.[11] Both Marnock and Robinson were gardeners trained through the apprenticeship system and through working on landowners' estates; Jekyll, Hole and Ellacombe were middle-class owners of substantial private gardens, and it is possible that the stiffness which accompanied the later dealings between Jekyll and Mawson may have come from the awareness of class differences which originated in this 'customer and supplier' relationship. Later, Mawson's role entailed visiting the firm's wholesale customers around London and talking with nurserymen such as Waterer's at Woking, Veitch in Kingston Vale and Bunyard's at Maidstone. T.S.Ware offered an excellent training, where Mawson made useful contacts among garden owners and nurserymen. They offered him a junior partnership, but the firm had no landscape department and this was what Mawson most wanted. His future was about to change.

Mawson had found the woman he wanted to marry – Anna Prentice, a doctor's daughter from North Walsham in Norfolk. Anna was a nurse who worked in a hospital in Tottenham High Street in its emergency scarlet fever wing. She had noticed a slim, dark and handsome young man who passed the hospital regularly and made sure she was at the window to see him. Mawson contrived a way of introducing himself to her. Before long he was supplying fresh flowers for the ward in which she worked and soon after asking her guardian for her hand in marriage. Now was the time to look for a position in which he could follow his strong inclination to become a landscape architect, and the opportunity arose through an unnamed firm in Surrey which ran a 'compact, high-class, profitable business' as

BELOW A meadow opens out above pools at Wightwick Manor, near Wolverhampton, with Mawson's favoured silver hollies and yews making an avenue at the top of the slope. He was to plant the same mix of shrubs and trees at Yews, in the Lake District. Mawson's arboricultural instruction in London nurseries taught him about trees and he learned by observation how to design with them.

contractors for garden landscape work. A partnership was offered to Mawson.

As chapter one will show, this offer of a partnership collapsed while Thomas and Anna were honeymooning in the Lake District in 1884. Mawson assessed the chances of work in the Lake District for himself and his brothers and chose to stay. By February 1885 they had moved into Wenderholme in Ellerthwaite Road, Windermere, and had a workplace in College Road and some land for a nursery.

What sort of world would Thomas Mawson – a gardener and nurseryman who had left school at twelve – enter when he set up Mawson Brothers (later Lakeland Nurseries) in Windermere? Each part of Edwardian society knew its place, where aristocratic landownership was seen as the peak of respectability – though few attained the 10,000 acres sought by what John Bateman called the 'Acreocracy of England'.[12] Agricultural dominance was beginning to crumble, with steam ships and steam trains transporting cheaper wheat and meat from the colonies, but new men, who made their money from industry, were coming to the fore and demanding large houses and crafted landscapes to compete with those owned by old money. Within the hierarchy of landowner, gentry and labouring classes fitted the hierarchy of land agent, butler, and head gardener, who in turn looked down to steward, cook, gamekeeper and gardener. Ownership of estates was signalled in the countryside by the colour of the paint on cottages and the lord of the manor's coat of arms on the wrought-iron gates. How could Mawson, from the bottom of the social ladder and with no professional training, succeed in this world – a world where garden design appeared to be the domain of the architect?

Such architectural training was available to the respectable middle classes. Their men could be articled to architects under a system of pupilage for four or five years, or they could go to the Architectural Association from its foundation in 1847, or be taught without fee at the Royal Academy School of Architecture in Burlington House, or attend the South Kensington School which taught architecture as a form of decorative art. Similar schools opened in towns beyond the capital, including Manchester in 1860. Some preferred the training of the Ecole des Beaux-Arts in Paris, and a number of English landscape gardeners such as Edward Milner (1819–84) had trained in Paris at the Jardin des Plantes. Many of the architectural schools' alumni would be engaged in building country houses and would think themselves fit to lay out the garden, at least next to the house.

As chapter two will show, Mawson became anxious to be considered as a landscape architect, not a gardener.

The Arts and Crafts Movement, with its approval of the hand crafted and the 'natural' as a key legacy from William Morris and John Ruskin, its use of the vernacular – whether local stone, plants or trees – its preference for wooden trellis, metal gates, brick and stone patterns in house walls and paths, and dry stone walls made by hand and its approval of plants scrambling unchecked or mixed with wild varieties, held sway after the departure from England's nineteenth-century revivalist gardens of several styles, often mixed up,

BELOW The water garden at Graythwaite Hall.

ABOVE Although Wood
Hall has been demolished
(as other houses where
Mawson was commissioned
to make a landscape) and
much of its stonework
removed, there is a haunting
beauty in its balustrading
overlooking the Cocker valley.

including the medieval, the Elizabethan and then the gothic. The 'natural' had also been adopted in France as the *jardin anglais* in Parisian public places such as the Buttes-Chaumont and the Bois de Boulogne. English gardeners trained in Paris and, in England, francophile William Robinson's influential book of 1870, *The Wild Garden,* had taken hold. But all of this was to be shaken in 1892 by the architects when they decided that 'the Ruskinian Gothic prejudice that the more academic classical architecture was, the more morally and artistically bad it must be' could be questioned and that it was time for some classical revivalism. Painters and writers had discovered the gardens and architecture of Italy, and now the architects had arrived at a point where it had to be realised that they were 'living in the Renaissance' with all its implications of formality in design.[13] The English Renaissance garden, which drew its strength from Francis Bacon's essay 'On Gardens' published in 1625, was based on Shakespearean allusions and a love of Queen Elizabeth I and came to be

associated with Penshurst Place in Kent. This garden, developed by architect George Devey, was much praised by fellow architect Reginald Blomfield (1856–1942). Landscape architects such as Mawson found themselves in a dilemma: whether to continue to design with 'natural' informality, or to take up the new trend towards the formality of classical design.

Allied to the argument between the styles – natural versus formal – was the argument for the control of the laying out of the garden. This was to rumble on, sometimes acrimoniously, from the end of the nineteenth century well into the twentieth. Who should be in charge? The most formidable supporter for the architects' cause was Reginald Blomfield, educated at Haileybury and Oxford, as was Francis Inigo Thomas (1866–1950), his co-author for their influential book *The Formal Garden in England*, which was first published in 1892 and reprinted in 1901. Blomfield was supported by John Dando Sedding (1838–91), whose *Garden Craft Old and New* was published after his death. In the preface Sedding confirmed his affinity for old gardens: 'The old-fashioned garden, whatever its failings in the eyes of the modern landscape gardener (great is the poverty of his invention) represents one of the pleasures of England.'[14]

Blomfield explained that 'the formal treatment of gardens, ought, perhaps, to be called the architectural treatment of gardens, for it consists in the extension of the principles of design which govern the house to the grounds which surround it'. He continued: 'the object of formal gardening is to bring the two into harmony, to make the house grow out of its surroundings, and to prevent it being an excrescence on the face of nature'.[15] David Ottewill has clarified what Blomfield meant by formal as:

a series of spaces divided by walls or clipped hedges, simply planned and proportioned in relation to the house, with raised terraces, gazebos, broad walks, alleys, lawns, flower beds and a symmetrically arranged entrance fore-court.[16]

To which could be added: some statuary and garden architecture, sunk gardens, and a very clear division between the garden and the parkland beyond.

After his quiet introduction, Blomfield soon waged war on the landscape gardener, blaming him for ignoring the house in his so-called natural designs and calling to account the writings of Edward Milner (1819–84) and, of course, William Robinson. Blomfield insisted that the straight line with its attendant geometric beds and rectangular lawns, was the only one possible to govern the layout of the garden, not the sinuous curves of the landscape architects. He accused them of being unable to define the 'natural', and of copying what was natural and then calling it a style.

William Robinson (1838–1935) was the complete opposite of Blomfield and his associates in background, upbringing and attitude to garden making. Descended from middle-class stock which had fallen on hard times in Ireland, Robinson had to make his own way in life, and his training was as a gardener on estates, the National Botanic garden in Dublin and the Royal Botanic Society's garden in Regent's Park. In his 1906 book *The Garden Beautiful*, he challenged Blomfield's view that gardens 'should never have been allowed to fall into the hands of the gardener or out of those of the architect; that it is an architectural matter, and should have been schemed at the same time and by the same time as the house itself'. He scoffed at plans as feeble substitutes for the garden; plans were for men who worked in offices. Gardens should be designed by men who knew the ground and knew their plants. (Although elsewhere he states that the garden plan should be made before the house was built.)

He challenged the cost of elaborate gardens, including Chatsworth and Castle Howard, and especially Versailles and the Crystal Palace. Even where there was no money to waste in needless walls and gigantic water-squirts, the idea of the terrace was still carried out, he claimed. Criticising headless Jupiters and goddesses in lead and nymphs in cement, he announced the only true ornament was living nature, with its changes of season in tree, shrub and flower, all other things should be subsidiary. There was no such thing as a style for every situation. Trees should be set in picturesque ways and allowed to take natural forms. He saw plants, shrubs and trees with the eyes of an artist, frequently commenting on the play of light and shade and the charm of colour. Group the plants as you may, he claimed, the lines of beauty are ever there. Arrange them as you may, the mystery and indefinitiveness which constitute beauty of vegetation in its highest sense cannot be extinguished.[17]

Robinson's long borders conserved the hardy perennials which he feared were being lost by the fashion for bedding out tender annuals. Wildness was a quality which he relished, and also wild plants mixed in with cultivated plants. Robinson, the vitalist, seeing that every organism had an innate spirit pushing it to survive, had a great respect for plants, forbidding their cutting and letting them grow freely. His garden at Gravetye Manor mixed the exotic and the native, the cultivated and the wild, making pictures which were very English, and with a minimum of digging and management. Robinson was Gertrude Jekyll's mentor, and, in the end, was better known than Blomfield.

Such were the guides that Mawson could follow as he read the *Gardeners' Chronicle* and the *Garden* and made his way through the invective between architect and landscape gardener towards a landscape of his own making.

As Mawson prospered and ambition led him to Europe and North America, other questions were to follow him, this time concerned with national identity. These aspects of culture were associated with the British Empire. Joseph Chamberlain was, as Niall Ferguson has pointed out, 'Britain's first, authentically, self-consciously imperialist politician'.[18] This Birmingham manufacturer of wooden screws had risen through national politics to become Colonial Secretary. In the last days of the nineteenth century, he spread the concept (not his own) of 'Greater Britain', urging that all the colonies should join together under the rule of London's parliament. Such a policy had broader implications for architecture and town planning, and a danger that Englishness would be adopted without any consideration that settlers in new lands would want to evolve a style of their own. There were mixed reactions to English imposition, and these were to emerge as Mawson moved through North America. Did his plans for colonial cities show him to be a carrier of the colonial torch?

The book will explore different aspects of Mawson's life in the British Isles, Europe and North America – as garden maker, park maker and town planner – and for different ranks of client. He was to work for *arrivistes* in the industrial world, and for royalty and the aristocracy of the traditional world of the landed estate; his clients included suburban house owners and local authorities. What follows is an exploration of the life and work of an extraordinary man, through the different spheres in which he was to work – garden making, park making and town planning.

CHAPTER ONE

Forging the style:
Lakeland 1885–1921

LEFT At Cringlemire
Mawson made a garden for
Henry Martin, a compulsive
plant collector. Some of his
rhododendrons and acers
remain by the informal walks
which wind round the edge
of the estate.

IN THE YEAR 1885 began one of the most important international landscape gardening careers of the Edwardian period. Thomas Hayton Mawson was an ambitious young man with prospects. He had gained considerable skills in horticulture from his work in several nurseries in the south, where he had had dealings with the fashionable garden makers of the middle classes. At twenty-three he had been promised a partnership with a firm of nurserymen in Surrey who wanted to develop their landscape work, offering exactly the career in design which he was keen to pursue. Seeing the time right, on 1 August 1884, in Trunch Church in Norfolk, he had married a North Walsham doctor's daughter Anna Prentice, to whom he was to dedicate his autobiography with the words 'to whose discernment and encouragement I owe any success I may have achieved'.[1] All seemed set for success.

However, an unexpected 'bolt from the blue' changed the perspective for Mawson, and his extended family.[2] On his honeymoon in the Lake District, he was informed that the owner of the firm which had offered him a partnership had changed his mind, but Mawson could work in the nursery. For a second time in seven years, he found himself faced with decisions which would affect not only his new wife, but his mother and brothers also. Should he stay employed in a job beneath his capabilities which offered him insufficient wages with which to support the widened family, should he look for another position in London, or should he return to the north where he had been raised and find a new direction for himself? This time, with characteristic decisiveness, he decided to reject a return to London.

Despite the siren calls of wealthy urban and rural customers in the south, he planned to set up a nursery and landscaping business of his own in Windermere in the Lake District. The intention, once again, was to take charge of the family by initially employing his brothers Robert and Isaac in the nursery, and then to start his own landscape design business. The two concerns would be run separately, but one would contract out to the other. As it turned out, both decisions were wise ones.

The close-knit Mawson family drew its strength from its bonds. Thomas' younger brother Robert, born in 1864, would marry Helen Prentice, the sister of Thomas' wife Anna. Helen and Anna Prentice had been made wards of their uncle, Thomas Bidwell, after their father, Edward Prentice, died. Anna, who would accompany her beloved father as he drove on his rounds in his pony and trap along the country roads of North Walsham, was just seven when he died. Just a few months later, Anna's mother died, too; she was only in her thirties. Isaac, Thomas' youngest brother, born in 1867, would marry Thomas Bidwell's daughter Rosa. Thus the young men and women of two families, and Thomas' mother Jane, were united through marriage.

Mawson must have assessed his potential market before instructing an estate agent to look for a site which would form the base for a nursery. Who would require the services of an aspiring young landscape gardener in Windermere? There were few long-established landowners with many acres who might be expected to commission him. Windermere's residents had been small farmers and craftsmen: the bobbin-makers who supplied half the textile industry of the north and who lived between Kendal and Windermere; the miners and quarry workers who hewed silver, lead, slate and granite; the woodcarvers of Kendal; the papermakers of Burneside and the linen makers of Keswick.

Since the eighteenth century the Lake District had drawn to it those who sought the spiritual beauty of its mountains and lakes and wandered its hills, who painted, wrote poetry and entered into the imaginary worlds of the Picturesque and the sometimes darker world of the Sublime. Nature and the God of Nature were worshipped by the Romantic writers. H.D.Rawnsley (later Canon Rawnsley), the vicar of Wray Church on the northwest bank of Lake Windermere, described the intermingling of 'a common perception' of these worlds in the lives of the two most influential Lakeland poets, William Wordsworth and John Ruskin:

If ever two minds could walk together because they were agreed, it was in the assertion that men could only truly live in their highest and happiest spirit life here on earth in communion with Nature if first they could perceive that Nature was a revelation of God's spirit and then could wonder and love it with deepest reverence.[3]

Not only poets, but other Lakelanders were imbued with such sentiments. Annie Garnett, the founder of Bowness Spinnery, wrote in her diary in 1899: 'A country life is the life to live; in touch with God, nature controlling; surrounded with Nature; in the very midst of Nature; part of Nature.'[4]

This group of quiet, reverential writers and painters (but not so many of the pastoral workers) were to find themselves sharply opposed to the inevitable changes brought by the opening of the railway line from Kendal to Birthwaite in Windermere in 1847 and the introduction of steamboats in 1870 to join the inaccessible parts of the lake together. By 1846 it had been possible to travel from Lancaster to Carlisle; a year later a branch of this line joined Lancaster to Kendal. By 1864 a railway left the coastal line north to Carlisle to join Cockermouth to Keswick and Penrith, skirting Bassenthwaite Lake and Derwent Water; and in 1869 a station on the southern tip of Lake Windermere took men southwest to the ironworks at Barrow-in-Furness.

Inevitably the poets saw the railway as an intrusion which destroyed their revered nature and inflicted damage on the landscape. Wordsworth, resigned to the building of a station at Windermere, campaigned against an extension further north to Ambleside. Despite his earlier fulminations that the gentry would be replaced by the settling in of the lower class trippers,[5] the majority of the visitors who came and then stayed were middle class, much to the pleasure of the shopkeepers, hotel and lodging-house owners.[6]

From the late 1870s, opposition groups, backed by John Ruskin, campaigned against the threats to the 'most beautiful and varied scenery in England' from proposed railway extensions, Manchester's need for a reservoir at Thirlmere and further quarrying. This led to the formation, in 1883, of the Lake District Defence Society. The opposition groups were largely culled from an outside intelligentsia – public school masters, academics, poets and writers such as Alfred Tennyson and Robert Browning, the architect Alfred Waterhouse, and the eventual founders of the National Trust – Octavia Hill, Canon Rawnsley, Robert Hunter and the Reverend Samuel Barnett. The striking absence, as Michael Dowthwaite points out, of local support for the Lake District Defence Society can be explained by the fact that Lakeland was becoming increasingly attractive to incomers who had money to spend, and these were the people to whom the tourist industry, local builders and shopkeepers looked for support; and it was from these ranks that Thomas Mawson would find his clients.[7]

From the late nineteenth century to the first decade of the twentieth, the settlers were increased by a new type of man. These incomers, or 'offcomers' as they were known, were new-rich industrialists and businessmen escaping the grim, smoking sprawl and slums of the northern textile towns, mining and port activities. Industrial leaders from Yorkshire, Manchester, Bolton and Liverpool could now travel by train to reach Windermere after a journey of between two and three hours.[8] These men were the magnates of engineering, cotton broking, shipping, mining and textile making firms, eager to leave the town behind and escape to the countryside. Among them were Joseph Ridgway Bridson, owner of a bleaching firm in Bolton, whose family eventually settled on the west side of Lake Windermere at Sawrey, and who were to offer Mawson his first important commission.

They were attracted by the long, gleaming waters of the lake below its dark mountain frame and the startling beauty of views to be gained by capturing a site on its banks. Their motives were twofold: to rest and enjoy a rural retreat, and to join the fashion which had been lately established by other industrial leaders of employing imaginative and creative young architects to design them large houses by the side of the lake and to find local craftsmen to work within the houses. They could build on the sunny eastern slopes from Windermere south to Bowness, go north to Ambleside, or cross the water to the steep and wooded western slope of the lake. Many would call on the expertise of the landscaping skills of the Mawsons. It was not so very different from North America, as Thomas Mawson would discover, where industrialists followed the artists into New England, or New York businessmen built their weekend mansions (which they called 'cottages') in the Hudson Valley.

A combination of transport modes helped accessibility between home and work. Oliver Westall relates the Bowness anecdote about 'Henry Schneider, the Furness iron magnate, strolling across the lawns of Belsfield each morning to his steam launch, the *Esperance,* in which his butler served breakfast as it conveyed them down the lake to connect with Schneider's special train to Barrow'.[9] Belsfield was turned into an hotel in 1900, and Mawson would work there in 1912 and 1922.[10] Such men could make second homes by the lakeside, as did Manchester brewer Sir Edward Holt, who commissioned Mackay Hugh Baillie Scott to design Blackwell between 1898 and 1900. Though partly this was a move to monitor the health of his brewery by keeping an eye on the progress of the plan for Thirlmere. He was to fall foul of the Ruskinians because he cut down trees around the reservoir which he claimed were polluting the water with their leaves.[11]

The new second-home owners were able to build on the small estates which characterised the area, encouraged by the activities of the Pattinson family, builders who were to work with the Mawsons. The Pattinsons had bought up much land south of Windermere on the Heathwaite and Storrs estates. At the time of Mawson's arrival they were completing one house per day on the Heathwaite estate.[12]

It was this climate of expansion and expectation that Thomas and Anna Mawson detected as they looked around Windermere in the late summer of 1884. In February 1885 the family took over a cottage, shop and an acre of land for the nursery. The 1891 census showed Thomas and Anna living at 284 Bowness Road, south of Windermere, with their young sons Edward and John, daughters Helen and Frances, and servant Alice Clark. Mawson's widowed mother Jane lived with Isaac at nearby 12 Oak Street. Five more children were to arrive by 1901, though the youngest, May, died in infancy. Villas were built on the Heathwaite estate for the brothers, and by 1899 The Corbels, Thomas' home and office, was established in Park Road on the same estate. The nursery gradually expanded on land leased from the Pattinsons by the road between Bowness and Windermere. It was

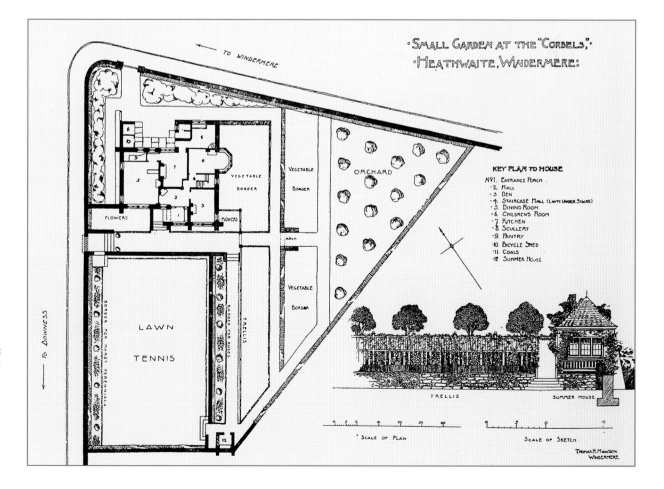

RIGHT This plan of The Corbels was used in the first edition of *The Art and Craft of Garden Making* (fig. 122) to show how a small site could be landscaped. The house was built in 1898 as Mawson's home and first office in Lakeland.

run by Robert and Isaac as partners from the early 1890s. This allowed Thomas Mawson to develop a career in design. The Mawsons were assisted in their building and nursery activities by members of the Mattocks family, related to Thomas' sister Sarah, who also lived in Windermere.

Annual catalogues, advertising Mawson's silver medal awarded in 1892 by the London International Horticultural Exhibition, offered seeds and spring bulbs, assuring customers that the staff visited Holland every year to choose the best stock. Roses, carnations, lilies and a wide range of perennials were listed; fruit trees, grape vines, figs, nuts and filberts; forest trees from alder, ash and elm to fir, poplar and willow. Country house customers could buy shrubs for game coverts, underwood and hedges. An impressive alpine garden was planted on an exposed rock face. Trellises and garden houses, pergolas, gates and decorative woodwork made for Mawson by Garden Crafts, which was housed in the old bobbin mill at Staveley, displayed Mawsons' stock in bloom and items to beautify the landscape.

Services such as landscape gardening and contract planting were advertised; with remodelling of old or laying out of new gardens, parks or cemeteries, the making of rockeries, waterfalls, ornamental lakes, land draining and road making. Mawson Brothers also offered horticultural buildings such as greenhouses and garden frames. In 1904 Shrublands, a house designed by Dan Gibson, was built opposite the nursery as a home and office for Robert Mawson, with its cool houses, frame ground, conservatory, plant houses, vinery and orchard.[13]

But their future was to be destroyed by illness; to the distress of the family Isaac died of a short but virulent attack of pneumonia in 1901, when he was only thirty-four. Nine years later, Robert was to die, at forty-six, of pernicious anaemia, exhaustion and cardiac failure. From 1908 his brother had taken on commissions in North America and Europe, and there is no doubt that Robert was overburdened. Isaac had had business skills and, with his brother, carried out the contracts for over half the garden designs. Both men had worked ceaselessly to make Mawson Brothers a success. Robert's widow Helen took charge briefly, trading as Mawson Brothers; Isaac's daughter Winnie, who married Toby Atkinson, and later the lively and business-like Frances, Thomas' fourth child, managed Mawson Brothers as Lakeland Nurseries from 1912. After Frances married, Thomas, Mawson's fourth son, born in 1899, took over, before setting up his own business in Morecambe Bay to sell sea-washed turf for bowling greens and golf courses.

Eventually, as demand for large garden work declined after the First World War, Shrublands was to develop as a smart restaurant and garden shop, with plants and cut flowers for sale, and seeds, sold in containers with small wooden shovels to fill the customer's bag. The family lived in a flat above the shop.

Mawson says very little about his four daughters. He took on female pupils after his career had widened further into teaching as well as practising landscape architecture, though he later regretted the lack of education he had given his own daughters in this field.[14] Helen, who married Colonel Smethurst of Thornton Hall in Lincolnshire, and Frances, married to Captain Guy Marshall, both had artistic ability and good business sense, and joined with their cousin Gladys (Robert's daughter) to run a successful cottage industry based on Thornton Hall, which made ornaments which they sold to prestigious customers such as Harrods. Frances, beautiful and vivacious, who loved plants and, like her father, could sell anything to anyone, was more like a secretary to her father, who appreciated her business skills. Helen studied sculpture and silversmithing at the Storey Institute in Lancaster, though she did not practise these skills; she played hockey for Lancashire and was a competitive swimmer.[15] Dorothy, who became a sister at

BELOW Shrublands, built in 1904 as the home of Robert Mawson and his family, was the business hub of Lakeland Nurseries. The plan appeared in the 5th edition of *The Art and Craft of Garden Making*, fig. 452.

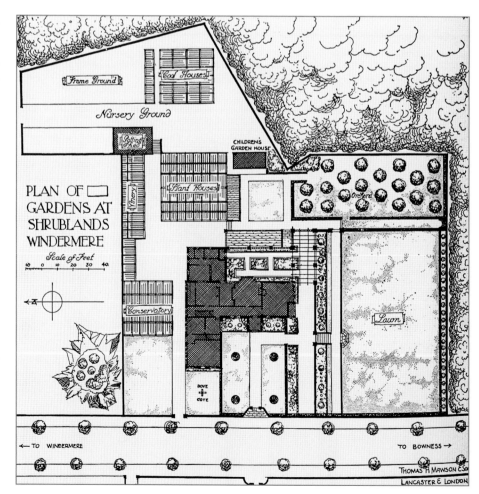

the Liverpool Royal Infirmary, and Millicent stayed at home with their parents. Anna Mawson, a cheerful, organised woman, very much in charge of the family (though not very interested in cooking – there were stories of porridge being quietly tipped down the drain), encouraged her family through the early stages of searching for commissions. At first the wider family of Jane, Thomas and Anna, Robert and Isaac met daily for tea, and if one of them suggested 'throwing up the sponge, he was at once decisively squashed by my mother'.[16]

Culturally, the Mawsons had arrived in the Lake District at a stimulating time. John Ruskin (1819–1900), moralist and social commentator, writer, artist, lecturer and Slade Professor of Fine Art at Oxford, had finally settled at Brantwood on Coniston Water in 1872, which he had bought the year before. In *Fors Clavigera: Letters to the Workmen and Labourers of Great Britain*, written between 1871 and 1884, Ruskin had urged the restoration of local crafts and rural industry, which led to a revival of the arts in Lakeland.[17] His inspiration was behind the foundation of Annie Garnett's Spinnery at Bowness, the Langdale Linen Industry and the Keswick School of Industrial Arts. Men (and women)

needed honest toil, in which they could take pride, and the provision of work in rural areas to halt the drift of the population to the towns. Shocked, as others were, by the degradation of the working conditions of industrial cities, he encouraged 'useful muscular work', where men could see the purpose of what they were doing and could enjoy the skills engendered by contact with tools. He took his Oxford students to dig a road at Hinkley and discuss the purpose for its creation. In Coniston he persuaded the boys in the local school to restore the school garden,[18] while at Brantwood he enjoyed making a terrace at the top of his garden and, at the bottom, where it dropped into Coniston Water, he dug a harbour for small boats.[19]

It was Joan Severn, Ruskin's cousin, who enabled Mawson to find his first major commission in the Lake District. In 1887 she introduced Mawson to J.R.Bridson at Sawrey. It is unlikely that Mawson and Ruskin ever met. For the last years of his life, Ruskin was subject to fits of severe mental illness; walking in certain parts of the Lake District brought on his own 'sublime' distress, though overwork joined the worm which constantly turned within his mind.[20] From 1889 his active life was ended, and he was nursed by his cousin until his death in 1900.

Mawson, while remaining Ruskin's 'admiring disciple' and adhering to local 'architectural traditions' as part of his 'passion for the works and views of Professor Ruskin', had a somewhat different approach to the natural in garden and park making.[21] Ruskin had no interest in design and the artificial, being committed to the observation of the 'specific, distinct and perfect beauty' of each plant.[22] He hated the bright colours of Victorian bedding, and hovered over his gardeners in his conservatory to make sure they did not replace pinks and strawberries with 'nasty gloxinias and glaring fuchsias'.[23] Neither did Ruskin like topiary, commenting that 'the great beauty of all foliage is the energy of life and action, of which it loses the appearance by formal clipping'.[24] Ruskin's view of the natural was one of awe and admiration, it did not require rearranging by man.

At first sight Mawson's conflation of nature and art – 'The stronger a man's love of art is, the more he will appreciate Nature' – seems to resonate with Ruskin.[25] Not a lover of Lancelot Brown, the maker of the English landscape garden, whom he saw as an imitator of nature and the instigator of a theory that 'nature abhorred a straight line',[26] Mawson admits that the landscape architect would:

> although preferring invention…have a care for the natural features having sufficient interest to warrant their preservation [and] bring them into harmony with the general composition. …This brings us to one of the most difficult problems with which the park and garden designer has to deal, viz: how much of Nature it is right to admit within the park or garden, and how far, if at all, it is right to assist it.[27]

Here is Thomas Mawson, landscape architect, with clients to consider, treading the middle ground between the two poles: the formal and the natural. It takes the argument beyond the reach of John Ruskin, who would have disapproved of Mawson's 'invention', and also beyond the other at times fierce current debate between the followers of Reginald Blomfield, the supporter of geometry in garden design, and William Robinson, who introduced the wild garden with its meadows and indigenous flowers. Next to the house Mawson admitted that he would consider 'a formal treatment the one most likely to give satisfactory results', but he did not think that '"The Art and Craft of Garden Making"' was advanced by a 'slavish adherence to style or tradition'.[28] As it will emerge, Mawson's gardens easily combined the formal and the natural, in what he called the composite style, without the histrionics of some of his contemporaries.

How much influence did Ruskin have on the newly arrived landscape architect? Ruskin was concerned for the place of nature in the wellbeing of mankind, while at first Mawson was more inclined to consider the significance of the 'natural' as an important element of the garden. Later, when he began to design city landscapes, he recognised the power of beauty as a vital force for the happiness of those living in towns. At the end of the 1890s Ebenezer Howard had written *To-morrow: A Peaceful Path to Real Reform,* which became a blueprint for the Garden City Movement. Mawson's later interest in the restoration and replanning of settlements and cities surely evolved in part from Ruskin's Christian socialism, reinforced by the sermons preached by the pastors of the Carver Memorial Church in Windermere, Doctors Taylor and Adamson, who played a significant part in moulding the young man's character.[29]

Indirectly more significant for Mawson was Ruskin's *The Nature of Gothic* of 1853, which led William Morris (1834–96), via a dreamworld of the idealised medieval craftsman, through tapestry and wallpaper making, painting and woodcraft, pottery and metal working, towards what became the Arts and Crafts Movement. From its urban beginnings at the first exhibition of the Arts and Crafts Society in London in 1888, where Lakeland crafts were shown, it gathered support in rural areas, not least in the Lake District itself. Soon there were Art Workers' Guilds and Exhibition Societies, with Kendal holding its own Arts, Crafts and Loan Exhibition in 1891. Mawson joined the Art Workers' Guild in London in 1905, resigning in 1929.

Thomas Mawson accepted the Arts and Crafts Movement as the obvious ambience in which his gardens and landscapes were to be made. They were to abound in good craftsmanship that would never appear in exhibitions: dry stone walls with careful planting; stone stairways linking terraces, and stone paving round pools; wooden trellises for roses and wooden gates with their half-circle tops and art nouveau hinges; wrought-iron gates with patterns like sturdy lacework; intricate brick and tile designs in walls and paving; topiary shapes; displays of horticultural expertise in herbaceous borders, rose gardens, green swards, avenues lined with trees and formal beds close to the house.

The same attention to craft standards could be seen in the design of the kitchen garden with its wooden bothies, arbours and trellises for the training of fruit

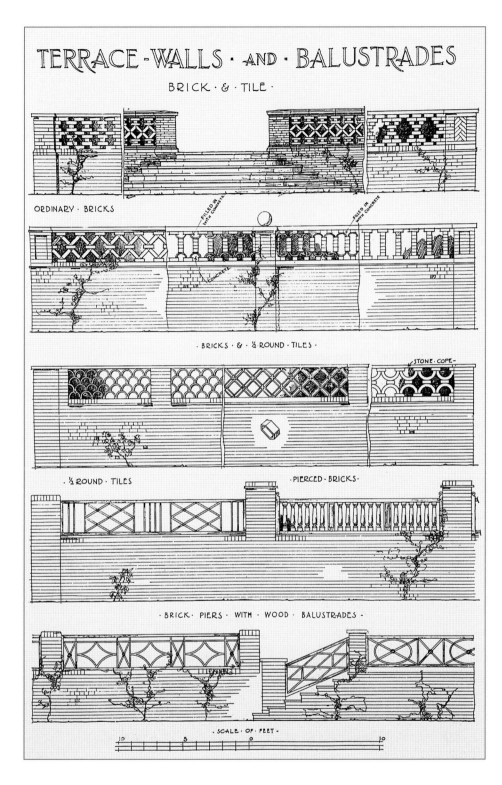

TERRACE·WALLS·AND·BALUSTRADES
BRICK·&·TILE·

ORDINARY·BRICKS·

·BRICKS·&·½·ROUND·TILES·

·½·ROUND·TILES·   ·PIERCED·BRICKS·

·BRICK·PIERS·WITH·WOOD·BALUSTRADES·

·SCALE·OF·FEET·

ABOVE Mawson's gardens are characterised by their brick and tile work, especially on balustrades, beside steps, on terraces and along drives. This is from the 5th edition of *The Art and Craft of Garden Making* (fig. 123).

Having…had considerable opportunities for studying gardens, more especially garden design, in its relation to the house and its architectural character, I have realised the fact that one must be a compliment [sic] of the other. I can therefore, sympathise, on the one hand, with those architects who claim the right to design the setting or garden frame to the house they have designed, and, on the other hand, with those landscape gardeners who have felt…that to ensure a successful garden it is necessary that the designer has some say in the arrangement and disposal of the house on the site, and also of the selection of the site itself.[30]

In this diplomatic manner, and probably to secure clients on both sides of the divide, Mawson introduced the modern approach to the garden which saw it as a part of the design of the house, and highlighted the arguments which had been circulating around the landscaping world between architects and plantsmen as to who should be master of the garden. Less obviously, he implied the tension between the professionally qualified, such as Blomfield, and those who had come up through the apprenticeship system, as had William Robinson. There was, for Mawson, a lifelong desire to attain both architectural expertise and a plantsman's training, to have served his apprenticeship and to have gained professional status. In the playing out of these ambitions, his sons were later to become a significant part.

Mawson's working methods enabled him to take on as many commissions as he was offered. In a division of labour between all concerned, he planned to visit the site and make drawings on the spot while talking to his client and accommodating his views and aspirations. He would then return home and make a sketch, which went back to the office in Windermere to be drawn up. Often there was more than one plan, but even so, alterations and 'improvements' took place on site as the work progressed, and costs sometimes precluded the finishing of the job. As Mawson commented in the preface to the first edition of *The Art and Craft of Garden Making*, none of the illustrations should be taken as the finished garden, and while some of his clients had rejected the plans he had put forward, they were happy for the plans to be published.

Soon Mawson was to acquire the services of young architects who were good draughtsmen and looking for extra income. They drew out the plans with skill and with colour – similar to today's glossy brochure – to suggest the best possible use of the client's land. If this was

trees, and its careful containment within walls. The provision of the hard landscaping lent itself to another of the unwritten rules of the movement: the use of the vernacular. Local stone, wood, plants and trees (though Mawson happily used 'foreign' plants where necessary) were used in the gardens, and local craftsmen were hired. The greatest affirmation to the movement is seen in the title given to the five editions of Mawson's textbook for his many followers: *The Art and Craft of Garden Making*. In the preface to his first edition in 1900, Mawson tackled the most difficult issue in which his bombastic contemporaries were engaged:

acceptable, a foreman was put in charge. However, the man was not to exercise his own discretion, as shown on a set of instructions for the foreman in charge of making gardens at Beechmount on the Graythwaite Hall Estate in 1904 for Colonel Sandys. After clear directions on how to make a dry stone wall, to preserve the apple trees and to lay out a level walk with edging stones, the foreman is told by Mawson that 'all work north of the tennis lawn to be left until I visit the site' and that 'Miss Hall must be consulted' about the work in the old kitchen garden. Exact details are given for the setting out of raspberries, blackcurrants and gooseberries, and 'Mr Stanton is to be consulted as to all planting of New Trees'.[31] For his first commissions he frequently visited the site to assess and direct operations. As he became busier, this function devolved to his sons.

The first call for Mawson's services came from the Bridsons at Bryerswood in Sawrey, on the wooded western bank of Lake Windermere. (There had been a small commission from Sir H.Moore at Crook on Windermere in the same year, 1887.) The house, recently built by Bolton-based architect Richard Knill Freeman for his Bolton neighbour J.R.Bridson on a slope overlooking the lake, was demolished some years ago. Bryerswood was a substantial, L-shaped gabled house with timbering across its upper floor, perhaps more influenced by Cheshire beams than the local stone. The large, bow-shaped ground floor windows faced west, ready to capture the sun and glimpses of the lake; they also overlooked the grassy platform on which the house stood, below which the Bridsons wanted a garden.

No plans survive for Bryerswood, but the site, gently decaying, reveals fragments of its past. Photographs from the 1930s show herbaceous borders by the lawn. The slope near the site of the house, contained by a stone terrace with a wide arched alcove above the remains of a metal fountain pond, squelches underfoot in the boggy meadow which now conceals the pleasure garden. Nearby, on a better drained site under the new house, the kitchen garden survives, with part of its original greenhouses intact. A boiler of indeterminate age aids the continuation of their use by tender plants. Below the greenhouses the kitchen garden thrives with cardoons and roses cheering the vegetables within; stone walls contain the whole, and a stone arch frames the wooden gate which leads through to the orchard.

With money from the bleaching works at Bolton, J.R.Bridson became a substantial figure in the social life of Windermere. He was a founder member in 1860 of the Windermere Sailing Club, which took the title of the Royal Windermere Yacht Club in 1887.[32] The club became a hub of activity for this new rich élite, whose members, such as the Pattinsons from Rayrigg Hall, might individually entertain on hired steamboats, and test their skills and sense of power in regattas.[33] Being employed by the Bridsons gave Mawson contacts in other parts of the Lake District and beyond, for a number of wealthy men who belonged to the yacht club also had property elsewhere in the north. Such a contact was Bolton 'offcomer' Sir James Scott, commodore of the yacht club in 1903, for whom Mawson landscaped an upper drive with hollies, and planted limes and possibly a herbaceous border on the lower drive in 1902.[34] The house, Yews, was extended from its earlier beginnings when the Storrs estate south of Bowness had been put up for sale in 1896. Sir James' sons Samuel and Francis – the latter a sailor – owned and managed the Provincial Insurance Company of Kendal, for which Mawson Brothers made a garden layout.[35]

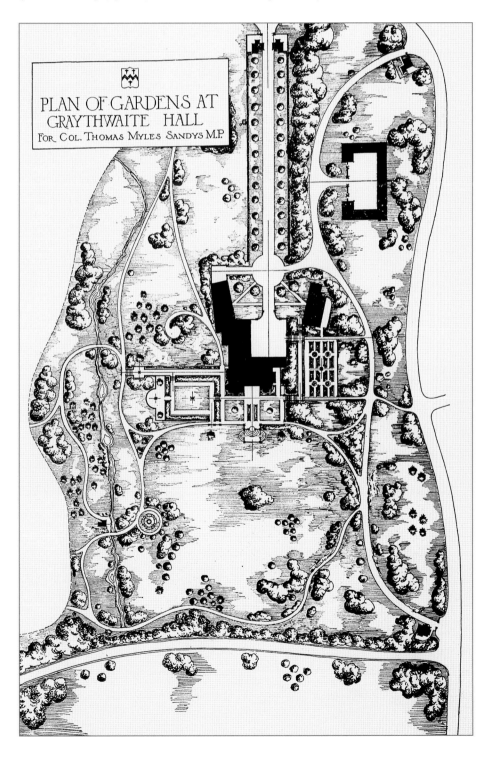

BELOW Here is Mawson's first significant design for his 'composite' garden. Graythwaite Hall's formal green garden is close to the house with informal woodlands and water garden blending into the distance. The drawing is from the 1st edition of *The Art and Craft of Garden Making* (fig. 141).

PLAN OF GARDENS AT
GRAYTHWAITE HALL
FOR COL. THOMAS MYLES SANDYS M.P.

At Bryerswood Thomas Mawson met Captain Josceline Bagot of Levens Hall, where in the 1920s he designed a water garden for the tenant, Lt. Colonel Sir James P. Reynolds.[36] More importantly, he met Bridson's neighbour in Sawrey and Member of Parliament for Bootle, Colonel Sandys of Graythwaite Hall, who wanted some improvements to his property.

Such a commission was the making of the man, as much for the chain reaction of professional contacts he enjoyed while engaged in the work, as for the showcasing of his skills. Mawson employed Richard Knill Freeman (the architect of Bryerswood) to make additions to the house and gardens. However, Mawson was particularly impressed by the skill and dexterity of Freeman's Lincolnshire architect colleague, Dan Gibson (1865–1907). 'One of the handsomest, most courtly, and able men I have ever known',[37] Gibson was, in addition, an impressive draughtsman, metal worker and figure maker: his sundials and wrought-iron gates raised the standard of decoration and ornamentation on Mawson's work above the ordinary. He was to work as a pupil in the London office of Ernest George and Peto. Gibson was a colleague and friend of Arthur Simpson (1857–1922), a Quaker woodcarver from Kendal, who made furniture for Mawson. Simpson had trained locally with a cabinet maker before working for Gillows of Lancaster, and then trying, unsuccessfully, to make a living in Kendal. No luckier in London with William Aumonier in the early 1880s through the low pay he received, he walked home to Kendal – some 250 miles. Mawson did not always credit the men he employed, and it is possible that Simpson may have worked for him in the role of 'Architectural and General Woodcarver', a title Simpson adopted, perhaps making garden furniture, after his second and successful return to Kendal in 1885. Simpson had provided the carved choir stalls in St James' Church in Staveley, near one of Mawson's garden commissions. Simpson knew Charles Francis Annesley Voysey (1857–1941), the architect for Moor Crag, which was landscaped by Mawson, and Charles Edward Mallows (1864–1915), architect and draughtsman, one of the illustrators of *The Art and Craft of Garden Making*, and who also designed gardens.

Sandys took on Mawson from 1889 to about 1905 to improve his garden, park and, later, parts of his estate, which lay between Lake Windermere and Esthwaite Water. This was 'almost impossible' territory in which to work, for the soil was thin – in some places only a few inches covered the rocky outcrops.[38] Trees shrouded the house, which dates back to the fifteenth century; there

was only one entrance, and the ground fell sharply along the drive, which made the house appear to be sitting in a hollow. Mawson was to show his skill in landscaping, and rehearse features which would return in other gardens but adapted to their sites.

By 1896 excavation had been carried out along the drive to remove its hillocks and give a better picture of the hall and plans had been made to return the drive to the north side of the house. Rock was hewn away from the encircling crags to make another side entrance. Notably, terraces constructed along the west and north

fronts gave more height to the house. Mindful of the work of Humphry Repton, whom he admired, Mawson cleared some old oaks to open views out across the park and the surrounding countryside. Further removal of old farm buildings and the resiting of the stables away from the house revealed a rocky hillside to the west, which Mawson planted with Scots firs.

From the terraces facing west, a grassy sward dropped to the boundary marked by established trees, which masked a road. Old yews near the house and old beeches, which Mawson was keen to protect, remained

ABOVE Mawson realised that Graythwaite Hall would gain a greater presence in the landscape by excavating the land around it and setting it on a shallow terrace. He was to use this method of enhancing the setting of a house for many owners.

in the sward, and other trees were moved to new sites. Round the edge of the park conifers were planted for shelter and acid-loving rhododendrons, azaleas and acers to provide colour in spring and autumn. Winding its way through the trees a sinuous path gave different viewpoints inwards to the hall. A stream which ran from northeast to southwest along one side of the garden invited the development of a water garden, its banks planted with daffodils, iris, Japanese anemones and spiraea. Mawson and Gibson designed an oak bridge to cross the stream, which was drawn by C.E.Mallows in

1899 and printed in the first edition of *The Art and Craft of Garden Making*.[39] All of this was typical of Mawson's early work – a plan to rearrange nature without imposing geometry, a transition between the 'natural' parkland and the formality which he was to introduce on each side of the Hall.

Freeman's archway enclosed Dan Gibson's beautiful wrought-iron gate (which has recently been moved to the other side of the courtyard), through which access was gained to an enclosed formal green garden on the north-east side of the hall, with neat box hedges forming low

LEFT The green garden, on the east side of Graythwaite Hall, with its sundial designed by Dan Gibson, is flanked by box parterres and Mawson's 'mushroom' yews, where golden tops are grafted onto green bases.

RIGHT AND BELOW The drawing of Dan Gibson's wrought-iron gate appeared in the first edition of *The Art and Craft of Garden Making* as fig. 140 and shows the original position by the house. Now facing it across the courtyard, the gate displays the importance of wrought iron to Arts and Crafts garden makers.

GATEWAY AND STEPS TO FORECOURT.
Graythwaite Hall.
Sydney R Jones · 1906

compartments. Within were placed specimen yews, each with its golden top trimmed into a ball which was grafted onto a green yew base. This was to become a Mawson speciality. In the centre, Gibson had devised a tall sundial whose square head rose above the viewer. This was to be one of many Gibson references to seventeenth-century garden making. Stone figures of children topped pillars at the exit which led through grass into trees. On the northwestern side of the house was a more relaxed, sunk garden, enclosed by balustrading and flower borders, overlooking the round rose garden, the trees and greensward falling away from the house and dropping to the stream. Further terrace schemes were made following Colonel Sandys' death in 1912.[40] The Gibson sundial became a striking feature on the covers of the last three editions of *The Art and Craft of Garden Making*.

Colonel Sandys was to call on Mawson for further work on the Graythwaite Hall Estate at Beechmount, in 1897, to make an oak bridge over a stream in its grounds, rather similar to the one at Graythwaite, and to make a long wooden trellis between flat-topped stone pillars that were to be crowned with rough stone.[41] In 1904 Mawson was called again to Beechmount. The days of driving to Graythwaite three days a week in a small open trap to supervise the work, were now gone, and keeping an eye on daily events was the job of the foreman.[42] The plans for Beechmount notably show a continuing craft and regional influence, with emphasis placed on the most ubiquitous functional – and beautiful – feature of the Lakeland landscape, the dry stone wall:

A. Remove bank at A and prepare foundations for a dry wall. Build dry wall to height of path giving slight batter on face. Build in suitable wall plants and provide ample soil at back. Select good square stone from local or Coniston quarries for coping. Set coping 1 foot 4 inches wide and the depth of itself above the path.

B. Allow wall to remain in present position but remove bank in front of other wall thus to support same or otherwise underpin wall.

There are diagrams for wooden fence palings, how stepping stones are built into a wall, and drawings of arches and gates. The kitchen garden, that other functional and beautiful part of the Edwardian landscape, was given detailed attention, as was the renewed kitchen garden at Graythwaite Hall.[43]

Mawson praised Colonel Sandys for being 'a beneficent paternal[ist]'…'in advance of the Liberal policy of better housing', for providing free medical care for his estate workers, and for paying a living wage.[44] Mawson was called to lay out the grounds around three cottages at Sawrey for Colonel Sandys for his estate workers, with their yards, wash houses, and drying grounds, all set

before an orchard.[45] Thomas Mawson acknowledged the benefit of the paternalistic encouragement of his client by dedicating the first three editions of *The Art and Craft of Garden Making* to Colonel Sandys.

The history of Graythwaite Hall encapsulates much of what was to come: the importance of 'raising' the house by means of terracing; Mawson's 'composite' layout of formal and informal; the appreciation of the regional characteristics of the landscape, in site, rocks, soil, plants, and trees; the love of the local crafts, in wood, stone,

ABOVE One of Brockhole's well established dry stone walls, with plants in some of the crevices. Such walls are found throughout Lakeland, and Mawson gave instructions on how to make them in *The Art and Craft of Garden Making*.

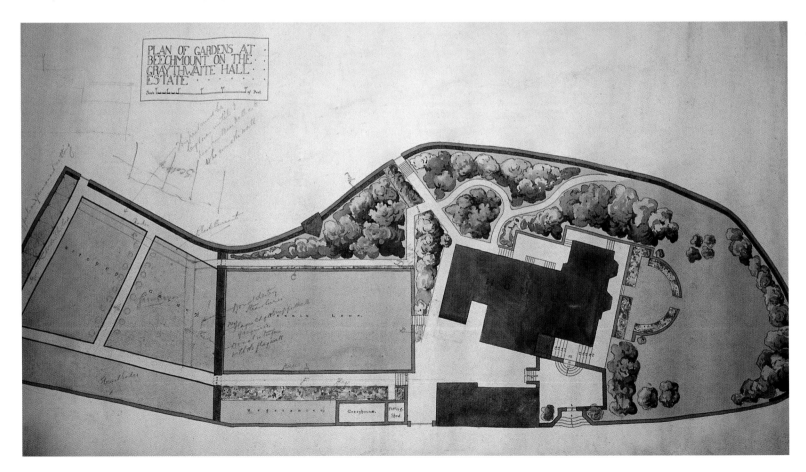

ABOVE Holehird, where
Mawson had a small
commission to build
glasshouses for brewer
William Grimble Groves.
On a slope above the gothic
mansion, built in 1854,
little remains of the original
glasshouses except the
surrounding walled garden.

LEFT A plan of one of the
houses on the Graythwaite
Estate, Beechmount,
with its simple but effective
garden plan, and space for
tennis courts behind.

and design; the infinite care with which sites were surveyed, plans drawn up, and directions given. No wonder Mawson was to be recalled by his employers and recommended to others.

With a well-developed system of foremen and workmen, it was possible – and wise – to take on small commissions. One such was at Holehird near Troutbeck Bridge, an enlarged gothic mansion bought by a local brewer, William Grimble Groves, in 1897. There were extensive glasshouses already in place, but Groves had a large orchid collection for which he wanted special conditions, and for this work he commissioned Mawson.[46]

Either the circle around the yacht club or the Pattinson connection led to Mawson's introduction to Mrs Edna Howarth of Low Wood Lodge beside Lake Windermere. Her Manchester businessman husband had bought the 11 acre site in 1890 for a modest retirement property but had died, leaving a widow who had grander ideas.

She commissioned the Manchester architect, Joseph Pattinson, to design a house with six bedrooms, a servants' hall on the ground floor, a conservatory and verandah. Later a billiard room was added. The house was built of Brathay blue stone by Grissenthwaite of Penrith, and was the first house in Windermere to have electric light.[47] Edna Howarth changed the name of the house to Langdale Chase, planned a boathouse in the same blue stone and gave the lodge to the head gardener. She commissioned Brockbank of Bowness to make a 50 foot steam launch, Thomas Mawson to lay out the

grounds, and began to entertain in the grand manner.[48]

The house was ready for occupation in 1894 and the gardens were probably laid out at that date. Mawson had provided three gardeners, who stayed at Langdale Chase from then on, to be joined in time by five others. It is likely that Howell Harrison, the head gardener, had been Mawson's original foreman for the job. The landscaping which evolved was aimed at providing status and amenity, rather than floral display. The oaks which lined the carriage drive in the front were preserved, giving dignity to the house. At the back, a steep drop to the lake was smoothed into a gentler slope which was planted with rhododendrons and azaleas for spring colour. Steps were made leading down to paths through shrubs, roses and a water garden where Edna Howarth, her daughter Lily and their guests could enjoy the flowers of summer. Visitors could delight in the views of the Langdales and watch the yachts on the water while strolling along the newly made gravel paths round the lake. There was tennis and croquet on the lawn below Mawson's balustraded terrace.

During Edna Howarth's ownership, Langdale Chase, with its grounds well suited to entertaining, became a social centre, hosting garden parties and a fashionable annual Chrysanthemum Tea in a marquee on the lawn.[49]

Later the upper room of the boathouse was turned into a tea room. However it was not until 1930, long after the death of Edna Howarth, that the building became an hotel, though the grounds have not been altered much since they were laid out by Mawson.

In 1898 Mawson asked Gibson to become his partner. Mawson saw the merit in having some recognised architectural qualification within the firm, and the multi-talented Gibson had already become attractive to those looking for well-designed houses. The partnership was short-lived, lasting just under two years, but only because Gibson wanted to set up on his own. Thomas Mawson's second son, John, was eventually a pupil in Gibson's office in Windermere.[51] Gibson continued to collaborate with Mawson afterwards, especially at the Heathwaite villas and The Corbels in 1899, and Shrublands in 1904, for his brother Robert Mawson – all had stone balls on the chimneypots. These two houses, with Brockhole, 1898, show the strong Lakeland influence of local stone and slate, uneven rooflines which catch the eye, the rounded chimneypots on chunky chimneys, and houses more akin in design to cottages than classical mansions. It was a loss to architecture that Gibson was to die in 1907, in his early forties; he remains an intriguing figure about whom very little is known.

ABOVE Originally Low Wood Lodge, Edna Howarth enlarged the house, calling it Langdale Chase, and employed Mawson to landscape the grounds. She entertained her sailing friends, and held garden exhibitions here.

RIGHT The boathouse at Langdale Chase, where an upper room was turned into a tearoom. Here the guests at chrysanthemum shows and other garden functions were entertained.

ABOVE Brockhole was
designed by Dan Gibson.
Clever terracing, begun
by Mawson, disguises the
difficult asymmetry of
the site below the house.

LEFT Lake Windermere's
shore below Brockhole.
Conifers around the
boundaries helped to shelter
the house and grounds.

The pair were busy from 1897 to 1900 at Brockhole, on the east bank of Lake Windermere between Windermere and Ambleside, for Manchester silk merchant William Henry Adolphus Gaddum. There were family connections in the area. Gaddum's wife Edith was Beatrix Potter's cousin. The substantial front of the house, with its reception rooms which face the lake, has four semicircular Jacobean gables over the bedroom windows, which was not unusual at the time. C.F.A. Voysey used them, too, although this was not a Westmorland style. The back and sides have the Lakeland pitched slate roofs, and there are stocky chimneys with rounded tops. The building was put up relatively quickly

as the stone was quarried locally. The Gaddums had bought thirty acres of land, and a magnificent site, which gently slopes westwards to the lake. The only difficulty appeared to be a shortage of water, which had to be pumped up from a well near the kitchen, while there were tanks to collect rainwater for the house and the orangery at the south end of the house.

Mawson planted conifers around the edge of the land to shelter it, as he had done at Graythwaite – a practice favoured by Repton and others, and which supplemented the natural woodland to the north and east of Brockhole. He planted Wellingtonias (*Sequoiadendron giganteum*), Caucasian firs (*Abies nordmanniana*) and

Douglas firs (*Pseudotsuga menziesii*). Then he terraced the south- and west-facing slopes, stressing that terraces 'should not be considered merely as one long promenade, but rather as a series of gardens, each division having its own particular charm; the whole being in connection with the best apartments of the house and forming a series of changes'.[51]

Walls of squared stone and slate with coping stones to drain off the rain were made near the house to strengthen the design of inner enclosures defined by yew and divided by stone steps. Two formal layouts were planned, at the east and west ends of the top terrace. As with all designs, the client had his own ideas, and the east garden was not implemented, but left as a lawn. Historian Hilary Taylor thinks this was intended as a rose garden.[52] She also suggests that a rustic pergola seen in contemporary photographs on the top terrace was Gaddum's work, and 'not very successful'. Asters, phlox and kniphofias were planted, colourful shrubs such as ceanothus, pyracanthus and *Chaenomeles japonica*, and aubretia, London Pride, *Dianthus lithospermum* and *Erinus alpinus* were tucked in the rockwork.[53]

Further down the slope the stone used for the walls changed to locally found boulders, and the formal garden merged into a wild meadow and woodland next to the lake. The kitchen garden, carefully placed behind beech hedges so it would not be seen as part of the flower garden, used its sheltered, sunny site to produce fruit, vegetables and espaliered apple and pear. The parkland retained its original oak and ash, to which Mawson added copper beech and limes along the drive.

The *International Studio Magazine* for May 1899 showed illustrations of three houses designed for owners in the North West by C.F.A. Voysey.[54] They were for H. Rickards at Windermere, W.E. Rowley at Glassonby, Kirkoswald in Cumberland and Currer Briggs at Broadleys, Gillhead, on the Storrs estate. Only Broadleys was built. The illustrations demonstrated a new approach to the architecture of middle-sized country houses: they were long and low like the Lake District longhouses, with clean lines and walls which sloped gently outwards and were accentuated by slim buttresses, and grouped rectangular windows set in bowed or rectangular bays. There was none of the nineteenth-century classical revivalism and decoration which Voysey abhorred and called 'shirt-front architecture'.[55] These were larger versions of the cottage farmhouse, which fitted the current building trend in Lakeland, but were also what Voysey wanted to design. Later came plans for G. Toulmin, of Windermere (again, the design was

not realised), Moor Crag on the Storrs estate south of Windermere in 1899 for J.R. Buckley, and Littleholme at Kendal in 1909 for the woodcarver Arthur Simpson. Of these, Moor Crag is considered to be the best house he ever designed.[56] Littleholme, with its garden made by Simpson's wife Jane based on her floral embroidery patterns, was the simplest.[57]

Voysey began his own practice and married at the same time as Thomas Mawson, and there was, briefly, a similarity of approach between the men. Voysey attracted interest in the Lakes from those who wanted smaller homes in the vernacular style, which were utilitarian as well as simple, and yet were well designed. 'The essential characteristic of Mr Voysey's work', said Baillie Scott, 'is its absolute sincerity.'[58]

On 23 June 1899, a third and final design for Moor Crag was shown to the client, J.R. Buckley, a textile manufacturer, at Rigg's Hotel in Windermere, and was 'approved by him and Mrs Buckley in the presence of Mr Mawson'. This comment was then written by Voysey and signed under the design.[59] The builder was a Pattinson. Clearly Mawson and Voysey worked harmoniously together, planning house and garden as one piece.[60] The approach to the house was hewn out of rock, and the drive curved round to the left suddenly to reveal the house on the hillside above. In many ways Moor Crag startles the viewer: it is long and low and anchored to its site in a way that prefigures the work of Frank Lloyd Wright (1869–1959). The east/west line of the house is at right angles with Lake Windermere below to the west, and the slope of the roof at this end follows the lay of the land like an extended bird's wing.

BELOW An early view of Moor Crag. Many sites in Lakeland needed rock to be removed from drives and banks.

ABOVE Moor Crag's woodland setting and shrubs helped to disguise the domestic arrangements for the house. The laundry lay to the left, below the house.

RIGHT Voysey's front of house makes a dramatic picture as the visitor rounds the drive from below and Moor Crag comes into view. Mawson's landscaping here was simple and natural.

LEFT Broadleys was built at much the same time across the road from Moor Crag, on the lakeside; Voysey's rounded windows look towards Lake Windermere. Stone terracing accommodates rhododendrons, and steep, stony paths drop towards the lake at the back of the house.

RIGHT Stone paths above the lowest terrace at Broadleys give fine views of Lake Windermere.

The natural surroundings of the house were wooded and Mawson intended a simple setting for its front on the north side, through grass, boulders and some of the original trees. There was some cultivation of flowering shrubs on the slope below the house, partly to hide the laundry and the path for the domestic staff. The garden for the house lies on its south side. It is small, divided into two halves by hedges which aligned themselves with the unequally divided house. Voysey had brought the roof very low in the middle of Moor Crag, interrupting it with a tiled, rectangular bay. By contrast each end presented to the sun a white gable with rectangular groups of windows.

The garden rises from the house, where the level was eventually broken by a stone wall, and further cultivation extended southwards. As there are no Mawson plans for this garden, it is impossible to tell what he intended for this side of the house. However, he designed a wooden playhouse with its stained-glass windows which once stood higher up in the trees on the southeast corner of the garden, beyond what must have been a lawn. The house itself is now in divided ownership.

Did Mawson lay out the garden at Broadleys? He does not say so in *Life and Work*, and there is no written evidence, but family sources say he did. Broadleys may have been finished before Moor Crag; its rock gardens and terracing suit the Mawson approach, and it is tempting to imagine the landscape architect moving between the closely situated houses to compare notes on the two Voysey houses.

If Moor Crag was predominantly an architect's province, Mawson's Yorkshire manufacturer client, Henry Martin, was more interested in collecting trees than good design. His house, Cringlemire, is set about one mile west of Langdale Chase, on a hilltop with a distant yet clear view across Lake Windermere. Mawson prepared a plan for a sunk formal garden contained within yew hedges, with flower borders by steps which led down to a green parterre with a central sundial.[61] The present garden was realigned later with its centre defined by geometry, and there are terraces on the eastern side of the house and a pergola on the north. As Mawson explained in *Life and Work*, Martin's real requirement 'was not a pleasaunce, but an arboricultural museum', and the implementation of the plan was handed over to Thomas' brother Robert.[62] The wide landscape beyond the house was given a circle of conifers for cover, and Martin would gather up Robert in Thomas' absence 'and in would go another hundred conifers, whilst another twenty men would be set to work on an extension to the rock garden'.[63] Even Thomas Mawson would admit that there was an exceptional collection of shrubs and conifers. Cringlemire's garden house was designed by Gibson, with its pillared verandah protecting an inner room poised above the much extended rock garden.[64]

Mawson's absence from Cringlemire gave him the opportunity to join forces with another respected architect whose practice included fine work on smaller houses – Mackay Hugh Baillie Scott (1865–1945). Blackwell, built for Manchester brewer Sir Edward Holt, later Lord Mayor of Manchester in 1908 and 1909, was finished around 1900. Holt wanted a holiday home in a country setting and commissioned Scott, who had been articled to an architect in Bath in 1886. Scott had written for *The Studio* and knew and admired C.F.A. Voysey's work – in fact his statement about interior design which should be 'without reference to conventional ideas or the dictates of fashion' sounds remarkably like Voysey.[65] His style developed on the Isle of Man, where he lived after his marriage, and he was commissioned by Ernst Ludwig, the Grand Duke of Hesse, to work on the interior of his palace at Darmstadt in 1897. As such work was recorded in contemporary journals, Holt recognised Scott's worth.

BELOW Cringlemire's bastion, with its simple yet elegant balustrading, gives a panorama across the formal garden, lawns and trees to Lake Windermere beyond.

ABOVE An early photograph of Cringlemire's splendid summerhouse, reproduced in the 5th edition of *The Art and Craft of Garden Making* (fig. 205).

RIGHT A photograph from the 1930s showing Cringlemire from the back.

Sited on the Storrs estate, Blackwell benefited from its singular views due to its position high up on the east side of Lake Windermere. Very much an Arts and Crafts building, its walls are roughcast and whitewashed. It has sandstone mullions to its windows, slate roofs, round chimneys and a host of references to the natural in its interior decoration. Local workmen and local materials abound. Simpson of Kendal's carvings of trees and flowers can be seen in the minstrels' gallery, and in rowan berries along the oak wainscot. The windows, as in Frank Lloyd Wright's houses, carry the shapes of flowers in coloured glass defined by lead outlines. Perhaps the most telling connection with the roots of the Arts and Crafts Movement is the revival of a large medieval hall, which successfully becomes the heart of the house.

There is little information about the garden. Edward Holt left no papers and no plans have emerged from Mawson's archive, though he refers to making the gardens in his autobiography. Mawson was working at Yews, close by, in the same year, 1902.[66]

The publication of *The Art and Craft of Garden Making* in 1900 and its second edition in 1901 helped to establish Thomas Mawson as a garden architect and from then on his list of commissions expanded, both in Britain and abroad. For this reason his autobiography speaks less of his work in the Lake District, though commissions there continued to be taken up by Mawson Brothers' Nurseries from 1889.

BELOW Blackwell's lower terrace has a small bastion which overlooks Lake Windermere.

LEFT Baillie Scott's Arts and Crafts house, Blackwell, built for Sir Edward Holt in 1900. Neither Holt nor Mawson left papers for Blackwell, so the layout of the garden remains something of a mystery. The buttressed wall supports the upper terrace, which today has a lawn and planting round the edges and close to the house.

BELOW One of several plans for garden alterations at Rydal Hall, made c.1909.

Strangely, he does not refer in his autobiography to work at Rydal Hall which began in 1909. Stanley Le Fleming was a descendant of a long line of aristocrats whose home, Rydal Hall, was rebuilt several times, and now lies on an oak-rich wooded slope, with ash, sycamore, elms and late added conifers, north of Ambleside. From the terrace on the south the valley of the river Rothay fills the foreground as it makes its way to Lake Windermere, a hazy blue on the skyline. Rydal Water is nearer, but screened from sight on the west. Rydal beck, which descends its boulder-strewn valley by the eastern side of the hall, falls suddenly as a white, divided cascade between dark rocks into a plunge pool before continuing through a ravine into the lower park. The Low Fall, as it is called, was a great attraction for lovers of the Picturesque, and in the seventeenth

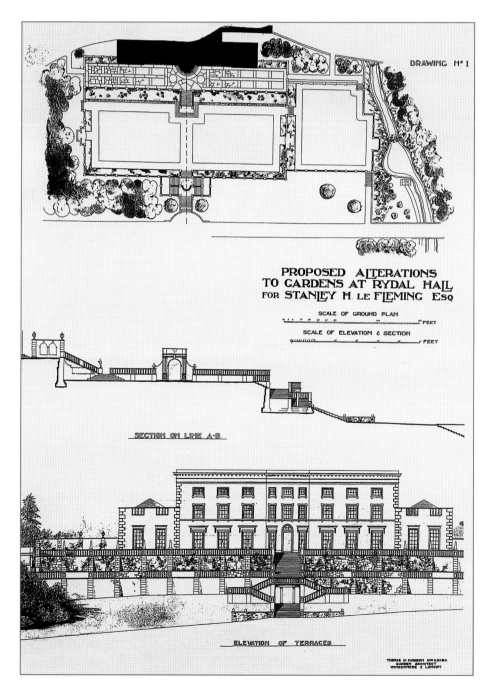

PROPOSED ALTERATIONS TO GARDENS AT RYDAL HALL FOR STANLEY H LE FLEMING ESQ

SCALE OF GROUND PLAN

SCALE OF ELEVATION & SECTION

SECTION ON LINE A·B

ELEVATION OF TERRACES

century a small hut was built as a 'station' from which visitors could gaze and marvel at the water or paint the falls. One of the best representations of *Rydal Waterfall* is by Joseph Wright of Derby in 1795. The valley of the beck with its light and shade, green leaves and sparkling water, and the approach to it through a dark archway, was left intact by Mawson, whose appreciation of the Picturesque was not in doubt. A quiet or wild garden (which dates back to Mawson's time and is now home to some modern sculptures) lay below the lower terrace with ponds and a rivulet fed by pumped water.

Mawson's attention was drawn by Le Fleming to the wide site below the back of the house, which faces south, and he determined to change the entrance to the house from the south to the west, so the main rooms would have full view of the gardens. The *Westmorland Gazette* in 1887 had described Rydal Hall as 'embowered in and overhung by old English gardens. There is no "perkiness", no modernism about it, and above all, no mathematical flower-beds.'[67] The Ordnance Survey map for 1898 shows that two terraces had been made below the hall, the upper terrace divided by steps.[68] It is possible that the slate walls which support the terraces were also built at this time. Mawson's survey indicated a croquet lawn already in place to the east of the terraces that was to become a tennis lawn.[69]

Two plans were drawn up by the firm, and a medley of them both was implemented over several years. The design was surprisingly more akin to the Italian revivalist style of the nineteenth century and out of step with contemporary thinking on gardens, perhaps at the wish of Le Fleming. The hall was to look very grand, with a long and narrow upper terrace laid to concrete slabs, now replaced by turf. Semicircular steps from the hall echoed the bowed shape of the front of the building.

From the upper terrace the descent led via an Italianate staircase with its paired, divided flights of steps (similar to those Mawson must have seen on his first visit to Italy in 1905 with Reginald Cory, the owner of Dyffryn in Wales). These stairs converged in front of a pool and fountain on a wider terrace with inset sheltered seats under short pergolas against the walls. The pergolas divided flower beds made against the terrace walls on the north side. There were trimmed golden yews, as points of interest; box-edged beds formed corners on each side of the lawns which were divided by the pool. These were later planted with standard roses and dahlias, similar to the German *Jugendstil* gardens Mawson must have seen when he visited Dresden and Berlin after the Vienna National Housing and Town Planning

LEFT ABOVE The lawn at Rydal Hall below the house, enclosed by balustrading with scooped hollows to accommodate pots.

LEFT BELOW The fountain pond at Rydal Hall, overlooking the tranquil fields beyond. The wrought-iron gate leads down to a grotto, made from concrete, like the pots and balustrading. The concrete was made on site from sand and gravel from the lake. Rydal still has the original moulds.

ABOVE Steps lead up from the bowling green (which predates Mawson) on to the lawn, with its row of short pergola seats and long herbaceous border.

Conference in 1910. From this terrace another Italianate staircase enclosing a tall, pillared grotto led steeply down to a road to Rydal. The plan was distinctly axial, at a time when such a concept was being quietly abandoned. Concrete balustrading round the terraces was crowned with urns which were made in moulds (which the estate still has), some being painted to resemble terracotta.

Carlisle Diocese, in conjunction with the Cumbria Gardens Trust and English Heritage, has recently restored Rydal Hall's garden and celebrated the end of the work with an Open Day in 2007. Rydal's main problem lay with its decaying concrete. Made since Roman times, Voysey had incorporated it into his houses, and Mawson was one of the first to use such material for garden landscaping. Constructed from Portland cement and Windermere dredged sand and gravel, it was cheaper than stone and produced more quickly.[70] Ornaments and balustrading were manufactured rather than crafted, thus putting them within the reach of the more affluent middle classes. But the artificial stone did not last as long as it should have done. Balustrading and flights of steps weathered, breaking open the initial smooth surface, and cracking to allow rain to percolate and open them even further.

The stonework is now restored, lightening the garden with clearly-defined hard landscaping, and planting has softened the formality of the lower terrace. Gradually Mawson's familiar choices of herbaceous plants will include hemerocallis, phlox, penstemon and poppy, campanula and coreopsis, verbascum and lobelia, peony and delphinium. To these will be added bedding plants such as viola, muscari, primula and arabis. Climbers such as clematis and rose will fill the pergolas, and the blooming of the standard roses in the corner beds will be followed, in late summer, by the bright colours of the dahlias.

The last member of the Le Fleming family to bear the name died in 1939 and the estate is in divided ownership. The Diocese of Carlisle purchased the freehold of the hall for a retreat in 1970.

In 1910, a year after Mawson began work at Rydal, he was commissioned by Edward T. Tyson, who had bought a gabled stone mansion near Cockermouth, built by the Fisher family high above the Cocker valley on the northwestern edge of Lakeland. Wood Hall was enlarged by the Tyson family, who then asked Mawson to landscape the south-facing site. The view had been painted by Turner, and every major incident in the structure of the garden was to lead the eye towards the deep valley below and its meadows and woodlands with the lazy coils of the river reflecting the sky. Mawson's aim was to increase the sense of space and to link the house with the landscape by enabling views from the house, from sites in the garden and from a key point on the front of the garden. The site was horizontally long and narrow and well wooded, and Mawson's design was to spread the terraces asymmetrically down the slope, with different land use on each level, but focusing the whole site on a semicircular 'balcony' or bastion with a sundial overlooking the river.

High on the slope above the house was the kitchen garden, stableyard and orchard, well above the frost pockets lower down; all were accessible from the back road to the house. To the west of the hall, a two-arched stone summerhouse was set by steps which climbed up from the drive below, the path planted with ferns, lobelia, campanula and alyssum. The steps were built as a repeated series of two long stone slabs set on unmortared rubble, beside dry stone walls. It took forty-one stonemasons to complete the work at Wood Hall. A contemporary photograph shows these craftsmen, two with balusters, one with a hammer, another with a

ABOVE The newly made herbaceous border at Rydal Hall, using plants from Mawson's original list, softens the grey stone under the house. Visitors celebrate the reopening of the newly restored gardens in August 2007.

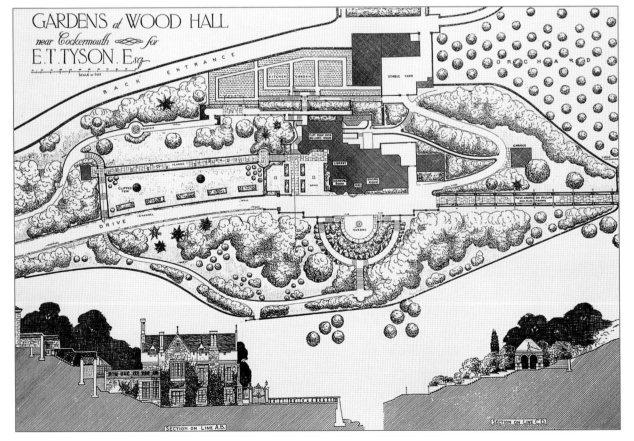

LEFT Mawson's landscape plan for Edward T. Tyson for Wood Hall, Cockermouth, which overlooks woodlands and fields and the valley of the River Cocker. The attractive perspective drawings helped to give the owner of the garden a good idea of its possibilities. *The Art and Craft of Garden Making.* 5th edition, fig.506.

ABOVE An early photograph of the lower summerhouse at Wood Hall. It appeared in the 4th edition of *The Art and Craft of Garden Making*, fig. 433.

Both summerhouses gave extensive views east and south across the valley below.

Flower beds were placed to be visible from the main rooms – the library, drawing room and dining room. Again, contemporary photographs show rectangular rose beds, and herbaceous borders filled with verbascum and pinks, with vines trained up the high retaining wall that led to the kitchen garden. Beyond the house to the east, paths led through trees to the service areas. At the end of the drive, and to finish the design on the east side, a gated pergola with round stone pillars and sturdy wooden cross beams led to steps down to the wild area beyond. Clematis and roses clothed the pillars, and herbaceous perennials filled the spaces between.

Surrounding the gardens was a woodland which needed little attention beyond thinning and the improvement of paths to make easier the walks among the trees – 'as in most hill side gardens there were few walks which ministered to comfort or leisure'.[71] Below the sundial bastion, shade-loving plants and shrubs eased the transition from formal to informal, as trees gave way to the river meadows below.

Today Wood Hall is no more, having been demolished. Its footprint is visible in parts of the foundations, and another, smaller house has been built higher up the slope. The remaining domestic buildings have mixed occupation. Some of the garden has remained, its hard

set square, and another with a pot of plaster. Beside the summerhouse, a grassy bank descended from a retaining wall at the top of the slope, cut in two by a path to the house, with grass and trees on one side and flower beds by the drive below. Above, a three-arched summerhouse was set into the retaining wall. Perhaps Mawson was thinking of the pavilion at the Villa Lante which he had seen on his travels in 1905, and whose form Harold Peto had used in some of his garden designs.

RIGHT The cultivated garden at Wood Hall soon tails off into woodland walks which surround the sloping site.

landscaping conserving the overall shape and its focus southwards towards the river Cocker. The concrete balustrading is now bereft of its many figures and urns which stood on top and the sundial which marked the centre of this promontory. Nevertheless this simplified bastion and its view beyond retains its quiet beauty, especially when seen from above.

Did Mawson, together with James Pulham & Son, make a Japanese garden for the Rea family of Gate House in Eskdale where Mawson worked in 1914? There is only family anecdote to support the claim. (A Mawson plan with a Japanese garden was made for Samuel Waring at Foots Cray in Kent in 1904, see page 69).

The First World War curtailed the activities of the Mawson family, but more commissions were to follow afterwards in the Lake District, completed by the managing directors of Lakeland Nurseries – firstly Thomas Mawson junior, then Harry Pierce, James Walker and Alec Mawson, Robert's son, who would become the chief officer for the London parks of the Greater London Council. The plans for some thirty or more Lakeland

gardens in the second two decades of the twentieth century were usually quickly sketched with a minimum of information and no detailed watercolour insets of houses, gates and coloured layouts as before; often they are neither dated nor signed. There was, no doubt, discussion with the owner as the men surveyed the garden, with decisions made 'in the field'.

One such garden, for Mrs Braithwaite of Far Park, Staveley, was laid out by Harry Pierce in 1921.[72] Far Park, a long, low farmhouse of eighteenth-century origins, has been enlarged by recent owners. It sits with its back towards a slope, on which is an old orchard and possibly the original kitchen garden. Set on a shallow stone terrace and enclosed by steps and dry stone walls, it is open to meadowland on one side and woodland behind; its garden lies before the front of the house. Here a long lawn runs its feet into trees at the far end of the garden.

An undated plan suggests a more rounded shape to the garden, the lawn with its half-circle end and right-angled turnbacks enclosing clipped balls of yew, reminiscent of many of Edward Prentice Mawson's

ABOVE A Japanese-style garden in Eskdale on the Gate House Estate. Family sources suggest it may have been designed for Mawson and Sons. Chris Jones has researched this garden.

architectural drawings. Fences on the outer edges contain shrubs, then box hedges, with two long herbaceous borders enclosing a tennis court in the middle of the lawn. Near the house, wedge-shaped rose beds with lavender between form a semicircle. There were rounded steps to the house, and figures to be set on the terrace. Beside the main garden is a wide area to the right of the front, which was planned for fruit trees and spring bulbs.

Though the overall shape is now rectangular rather than rounded, the herbaceous borders too labour intensive to be maintained and the tennis court never made, the garden has much of the spirit of the original. Within the amphitheatre at the far end of the lawn is a stone plinth with a female figure contained by green hedges; there are laburnums and prunus in the woodland behind it; many of the originally suggested shrubs such as lilac, *Chaenomeles japonica*, philadelphus and deutzia can be recognised close to the house, and there is a predominance of native trees such as hazel in the hedges. Bulbs have been planted in the grass, as in the Mawson plan.

Harry Pierce left an unexpected legacy to Lakeland. This landscape architect, who was steeped in Thomas Mawson's composite form of garden making, befriended

Kurt Schwitters (1887–1948), a German Dada artist who fled Nazi Germany and was interned on the Isle of Man before making a new life painting in the Lake District. In Germany Schwitters had made collages and created works (*Merzbilder*) and bigger constructions (*Merzbau*). Pierce gave him a barn on his land in Ambleside, on which Schwitters was to make his last *Merzbau*. This is now preserved in the University of Newcastle.

There is little doubt that Thomas Mawson's style was shaped by the slopes of Lakeland, and that key elements in his designs owe most to the best use of the site. 'Site' is the first item in his directions to landscape gardeners, made in the five editions of *The Art and Craft of Garden Making*. Not only did he urge architect and landscape gardener to work together so the rooms within the house could often be echoed by the arrangement of compartments outside, but more often the house and garden could gather to themselves the startling views across sheets of water whether blustery and slate-coloured with white curling tops, a contemplative rainy grey or blue and mist-hidden, but often dazzling in the sun. Clearing a selected group of trees would open out pictures of the hills beyond or the river meadows below.

BELOW Far Park, where the original long axis into woodland in front of the house has been tempered by horizontal beds parallel with the terrace.

LEFT Present-day planting on Blackwell's steep walls.

BELOW Lake Windermere beyond Moor Crag. Every new country house owner desired such a view.

The new landscape would need protection, also, and conifers were planted around the boundaries to shield it from the wind and driving rain.

The need to terrace the slope gave opportunities for balustrading and flights of stone steps to decorate, dignify and make accessible all parts of the garden, the style of architecture reflecting the requirements of its client – functional vernacular for Langdale Chase, slim Italianate for the Le Flemings, romantic adornments to absorb the views at Wood Hall, Cockermouth. The designs were not necessarily geometric, with the asymmetry of some, as with the use of concrete, pointing to Modernism rather than Arts and Crafts. Added interest was provided by pots, urns and figures, made, as the balustrading, from concrete intended to look like stone, and which cost its owners less than the real thing – though occasionally an antique piece was bought for the garden. Was this a departure from the Arts and Crafts philosophy of the nobility of work done by hand? Perhaps, but quarried stone from nearby was used to make walls, summerhouses and sundials, and was shaped by stonemasons. Bricks were laid on some paths, wood was crafted into pergolas and arbours, and iron wrought into gates. Rock gardens could be fashioned, and water shaped into falls, canals or pools.

Mawson's planting took into consideration the acid soils and the aspect of the site, so rhododendrons, acers, azaleas, kalmia and heather were frequently planted, a managed informality encircling a formal centre near the house, beyond which were conifers adding to the vernacular spread of Scots firs, oak, ash, beech, birch, hawthorn and hazel. Close to the house was the orderly neatness of geometric beds, parterres and compartments, including the de rigueur rose garden, and often next to hedges which divided the garden into compartments were long herbaceous borders with perennials such as hemerocallis, aquilegia, coreopsis, crambe, delphinium, hollyhocks, poppy, phlox and iris, arranged in asymmetrical masses. Gertrude Jekyll was not the only maker of flowering borders at this time, though Mawson planting did not use drifts of herbaceous plants, as she did.

Mawson's Lakeland gardens contained his clients' functional requirements – the tennis courts, bowling greens and ranges of efficient glasshouses built by his contracting firm, Mawson Brothers, later Lakeland Nurseries. All of these features were easily transferable to other parts of Britain, as the rush of potential clients made clear, and adapted to lower gradients, less acidic soils and sunnier climates. Thus the Arts and Crafts landscape gardener found himself very much in demand.

CHAPTER TWO

Widening horizons: clients with power and prestige

1900–1923

THE FIRST DECADE of the twentieth century brought Mawson rich opportunities, both at home and abroad. His sons were gathered more tightly into the family firm and in order to travel faster to London and the far corners of Scotland, Wales and England the centre of his business activity moved southwards to Lancaster. Mawson also made the ambitious decision to open another office, in London. There were new architects and draughtsmen with whom he worked, and he began to set himself up as a town planner and park maker as well. He collected a wealthy clientele of industrialists, self-made millionaires who became his friends and would continue to give him work over the decades. The aristocratic owners of large estates whose money had come from agriculture were suffering from the decline in farming incomes which had begun in the third quarter of the nineteenth century; they were in the minority of Mawson's clients. This chapter, then, will be concerned with men of industry and commerce, whose landscapes were commissioned for many reasons: for entertainment, for peaceful solitude, for a show of wealth, as well as from an appreciation of beauty. And it also introduces Mawson's work for the royal houses of Europe, which began with Samuel Waring's recommendation to Queen Alexandra, the wife of King Edward VII.

But the movement from the Lake District at the turn of the century was not achieved without anxiety. Money was short, as the Mawsons now had six children. Thomas Mawson had just finished building The Corbels for himself in Windermere and it had been a costly enterprise. Though Mawson does not mention this, Anna decided to work as a midwife to supplement the

family income, and this may have provided resources to build a bungalow at Hest Bank as a second home. There was also personal soul-searching about his adoption of classical revivalism and the direction in which his career was going. He was being drawn closer to an appreciation of formality and his need to relate to architecture, while not abandoning his appreciation of nature in the landscape. He did not want to be considered as a gardener and nurseryman and he wanted to be taken seriously by architects. He sought to establish his position, and that of landscape architecture as against landscape gardening, by writing a manual. Having been rejected by publishing houses, he had just taken the risky decision to pay £660 for the publishing of 1,000 copies of *The Art and Craft of Garden Making*, though Batsford and Country Life agreed to market it for him.[1]

The mental turmoil which accompanied his change of direction provoked a breakdown, which laid him 'aside for many weeks during one of the most critical periods of my career'.[2] He feared that public perception of his work was being distorted by his association, as a nurseryman, with horticulture. In discussion with his partner, Dan Gibson, he admitted that his early work had concentrated too heavily on the natural landscape and had ignored architecture as an art form, though he recognised there was an 'extreme cult' of architectural gardening. Even in his report on the making of Hanley Park in 1894 he had commented that the work he was doing should be 'a subject to be ruled by art and not merely an imitation of nature'.[3] The turning point was in 1900: before this date 'Nature was the conductor, and Art first fiddle'. Now the position was reversed.[4] Nevertheless Mawson was

LEFT The pergola at The Hill gave shelter from Hampstead Heath for Lever (shortly to become Lord Leverhulme) to entertain his friends and constituents.

disturbed by the attitude of some of his established clients who still 'thought he could do good landscape gardening and copy nature' and who now considered him to be 'a heretic'. With great discomfort he saw himself to be 'losing caste as a landscape gardener', but he had 'not yet arrived as a landscape architect'.[5]

Mawson need not have worried as his new book had good reviews and sold out in three months. On the strength of it he gathered in many new clients, including Lawrence Johnston, for whom 'the author's principles became Johnston's guiding light in developing Hidcote'. Mawson's preferred style of a formal core close to the house, and its more natural surroundings further out, was widely accepted; and his calm and efficient wife Anna nursed him back to health.[6]

In order to feel more secure, the family drew close together. This strong clannishness, with Thomas Hayton Mawson at its centre, surely has its roots in the predicament of the young man of sixteen, who had to take on the responsibility usually shouldered by the father of the family. He had had to look after his mother Jane Hayton and his two sisters and two brothers when their father died in 1877. His protective role became part of his being, as he cared for his mother, brothers and sisters as

well as his wife and, eventually, nine children, encouraged by a Protestant work ethic and a sturdy individuality. But there may also have been an element of self-protection, as Mawson had made his own way without the benefit of a university education or articles with a firm of architects; to some extent, his family became a surrounding wall of armour: professional partners on whom he could rely. He could stand away from the arguments between the architects and landscape architects about the primacy of garden design, as his own firm could produce both types of professional and many other skilful experts. The strong element of class distinction in Britain before the First World War perceived Thomas Mawson as 'trade', the gardener/nurseryman. Gardeners did not come from the upper-class certainties which bred 'gentlemen and ladies', nor the middle classes who raised professional architects such as Lutyens and Blomfield, nor the middle classes with money who did not have to work for a living such as plantswoman Gertrude Jekyll. Even William Lever made him enter by the back door.

From 1900 commissions were coming in, ever more plentiful, and Mawson found that his three-roomed office in Windermere offered insufficient accommodation. He looked at the place with regret, for most of his

ABOVE The Bungalow built at Hest Bank as a holiday house for the children and a musical centre for the family with a tennis court on the foreshore. Later the Mattocks family built a house adjoining the music room.

ABOVE RIGHT Thomas Mawson and Charles Mallows working on plans at Hest Bank. Mawson would have liked Mallows to be his business partner, but could not persuade him to agree.

BELOW RIGHT The Corbels, the Mawson home on the Heathwaite estate in Windermere at the end of the 1890s.

children had been born in The Corbels, a house he had built with Dan Gibson on the heights of middle-class Heathwaite, with a garden he had landscaped; his sons had gone to the grammar school at Windermere. The house was to be let to a Miss Forshaw, who paid a half-yearly rent of £34 10s.[7] But there was much travelling to be done to meet his clients, some of whom lived in the south and others in Scotland; he was soon to be covering some 20,000 rail miles a year. Consultations were followed by surveys, arrangements with contractors and directions for foremen. The train journeys and the evenings – in hotels or in his client's house – were spent poring over the day's notes and sketches and making reports to be worked up in the Windermere office. Train journeys from Windermere to the south were lengthy because the route was diverted via Preston. Not only did he write up his reports on the long journeys, but he used a folding portable drawing board made for him by the woodcarver Arthur Simpson, so he could draw diagrams and make plans as well.

In 1901 Mawson took a lease on offices in 28 Conduit Street, off Regent Street in London. This prestigious site was both a mark of his ambition and of the type of client he now attracted. It was also a good tactical move, for the RIBA and the Architectural Association shared premises at number 9. The office was in the charge of James Crossland, Mawson's first pupil, and Mawson would visit from time to time and meet new clients there. He sometimes stayed at the National Liberal Club in Whitehall Place (near Charing Cross railway station), another useful meeting place. Later, Edward Prentice would become a member. From about 1906 the firm had its main office in High Street House, Lancaster, though later Mawson's greatest regret was that he chose to locate his head office in Lancaster rather than London.

The family's bungalow at Hest Bank, on the edge of Morecambe Bay in Lancashire, was set back from the shore (but with enough space for a tennis court), overlooking the cool greys and blues of the sea which withdrew to a hazy distance to reveal miles of pools and sandy ridges at low tide. Sheep grazed on the banks, their fleeces the same tawny colour as the sands that sur-rounded them. It was a short walk to the station over the railway bridge beside the bungalow, and the saving of half a day's travelling to London compared with his journeys from Windermere. Travelling first class (with a *Bradshaw* in his bag), partly for the space to spread out his drawing board and plans, but mainly because he found more interesting people with whom to chat, Mawson would often return home with some worthwhile guest to

ABOVE An 'Elizabethan'
garden at Dalham Hall,
designed by Charles Mallows
for Cecil Rhodes. Rhodes
disliked the garden and died
before it could be made.

entertain to a meal. Persistently late in setting off for the station, there is a family tale which recounts Anna telephoning the station master to persuade him to hold the train while Mawson sprinted hopefully.

The long, low, spacious bungalow had its music room with an organ which Mawson played, and mother and children had good singing voices: Anna alto, Frances soprano, John tenor and Edward bass. They were in demand as a quartet to entertain at village events. A rumbustious family, prepared to leap up from the break-fast table leaving the washing-up and the bed-making undone while they rushed into the music room for an impromptu concert, they shocked the Lincolnshire Smethursts, there on a visit, with their behaviour. However this was also a mark of the difference between the Lincolnshire side of the family, who were wealthy and proper, and the unsophisticated Mawsons. The mar-riage of Helen Mawson and William Smethurst in May 1911 took part in two stages: first, in Grimsby, with only the groom's family present, and the second, in Lancaster, with only the bride's family attending. Anna referred to

the Lincolnshire side as 'big frogs in little puddles'; though later Mawson & Son shaped the gardens at the Smethurst family home at Thornton Hall in 1919–20.

Dan Gibson's ending of his partnership with Mawson gained the latter another amicable working companion – Charles Edward Mallows (1864–1915), who rented his London office at 28 Conduit Street from Mawson. The son of a Bedford boot-and-shoe-maker, Mallows had been educated at Bedford Art School and articled to the local architect F.T.Mercer before attending the Royal Academy Schools. A considerable artist, he also designed gardens, as well as illustrating Mawson's commissions. Mawson and Mallows were strongly influenced by the seventeenth century, and its belief in the combination of house and garden design. It is likely that Mallows encouraged Mawson to exhibit the firm's designs at the Royal Academy, where fifty were shown from May to August, between 1900 and 1932. Mallows was asked by John Pyghtle White, the Bedford maker of garden furniture, to design White's house and garden, and he illustrated White's catalogue. Mallows and

Mawson worked together in 1901 on an inauspicious commission for a garden in the Elizabethan style at Dalham Hall in Suffolk for Sir Robert Affleck, though Affleck lost his money almost immediately and the hall was bought by Cecil Rhodes (1853–1902), who was rude to Mallows and whose death removed the need to finish the work.[8]

Another London compatriot was Robert Atkinson (1883–1952), who was born in Wigton, near Carlisle. The son of a cabinet maker, he had worked in Mallows' office as a perspective draftsman after training part-time at Nottingham School of Art and began to work for Thomas Mawson in 1906. Later he set up offices in London, became an associate of the Royal Institute of British Architects in 1910, and was soon after awarded a fellowship, before becoming the principal of the Architectural Association in 1913. Atkinson's remarkable drawings and watercolours helped to illuminate plans and diagrams in the pages of *Civic Art* (published in 1911)) and editions of *The Art and Craft of Garden Making*.[9]

Mawson had the ability to cultivate wealthy industrialists. Throughout his working career he kept the respect, and the commissions, of a band of newly rich men: industrialist Andrew Carnegie, furniture maker and decorator Samuel Waring, manufacturer Lord Leverhulme, and, briefly, the store owner Gordon Selfridge. These men had the restlessness which accompanies ambition and were constantly making changes to their properties. Mawson & Sons could meet their demands and Mawson Brothers or Lakeland Nurseries would carry out the contracts.

Andrew Carnegie (1835–1918), whose early life bore an uncanny resemblance to that of Thomas Mawson, was born in Dunfermline. His father, a handloom weaver making damask in the small cottage in which the family lived, found his livelihood threatened by the advance of steam-driven looms and the factories in which they were housed. In 1848 the family emigrated to the United States. Carnegie senior found work as a handloom weaver in the cotton industry in Allegheny City, with his son Andrew as a bobbin boy. In his autobiography Andrew Carnegie, like Thomas Mawson, stressed the need 'to get to work that I might help the family'.[10] From bobbin boy to messenger boy to telegraph operator for the Pennsylvania Railroad, the young Carnegie's shrewdness, hard work and self-taught understanding of business took him swiftly from manager and investor in the railroad industry and in oil-rich land to ownership of the largest iron and steel works in the USA. By his early thirties he was a millionaire and had no need to work any further.

BELOW Skibo Castle, Andrew Carnegie's Scottish home in the summer months. Mawson was responsible for the terracing and balustrading, and for the layout of the land in front of the hedge.

Carnegie had never lost the love for the land of his childhood and rented properties in Scotland with his wife Louise late each summer; the early summers were mostly spent travelling in Europe. After Margaret was born in 1897, Carnegie decided to make a home in Scotland and bought the ruined Skibo Castle in Sutherland from the Duke of Sutherland. Before he had rebuilt the castle, however, he was able to buy another site which had made a lasting impression on the Carnegie family history: Pittencrieff Glen in Dunfermline. This, and Skibo, brought Thomas Mawson and Andrew Carnegie into contact.

Mawson had lost out in the competition to design Carnegie's park for Dunfermline in 1904 (as described in chapter seven), but Carnegie clearly respected his talent for landscape architecture, and asked him to make alterations and additions to the landscape at Skibo. The Scottish baronial remaking of the castle is attributed to the firm of Ross & Macbeth between 1900 and 1905, and Carnegie made early improvements such as the installation of electricity and running water so that he and his family were able to spend nearly every summer and autumn in Scotland before returning to New York for the winter. Here he entertained men such as Lloyd George and Woodrow Wilson, his great friend and English cabinet minister John Morley, Paderewski and Rudyard Kipling, and, more significantly for

Mawson, the American ambassador to Germany, Andrew Dickson White (1832–1918), who was the American delegate to the first Peace Conference at The Hague in 1899.[11] As Louise Carnegie described, visitors would arrive through 'a beautiful undulating park with cattle grazing, a stately avenue of fine old beeches, glimpses of the Dornoch Firth, about a mile away, all seen through the picturesque cluster of lime and beech trees'.[12] A circular carriage court and roomy *porte cochère* led into the impressive spacious interior of the castle with its patterned stonework and the art nouveau stained-glass windows depicting the lairds of Skibo gazing down the staircase at the visitors. It was all very similar to what was to come in the interior of the Palace of Peace in The Hague.

Set high on a terrace on the north side of the Dornoch Firth, Skibo Castle's pink stone came from nearby quarries, but there was also steel from Pittsburgh in its structure. Its great appeal remains in the magnificent views southwestwards, across the Dornoch Firth to the ancient, rounded tops of the mountains of Easter Ross. The castle is still sheltered by mature deciduous trees which give displays of colour in spring and autumn. The 30,000-acre estate was almost enclosed on the west by the river Shin and the east by the river Evelix, and Carnegie dammed the Evelix to make Loch Evelix and the Allt Garbh to make three other lochs: Ospidale,

LEFT The formal garden at Skibo around the fountain below the grotto.

Margaret and Lake Louise. These introduced the salmon and trout for which he liked to fish. He had already added buildings including a conservatory and a swimming pool enclosed with a glass roof and its gallery-like viewing platform, before summoning Mawson in the autumn of 1903 to come 'at once' to Skibo.

Mawson was horrified at Carnegie's 'feeble attempts at artificial rocky streams and rock gardens, and other mistaken attempts at garden-making scattered about in all directions'. The 'bath-house', he reckoned, 'must have cost a fortune', and it introduced 'a persistent jarring note'. Mawson walked the grounds with Carnegie, suggesting landscaping improvements, including the planting of trees on the west. Perhaps Carnegie asked Mawson about the golf course he wanted. Plans sent to Carnegie's New York home gave details of the balustraded terrace steps and the planting which Mawson carried out close to the front of the castle in 1904.[13]

Skibo's plans are now missing from the Cumbria archives and there are no Mawson plans at Skibo. But rough paintings in the archive and one small drawing for a stone archway in a walled garden, possibly to a kitchen garden, in the fifth edition of *The Art and Craft of Garden Making* show that there was more Mawson input into the general plan for the gardens than the balustrading which spans the wide south front just under the windows of the first floor and finishes the grass bank supporting the terrace like a band of lace edging a garment.[14] Mawson added a bastion which looks across the Firth and tops a planted, grotto-like feature between two flights of stone steps leading down to a rock garden. The paintings show a round pool with a fountain to the south beyond the steps, which may predate Mawson, set in the grass below the bastion. Today this is surrounded by eight beds, typical of Mawson, planted with dahlias in the autumn and bulbs in the spring. The ground rises eastwards, with herbaceous borders leading towards a walled kitchen garden. Today the beds within are partially planted with heathers and small coniferous shrubs beside a long range of glasshouses.

Carnegie had retired from industrial life in 1899 and while at Skibo developed his resolve to give away his fortune of some 40 million dollars. It was, in his words, a decision 'to stop accumulating and begin the infinitely more serious and difficult task of wise distribution'. This wise distribution eventually found its way into ventures for education, welfare and peace. He had been approached by the pacifist British journalist W.T. Stead to join the peace movement at the time of the first International Peace Conference in The Hague in 1899, but it was 1910 before his Carnegie Endowment for International Peace was established. In the meantime, Andrew Dickson White and the lawyer Frederick Holls (1857–1903) visited Carnegie at Skibo. White, in colourful and evocative tones, tried to persuade Carnegie to fund a 'Temple of Peace' in The Hague which would accommodate conferences, while Frederick Holls in more measured words pursued the need for an international Law Library in the same building, which would eventually serve a permanent Court of Arbitration. By 1903 Carnegie had agreed and at Skibo signed a draft for a bill of exchange for the transfer of 1.5 million dollars from New York to The Hague.[15]

However, the wrangling and disagreement about the choice of site, the status of the Peace Palace, which was considered at length as a 'world capital' that might rank 'next to the Vatican as a symbol of global unity in earthly matters', and then the struggles over the choice of design, delayed the beginning of construction until 1908. A competition was held in which architects including Otto Wagner, H.P.Berlage, Saarinen of Finland and Greenley and Olin of New York produced designs with which the jury found fault. Eventually they chose that of the Beaux-Arts educated Louis Cordonnier from Lille. His neo-Flemish building, based on 'a mix of baroque and gothic', was modified with the help of the Dutch Van der Steur of Haarlem, later the architect in charge of operations. The palace, with its red brick and white sandstone façade and steeply sloping roof of grey Welsh slate, was built on a square with an inner courtyard. A tall clock tower, topped by a turreted belfry, dominates the southern end, with a central needle-like spire, small dormer windows and a slim northern belfry adding decoration to the roofscape.

It was decided to invite only three suitably qualified men to compete for the layout of the grounds. They were L.Springer of Haarlem, H.de Wilde of Ghent and Thomas Mawson. Mawson's selection as one of the perceived three best European landscape designers, and his winning of the competition, were significant indicators of the importance of his career at this point.

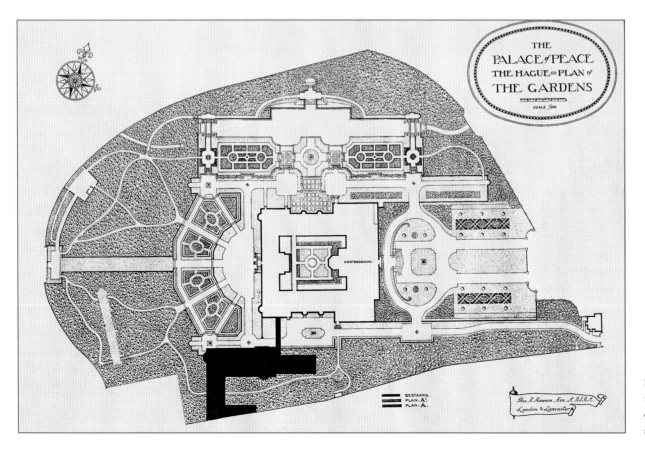

LEFT One of several plans for the Peace Palace grounds, drawn up to Mawson's specification in 1908.

On 26 May 1908 Mawson signed an acknowledgement of £941 7s.8d. sent by the Carnegie Foundation for his design for the grounds surrounding the Peace Palace.[16]

The Peace Palace was built on land in the old Zorgvliet and Rustenburg estates, a wooded area on the edge of the sand dunes to the southwest of the North Sea resort of Scheveningen. There were many old oak, beech and lime trees, some oaks dating back to the avenues planted by the seventeenth-century owners of the grand Zorgvliet estate, including King William III's personal adviser and head gardener, Hans Willem Bentinck. One of the requirements of the competition was that as many of the trees as possible should be left standing, especially on the north side of the palace, to maintain 'the somewhat forest-like character of the park'. The competition imposed few other stipulations: these related to the carriage court, views of the building from the Scheveningen road, and the terrace and balustrading in front of the palace; but the plan could 'freely deal with the foreground of the building', in keeping with its 'monumental character'.

Mawson was governed by his desire to enhance the meaning of the Peace Palace, and to create an iconography of 'peace and rest by breadth of treatment and noble, happy and dignified features and adornments'. There should be 'clear, tranquil pools of water', carefully chosen trees and shrubs with wide, smooth leaves and restrained schemes of colouring. The front of the palace faced east and the spaces surrounding the palace were to be treated differently. Mawson planned two main axes to the leading features: one from the Carnegieplein on the east through entrance gates to a fountain of peace continued via the palace across the inner courtyard and out to the western garden. The second began in a garden pavilion – 'the Temple of Peace'– on the north, crossing the canal to the palace and its courtyard. Two pergola bridges spanned the canal at each end of the garden, enabling reflections of the temple to be seen in the water.[17]

The garden, beautifully illustrated for presentation at the competition in a perspective painting by Robert Atkinson (which hangs with Atkinson's other architectural drawings in the palace refectory), appears to have been partly influenced by J.van Avelen's engraving of the gardens of Zorgvliet of about 1692-98, with its double avenue of trees leading to the palace and its parterres punctuated with conical trimmed evergreens and a large fountain in the middle. Atkinson depicted the approach to the building flanked by avenues of pleached limes, forming a green, covered walk, an ornate stone fountain dominating the square court before the terrace leading into the palace and gardens on the north side. These were divided by shallow terraces into an upper level with a parterre on the western end. The lowest terrace overlooked a canal which was fed by the Beek stream that flowed through the grounds.

Mawson's detailed ground plan was needed to enlarge on the tone set by Atkinson for presentation to the competition. Mawson intended sculptures to stand throughout the grounds, and Atkinson had indicated recesses for figures in walls and plinths on which they could be placed. The western end of the garden fanned out past a semicircular parterre, with three long walks ending in shrubs and trees; here the outer paths meandered informally. The southern garden was set in shrubs. Leeuwin drew attention to the shape of the ground plan which he likened to a cathedral with a nave, side chapels and an apse, reflecting Mawson's Christian principles. However, as the 'apse' is pointing to the west, this is somewhat fanciful.[18]

But, when the garden making began in 1911, the ground conditions were more difficult than Mawson had expected. Bills for soil from nurseryman M.Koster from Boskoop appear in the accounts in December 1911. In his autobiography Mawson explained:

> the soil was almost pure sand, into which had to be incorporated peat soil brought from a distance. The water level, which was publicly controlled, was only two feet below the surface over a large section of the ground; and, lastly, the varieties of trees and shrubs which could be relied on to flourish under these conditions were limited and different from those we usually planted in any of our home gardens.

Mawson could have added that the salty water from the dunes killed off many of the plants and they had to be replaced.[19]

BELOW The rose garden parterre at the Palace of Peace, 2005.

These difficulties added to the cost and Mawson had to amend his plans. Most of the architectural decorations to the garden had to be abandoned and the plans for the Temple of Peace shrank first to a stone seat in an exedra, then, lastly, to a semicircular seat set back from the canal, and the fountain in the approach to the palace was omitted. In a letter to A.P.C.Karnbeek, the president of the Peace Palace, on 6 December 1909, Mawson regretted the cost-cutting which was imposed upon him and the placing of the architectural scheme of the garden into Dutch hands, saying that 'the result will fall far short of that which I had hoped to secure for you, and also far short of what my contemporaries in this country [Britain] will expect of me'.[20]

Economies included the use of brickwork instead of stone for the pergolas on the bridges, the paths and the terraces, though the finished work was much praised by Mawson. Even so, expensive York stone was delivered from Bradford in England for some paving. The rose garden was extended to the limits of the north terrace (presumably to save on stone) and younger (and cheaper) members of staff were employed. Howard Grubb took over from Edward Prentice, followed by a homesick Norman Dixon, as the representatives of Mawson & Son on site. Edward Prentice or the Lakeland Nursery manager J.B.Walker visited with Thomas Mawson every six weeks or so, checking the accounts and bills for tools, soil, matting, plants and other purchases and writing where

they were to be placed on the bottom of receipts for plants.[21] Mawson's site and planting plans were drawn up by the Dutchwoman Sophia Luyt, who supervised the planting 'of every shrub and tree, perennials and bulbs'. This explains the strong link to art nouveau in the final ground plan, despite Mawson's dislike of the style.[22]

The great majority of plants for the Peace Palace grounds came from the Hollandia Nurseries of M.Koster of Boskoop, who supplied box for the edging in the rose garden and elsewhere and larger plants for corners, yew and beech for hedges, and rhododendrons, azalea, kalmia, andromeda, erica, skimmia, gaultheria, berberis, pernettya and *Mahonia japonica* for the acid sandy soils – a list similar in kind to many required for Mawson's patrons in the Lake District. These were planted plentifully in the west garden, the terrace and the service court. As work progressed, Kosters provided olearia, Japanese maple, hypericum, spiraea, forsythia, lilac, holly, viburnum, prunus, and crab apple for planting 'outside formal lines', south of the main entrance and north of the lake. Colour in leaf and flower was supplied in trees and large shrubs such as betula, mountain ash, liquidamber, robinia, purple beech, Norway maple, scarlet chestnut and philadelphus, with *Magnolia soulangeana* being added at the main entrance in 1913.

Bonne Ruys had founded his internationally known nursery at Moerheim, Dedemsvaart, where it is still run today by his grandson, Theo. They supplied herbaceous

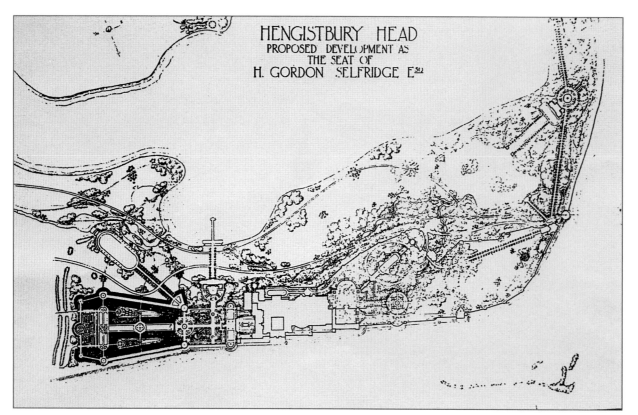

HENGISTBURY HEAD
PROPOSED DEVELOPMENT AS
THE SEAT OF
H. GORDON SELFRIDGE E⁵ᵠ

LEFT The proposed Mawson landscaping for Gordon Selfridge's dream castle at Hengistbury Head. It was never built because of Selfridge's financial losses.

perennials and biennials on 14 October 1912, and there are photographs of a long border for which these flowers would have been ideally suited. The list included many species of poppy, *Anemone japonica*, aster, delphinium, phlox, lupin, coreopsis, iris, rudbeckia, aquilegia, hemerocallis, monarda, geranium, verbascum and digitalis. As the separate parts of the gardens were finished, Lakeland Nurseries supplied bushels of special mixture lawn grass seeds on 5 May and 16 July 1912, indicating that the job was nearing completion. The Peace Palace was formally opened in 1913. The garden was favourably received by the critics after a garden party on 29 August. They agreed that the lawns were a feast for the eyes, and praised the scent and colours of the rose garden and flower borders. This was the last time Mawson saw Andrew Carnegie, who died in 1918.[23]

Palace and gardens show a close link, with the designs and decorations of the interior reflected by the compartmented exterior. A large tiled plan of the gardens adorns the wall of the corridor opposite the library. The careful workmanship speaks of the Arts and Crafts Movement, the designs and colour of art nouveau. Much of the iconography of peace and justice in the grounds, which can be seen in the gates and stonework of the entrance from the Carnegieplein, were added to the gardens after the end of the First World War. Metal from melted down weapons was given by the Germans in the form of brass medallions of *Amicitia*, *Pax* and *Justitia* and made into gates.

Mawson does not recount how he met Samuel James Waring (1860–1940), though the latter's connections with the manufacture of furniture, whose factory was in Lancaster, may have provided the link between the two northerners, who were both interested in the craft of woodwork. Waring's father, Samuel senior, had set up a furniture manufacturing and upholstering business in Liverpool in the nineteenth century. By 1897 this was sufficiently successful to have a branch in Oxford Street, London, run by his son Samuel James junior, and to warrant the amalgamation of Warings with Messrs Gillow & Co. of London, Liverpool, Manchester and Lancaster. *The Times* of 10 July 1897 eulogised the two firms as 'leading establishments in Europe in the highest class branches of the Furniture and Decorating Trade, and they possess a world-wide reputation'. Waring was to number on his list of contracts work for the royal apartments at Windsor Castle and Buckingham Palace, Aridore Villa (Hvidöre) for Queen Alexandra, a palace for Prince Nicholas of Greece, and the yacht belonging to the German emperor. He was indeed a good person to know.

Samuel Waring enjoyed business expansion. He directed a building firm, Waring and White, with premises adjoining those of Gillow, in 406-8 Oxford Street, which ran estate agents' and importers' businesses as well as its furniture firm from the same site. In 1906, Waring and White were completing the building of the Ritz and the Waldorf Hotels. In 1906 Harry Gordon Selfridge (1856–1947), an American who had pursued a successful career in retailing, especially with Marshall Field's in Chicago, came to England with the idea of building a leading store. He was directed to the site in Oxford Street occupied by Waring & Gillow, and wasted no time in coming to an arrangement with Samuel Waring. That year Selfridge & Waring Ltd was formed in order to clear the site and build Selfridge's new store. Tenants were bought out and compensation paid. But Waring was alarmed by Selfridge's grandiose plans, with a tower or a dome which breached the London Building Act and fire regulations, and pulled out of the deal. Selfridge & Waring Ltd was wound up between 1908 and 1909.[24]

However, these financial complications did not hold back the ambitions for personal aggrandisement of the combatants. Waring had married Eleanor Bamford, who inherited property in Cheshire and Denbighshire. He bought a farming estate at Gopsall Hall, Leicestershire, parkland around a Palladian mansion at Foots Cray, Kent, and a London home at 13 Portland Place. Selfridge rented 32 Orchard Street (beside his store), a town house near the Ritz, and, briefly, was Waring's tenant at Foots Cray Place. Having seen Mawson's work there, Selfridge wanted to employ Mawson, and the architect Philip Tilden, at Highcliffe in Dorset, where he had yet another home, planning in 1919 to build a castle on Hengistbury Head. Drawings were made by the Mawsons for gardens for the castle and its outlying buildings. Mawson was excited by what he saw as one of the biggest private commissions with which he had ever been entrusted. But Selfridge lost his money in the 1920s and the dream castle was never built.

Waring called in Mawson to model the garden at Foots Cray Place and its estate of some 1,000 acres in the Cray valley in Kent, of which he had taken the lease in his wife's name (to avoid taxation) in 1898. He bought the freehold in 1917. The house was within easy reach of London and from 1900 Mawson was taking the train to Sidcup where a carriage would meet him (Mawson never learned to drive) to visit Waring and to make preliminary surveys and sketches. He had been commissioned initially to create gardens close to the house, and Waring planned a new lodge, drive, stable block and drainage system.[25]

Waring's new house was set in a beautiful estate of woodland, river and meadow, which had been altered in the eighteenth century by a London pewterer, Bouchier Cleve. Cleve commissioned Isaac Ware in 1754 to build a domed Palladian villa with a pillared portico in place of the earlier house. After the removal of the formal gardens of the seventeenth century, the grounds had been landscaped by 'Capability' Brown in 1781, with grassland rolling away from the walls of the mansion. There had been few changes since. The River Cray had been widened, with small barrages, into a canal, there

RIGHT The plan of the garden at Foots Cray Place for Samuel Waring's country estate on the edge of London was made *c*.1901. The plan appeared in the 5th edition of *The Art and Craft of Garden Making*, fig. 504.

TERRACE · GARDENS · FOOTS · CRAY · PLACE · SIDCUP
for S · J · WARING · ESQ

Thomas H. Mawson Hon A.R.I.B.A. in connection with the late Dan Gibson:- Architects.

were groups of fine old trees, and there were views across to the villages of Foots Cray and North Cray. Mawson found the 'architectural merits of the house…exceptional…the site…splendid' and the landscape…'forms a setting which is quite enchanting'.[26]

Plans made by Mawson with Dan Gibson and published in the second edition of *The Art and Craft of Garden Making* in 1901 altered the setting of the house quite radically by placing the carriage court on the north side. Not only would the principal rooms overlook the new garden, the new elm avenue and the river, but ground would be released around three sides of the house for formal gardens (the designs changed in the later editions of the book). Mawson introduced two terraces with broad steps leading down from the house, from which the designs of the panel gardens could be admired. The second terrace was marked at each end by lead figures and cryptomerias. On each side of the house there were clipped yews (some of these still remain in an overgrown state), box-edged beds planted with hardy perennials and paths made of gravel. Croquet and tennis lawns occupied the lowest level. Thus the gentle Georgian slope from the mansion disappeared and was replaced by orderly terraces with 'variety and change of scene'.[27]

Mawson's plans clothed the paths with pavilions, figures at intersections, a fountain pool and other diversions, but Ordnance Survey maps of 1909 and 1933 show only a large round pool (now vanished) to the northwest of the house. But a large, rectangular formal garden was made behind the red brick Georgian stables

and its cupola, with a pool in its centre, in which a fountain from the Mawson period still jets water into the air. The surrounding walls are arched, punctuated by pillars and the original metal gates, through which a kitchen garden can be seen. Alongside the formal and kitchen gardens is a narrow bowling alley with its domed teahouse.[28]

There was an abrupt change of tone from formal garden to natural parkland at the foot of the terraces, which bordered the Brownian grasslands with its clumps of trees. A double avenue of trees still marches down towards the lake, where Mawson planned a garden

RIGHT By 1928 Waring
had added a 'Dutch' garden
to the back of the stables
at Foots Cray Place.

house, part boathouse. Here there is Brown's five-arched brick bridge, with its cascade created to back up the waters of the Cray into a canal.

A second batch of plans was made in September 1904. There are two of the plantations on the northeast of the house, which were divided by mown grass paths running diagonally across compartments of woodland, which were full of bluebells in spring. These spaces, meant for strolling, could be reached by paths leading through the trees to a statue on its boundary. A semi-wild garden, divided by a hornbeam hedge, was edged by scarlet maple, purple hazel and *Berberis thunbergii*, and planned to include roses, primroses, daffodils, foxgloves and epimedium growing amongst them. These graded eastwards to a lily pond and a bog garden beside a stream. Another plan concentrates on the arrangement of the trees within their compartments, including Mawson's preferred indigenous species such as elms, sycamore and thorn, and chestnuts. Mawson's semi-wild zone between the parkland and the natural woodland beyond can be seen on the 1:2500 Ordnance Survey map of North Cray for 1909.[29]

There is also a 1904 plan for a Japanese garden. The British had been introducing anglicised versions of these landscapes since the relaxation of diplomatic and trading relationships with Japan from 1853. Between 1880 and 1910 the Edwardians made many such gardens, sometimes with the help of Japanese gardeners. Waring

was a socially well-connected man and would have been anxious to entertain his visitors in this setting. Set around a lake, there is a torii, or Shinto entrance to the garden, with two uprights and two cross-pieces. By the entrance is a hollowed stone for ritual handwashing. From this a 'bridge of friendship' leads on to an island, on which there is a stone lantern, a tea house, a Judas tree, bamboo and willow. Another island lies to the west, its margin 'to be built up with stonework'. There is a mix of English and Asiatic plants: plants and shrubs such as gunnera, spiraea, and rambling roses – Dorothy Perkins 'to be trained to overhang the water' – combine with the iris, bamboo, willow and Japanese cherries. There are mounds to north and south, which were to be planted with dwarf conifers among groups of boulders. A 'moonshadow stone' is set on one hill, a 'tree of the setting sun' on another, this to be beside a 'pool of reflection'. The southern shore has a 'garden of the dead', and three more stone lanterns.[30]

The plan is fascinating, as it is one of only two for Japanese gardens designed by a Mawson hand yet discovered. It is clear that Mawson employed James Pulham & Son to make Japanese gardens when their clients so required, but they would give directions to Pulham, and Pulham would make Japanese artefacts including lanterns for the client. Neither Waring nor Mawson had ever been to Japan. Was this garden ever made? There are no pictures of it among later photographs.

The house was requisitioned in 1939, a year before Waring died, as a naval training establishment, and much of the original landscape was obliterated. In October 1949 the house caught fire and was so badly burned it had to be pulled down.

Waring had moved into the production of aircraft and war equipment during the First World War and was made a baronet in 1919. At his elevation to the peerage in 1922 there were accusations recorded in *The Times* of 20 July that he had pocketed money from his government contracts, despite having received thanks from the War Office, Ministry of Pensions and Air Board. Others suggested that he had 'bought' his peerage from Lloyd George. Was this spiteful war between aristocracy and commerce? Whatever the truth of these matters, Waring was wealthy enough to fill Foots Cray Place with fine period furniture, make property deals, and open branches of Waring & Gillow in Paris and Brussels and invest in hotels in Europe. Such trading eventually lost him money in the recession before the Second World War, but for the moment it led to connections with the rich in many parts of Europe.

One such man whom Waring introduced to Mawson was Lazare Weiller (1858–1928), raised in Sélestat in Alsace. After the French defeat in the Franco-Prussian War in 1870-1, Weiller's homeland was handed over to the Germans, and his mother sent him to study first in Angoulême, and then Trinity College in Oxford. He returned to Angoulême to what became a remarkably successful innovative career as an electrical engineer, working with copper wire for telegraphic communication, and then in the early days of television. He had stood, unsuccessfully at first, as a deputy for the French Parliament as a republican in the department of Charente, visited the USA and knew the Wright Brothers, and had become a founder member of a company for electrical navigation systems for aircraft.

By the time he met Mawson in 1908, he owned several chateaux and was interested in their landscaping. His English education was likely to have reinforced his preference for natural gardens and the *jardin anglaise*, which was the opposite of the *jardin à la française*, which referred to the style of Le Nôtre in France. He bought the Château de Grouchy in 1898 at Osny in the Val d'Oise which had an English-style garden with a large lawn and a lake, and had made many alterations before a fall in the price of copper made him sell up in 1901, with some of his other property and his art collection. He still had the villa Isola-Celesta in Cannes (bought in 1893), where his rose garden was considered one of the finest

in Europe, and a town house in Paris in the wealthy rue de la Bienfaisance.

Mawson, who referred to his client as 'a Parisian banker and financier' – which may be a slip of memory or perhaps he did not know the full nature of Weiller's many-faceted occupations – spent some pleasant hours with his client looking for a country property which was no more than an hour and a half's car journey from Paris.[31] They hit on an estate in the small village of Angervilliers, to the southwest of Paris, between Dourdan and Limours.

There had been a chateau on the site which dated from the seventeenth century, and Mawson's excitement rose when he found plans by Le Nôtre in the archives of a 'moderate sized villa, evidently intended as a dower house' still remaining on the estate.[32] This was exactly the type of garden in which Mawson delighted – radiating avenues with a long central canal (which had been filled in), and with the help of Weiller's Parisian architect he was determined to create a plan with the canal as the main axis and with 'every favourable vista which Le Notre's scheme sought to emphasise'. Mawson's design approached the house by a double avenue, with geometrically patterned rose gardens and long herbaceous borders leading south from an octagonal carriage court.

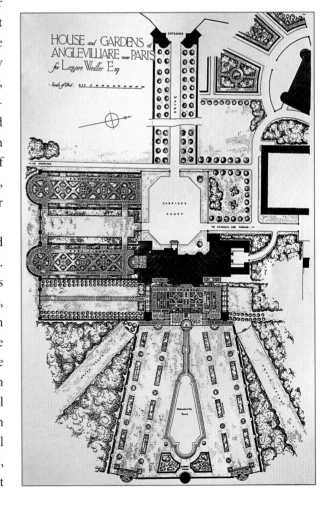

LEFT Hvidöre, the seaside villa belonging to Queen Alexandra and her widowed sister, Marie Federovna. The window trellis could well be Mawson's work.

A terrace faced east from the house and looked over the canal which had now been widened at its eastern end and from which the view could be enjoyed from a garden house. Columns of narrow flower beds punctuated with round ones fanned out from the house, with woodland and grass glades between them.[33]

Little is said by Mawson about what happened next, though, as other plans that he had prepared for clients showed, the grand design was not taken up. Was he left to make his own decisions concerning the landscape, or had he overridden Weiller's preferences? As *Les Beaux Domaines* of December 1913 showed, nothing of Mawson's plan for Angervilliers was adopted. The working arrangement between the men was paradoxical. Mawson sought to make the French landscape which he thought Weiller wanted. Instead, having sought inspiration in England 'for a manor house of the Elizabethan period' Weiller built 'a vast cottage'[34] which would have passed for an Edwardian country house, with gables, deeply pitched roofs, tall chimneys and mullioned windows. He kept the small house (Mawson's dower house) for his son and preserved the original, wooded landscape. The house had a symmetrical carriage drive, a simple terrace with a formal bed to one side below a loggia, and a pergola which sheltered the house from the drive. As *Les Beaux Domaines* said: 'it is an English

landscape that you have before you, a complete English landscape that seems to have been brought from across the Channel and placed in the midst of the Ile de France'.[35] Weiller was to live here until 1921; after being elected senator of the Lower Rhine in 1920, he went back to live in the town of his childhood, Sélestat.[36]

In the same year, 1908, Mawson received another prestigious client from Waring, this time with success. Waring had returned from visiting Queen Alexandra and her sister Dagmar (Marie Federovna), the Dowager Czarina of Russia, where his firm had been working on the interior of Hvidöre in Copenhagen. He had recommended Mawson to replan the royal gardens here. The queen was the daughter of King Christian IX of Denmark and his wife Louise. Marie Fedorovna had married Emperor Alexander III of Russia, who had died in 1894. When Alexandra's father died in 1906, she wanted to find a holiday home by the sea in Copenhagen to share with her widowed sister, Marie. As her biographer noted, 'cut off by deafness from things both intellectual and social, she tended to make her home and her children the central interests of her life whilst for amusements she turned to dogs and horses and the undemanding pleasures of the countryside'.[37] Her new home also distanced her from the infidelities of her husband, which she chose to ignore. There were no reported

ABOVE RIGHT Ernest Rowe's painting of Hvidöre in Copenhagen, *c*.1912. It shows the colourful massed planting of perennials along the borders, climbers on trellises and patterns in the stone of the paths. Shelter from the wind was essential as Queen Alexandra's garden was by the sea.

RIGHT This may be the entrance to the tunnel which led under the road to the lower garden. Queen Alexandra (left) and her sister, Marie Federovna (right) pose in the stone archway planted with rockplants at Hvidöre.

contacts between the queen and the landscape architect, and Samuel Waring dealt with the payments between Alexandra and Thomas Mawson, including July 1910, for £94 2s.3d; 10 June 1911, for £94 2s.3d;18 June 1912, for £49 3s. 6d, and 8 May 1916, for £19 5s.6d, the balance of her account.

Hvidöre was a two storey, white building with a basement, set on a terrace with a viewing tower and cupola on its gently sloping roof. It had large windows; those on its first floor were set back behind caryatids and rounded trellises full of climbers. A road divided the garden. Alexandra, whose poor hearing left her undisturbed by traffic passing, was delighted with her holiday home; Lord Hardinge of Penshurst (husband to the queen's lady-in-waiting) called it a 'ghastly property', with its lack of privacy and commented acidly that 'access to the sea could only be obtained by crossing the road'.[38]

Though the garden was divided in two, a subway under the road joined the parts together. The house and formal terraces occupied the higher garden, and Mawson was required to model the lower portion of just over two acres of sandy soil which ran down to the seashore. The main problem was the wind from the sea, which was checked by tamarisk and sea buckthorn, tall hedges, trees and trellises. A boundary between sea

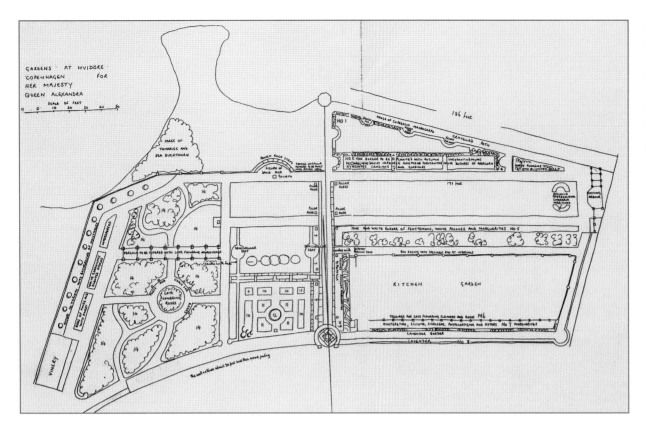

and garden was marked by a characteristic Mawson wall, with its materials probably imported from England, of interlocking half-circled terracotta tiles with a stone capping. Rough rock steps led down to the sea.

The watercolour by E.A.Rowe of a corner of Queen Alexandra's garden gives an accurate impression of Mawson's planned flower borders and pillars and trellises swagged with roses. The plan shows that Rowe's easel stood on a patterned, paved circle at the joining of two gravel paths: one with lavender-edged borders, full of lilies, sidalcea, asters and marguerites, and the other with phlox, achillea, gypsophila and marguerites. Late-flowering clematis and roses filled the trellises.

Tucked away behind this heady mix of flowers, however, was the kitchen garden, and contemporary photographs show how much the sisters appreciated inspecting their own fruit and vegetables. A box hedge divided the kitchen garden from a gravel path, shrubs, and then a further border. A planting plan for an unspecified border suggested a theme for pink and white dahlias, asters and sweet peas forming the backdrop for *Campanula pyramidalis*, *Lilium auratum* and summer chrysanthemums, with phlox, lavatera and lavender lining the front of the border. The trellises behind were to be planted with Japanese hop, *Cobaea scandens*, and *Tropaeolum canariensis*. A third, triangular space with lawn and flower borders formed a boundary, with recesses for seats in a clipped hedge. Behind E.A.Rowe's easel was another series of varied gardens: a formal parterre was

set beside informal paths surrounding a circular bed filled with late-flowering roses, and divided in two by a pergola covered by late-flowering honeysuckle. At the outer corner of this garden was space for a vinery. It would have been covered to shelter it from the wind.[39]

The entrance to the tunnel was improved with rockwork, ferns and flowering plants. The garden was a haven for the two women, who could come and go as they pleased, pick fruit, sit and talk together on the seats beside the long gravelled paths, or wander off along the shore to find pieces of amber. In 1909 Edward Prentice Mawson designed a tower as a look-out for the garden. After Edward VII's death in 1910, Alexandra visited Hvidöre until the war, when her access to her sister was denied because of her marriage to the Czar of Russia and she could not cross the sea to Copenhagen either. She died at Sandringham in 1925.[40] The grounds of Hvidöre are now taken up with the offices of the Novo Nordisk House of Education.

Despite the lack of any contact between the queen and landscape architect, work for a royal patron gave Mawson considerable status in the hierarchical world of the Edwardians, and, as chapter six relates, this particular patron was closely linked with the Greek royal family, who were to give Mawson & Sons their last prestigious commission as a family.

Thomas Mawson's most constant client was William Hesketh Lever (1851–1925), created Baron Leverhulme (1917) and the first Viscount Leverhulme (1922), whom he asked, as another 'High Church Nonconformist', for a donation for a screen in the church at Hest Bank in 1905. The much-related response was, 'Now that you have had the courage to ask me for a subscription, may I be so bold as to ask you to come and advise me upon the improvement of my garden at Thornton Manor?'[41] The manor, sited in the Wirral, south of Birkenhead, was the hub of Lever's activities, both social and administrative, to which he regularly returned. The son of a Bolton wholesale grocer, William Lever's childhood had been relatively comfortable, though he was aware of the poverty of working-class Bolton. Lever was to employ Mawson in park making and garden city planning and in some housing developments in the Western Isles. Lever had several other homes besides Thornton Manor: Roynton Cottage in the Pennines and The Hill, Hampstead, made dramatic statements in their landscapes. Mawson was involved in each one.

Lever became a partner in his father's wholesale grocery business in 1872. Within twelve years he had made his fortune by using the new methods of mass production to manufacture soap, and the aggressive sales techniques which he learned from the Americans to market the product. From 1885 Sunlight Soap, made from palm kernel and cotton seed oils, replaced the old soap made from tallow and chemicals which irritated the skin. Lever had married Elizabeth Hulme in 1874, and after the birth of their only surviving child, William Hulme Lever (1888–1949), the family moved from Bolton to Thornton Manor, Cheshire, on the edge of the village of Thornton Hough. Here Lever could see himself in the role of benevolent lord of the manor and paternalist employer. The Hough, as Mawson described for his American readers in 1917, had been laid out as a garden village, with a double line of trees on each side of the road making an avenue leading to Port Sunlight, Lever's enormous soapworks, on an inlet on the west bank of the river Mersey. The gardens of Thornton Manor had been made for Lever to entertain his huge workforce from the factory (a garden party usually accommodated at least 2,000 guests), which had implications for the layout of the garden – wide paths and many shelters were essential. Begun in 1906, interrupted by the First World War, house and garden were continuously altered and extended.[42]

Thornton Manor's south face, which was originally its front, is open to constant winds from Wales across flat plains, so shelter became an important factor in the garden's design. Pleached lime avenues were planted, 'extended green wings to the house', which in turn protected parallel lines of pillars making a rectangular 'forum' along part of the south front. Inside the forum a

RIGHT The entrance to Thornton Manor, the home of William Hesketh Lever.

WIDENING HORIZONS 75

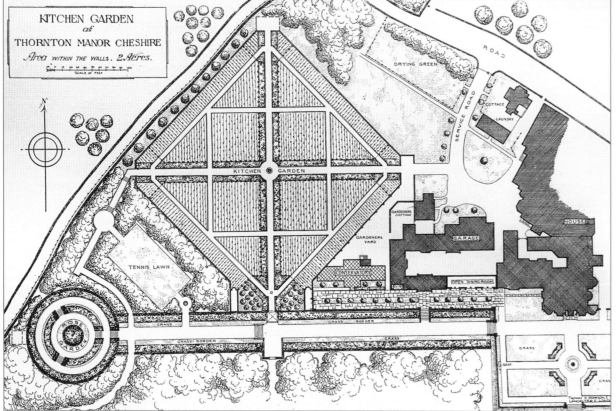

ABOVE The windy south front at Thornton Manor – the forum to the left.

LEFT The diamond-shaped kitchen garden at Thornton Manor. This plan appeared in the 5th edition of *The Art and Craft of Garden Making*, fig. 365.

RIGHT The rose garden at Thornton Manor.

large marquee would be pitched to accommodate the guests on a blustery day. Nevertheless Lever had asked for an open-air dining room to be made close to the house, where tables could be set under the trees. Along the south wall shelters were built, sombre and heavy in style, with the exception of the colonnade that led towards the kitchen garden. Here was a view from the roof of the colonnade, below which chairs could be placed on a sunny afternoon, and the Mawson and Lever ladies could pass their time over tea and conversation.[43]

But the long walks throughout the garden were a reminder of Lever's restless personality; he paced up and down similar pathways at Roynton Cottage and Hampstead, in conversation, or contemplation. Mawson

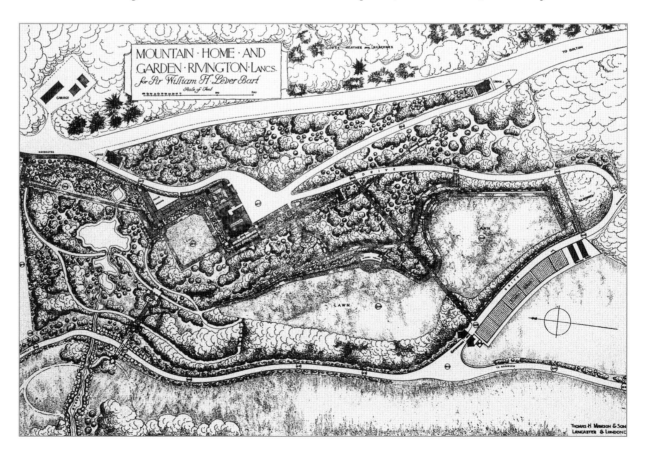

RIGHT A plan of Rivington drawn by Edward Prentice Mawson. This plan was shown in the 5th edition of *The Art and Craft of Garden Making*, fig. 491.

described Lever's arrival at 6.15 a.m. in the manor garden on the first day of his visit, after his host had answered his post and enjoyed his morning's ride on horseback. He had bundles of plans for the extension of the garden which he had drawn up himself. 'I began to wonder how many hours' sleep he thought necessary,' Mawson confided to his autobiography.[44] All Lever's houses had a bedroom for him somewhere in their roofs, open to the stars, where he would sleep even on a frosty night.

Sheltered herbaceous borders led westwards to a figure-of-eight sunk garden, originally planned for roses but later for a fountain pond and for bedding plants. Smaller gardens led from this meeting point. Northwards from the colonnade was a two-and-a-half-acre, brick-walled, diamond-shaped kitchen garden, adorned by semicircular trellis-heads from which hung small-flowered rambler roses. Another fountain marked its centre. Mawson explained to the Americans that kitchen gardens were ornamental because enclosed, sheltered spaces were welcome places in which to stroll on wintry days.[45]

The south front looked on to meadowland and a cricket ground with a rustic pavilion.[46] To the west, beyond the formal garden, was a lake with a boathouse, in part engineered for boating to entertain Lever's party guests. A drawing by Robert Mattocks, Mawson's nephew, with its delightful small pavilions for the observers, planned a canal to lead from the lake towards a bathing pond with a water pavilion behind it.[47]

Lever's next venture into property involved Mawson & Sons in landscape design in the Pennines. In 1899 the owner of the Rivington Hall Estate northwest of Bolton had put up his land for sale, offering Lever the 2,110 acres of land between the long and narrow Rivington Reservoir on the west and moorlands on the east. Lever saw its potential for himself, and for Bolton. He wanted 45 acres on which to build a home just below the summit of Rivington Pike and to conjure the wild landscape into a mountain garden. He asked Mawson to design this for him.

The purchase did not go smoothly as Liverpool Corporation, jealous to conserve the purity of its catchment area for water from the reservoir, did not want Lever to buy the land. This was no isolated example of 'water wars' at this time; Lake District entrepreneurs including the brewer Sir Edward Holt, found themselves opposed by administrative and conservation bodies with other claims on lakes and reservoirs. Lever had bid a sum which he realised the corporation would not match, and donated the land, less his own 45 acres, to Bolton for use as a park. Not to be thwarted, Liverpool Corporation engineered a bill through Parliament which would give it control over the catchment area. Lever countered

BELOW The Romanesque bridge at Rivington, designed by Lever, which separated the public park he had made (to the left) from his private grounds (on the right).

RIGHT Rivington's scenery was transformed by the Pulhams' construction of ravines and waterfalls.

with a legal fight which was settled by a Commons Select Committee. By 1905 Lever would win his battle; Liverpool Corporation was offered the new Lever Park at double the price paid by Lever, and was to maintain the park as a public amenity with free access. After an unsuccessful appeal, the corporation admitted defeat, and Lever improved the drainage and road systems, altered and improved several estate buildings to provide a museum, art gallery and refreshment rooms, and even an outdoor zoo. By this time he had already begun to make a home there.[48]

Anyone expecting to see builders moving along the tracks towards the footings of a large mansion would have been taken aback, as in 1901 a single-storey wooden bungalow, designed by Lever's schoolfriend Jonathan Simpson, rose quietly in the shadow of the Pike. Called 'Roynton Cottage' after an old name for Rivington, the bungalow was intended for weekend visits and shooting parties. At the time Mawson was beginning work there, in 1905, Lever was adding another storey, as he began to see the possibilities for entertainment. Despite Lever's presiding over a public meeting of the Birkenhead and Wirral Women's Suffrage Society in Hulme Hall in 1903, an act of arson by suffragette Edith Rigby burned down

the wooden bungalow in July 1913. She knew her act would publicise her cause (Lever and his wife were dining with King George V, Queen Mary and the Earl and Countess of Derby at the time). Lever determined to build another, stone house to replace it. Despite his wife's death in the same year as the fire, Lever's new home was to be a place for entertaining, with a round ballroom, and a glass-roofed pergola and winter garden which stretched along the south and west sides of the zigzag-shaped building: here was the customary long walk for pacing up and down.

It would be wrong to attribute the design of the mountain gardens of Rivington entirely to Lever. Edward Prentice made the overall design; there were illustrations in *Civic Art* (1911) drawn by Robert Atkinson. The southern approach from Lever Park is steep, wooded and rugged; a ravine with waterfalls, made in 1921 by James Pulham, can convince the visitor that it is natural. Many stone stairways join crazy-paving paths which make their way diagonally across the contours to form terraces, planted with rhododendrons. There are capacious, somewhat gloomy shelters (a Mawson design, but rendered heavier by Leverhulme) made in appropriate places to pause, with round, tesselated pillars supporting

BELOW Part of the Japanese-style garden made by James Pulham at Rivington and shown in the 5th edition of *The Art and Craft of Garden Making,* fig. 312.

stone lintels. Halfway to the bungalow, Roynton Lane cuts across the moorland, a seven-arched Romanesque bridge, designed by Lever, taking walkers over the road and dividing Lever Park from his private territory. Access for cars was by a road from Bolton to the north of the bungalow.

On the eastern extremity was a Japanese garden of about 1922, which can probably be attributed to a cooperative design from Lever, who had been to Japan, and Mawson, who had designed one for Waring in 1904 – though the plan in the 1926 edition of *The Art and Craft of Garden Making* does not include it. Serving also as a supply of water for the falls below, a lake was carved from the horizontal sandstone, with teahouses on its northern, eastern and western shores. On its promontories stood stone lanterns; in Leverhulme's time there were flamingoes and swans on the water.

The rockwork and Japanese garden were made by James Pulham, and Edward Prentice Mawson had as much to do with the planning and management of the project as his father. Stripped of all references today, the lake remains in its austere but peaceful setting.[49]

To the west of the Japanese garden, some hundred feet below the bungalow, was a site excavated and made flat for entertainment; rock was transported to and from the area by a narrow-gauge railway built for the purpose. The Great Lawn, divided into two large grassed areas, provided the astonishing summertime sight of Lever's guests dancing to a band which was playing on the flat roofs of the shelters at the back of the lawn. Above the lawn an isolated tall lookout tower, with a room under a dovecote, loomed strangely over rock gardens below. There is a 1910 drawing by Robert Atkinson of the tower, linked by a stone, arched screen to the bungalow.[50]

Of Roynton Cottage nothing remains today except stone patterns set into the ground, marking the floor of some rooms. Below to the west is the site of the 1906 bowling green; there were tennis courts, greenhouses, and lodges. Abandoned after the death of its last owner in 1939, Liverpool Corporation pulled it down in 1947. There has been recent interest in this strange and deserted site, with its views across to the Rivington reservoir and beyond, and something of its wild beauty is now being revealed with the clearance of paths. Recent attacks by an insect which kills rhododendrons and affects oak trees resulted in a decision to remove these colourful shrubs for the benefit of the oaks, and the clearance of vegetation is having a beneficial effect in revealing the design too long hidden in the overgrown landscape.

At the same time as work was begun on Thornton Manor, Lever had bought a house in Hampstead. Elected to Parliament as a Liberal Member for the Wirral Division of Cheshire at the beginning of 1906, he needed a London base for entertaining his parliamentary colleagues. Like

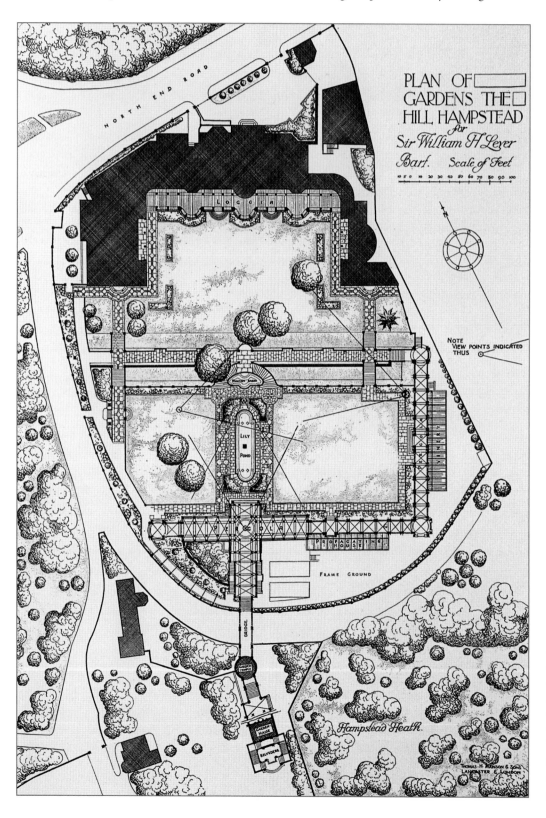

LEFT Edward Prentice Mawson's plan, made after1911, shows Lever's expanded landscape at The Hill with a bridge across the road which extended the pergola to a belvedere. This plan appeared in the 5th edition of *The Art and Craft of Garden Making*, fig. 458.

Mawson, he travelled between the northwest and London. The Hill was an appropriate name for a house on a high, sandy rise; enlarged by architect E.A.Ould, it needed a dignified and decorated space with sufficient privacy to hide the guests from the eyes of the public on Hampstead Heath below. The Hill was to provide Mawson with the third of his 'ideally balanced trio of studies in landscape architecture' for Lever – the country house, the mountain-side garden, and the suburban garden.[51]

Mawson had learned how to utilise spoil from making lakes in his first major public park in Hanley in 1894. He saw the advantage of material offered by the excavation of the new underground railway to Hampstead, especially as the railway company paid for dumping their material on Lever's land. A considerable feat of engineering by Mawson Brothers was needed to build containing walls, which served to make possible level lawns on a slope which dropped 30 feet in 250 feet. More spoil could then be fashioned into walls around the site, somewhat reminiscent of a medieval castle, on top of which would be built a massive pergola to act as a screen, but one that would 'keep open the panorama from The Hill'.[52]

The plan of the garden, made by Edward Prentice, shows a strong axis running from the house, across a wide lawn edged by herbaceous borders, to steps down to a rectangular lily pool, forming a feature in the midst of the lower lawn. The axis continues into an open wooden 'temple' dome, itself a meeting point for the raised paved walk which extends south, east and north around the house. The colonnade made by the pergola had an open wooden trellis roof supported by concrete pillars, and gathered varied climbers including roses and clematis. Low-growing shrubs made a contrast to the paving on four corners of the lily pond. Neat flower beds edged the lawns. The pergola and temple domes were made in Garden Crafts' workshops in the converted bobbin mills at Staveley, and set up by Mawson Brothers, who were also the providers of Lever's instant flower garden.

In 1911 Lever bought and pulled down the adjoining house, Heath Lodge, adding its gardens to his own. In order to achieve a smooth combination of sites, the southern part of the colonnade was extended over a public footway to a belvedere above a descending staircase. Unsurprisingly local people objected strongly and litigation took place with Hampstead Borough Council. The original colonnade had ended at a large conservatory, which was removed to continue the path. Now it was possible, from the bridge, to look down at the glasshouses and propagating frames which lay below the house.

Lever's later years were spent travelling. During the war his homes became hospitals and his factories produced glycerine for explosives and margarine. After being made Baron Leverhulme of Bolton-le-Moors in 1917, he bought land in the Western Isles of Scotland in a seriously ill-judged venture. Attempting to wean the inhabitants from their low-yielding crofts, he assumed that the local people would welcome work in a canning factory and an ice plant at Stornoway on Lewis for Macfisheries, a firm he established to provide the market with kippers and herrings. He built houses and began a new road, but the islanders resented what they saw as a foreign landlord telling them what to do, and Leverhulme admitted defeat, made a gift of the island to its inhabitants, and moved on to Harris. Here he planned a village called Leverburgh, a new harbour, new roads and an hotel. At Tarbert a housing scheme was drawn up by a local architect and surveyor, Don Cattanach, with eleven houses in a crescent and a church. Leverhulme tried to establish himself as the local landowner in a house called Borve Lodge. Two circular garden plans were made by Mawson & Partners for the lodge. One had steps descending to a rose garden. The other sunk circular garden plan had steps leading down into a walled orchard, this time to take fruit trees sold by the horticultural firm of Croux et Fils. Ranged around the walls were gooseberries, apples, pears, plums and Morello cherries.[53] Briefly, Leverhulme was joined by John Mawson as a technical secretary, after John's work in Canada had ended with the closure of the Vancouver office in 1921.

Unfortunately for Leverhulme, the islanders did not want to change their lives. In 1923, with unconnected problems in the main works and after some vandalism, he decided to abandon his efforts and left the Western Isles. Two years later, Leverhulme was dead; the firm no longer had spare funds, and all attempts to help the islanders were stopped.

The majority of Mawson's main clients worked in 'trade' in the terms of the early twentieth-century social hierarchy; that may account for his successful collaboration with these three influential men. They established him as a landscape architect with a world-wide reputation, recommended him to other clients, and kept his order books full with their constant demands. At the same time, running parallel with the work described in this chapter, Mawson and his sons and partners were making gardens for country houses throughout England, Wales and Scotland. These will be explored in the next two chapters.

CHAPTER THREE

The landscape architect in demand: 1890–1910

M AWSON'S REPUTATION as a landscape architect was soon established in the Lake District in the 1890s and spread rapidly in northern Britain. With the assistance of his brothers' contracting and nursery business, the provision of garden furniture and statuary by Garden Crafts of Staveley, and the expertise of James Pulham & Son in the handling of stonework in streams and for rock gardens, Mawson was able to cope with many commissions at the same time. Over this long spell he was assisted by able men, especially Dan Gibson and Charles Mallows, while his sons were reaching

manhood. Mawson was soon able to embrace a clientele in the southern counties.

Mawson's clients appreciated the way in which he carefully surveyed each site, assessing its possibilities, including cross sections in drawings so they could see what he had in mind. He had discovered how to use the contours in his favour, lifting a slope from the ordinary to the spectacular by the use of steps and terracing, and thus placing the house near the top in a dramatic setting, or, if the house was set into the hillside, creating walks and vistas to make it visible with the ascent. On the

LEFT The summerhouse at Little Onn, situated on an island in the moat, is likely to have been made by Garden Crafts of Staveley.

RIGHT Garden Crafts Ltd at Staveley, housed in an old bobbin mill, made garden furniture for Mawson Brothers.

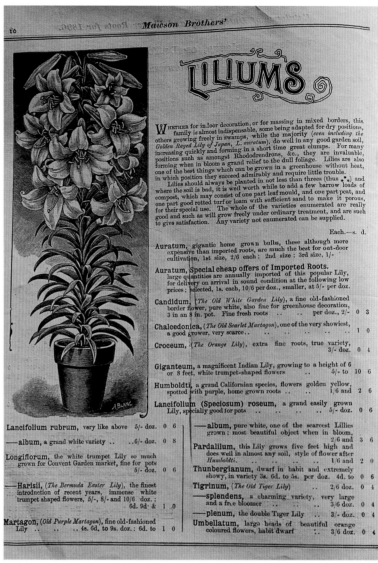

lower ground he augmented the qualities of the 'natural' along streams, enlarging pools, encouraging falls of water and installing rockwork, and widening rivers into canals. These skills, learned and honed in the Lake District and Scotland, were adapted to the special requirements of new sites, local materials and new clients. Mawson's plans were site-led, each garden and landscape subtly different from all the others, and his ideas were always three-dimensional – unlike those of many of his contemporaries, who relied on plans drawn up in the office without a preliminary survey.

Working in Scotland with Dan Gibson in the late 1890s, his abilities (and those of Gibson) were recognised by the 'tyrannical' but generous Sir William Cunliffe-Brooks of Glen Tana in Aberdeenshire, who wanted improvements on his estate.[1]

Before he died, Sir William had recommended Mawson to three further clients in Aberdeenshire: Mrs Mary Grenville Pickering of Kincardine House, for whom Mawson made garden plans in 1898; Sir Alan Mackenzie at Brackley, in Ballater, for whom the harmonious partnership of Mawson and Gibson worked in 1900, adding terraces and an avenue as well as gardens and extensions to the house; and Lord Erroll of Slains Castle, Cruden Bay, for whom they made gardens and landscaping around the castle.

On the west side of Scotland, Mawson again worked with Dan Gibson at Mount Stuart, the home of John, the third Marquess of Bute, a devout convert to Roman Catholicism. The house had been built with views through the trees eastwards to the Firth of Clyde. The hilly island of Bute, with its woodlands and nearness

LEFT Woodland walks on the Isle of Bute were brightened by the occasional planting of lilies and irises among the ferns on the estate of John, Marquess of Bute. The photograph is from the 1st edition of *The Art and Craft of Garden Making*, fig. 131.

to the sea, provided the scholarly marquess with an atmospheric setting for a plan that he discussed with Mawson in 1898 for a route to the top of the slope behind Mount Stuart House. This was to be designed as a devotional Way of the Cross, with Stations along the route, a Calvary at the top, and a Church of the Sepulchre below. At much the same time, the marquess was also discussing with the Scottish architect Robert Weir Schultz (1860–1951) how a meditative garden dedicated to St John the Baptist could be made in his London garden in St John's Lodge, Regent's Park.

Mawson's Protestantism saw no problems with Bute's Catholicism, and the route was planned through beech trees and mossy ground in Torr Wood to the north of the house, within earshot of the waves breaking over the shore below. Dan Gibson made designs for the oratories, but the marquess, aged only 59, died in 1900 before these could be built, though Weir Schultz completed his garden in St John's Lodge some time before 1897. Here Bute had spent his last years in 'a life of long walks and long conversations on the mysteries of the world unseen'.[2] However, Mawson did complete work on the island landscape, transforming Racer's Burn, the stream which flowed through Torr Wood, with pools and cascades which could be viewed from a bridge, and a rock garden which was made on the west front with some later alterations.[3]

Through the agent for the Bute estate Mawson met Major Macrae Gilstrap, who in 1899 had bought the several hundred acre Ballimore estate on the east shore of Loch Fyne – a setting protected by the long fingers of the Argyll and Kintyre peninsulas and the warm currents from the North Atlantic Drift. As a keen horticulturist and collector of plants, Gilstrap had found a good location. First he employed William Leiper to make alterations to the house, built by David Hamilton in 1832, then from 1900 Thomas Mawson designed a landscape to complement the building to his client's satisfaction. Mawson was pleased with his own work here, too, for *The Art and Craft of Garden Making* carried the full account of Ballimore through the second, third and fourth editions.

Mawson's plan for the hillside site was adopted in its entirety apart from some minor features. The fall in height from the south of the mansion to a central valley, and its rise on the far side were used to accentuate the difference between the formal and the informal treatment of the landscape. He placed the formal elements – the panel gardens to the east and west of the south front, the straight walk to the garden house on the east, and the

descending terraces to the stream below – on the high points near the house, with a round rose garden encircling a temple where the ground climbed again on the far side of the valley. Mawson's intention 'to lay out certain prominent lines which would grip the landscape, and give a feeling of connection between the mansion, garden, and park' included long, solid terrace walls built of local ragstone incorporating a domed summerhouse.[4]

By contrast, below and around the house were winding walks out of sight of the formality above, keeping close to the stream whose bed had been shaped into pools to encourage fish, and cascades and waterfalls to delight the eye and the ear. Here, as in other commissions, Mawson used James Pulham & Son. Water plants such as nymphaeas (water lilies), iris, caltha and spiraeas were planted in pools and along the edge of the water garden, and spring flowering bulbs were planted to naturalise in the grass.

The estate was well wooded with beech and sycamore and Mawson noted, for preservation, the old hollies and oaks on his plan. Gilstrap soon filled the new gardens with a significant collection which would have rivalled a botanic garden – at least one of every available species of plant and shrub was said to have been planted at Ballimore. The terrace beds contained hardy perennials and roses, and their walls were covered in honeysuckle, wisteria, clematis, roses and magnolia. Other specialities

LEFT Mawson employed James Pulham to enliven the stream below the house at Ballimore with cascades and falls which could be viewed from a wooden bridge. *The Art and Craft of Making Gardens*, 1st edition, fig. 131.

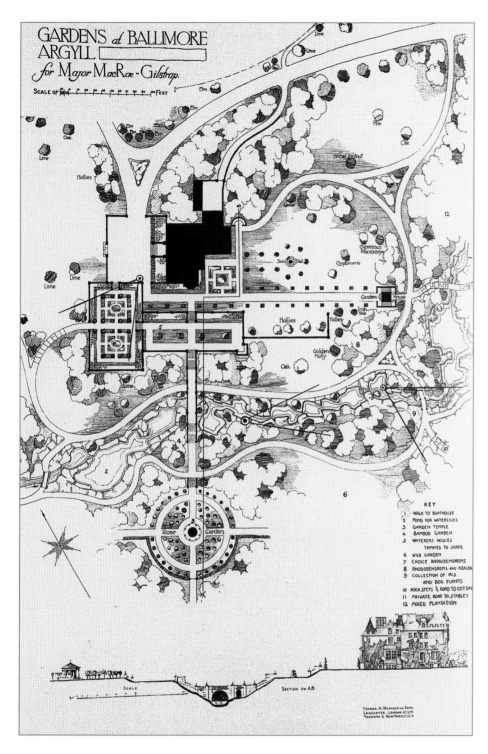

GARDENS at BALLIMORE ARGYLL

for Major MacRae-Gilstrap.

SCALE OF FEET

KEY
1 WALK TO BOATHOUSE
2 POND FOR WATERLILIES
3 GARDEN TEMPLE
4 BAMBOO GARDEN
5 WATERERS HOLLIES TRIMMED TO SHAPE
6 WILD GARDEN
7 CHOICE RHODODENDRONS
8 RHODODENDRONS AND AZALEA
9 COLLECTION OF IRIS AND BOG PLANTS
10 ROCK STEPS & ROAD TO COTTAGE
11 PRIVATE ROAD TO STABLES
12 MIXED PLANTATION

SECTION ON A.B

THOMAS H. MAWSON AND SONS
LANCASTER, LONDON
TORONTO & NEW YORK

ABOVE The Mawson
plan for Ballimore, home
of Major Macrae Gilstrap,
a keen plant collector who
asked Mawson to landscape
his estate in 1900. The
plan is from the 1st edition
of *The Art and Craft of
Garden Making*, fig. 130.

Mawson, who not only used the firm to construct cascades and rock gardens, but instructed them in the laying out of Japanese gardens. But even before the turn of the century with his newly located office and home, Mawson had been offered commissions further south which whetted his appetite for more.

One such commission was for Little Onn, near Gnossall in Staffordshire, owned by the Misses Ashton, though how they heard about Mawson is not explained. Their father, Colonel Ashton, had built a mansion in 1850 from local stone which the two ladies enlarged after his death. The gabled fronts and mullioned windows eventually sheltered ten main bedrooms and additional servants' accommodation. They commissioned Mawson to lay out the garden for them some time in the early 1890s.

Because the house sat on level ground, it had 'a depressed appearance, and suggest[ed] dampness'.[6] Mawson saw the advantage to be gained in elevating Little Onn by excavating the surrounding ground and resting the house on a terrace some four feet above its south and east sides; this successful method of rejuvenating a house he would use elsewhere. The land fell away naturally on the east – the terrace here overlooks the tennis court – and on the west, which added outward vistas to the improved siting. He also moved the approach to the house, which previously led into a yard on the north side. Now a drive advanced in a more dignified manner towards a carriage court on the west front. Panel gardens lay close to the house on three sides, and a grass parterre centred by a sundial to the south; square stone summerhouses marked the boundary with pastureland beyond. Here Mawson was asked to plant specimen trees including cedar, rhododendron, oak, beech, Scots pine and redwood.

An unusual feature was a moated island to the northeast, a relic of the medieval monastic landscape on which the house was built. Mawson planned bridges to cross to the island on which was placed a rustic summerhouse, now sheltered by willows and rhododendrons. Advertising the skills in woodcraft of Garden Crafts at Staveley, the summerhouse was decorated with close-knit patterns made from wood, tiny gothic windows and a wooden tiled roof. These garden houses were popular: another (now gone) was used by children as a playhouse at Moor Crag in the Lake District. The present owner remembers it having 'stained glass'. There was a pair of similarly patterned summerhouses at Humphry Ward's (1845–1926) Stocks, at Aldbury, in Hertfordshire. Ward, a fellow of Brasenose College, Oxford, and a writer for *The Times*, visited Mawson at his office in Conduit Street.

such as the *Eucryphia glutinosa* were safely planted within the walled garden on the east of the house.[5]

Mawson, though satisfied with his northern achievements, was keen to expand his clientele in the south, which became easier with the faster rail connection from Lancaster and the firm had a large office there, at High Street House. Once the London office had been established in Conduit Street, nothing could hold them back. The advantage of a London office was also recognised by James Pulham & Son, whose firm had made artificial stone for landscape work before changing to the use of the real thing in the 1870s. In 1902 Pulham moved to 71 Newman Street, off Oxford Street, not very far from

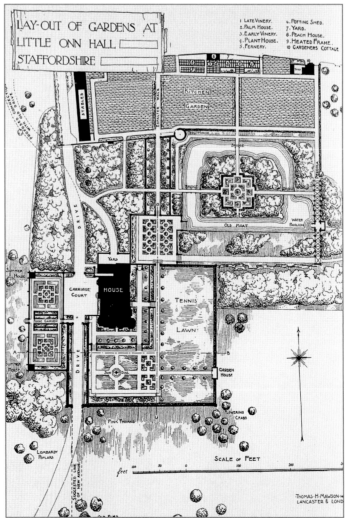

In 1909 Ward asked for plans for the garden at Stocks, near Tring, which they had bought in 1896, where his wife Mary, known only as 'Mrs Humphry Ward', a successful novelist and friend of Edith Wharton, was 'magisterially hospitable'. (Mawson found her conversation demanding and her dislike of Liberalism surprising, but nevertheless fell under her spell.) Many of his garden proposals were not accepted, but wooden summerhouses, a carriage court and rose garden were made.[7]

Much further south, on the northern edge of Dartmoor, the Lethbridge family had owned a farmhouse and worked the land at South Tawton since the seventeenth century. In 1898, when Wood House and estate were inherited by William Lethbridge, a wealthy lawyer and a bachelor, it was decided to rebuild the Victorian house which had replaced the earlier farmhouse and remodel the grounds. Though Mawson gives a later estimate of when he was approached to work here evidence suggests that the first contacts were made at the end of the 1890s.[8] Mawson gave Gibson the Lethbridge contract for the house just before the Gibson/Mawson partnership ended in 1899. The work lasted for nearly a decade: the last payment into Mawson's accounts from 'Lethbridge – late' was made from Wood on 30 June 1910 for £60 lls. 4d.[9] William Lethbridge died in 1910 and was succeeded by his cousin, another William. Once

ABOVE Little Onn in 2006, with its terrace lifting it from its flat surroundings. The rose parterre is at the front, with the lawn to the right.

LEFT Mawson's plan of Little Onn re-routed the drive so that visitors saw the formal gardens close to the house as they drove in. The final design simplified Mawson's late 1890s plan for the island. Plan from the 2nd edition of *The Art and Craft of Garden Making*, fig. 168.

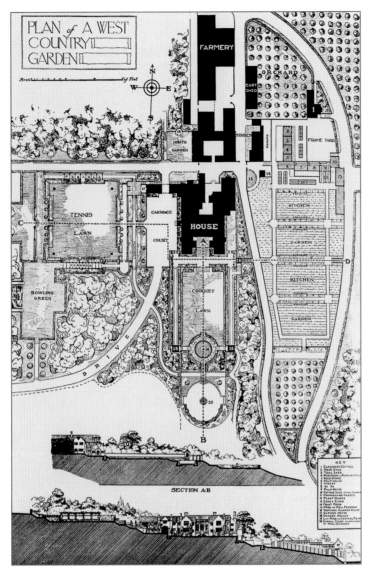

more, typical of the times, the client was a man who had made his wealth from business and not from farming.

The house, when rebuilt, would occupy the place of its predecessor – in a hollow on the side of a slope, with its southern face looking past the lake towards a distant Dartmoor, and its western side fronting a carriage court and rising ground beyond. Mixed woodland and pasture surrounded the estate and a stream flowed along the eastern boundary. Mawson's plan for the house and garden would be implemented by Mawson Brothers under the direction of Robert. Gibson was to remodel the entrance lodge and the house: the lead drainpipes, decorated with leaves and stems, relating interior and exterior Arts and Crafts designs, also bore what might have been his finishing date of 1904.

The house was built on an H-shaped ground plan from Dartmoor granite. Its pitched roofs carried the Gibson signature of rounded, chunky chimneys. The house appeared long, boxy and low on its western side, its rectangular, mullioned windows, with exposed granite frames close under the roofline, facing the hill slope. Mawson changed the entry from the south to a new carriage court on the west side in order to develop the garden on the south. A projecting wing to the west opened, through an arched entrance, to the north court and the domestic quarters; on the end of the west wing was a garden house. The eastern side faced a walled kitchen garden, glasshouses and stables. The southern

ABOVE Plan for Wood House in Devon, a partnership of Mawson and Gibson who made the gardens and house respectively at the end of the 1890s for William Lethbridge. Figure 480 in the 5th edition of *The Art and Craft of Garden Making*.

RIGHT The west court and wing of Wood House in the early 1900s. The round, chunky chimneys are characteristic of Gibson's work.

ABOVE LEFT Wood House, the sunk garden at the back, ending at a pool with F.Derwent Wood's statue of a boy spearing a fish.

BELOW LEFT Steps down to terraces below at Wood House in an early photogrph which appeared in the 4th edition of *The Art and Craft of Garden Making*, fig. 365.

side, with its sheltered courtyard between its gables, now overlooked the more extensive landscaped front which led down to the lake.

Entrance to the house was by a porch on the west, across a threshold paved with stone decorated with fan-shaped corrugations. Inside the house, stairs opened to semi-landings and descended to a wood-panelled, gallery-like hall. In the main rooms wood panelling carved in seventeenth-century designs, and plasterwork on the ceiling composed of flowers and leaves, referred to the earlier origins of the first Wood House. Low mullioned windows, closed with ornate metal catches, spoke of the Arts and Crafts interior which Dan Gibson designed. He had skilled knowledge of antique silver-ware and china, and selected these and the appropriate linen for the house.[10] Many of the architectural features were similar to Brockhole in the Lake District, which was being built for the Gaddum family at about the same time.

Mawson used the rectangle and circle in his design for the garden close to the house on the southern front. The walled, rectangular croquet lawn, surrounded by rose borders and a raised walk leading towards two square garden houses, evoked the seventeenth-century house. Looking towards the horizon, Mawson slowly built up anticipation for the view. The focus at first was on F.Derwent Wood's bronze figure of a boy spearing a fish in a round lily pool, and then the view downhill

was glimpsed through metal gates held in a semi-circle of pillars with climbing plants marking the edge of the high ground.[11] On the other side of the gates, the 'Tors of Dartmoor and the famous Doone Glen, [could] be viewed, across stretches of restful lawn, unbroken by drives or gravelled spaces'.[12] Steps led down through two turf terraces supported by semicircular granite dry-stone walls with rock plants tucked in the crevices. On the lower terrace stood a square granite sundial. More steps led down to the grassy sward ahead. Mawson was particularly pleased with this form of terracing. 'The success of this work has inclined me still more towards simple retaining walls in preference to expensive pierced work and balustrades', he wrote, 'which, though necessary to mansions designed in the grand style, are not essential to houses of moderate dimensions; and the money thus saved could be more effectively expended upon good modern sculpture.' He used this view of the formal garden as endpapers in the fourth and fifth editions of *The Art and Craft of Garden Making*.[13]

Downhill, a lake in the distance was approached by a path through trees on the east. Mixed conifers and broad-leaved woodland trees may have been planted by Mawson here as his policy was to create a shelter belt around the edge of the park. James Pulham was employed to construct a water garden among the trees with massive boulders interrupting and creaming the flow of the stream, and with cascades overlooked by a

RIGHT The lawn looking towards a garden pavilion near the pool at Wood House.

simple wooden bridge; in 1903 a payment certificate for £200 and £39 2s. 10d. was issued by Mawson's office to James Pulham.[14] Facing the house from the far side of the lake was a thatched shelter with a stone seat giving a peaceful view of the lake and the stone terraces on the rising ground beyond.

The north court had a smaller thatched shelter on two stone pillars, this time set in the wall round the courtyard by a small lawn, which was overlooked by the billiard room, and similar to one in Major Bolitho's Hannaford at Poundsgate in Devon, which was made from 1906. Both shelters were products of Garden Crafts of Staveley. The wall also had large niches, big enough to hold figures or urns. On the northern, outer side of the wall was a fountain, spilling into a basin, again similar to one at Hannaford.[15]

From the western side the ground rose quite steeply, above the height of the house. Here Mawson intended a 'quiet and restful scheme' with no flower beds. A stone staircase climbed with several breaks.[16] One landing opened to two tennis lawns, hedged with yew, and a bowling green. Above this was a green bank as a viewing terrace for the courts. At the corners of this bank

Mawson suggested planting Japanese crab apple, *Malus floribunda*, and placed curved seats.

On the west of the bowling green was an astonishing balustraded viewing terrace. Not only did this startle with its sophisticated design on the edge of a simple layout, but it appears to contradict Mawson's preference for simple ornamental detail. Maybe it was a late addition to the garden, for Mawson says very little about it. Stairs led to the viewing terrace through arched entrances, and there was an arched recess or loggia underneath as a shelter.

ABOVE The tea house at the top of the west slope at Wood House.

BELOW Mawson frequently used a half-circle of stone or brick at the front door. Hannaford's was made of different coloured brick; Wood, north of Dartmoor, was made of grey stone, with a fan of crenellations.

ABOVE The canal at
Kearsney Court was widened
into a circular boating pool
by concreting the bottom
and sides of the canal to
stop water sinking through
the chalk below. The bridges,
and boathouse on the left
may have been inspired by
those in Joseph Paxton's
Birkenhead Park, designed
in 1843.

However, the most extraordinary architectural feature in this garden was the teahouse, which was reached from the central stone stairway, a little more of the building coming into sight at each landing on the stairs. Beyond a lawn planted with cedars, the teahouse was a large, curved building made of granite ashlar walls with a tiled roof of Cotswold stone, peaked in the middle. The ends of the curve were recessed, like those in the north court. Behind stone pillars was a glazed space intended as a large sitting room with a fireplace. Something of the same sort was made for Mrs George Hamilton Fletcher at Leweston in Dorset in 1910.

This was one of Mawson's finest gardens, succeeding through an empathetic relationship with Dan Gibson, their appreciation of the nature of the landscape, the simplicity of the design, and their sympathy with the arts and crafts with which they worked. Mawson enjoyed the realisation of the plan, particularly working with granite: 'local materials and building methods should invariably be adopted wherever possible,' he wrote, and 'much ornamental detail is generally unnecessary, while such as is allowable should express as simply as possible the character of the constructive material'.[17]

Wood House remained in the hands of the Lethbridge family until 1969 and, despite a mixture of owners since, much of the garden and landscape remains intact today, though its outward views have been obscured by the growth of many trees.

This was the last commission on which Mawson was to work with Dan Gibson, for in 1907 Gibson died suddenly at the age of forty-two; he had been seriously ill a few years before with an unspecified condition. Dan Gibson had been Mawson's respected partner, working on many garden, park and house commissions with him, and he had tutored Mawson's son John.

Projects had been crowding in, providing at least fifteen new commissions alone in 1901. Many of these would have to be begun as others were being completed or continued. Overlapping with work in Devon was work in Kent, as Mawson began a commission for Edmund Percy Barlow, the chairman of Wiggins Teape, a paper manufacturer, to landscape his steeply sloping site at Kearsney near Dover. Barlow's paper mills were downstream on the river below the house. Once again, Mawson was to use a sloping site to its best advantage. The curving spur above the river on which Kearsney

LEFT The top terrace at Kearsney Court, which opened to a semicircular bastion garden overlooking the canal. This photograph was the frontispiece in the 3rd edition of *The Art and Craft of Garden Making*.

Court was built by local architects Worsfold and Hayward lent itself to a bastion which would dominate the valley. An illustration in the *Architectural Review* in 1910 shows that Mawson terraced the house, opening the garden with a central, semicircular bed, shaped by circular paths filled with herbaceous plants, enclosing it all with a sweeping semicircular hedge. A central path opened to allow a descent to a small, rectangular lily pond between tennis and croquet grounds.[18]

Mawson wanted to draw attention to the handsome canal which he built to replace the once boggy and poorly drained valley at the bottom of the slope below the house. On each side of the canal existing mature elms were left to form a wide avenue; here he had French landscaping in mind. Gravel walks edged with grass stretched along the canal's banks. The clear stream

with its waving green weed flowed across chalky ground, occasionally disappearing underground. To canalise a section below the house and conjure a reflecting, constant lake, Mawson made two rocky cascades which dammed the stream but gave sparkling outlets, housing them under two handsome balustraded bridges with pillars supporting tiled roofs, one marking the inlet and the other the outlet. The lake bed was lined with concrete and widened in the centre into a circular pool, where he built a boathouse in the same style as the bridges. Recently restored, the lake's reflections of the red and white bridges, and the gently rocking mirror of sun and leaves is magical. Mawson, lamenting the lack of large-scale water features such as Kearsney's, put it down to 'the teachings of the early-Victorian school of Landscape Gardeners who maintained that, in no case could a formal arrangement be beautiful'. He urged the making of the 'architectural' canal which suited the building and reflected the sky.[19]

Edmund Barlow died in 1912, and after several new owners including institutional establishments, the estate was bought by developers in the 1950s. The house was divided up between seven residents, new houses were built beside it, and the lower, canal area became a public park called Russell Gardens. Only the paired lodges at the entrance to the housing development give any indication of the presence of the erstwhile Kearsney Court estate, though old orchard trees and pampas grass grow along the river bank, and the rectangular lily pond is now filled in as a flower bed between the tennis courts.

The value of Mawson's many working arrangements made it possible for him to venture into Wales in 1901. A small entry in *Life and Work* makes reference to his invitation to work at Wern near Porthmadog, now in the southern part of Snowdonia's National Park.[20] There is no further entry in any of the editions of *The Art and Craft of Garden Making*, suggesting that most of the work was left to Mawson Brothers. Mawson wrongly attributes his commission to W.G. Greaves, but he was in fact employed by Richard Methuen Greaves (1852–1940), who had bought the Wern estate in 1886. Greaves, another Victorian 'new rich', the uncle of architect Clough Williams-Ellis, ran the Llechwedd slate quarry in Blaenau Ffestiniog with his brother John, who had built

himself a house called Bron Eifion near to Wern in 1883; it is possible that Mawson's firm was involved with this garden, too. The house's slate-paved terrace announced the source of the family's wealth; they were also involved in the construction of the Ffestiniog railway down to Porthmadog which took their Welsh slate for export in their own ships from the port on Cardigan Bay which they had helped to expand.

Richard Greaves had travelled the world as a young man and a letter from Japan written to his father when he was twenty-one indicates an interest in horticulture. He praised the colourful Japanese maples and promised to send plants and lily bulbs to Wales.[21] There had been a sizeable house at Wern since the seventeenth century. Richard Greaves showed all the signs of late nineteenth-century worldly ambition; in 1892 he employed an architect, John Douglas of Chester, to remodel and enlarge the house. This was made from roughly dressed local stone with a slate roof and mullioned windows framed in sandstone, and a new porch was added for the south-facing entrance. In the following years Greaves bought more land to enlarge his estate.

The house, set just below the crest of a hill, was built above the valley of a stream which wound its way across the estate to the south. Here woodland shielded the house from a railway embankment which crossed the southern part of the estate from west to east. To the north and northwest were the kitchen gardens, glasshouses and

RIGHT Wern in Snowdonia was owned by Richard Methuen Greaves, whose wealth came from a slate quarry. His interest in Japanese gardens is shown by the stone lanterns, which predate Mawson, who was called in 1901 to landscape the garden. John Douglas built the Italianate staircase.

stables, and the domestic entrance was on the west of the house. The glasshouses and the main entrance gates by the lodge had been made by Boulton and Paul of Norwich; they were opened from Douglas' lodge using machinery designed by Greaves, allowing the visitor to proceed up the drive leading to the house from the tunnel under the railway to the main entrance on the south.

Below the house on the south, Greaves set out stone Japanese lanterns and grew lilies, mindful of his earlier travels, but there was no attempt to develop this as a Japanese garden during Mawson's time. Greaves was more influenced by the current Edwardian delight in Italianate stone staircases, terraces and garden houses, seen especially in his garden pavilion. John Douglas had designed a terrace on the south side of the house. A photograph of about 1900 confirms the construction of plans made by Douglas of simple arched balustrading with balls on top of pillars, looking down to a formal, circular space defined by bedding plants in full bloom, with a spiky succulent placed on the top of a pyramidal bed in its centre.[22]

However, Douglas' designs were not what Greaves wanted. In 1901 Mawson was invited to develop part of the pleasure grounds, and between July and September 1902 the Windermere office was producing plans for both Richard Greaves and his wife, which showed three flights of stairs leading down from the south terrace and another leading to the east. The drawings show that the balls had been replaced by finials of the slender pyramidal shape, appropriate for the seventeenth-century origins of the house. In the end only two staircases were built; in 2006 both finials and balls could be seen on what remains of the stonework.[23]

The woodland 'wilderness' to the south, with specimen tree planting that predates Mawson's alterations, was to be left untouched. Greaves had purchased land on the east of the house, where an eighteenth-century ha-ha along the boundary emphasised earlier values placed on views across the fields to Tremadog and the mountain of Moel-y-gest to the southeast. Mawson's usual tendency to alter the alignment of the gardens towards outward vistas probably accorded with what his client wanted, and the focus of the pleasure grounds was now placed in an easterly direction, with a long walk which made its way to a round garden and ended at a garden pavilion.

The long walk was flanked by yew hedges, with flower beds on each side of the path. 'T.H.Mawson' appears on the design for the three-arched pavilion (but not in his hand) on 17 December 1901 and the 1903 on the lead guttering gives its completion date. Photographs show that it was made from ashlar blocks, with a pitched roof of slate. The building differed from the original design only in having a cornice below the roof, rather than a pediment. Stone steps led up to the open entrance and flanking arches, which had rose-shaped supports for the artificial stone rail above. A visit to Wern in 2006 failed to locate the pavilion inside a dense mass of scrub; it is extremely sad that such a building could be so neglected.[24]

The round garden was meant to be viewed from the pavilion and the photographs show that it was made after the building was completed. It was surrounded by a hedge and in its centre was an Italian wellhead, similar to the one at Leweston in Dorset, though Mawson's plan suggested a sundial. Even though completely overgrown, it is possible to make out box plants, now tall bushes, which once edged the three circular beds, but there is no evidence for the plants that grew in them. The paths were tiled, but these have disappeared, along with urns, ornaments, a sundial and all else that was portable in the garden. The ground dropped to the north from the round garden, and still visible, though badly silted, is a rectangular pool with apsidal ends made from cement. There is an unsigned plan for a lily tank, which, like the pool, might well have been made by Mawson Brothers,

who did not always sign or date their plans. The yew walk back to the house was bisected by another path which led between rose arbours supported by sixteen square slate pillars and linked by chains; here rambler roses still make a brave effort to bloom amidst the wilderness of the garden.[25]

As the pleasure grounds developed at the beginning of the twentieth century, the open ground in which they were made began to close as hedges thrived and spaces were defined by the rose arbour, the lily pool, the round garden and topiary. Mawson's provision of the long promenade along the yew walk was made colourful by tall sunflowers with massed bedding at their feet. There are photographs of the Greaves and Williams-Ellis families strolling here, including one with Queen Marie of Romania (1875–1938). Marie, whose grandmother was Queen Victoria, was one of a significant number of European royalty for whom Mawson made gardens and maybe she expressed an interest in Wern. There are undated records of Romanian housing being designed by the firm.[26]

Since the war, Wern Manor has had a variety of owners, including the present residential home, and the landscape has become badly neglected. It needs attention very soon, or its present state of dilapidation will decline beyond rescue.

RIGHT The pavilion and round garden and topiary at Wern in an undated photograph.

As Mawson finished shaping Wern in Snowdonia, he was asked to design for the 55 acres of gardens of the extensive Dyffryn estate in Glamorganshire, south Wales, for John Cory, his 'most notable client' in that year. Whether this was 1903 or 1904 is not quite clear, though Mawson had made 'the broad outlines of our scheme' before John Cory died in 1910.[27] Cory may have come across Mawson through Richard Greaves, as both were wealthy shipowners, and Cory a coal exporter. He had bought the 2,000 acre estate in 1891 and had the original house pulled down and another built by a Newport architect, E.A.Landsowne, which reminded Mawson of 'an Italian villa as interpreted by English architects forty years ago'.[28]

The front of the rectangular house faced north and the land to both sides was flat, with the river Waystock flowing in a culvert past the east front. John Cory had attempted to make a lake at the southern end of the pleasure grounds by damming the river. There were plantations of young trees, including larch, Scots firs, sycamores and elm. Cory's early garden consisted of a shallow terrace on the south front with flower beds, a tennis court and croquet lawn separated from a vast green sward by another shallow terrace with steps down, a panel garden on the east front and an herbaceous border. Mawson recognised that the main landscaping task was to banish the flat and uninteresting plain created by the lack of a horizon; there were no hills to look toward. Work was begun in 1905.

When Reginald Cory (1871–1934) took over after his father's death, Mawson found a good companion in the man only ten years younger than himself and with a great aptitude for horticulture. Cory collected horticultural books, financially backed plant hunters and later, in the 1920s and 1930s, went on expeditions of his own to North and South Africa and the West Indies. Vice President of the Royal Horticultural Society and a liveryman of the Guild of Gardeners, he donated plants to both the RHS and the Cambridge Botanic Garden. It was hardly surprising that his landscape at Dyffryn was to contain exotics from China, collections of trees including conifers and specimens of bonsai, water lilies, and some 600 varieties of dahlias, for which he was awarded a gold medal by the Royal Horticultural Society and made President of the Dahlia Society.[29]

Cory had some knowledge of landscape architecture and draughtsmanship as well as horticulture. Cory and Mawson discussed the new garden which had become a collaboration between the two men, and, deciding that they needed to educate themselves to implement their vision, set off on a holiday to Mediterranean Europe. Mawson had not been to Italy before, unlike most of his contemporary landscape architects, and both men sketched and took photographs. Not only did they

LEFT The Pompeian Garden at Dyffryn, with its fountain.

ABOVE Dyffryn, South Wales, the south garden with yews, which helped to break up the large expanse of green sward.

RIGHT A Mawson plan for Dyffryn which shows the many individual gardens around the central lawn and its canal, and the ill-fated lake to the right. *The Art and Craft of Garden Making*, 5th edition, fig. 47.

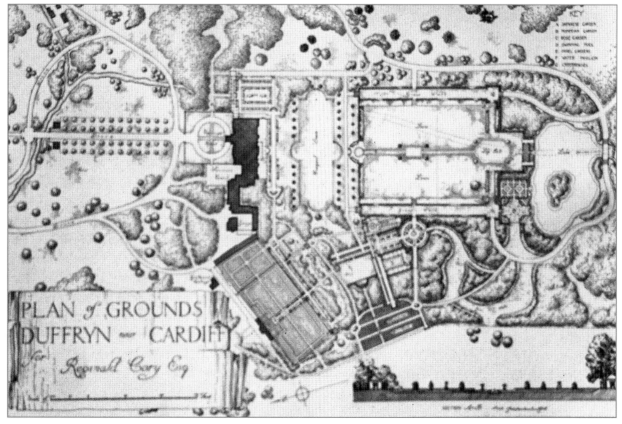

visit important villas and their gardens, but, as Mawson related, the picture galleries of 'Florence, Milan, Naples and Rome, for I realised that Italian gardens were but one phase of the expression of a great art movement which influenced all design'.[30] The journey was not only an adventure for learning, but also preparation for the shape and design of the gardens at Dyffryn.

As at Little Onn and Graythwaite Hall, Mawson saw the need to release the house from its flat dreariness on the south side. Below John Cory's shallow balustraded terraces and croquet lawn he set out 'to plan a great lawn extending from the old part of the garden on the south front, the object being to gain a sense of scale, a restful base to the house and a compensating expanse of view from the principal rooms, to make up for the lack of more distant landscape views'.[31] He excavated the site, making turf embankments on each side which contained and defined the central space. Mawson was not afraid of large greenswards and generally felt that they should not be enlivened with flower beds.[32] But to break up this large space, and to gather together the house and the horizon, he employed a long, stone-edged canal as an axis from the centre of the lowest terrace,

terminating before an octagonal pool, flanked by square pavilions. Later a crossing was added to the canal in which was planted some of Reginald Cory's collection of water lilies. The sense of formality near the house was encouraged with a long, colourfully planted terrace bed on the south front, beyond which were Irish fastigiate yews. A larger panel garden on the east side was linked by the same Irish yews to the south of the house. Both formal flower gardens were John Cory's, but reinvigorated by Mawson. Stone figures remained intact in niches along the walls on the south of the house; beds along the south and east fronts were punctuated with artificial stone figures and baskets of flowers. Some were later broken and replaced, moved elsewhere, or stolen.

What makes Dyffryn different from earlier Mawson work is the lively collection of small, discrete, interconnected but hidden gardens on the western side, reached via steps and through entrances in yew hedges. Each has its element of surprise and its own theme relating to ideas and plants collected at home and abroad and moulded by Cory and Mawson. Here were rooms to explore – a mixture of *hortus conclusus* and walled garden in a deliberate contrast to the vast green sward. This approach to the 'outside room' was being adopted elsewhere to show off collections of architectural pieces, as in Lord Astor's Pompeian Wall at Hever and Peto's own garden at Iford; but Cory wanted mainly to display his plants. 'We felt at liberty', said Mawson, 'to indulge in every phase of garden design which the site and my client's catholic views suggested.'[33]

The entrance from the house to the western 'rooms' was via a Moorish court, with keyhole arches, now filled in. To the massed and colourful herbaceous border begun by Cory's father were added Mawson's metal rose trellises. There was a Dutch Garden, and a yew walk called the Cloister, almost wide enough to be called an allée, that formed the beginning of an axis leading through a paved court to a round garden which ended the collection of rooms. Behind the Cloister on the west was a wide lawn with its semicircular tier of stone ledges, backed by dark green clipped hedges which formed a perfect foil for Cory's collection of bonsai and Japanese ornaments. At the back of the display was a tall pillar which was intended to support a sundial head. The rest of this lawned area, the Theatre Garden, was used for outdoor dramatics. The most arresting design was the classical Pompeian Garden, its Ionic pillars supporting flat roofs on which stood urns with plants; a fountain played in a central pool. Next to this were two gardens attributed by Mawson to Cory – the Paved Court and the Bathing Pool garden. Both had flower beds: the former with its stone lattice screen above a semicircular dipping pond, the latter now filled in as there were no pipes laid on here and the water became stagnant. The garden rooms ended with a circular bed defined by topiary which grew mainly roses, and from there a walk led south through flowering shrubs and trees to Cory's beloved dahlia collections.[34]

The southern end of the garden was finished later, interrupted by the First World War. It was intended that the axis from the canal should continue through a lake with an island, ending at a water pavilion on the far shore, and that a path should lead from the pavilion to the arboretum on the east side of Dyffryn.[35] Anecdotal evidence from a gardener suggests that Mawson's attempt to revive Cory's earlier sheet of water met with disastrous results: the dam on the Waycock caused the stream to back up in its culvert past the house and as the lake filled with water so did Dyffryn's cellars.[36] Further attempts at lake-making were abandoned but not before a round, red brick viewing tower was built, with its underground room from where visitors would have been able to watch the fish. By the observation

tower was the Lavender Court, a formal garden with geometric raised beds for dwarf lavender and small rose varieties, centred by a sundial. There were curved lily pools behind the flowers, brick paths and painted white trelliswork on the east.

The eastern side of Dyffryn had a totally different flavour; Cory's arboretum was a more relaxed area in which Mawson, a lover of trees, would have enjoyed wandering, appreciating his client's latest additions to the arboretum, with its *Davidia involucrata* (pocket handkerchief tree) and *Acer griseum* (paper bark maple), the many unusual acers and conifers such as *Nothofagus procera* .

Mawson's plans for the north side, the entrance to Dyffryn, were not carried out. Here Cory made the carriage court and drive and the craggy rock garden on the northeast side of the arboretum. In fact the only traces of Mawson are found in the mushroom-shaped yew trees which have golden tops grafted on to green bases.

Cory stayed in the house until 1931, adding to his collections and gardens. After his sudden death in 1934, Dyffryn was leased to Glamorgan County Council on the understanding that it should be used for educational purposes only. Post-war, many improvements were carried out and today the garden is well worth visiting to discover the various survivals of both architectural and plant landscaping created by two great enthusiasts, Reginald Cory and Thomas Mawson.

A 'lean year' for commissions, was what Mawson called 1906, but Major Bolitho, a banker who lived on the eastern side of Dartmoor south of Poundsgate, turned out to be another valued enthusiast for plants.[37] The hard landscaping indicates that he must have seen the garden of the Lethbridge family at Wood House, which was not that far away on the north side of the moor. Garden Crafts of Staveley and Mawson Brothers' Nurseries were employed to shape the landscape – a fact which was emphasised by the stamping of the firm's name on a metal drain cover by the back gate.

Hannaford Manor was constructed by A.Wickham Jarvis between 1904 and 1911 for Bolitho. Built of granite, its slate roofline has tall chimneys on the entry side and restrained gables on both sides; the house is rectangular and sits low and unassuming in the landscape. The Arts and Crafts house has its back (and entrance) to a slope and its main living rooms, on the other side of the house, look out over a steep but rounded valley side with pasture and woodland, and an equally steep rise beyond. Hannaford has a sheltered space above a dramatic southward bend in the River Dart, and its architect chose a spot where Bolitho could enjoy both sun and scenery.

A single payment of £216 19s. 2d. by Bolitho on 3 August 1907 in the cash book seems to suggest that this might have been a short-lived commission.

Mawson's plan does not show whether it was his decision to alter the entrance from the ancient route which ran across the lower ground to the present carriage court at the back of the house, but this arrangement was best for motor cars and gave better light to the main living rooms.[38] The slope above the house was to be occupied by the kitchen garden with the orchard below. Sections were drawn showing stone walls with arched doorways and hedges with entrances, dividing the activities in each part of the gardens. Beside the house on the east side would be a lily pond with a tennis court matching it on the other side. Terracing and staircases enabled several levels of the garden down the slope, and led an axis to a bastion overlooking the fields. Once

more Mawson was to employ his favoured architectural device for designing a viewpoint.

What emerged was very close to the plan. In reality an arboretum was made above the kitchen garden, the tennis lawn descended to occupy the ground on the west of the house and the lily pond, built to Mawson's design, was placed on the lowest terrace. Granite was the obvious material for the framework. The first terrace leads from the carriage court towards steps which enter an arched doorway towards the kitchen garden. The terrace is backed by a well laid wall, in which is set a semicircular granite basin where a wall fountain, fed by a stream, fills it to the brim. Below the terrace on the east side is a lawn with surrounding flower beds, enclosed by the second terrace topped with plain, rectangular pieces of granite. On the west side is a now altered thatched garden shelter. Further levels down open into a large lily

ABOVE The front of Hannaford in Devon.

ABOVE RIGHT Terracing at Hannaford, with a granite basin filled by a spring.

RIGHT A pool designed by Mawson but moved to a different part of the garden at Hannaford.

ABOVE Stone steps at
Hannaford to the country
below. To the left is a drain
cover marked 'Mawson
Brothers'.

pool surrounded by lawn and azaleas and rhododendrons; on the opposite side of the garden is a granite dovecote. The back door, once the front, has a square stone frame over which a flat sundial presides; on the floor is a fan-shaped pattern of red brick.

The garden, with its collections of orange, red and white azaleas and rhododendrons which would have been suggested by Mawson, is immensely pleasing in its balance of garden spaces on different levels. Bolitho must also have felt satisfaction with good craftsmanship as he turned at the bottom of the stairs to look upwards at the design of the metal gate in its square granite pillars, to admire the set of the semicircular steps and the rough wall beside them, with rock plants in the spaces, before turning again to gaze at the hills of Dartmoor and the green pastures below.

In 1907 Mawson was called to Hartpury House, a red brick mansion extended and remodelled by Guy Dawber, northwest of Gloucester. The farming estate in which the house was set was owned by the Gordon-Canning family, who had been in occupation since the eighteenth century, the surname 'Gordon' added in 1848 when the Canning heiress married a Scotsman, Captain Patrick Robert Gordon. It was Patrick's daughter-in-law Maria who summoned Mawson; he had made a fan-shaped carnation and rose garden enclosed by clipped yew hedges for Lord and Lady Beauchamp at Madresfield Court, near Malvern, in 1903. Both families were keen horticulturists and lived not far from each other. It is likely that their common ties engendered an invitation for Mawson.

The gardens had previously been laid out by the artist Alfred Parsons (1847–1920), and though Mawson praised his paintings, he had little regard for the 'natural' school which Parsons represented, with their looser designs led by colour and planting. 'The inability of the artist to realise the necessity, in gardens, for definite architectural motif and scholarly detail when working near the residence is most marked,' said Mawson, though he approved of Parsons' layout of the plantations and flowering shrubs.[39]

Mawson surveyed the garden in January 1907.[40] Hartpury was set on the top of a gentle rise, overlooking orchard and farmland, and with a view to the Malvern

Hills on the north. There was a square carriage court with panel gardens leading off to the east. On the north side of the house Mawson engaged in his 'Old English' style of formality, though Mrs Gordon-Canning seems later to have loosened this with her choice of planting. Steps led down to a geometric parterre planted with roses and lavender in small beds with a sundial in its centre. The path from the rose garden was softened by small plants growing in the crevices and Mrs Gordon-Canning encouraged aubretia, *Cerastium tomentosum* and *Dianthus fragrans* in wall spaces wherever she could.

The most memorable feature, however, was the arrangement of wall, pillars, gate and steps on the break of slope which 'divided the old garden from the new extension' below – similar features as found at Hannaford, but executed in a strikingly different manner. The steps which led up from the flagged terrace to the gate were laid in a four-sided fan, and the stone gate posts, topped by urns, were flanked by walls of close-laid limestone. In the walls were patterns made by half-circle terracotta tiles capped by a limestone coping – similar walls could be found around the carriage court of Madresfield Court.

In the middle was a beautiful wrought-iron gate, made by Mrs Ames Lyde, a lady blacksmith whom Mawson had met in Florence (presumably on his travels with Reginald Cory). The gates, made to Mawson's pattern, provided an elegant vertical screen. Mrs Ames Lyde, who also loved roses, carried out 'considerable work' for Mawson, from her home in Norfolk.[41]

Beside the gated terrace Mawson planned flower borders and, below it, lily ponds on each side of the long lawn ending in a garden temple.[42] This would have ended the axis which began at the house and came via the path to the wrought-iron gate. However, a curved stone garden seat was preferred to a garden temple and more flower beds ousted the lily ponds; one rectangular lily pond was made at the end of the gate terrace, at the foot of curved, solid-balustraded steps down. Shrubs were kept behind an edging wall of yew which emphasised the colours of the kalmias, rhododendrons, andromedas and azaleas mollis and Ghent, bursting forth in the spring with roses to follow.

Planting plans for Hartpury give an insight into what Mawson recommended for the garden, but the exact location of the borders is unclear.[43] The 'autumn' or 'top border' was to contain aster, *Galtonia hyacinthus candicans, Hydrangea paniculata,* Japanese anemone, white phlox, primrose (double mauve and white) and blue viola, with a note saying gaps should be filled with white and blue Canterbury bells, ageratum and *Salvia patens.* The 'spring border' was to have arabis, hesperis, blue and white hyacinth, white honesty, forget-me-not, narcissus pheasant's eye, double mauve and double white primrose, blue and white crocus and tulips. Here the reminder was to fill the gaps with forget-me-nots and white narcissus. Gorse, several varieties of acer, azaleas and *Fuchsia gracilis* were some of the suggested shrubs, all of which would have been available from Mawson Brothers' nursery. Later plans in 1907 show the continuing close interest shown by Mrs Gordon-Canning.[44]

In 1913 the *Gardeners' Magazine* showed the extended garden to be packed with flower beds with short stretches of clipped hedge and perhaps less lawn than Mawson suggested. A colourful and scented mix of jasmine, daphne and chimonanthus was added to eleagnus, escallonia and euonymus along the walls, iris reticulata and daffodils in the beds, and there were pillars with *Clematis 'Jackmanii Superba'*, 'American Pillar' and 'Dorothy Perkins' roses.[45]

The Gordon-Cannings used unemployed labour to make their garden; there are stories of these unskilled men being encouraged with mugs of Bovril as they sowed the lawn seed and dug and planted.[46] The Hartpury commission was a short one – Mrs Gordon-Canning had paid her last bill a year later on 16 January 1908. She herself had considerable knowledge of gardening and had nine gardeners and three men to maintain the horticultural buildings.

Hartpury went through the following years with a variety of owners and uses, and now it is part of the University of the West of England, where it offers sports and land-based studies. Some of the original trees and shrubs are identifiable and the bones of the garden are strongly visible, though much of the stonework needs attention, and labour-intensive features, such as the parterre above the terraces, have been modified.

Lees Court is a large house of stuccoed brick near Faversham in Kent built for Sir George Sondes in 1652. The building forms a square round a courtyard. It has been wishfully attributed to Inigo Jones, especially by Christopher Hussey, though the architect died in 1651.[47] The stables with their clock tower were built by Sir John Soane. The Sondes family, who had owned the house from the seventeenth century in its estate of 14,000 acres and some 5,000 acres in Norfolk also, had fallen on hard financial times in the early twentieth century and the third Earl Sondes, Lewis Arthur Milles, who inherited in 1907, had decided to let Lees Court and live elsewhere. The lease was taken on by a Captain Gerard Leigh and his American wife. Mrs Leigh's father and mother, Mr and Mrs Gerald Halsey, also lived at Lees Court, and it seems likely that they became the main lessees later in the twentieth century.

In 1908 Mrs Gerard Leigh asked Thomas Mawson to come to reshape the grounds. Mawson was excited by the design of the house, which appealed to his love for the seventeenth century and classical buildings; he asked Robert Atkinson to join him. Mawson must have seen a 1719 bird's-eye drawing of the house and its highly ornate and French-influenced ground plan by the surveyor Thomas Badeslade: such drawings represented the vanity of the owner, or his financial power, or both. Mawson delighted in the bedroom he was given at Lees Court with its 'panelling from floor to ceiling' and its 'fine old Tudor mantlepiece decorated with carriage and strapwork'. Strangely, a dream he had here which involved a murder which had taken place in the room centuries before, revealed a quality which would have made him a good medium, as a granddaughter later related.[48]

Lees Court was different from Mawson's other commissions so far: Gertrude Jekyll had been invited to set out the planting. Neither garden designer mentioned the other, and one senses a frosty silence. A general plan of the garden was sent from 28 Conduit Street for Jekyll to use, which to some extent gave control to Mawson. From 1909 to the autumn of 1910, when her papers ended, Jekyll filled thirty pages of her notebook with lists of plants – for shrubs, annuals and perennials for borders and an iris garden. Many, such as the iris garden, were crossed through, indicating, perhaps, a difference of opinion with Mrs Halsey. Other large plans carefully allocated long drifts to narrow borders, packed perennials into angular beds and roses into the borders of larger beds. There were rows of standard fruit trees with suggestions of suppliers such as Waterers and Bunyards.[49]

The planning of the new garden was begun and the work had commenced, when on the night of 26 November 1910, a fire began in a chimney and roared away, fed by the strong winds and timber which formed much of the furnishing. In four hours the flames had devoured all but the walls, and the southeast front collapsed the next day. The house at the time was in the

ABOVE The formal parterre
on the south side of Lees
Court in Kent.

charge of Mr and Mrs Gerald Halsey. Though it was possible to rescue many of the portable treasures, the family portraits and much else were lost. However, the house was fully insured, and it was decided to rebuild Lees Court to the original design as soon as possible, with the addition of electricity and an extra floor over the hall. The London architects Edward Hoare and Montague Wheeler were engaged, and Robert Atkinson was employed on the interior. Surprisingly, the American ladies supervised the rebuilding and paid for linens and furniture with their own accounts at Harrods and Harvey Nichols. Mawson persuaded the architects to move the entrance from the west to the east front, where Hoare and Wheeler made a new entrance hall with Tuscan columns on the ground floor and Ionic columns on the first floor, and a new carriage court outside.[50]

The grounds had been allowed to drift away from any style; successive Sondes had been taken up with shooting parties and the earls were more interested in field sports and cricket (there was a cricket pitch on the estate). Mawson had already seized the opportunity in 1908 to create a magnificent plan which reflected his

appreciation of French design, and it shows the house approached on the east side by a fan of three tree-lined avenues, two of which must have been there already as he labels them 'old avenues'. These 'green wings' to the house, which should have two lines of trees if the avenue was 'over five hundred yards in length' and should end some distance away so as not to 'monopolise the whole landscape', echoed the Badeslade drawing, and can be seen today.[51] However, unlike Badeslade, Mawson was concerned to raise the house above the surrounding flat land on the west and south sides by his usual method of excavating the space below.

The latticework of beds planned for the south front's rose garden were flanked on each side by box-edged herbaceous borders divided by yew hedges; but the main feature lay beyond the rose garden. Centred at the end of the lawn, as an eye-catcher from the terrace, was a wonderful piece of green sculpture, formed by four concave, clipped yew hedges, with each cavity on the lawn side filled by a curved, stone seat. In the centre of this sculpture rose a tall, pillar fountain, spilling into a pool. The pillar was topped by Mrs Halsey's preferred beckoning Mercury with a dart in his other hand, not the stately figure used by Robert Atkinson in his coloured illustration of this piece of green sculpture which formed the frontispiece for the fourth edition of *The Art and Craft of Garden Making* in 1912. These remain today, together with the pollard limes which have been shaped to form archways approaching the fountain from each

side of the garden. Pleached lime walks were favoured by Mawson as 'a favourite device of the artist gardener both in this country and on the continent'.[52] Beyond the fountain was a bastion and below it a tennis court.

The Halseys had taken Lees Court to their hearts – and purses. This extraordinary situation – of an American tenant with more generosity than the landed

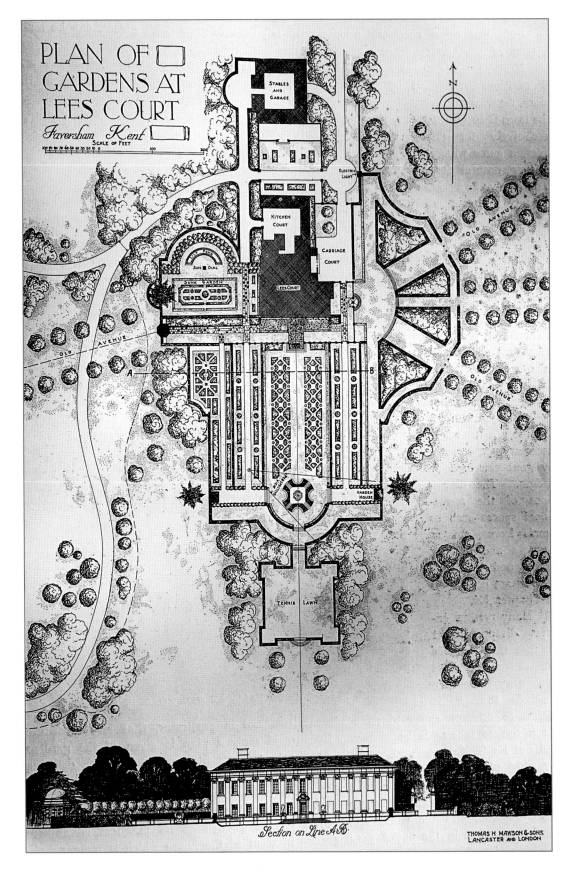

élite who owned the house and should have had responsibility for its upkeep – must have been unique to Mawson's list of clients. The view of the rose garden, the plan for the garden and the drawing for the gate piers were all made for Mrs Halsey, and she also continued to pay the rent for the lease to the Sondes.[53] Later payments in the Mawson cash book for £32 7s. 5d. on 25 June 1913 and £42 18s. 2d on 12 February 1923 show that the association with the Mawsons lingered on, until the Halseys gave up their tenancy in 1924. The third earl moved back into his house in 1932.

The house today is in divided occupation with tenants who have a strong interest in the history of the house and its Mawson garden.

LEFT Mawson's plan for Lees Court. It was reproduced in the 5th edition of *The Art and Craft of Garden Making*, fig. 134.

RIGHT Lees Court, Kent, in an aerial view showing the main features of the garden very much as Mawson had planned them. The mansion is the northernmost point. The old avenues, which still survive, are aligned on the mansion. This aerial view, made in 1960, shows the extraordinary closeness of the plan to reality at that time.

CHAPTER FOUR

Edward in partnership
1910–1924

MAWSON'S STAR continued to rise: his amazing success in finding clients, and his bold ventures into Canada from 1910 and Greece from 1913 described in the following chapters, meant that he had remarkable opportunities to offer his sons. Edward Prentice, Thomas' eldest child, born in Windermere on 16 July 1885, and his brother, John William, born in 1886, were to be groomed to work with the family business as landscape architect and town planner. Edward, capable and intelligent, would eventually take charge of the family firm and this chapter illustrates his quiet rise – via the interim 'Mawson & Son' which meant Thomas and Edward – after John had become the chief planner in New Zealand.

At this time there were no courses for landscape architects; men with such ambitions usually first trained as architects or civil engineers, and then sought to learn about horticulture elsewhere. Those who were only apprenticed to nurserymen were regarded by architects as artisans, inferior mortals, as Thomas Mawson learned to his cost; his sons were to be better educated for their chosen careers. Edward Prentice worked in a London architect's office for two years before going on to the Architectural Association School in Tufton Street, Westminster, between 1905 and 1907. He learned all he needed about plants and garden design from his father and the family nursery. One of his pupils later described him as a quiet, hard-working man, whose relaxed air and half-closed eyes misled his clients into believing that he was not listening when in reality he was on top of all the facts.[1] Following chapters will show how Edward and his brother, John, continued their education in landscape

architecture as they accompanied their father's journeys to Canada and Greece.

Thomas Mawson, having watched Edward's progress at the Architectural Association, found himself pulled into the midst of the debate which had been going on since the turn of the century in architectural schools and amongst leading architects. This concerned the direction in which teaching and the content of the courses were leading young architects away from formal structure to a freer, less disciplined way of working. The study of materials and techniques emerged as more important than the study of style. 'Young architects were taught everything except design', he said, 'and were submerged in details long before they had learnt the elementary principles of composition.' They were not taught axial planning, nor the relationship of a house to its site. Students were given exercises in drawing the 'quaint eccentricities and irregularities of medieval architecture' and were given 'predetermined details' round which a plan of a house evolved.[2] Mawson's was not the only voice speaking up for the return of classical principles. The *Builder* acknowledged Classicism as 'the most permanent element in civilized architecture' and gradually schools such as those at the Glasgow School of Art and Liverpool University (where Mawson lectured from 1911) turned to Neoclassicism.[3] Then, following the example of other landscape architects such as Edward Milner (1819–84) and his son Henry Ernest Milner (1845–1906), Edward Prentice was sent to Paris, to the Beaux-Arts School, where he was taught in the way in which his father approved and where he remained from 1907 to 1910. A further year working in another (unnamed) London architect's office was necessary before he could take his qualifying architectural examinations. This was a time which Edward Prentice did not enjoy: he spent it tracing structural steelworks drawings for his employer.

But in 1911, at the age of twenty-six, he was made a senior partner in his father's firm. Inheriting his father's business ability, he soon realised the advantages of having another office, as well as 28 Conduit Street, in London. This would be for himself, though carrying the name: Thomas Mawson & Sons, Architects. Walking along Victoria Street from the Architectural Association in Tufton Street nearby some years earlier, Edward had spotted the value of a location so well populated by firms supplying services to landscape architecture. In 1912 there were terracotta makers, suppliers of bricks, glazing contractors, a potash syndicate and manure merchant, concrete and ferroconcrete manufacturers and numerous engineers and quantity surveyors. Edward B. Milner, garden architect, established himself at number 7 by 1902, (this became Milner, Son & White, garden architects and experts in forestry and horticulture in the 1920s); Cheal & Sons, landscape gardeners, were at 53 Victoria Street; and Sutton & Sons, Seed Merchants, at 13. Seeing the advantage of his son's idea, Mawson & Sons moved into the seventh floor of Belgrave Chambers, 72 Victoria Street in 1912.

In succeeding years George Trollope & Sons and Colls & Sons supplied Mawson with cast and stone vases, Istrian stone wellheads, Roman terracotta oil jars and Verona octagonal wellheads from their Halkin Street, Belgrave Square office, just north of Victoria Street; H.W.Cashmore provided sundial bases, 'boy with a dolphin' fountains and 'Diana and hound' statuary from 32 and 96 Victoria Street and Hill & Smith took orders for metalwork from 8 Victoria Street (for their Staffordshire works). Garden Crafts of Staveley provided wooden garden furniture, and James Pulham made Japanese-style ornaments as well as terracotta stonework for clients who wanted them from their works in Hoddesdon, Hertfordshire. Metal, cast cement, lead and other manufactures could be provided by the Bromsgrove Guild of Applied Arts, and the J.Pyghtle White works in Bedford could supplement the locally-made wooden garden furniture. Mawson & Sons could successfully supply their clients in country houses and parks from their connections with specialist firms.

The Mawsons took other leases in Victoria Street, including numbers 25 and 26, opposite each other. Edward took on number 13 in the 1930s, which Suttons Seeds had occupied. During the Blitz this proved to have been a disastrous choice, as the Germans dropped a bomb which exploded on number 15 on 11 November 1940, killing two people, and badly damaging number 13, where the firm's records were kept. Edward was at first refused entry to the building by the air raid warden, but at the production of some cash, the warden turned a blind eye to Edward's rapid extraction of current drawings on which the firm was working and whatever else he could salvage. The loss of the rest meant that much valuable material about the firm and the staff are denied to the historian.[4]

High Street House in Lancaster remained the focus of Mawson & Sons. The staff included the able secretary John Dyer, who was also responsible for translating Mawson's erratic English into publishable books. James Crossland, the hard-working Irishman who went on ahead when Mawson travelled, taking slides for him and collecting data, and Howard Grubb, the young American who successfully persisted in asking Mawson to employ him, were typical of the many who respected Mawson's name. But Mawson could also be unkind if he did not think the work done by one of his thirty staff was good enough. The plans were prepared on linen and Mawson would run his thumbnail down the piece in question, effectively spoiling it, so the draftsman had to begin again.

LEFT A statue for sale at Lakeland Nurseries.

ABOVE Shrublands, painted by Ernest Chadwick *c*.1911, made a tasteful advertisement for the skills of Mawson & Sons as garden makers. It is possible that Mawson's daughters, Helen and Frances, with their connections in the world of the arts, encouraged watercolorists such as Chadwick and Ernest Rowe to paint the gardens made by Mawson for succeeding editions of *The Art and Craft of Garden Making.*

LEFT The rock garden at Shrublands showed visitors the best planting materials and methods to make a popular feature in the Edwardian garden.

LEFT High Street House, Lancaster, where the hard work on drafting plans was done.

KEY:

1   John Dyer
2   James Radcliffe Mawson
3   Hannah Richardson, secretary
4   John Shaw
5   Edward Prentice Mawson
6   Thomas H. Mawson
7   Bob Mattocks
8   T. Wearing Pennington
9   William Dean
10 James Crossland
11 Howard Grubb

The staff were used to travelling. The departure of the firm to visit clients in the south must have been an unwieldy performance. The long journeys were undertaken by train and heavy surveying equipment was carried to and from stations and the destined mansion by horse and trap. Mawson would stay with his client as a guest and would be collected by car from the station. Edward Prentice, and later, John, when he had finished his training, would stay in the nearest inn and the nursery staff in 'digs'. Because it was difficult to find competent landscape contractors, Mawson's nursery would take on the job on a cost plus fixed fee basis, which would include the services of a Mawson-trained foreman.

As Thomas took on other activities, Edward found himself representing his father at client meetings. He later related the story of one client in Yorkshire who, taken aback by seeing Edward, said, 'I thought yer Dad were coming!' To which Edward explained why he was representing his father and asked what ideas and preferences the man had for the scheme for the garden. The response was: 'Ideas! Look, it's the done thing to have a garden by your father, and I want one, too. Get on with it.'[5]

The year 1910 brought at least thirteen major commissions, including one for a man who wanted to live on London's fringe. Sir Robert Laidlaw, of Whiteway and Laidlaw, merchants in India, known familiarly as the 'Selfridges of India', was the Liberal MP for Renfrewshire and needed to be near Parliament. He bought Warren House in Hayes, Kent in 1909.

The house had been built by a Dutch stockbroker, Walter Maximilian de Zoete, in 1882, on six acres of Hayes Common which he had leased for 99 years from the Wickham Court Estate. The choice was a wise one, for down the hill half a mile away Hayes railway station was opened in the same year: the journey to Charing Cross took just under three-quarters of an hour. The house was built of red brick by George Somers Leigh Clarke, to designs by de Zoete, with Dutch gabling. The next tenant, a City banker, was to add an extra wing and a billiard room, and he had sufficient interest in horticulture to build glasshouses and a summerhouse. He was a keen carnation grower.

Laidlaw was a lover of trees, which was appropriate for the site on Hayes Common, described in a sales catalogue of 1909 as having 'glorious heather-clad spaces and wild woodlands'. The entrance to Warren House faced northeast and looked towards ground which fell southwards in rounded valleys. By 1909 the estate had grown to 22 acres. Mawson planned a parkland for him which stretched from southwest to northeast, an even stretch of well-wooded land. This was to be the heartland of Warren House's landscape. Much of the woodland was to be cleared, leaving clumps of Scots firs and silver birch and a group of three cedars of Lebanon as focal points. Trees were massed around the boundary with the common for privacy.

The main difference between Mawson's usual garden plan and the Warren House commission was that a considerable area of rose border specimens trained up pillars and interspersed with briars and other rose varieties were to be moved away to the far sides of the broad expanse of grass and trees in the large landscape to the southwest of the house. Here they made a rim, joined by a pleached lime walk, which was part of the sinuous path system which joined up the flower gardens around the outer perimeter. This was partly because, at the owner's request, tennis and croquet lawns took space close to the house, but it was also for aesthetic reasons: the views through the parkland would be spoiled – as Mawson put it: 'flower beds near the house

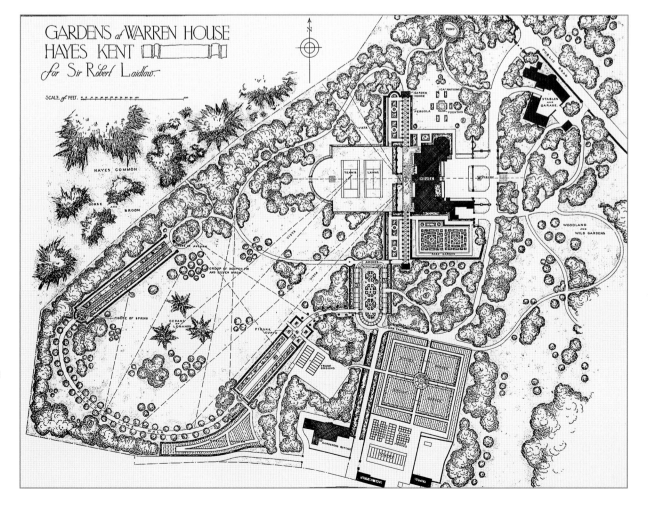

RIGHT Set on the common at Hayes in Kent, Warren House's trees had to be cleared to make the landscape garden in 1910. Flower beds were placed around the edge of the landscape at the owner's request. This plan appeared in the 5th edition of *The Art and Craft of Garden Making*, fig. 153.

would prevent a co-ordinated treatment of the lawns and accompanying groups of trees, which together form the vistas'.[6]

However, Mawson incorporated the formal rose garden enclosed by yew hedges which had been made by the Victorian gardener George Devey (1820–86) to the south of the house. Here he may have added red brick walls, as in a small court on the north of the house, where there are arcaded shelters. Whether the pergolas running north–south on each side of the building were made is not clear. But later photographs show pergolas along the panel garden which leads to the kitchen garden on the far south. Here also were curved stone seats – one has escaped the fate of other lost pieces of stonework – from which the plants in the centre could be admired. Paths connected the chain of gardens, heather and shrubs and mature trees around the estate, as they continued to do by the time of a sale advertisement of 1934.[7] Mawson's involvement with the tamed 'wild woodland' garden was a short one: the last bill, £114 4s. 9d. was for work done by 31 December 1910. Very little of the garden remains today as the building and grounds form the sports centre for the Metropolitan Police and Laidlaw's central parkland accommodates football pitches and the slopes below the house, a golf course.

In the same year, 1910, Mawson was engaged in west Dorset, at Leweston, two miles south of Sherborne, for the Hamilton Fletchers, a wealthy Catholic family. They had purchased a red brick Palladian mansion with a balustraded roof, built in the late eighteenth century, overlooking gentle, wooded valleys.

As he surveyed the grounds, Mawson's attention was captured by the wide, misty blue view over the river valley below and the woodlands beyond, and this was the area of landscaping to which he first directed his skills, building the expectation of the horizon to come. A long allée was cleared through the trees, beginning at a plinth surmounted by a stone wild boar; in the distance the bright sky illuminated two tall stone pillars, crowned by pineapples, and then the plain beyond. This was an original departure for Mawson. Paired, free-standing pillars had been used by Harold Peto, notably at the Villa Maryland in the Alpes Maritimes in 1904, though these had figures on the tops. Steps led down to a bastion which gloried in the view; on each side of the steps were curved, stone pavilions like the teahouse at Wood House over the border in Devon, but open, with stone seats behind the supporting, slim pillars. The bastion floor was paved and in its centre was placed an antique wellhead similar to the one at Wern, though, as at Wern, Mawson had recommended a sundial. A plaque on the pavilions (or shelters, as Mawson called them) recorded the completion of the terrace garden, avenue and approach in 1910-11.

Behind the bastion, a path led to a return allée towards the house through the original mature trees; Mawson's suggested treatment of these green walks was to turf or seed areas where roots had been removed and plant hedges with young trees behind.[8] Here the walks cut through established woodland. As the land dropped gently nearer the house, the allée was joined by a raised path. Today stone dogs and other beasts sit waiting in the

LEFT A wellhead divides two shelters on the bastion at Leweston.

shadows to be replaced in appropriate settings; sets of stone steps lead down the slope, which, like the one at Foots Cray, may have been screened by trellis and summer flowers. Closer to the house was a fountain in a rose garden, now heavily overshadowed by trees. To the side of the main entrance is a concrete lily pool, which has been rejected as a Mawson construction, but, as at Wern, it is very likely that the pool was built later by Mawson Brothers. The lantern-shaped glasshouse framed by wooden rose pillars and its pretty bedding plants reminded the staff that kitchen gardens can lift the spirits even on a grey day. Payments for £189 10s. and £5 8s. 10d. were made on 30 June 1911, and 18 April 1912 by the Hamilton Fletchers, which seems to be the last contact with Mawson. Today the house is a school, and although work needs to be done on the gardens the architectural features have been well looked after.

Mawson met the painter Sir Hubert von Herkomer while the landscape architect was looking for a studio not far from London. Herkomer had established himself in the midst of an artists' colony at Bushey in Hertfordshire, where he set up the Herkomer Art School in 1883 with money given to him by the guardian of one of his students. He had met an architect, H.H.Richardson, on a painting tour in the USA, and asked him to build a house in Melbourne Road in Bushey for his wife and his parents, not far from the school. This was called Lululaund, after his second wife Lulu Griffiths. It was full of elaborate wood carving by Herkomer's father, which reminded them both of their home in Bavaria, and much individually designed metalwork. Several hundred artists were taught at the Herkomer School before he ran

into debt and decided to withdraw in 1904. It existed for a while under the direction of a former student and was then called the Bushey School of Painting, but for some unexplained reason Herkomer bought it back again in 1912 and demolished it – just at the point when Mawson had heard of the empty studios and wanted to take them on. Herkomer, however, had decided to turn the space once occupied by the school into a rose garden, and when Mawson had made contact, Herkomer recognised him as the author of *The Art and Craft of Garden Making*. The two soon met, and discussed how the garden should be laid out. But before that was done, Mawson related, Herkomer proposed to paint his portrait in return for the price of the garden. The artist captured the restless – perhaps uneasy – spirit of his sitter; work began in 1913.[9]

The first sight of the rose garden brings to mind a sombre memorial: The Monument, a fountain made from Bavarian grey tufa brought in for the purpose, stands in the middle of a sunk garden. The fountain once trickled water through pipes into basins, forming a quatrefoil on a base of larger quatrefoils. Flanked by four columns, the Monument is joined to the top by a layered cornice, commanding the middle of a brick- and stone-laid circle, with creamy-pink brick walls forming raised beds around the edge of the circle. Stone steps rise to the panel beds, still planted with roses and with box hedging

containing their boundaries. Wooden rose poles topped with metal ornamentation for attaching ramblers were probably placed in the beds soon after they were made. The rose beds and Monument are set in the middle of a square which is paved with bricks, partly in a basket-weave pattern, and partly fanning into semicircles where seats were once placed, and from which paths radiate from the four quarters. An octagonal brick and tile column marks the end of one path, purpose unknown, and the summerhouse ends another. This is square, gabled, with an arched entrance and a tiled roof, and had a coved ceiling, a stone-flagged floor and a fireplace for the Herkomers to take refuge on a cold day. A square-topped door leads out to the pergola.

The pergola, once roofed by curving cross-pieces over square brick pillars, joined the summerhouse to Lululaund, and also divided the rose garden from the large lawn which Mawson knew as the kitchen garden. It was once clothed with climbing roses. No planting plans have been found for the rose garden, but Herkomer possessed a copy of *The Art and Craft of Garden Making* which listed suitable plants for all locations, and no doubt Herkomer discussed such things with Mawson as he sat for his portrait to be painted.

Hubert Herkomer died the following year and after the death of his third wife, in 1934, Bushey Urban District Council acquired the grounds and made it a public garden in 1937; Hertsmere Borough Council took

this on in 1974. This small but historic garden, with its wealth of craft skills in its brick, stone and wood, has been recently restored, with careful attention paid to the structure and replanting. It now presents a scented and tranquil space for local people to enjoy.

A country house near Wolverhampton, Wightwick Manor, built in the 1890s by Edward Ould for Theodore Mander, was to engage the attention of both Alfred Parsons (1847–1920) and Thomas Mawson. Set on a

ABOVE The Bushey rose garden with its tufa stone Monument (a fountain) before recent restoration.

ABOVE Mawson was not fond of topiary, but the yews under the house at Wightwick make a bold statement.

RIGHT Wooden bridges were frequently made by Garden Crafts Ltd. This one, at Wightwick Manor, spans a stream which leads into a lake.

BELOW LEFT At Wightwick Manor, wooden balustrading, unusual for Mawson, and brick piers make an ornamental feature above steps to the grass terrace below.

slope, with sandstone cliffs exposed along the approach road, Wightwick Manor's black and white beams with their decoratively carved wooden gables and stained-glass windows displayed an attractive example of an Arts and Crafts house. Mander, educated in science at both London and Cambridge universities, and a Liberal non-conformist, had made his money from the manufacture of paint and varnish. He rose steadily up the civic scale to become a councillor and then Mayor of Wolverhampton, and as a garden lover may have come across Mawson when he was engaged in work for East Park in Wolverhampton in 1895. In 1899 Alfred Parsons was approached to make the garden and some work was done, of which there is no record; but Theodore Mander died after an operation in 1901 and the house was shut up. Mander's wife asked Mawson to alter the garden layout in 1904, but the death of Flora Mander in 1905 again ended further planning for the garden.

Theodore's son Geoffrey inherited the house and his father's interests. He recalled Mawson and it is likely that Mawson went back to his earlier plan; his charges to 8 November 1910 were only £47 2s. 3d, which compares with Parsons' estimate in 1899 for 250 guineas for making plans for the garden. Mawson excavated earth to give the south front a clear presence in the landscape by setting it on a terrace above the lawn. The photograph in the fourth edition of *The Art and Craft of Garden Making* shows the terrace with its stone capped balustrading and oak balusters (unusual for Mawson) and tiered brick piers beside

a staircase leading down. Below the terrace, two pyramid yews are visible in the picture. Today these yews join others, trimmed as cones and much too wide for their site, marching down in pairs across a lawn towards a sun-dial, forming an axis which joins house and countryside.

Mawson's 1904 plan shows that he intended a circular ending for this axis, with trees and shrubs around it which would link the formality of the lawned area with the woodlands. The eastern side of the house would lead, via circular steps, to a lawn and an orchard, and a bridge over the road on Wightwick's eastern boundary would connect with the kitchen garden – now sold off. Across the carriage court, on the north, a Long Walk of yews led westwards. Further to the north was an elliptical garden with flower-planted panels forming fans. Today this is a rose garden with posts and swags. Leading northwest from the roses, Mawson planned an allée through pairs of lightly trimmed silver hollies and yews which make a beautiful and harmonious contrast. This leads into a wild garden and slopes which Mawson thought would be ideal for car-rying orchards and their ripening fruits, before dropping to water gardens along a stream leading into lakes. Much of this layout remains today, and is gradually being steered back to Mawson's original plan. Wightwick Manor was accepted by the National Trust in 1937, though Geoffrey Mander was able to live in it during his lifetime.

Tirley Garth in Cheshire turned the tables on the usual arrangements between Mawson and his architect colleague, Charles Mallows, as Mallows asked Mawson

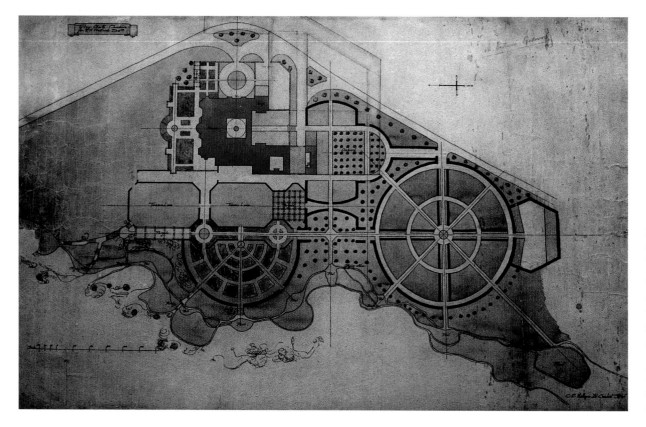

RIGHT The second of Charles Mallows' plans for Tirley Garth, Cheshire, drawn after he had asked Mawson to join him in a venture to make the garden for the house he had begun for Brian Leesmith in 1906. With a new owner, R.H. Prestwich, the house and garden were finished in 1912–14.

to work with him in a joint venture which concerned building the house and making the garden. Mallows was approached by Brian Leesmith, the director of a chemical firm, Brunner Mond, in 1906. Leesmith wanted a house on a slope overlooking the Cheshire Plain and the distant hills. The house of local grey and rose sandstone was begun in architect Mallows' preferred neo-Tudor style windows, gables and chimneys, but in 1911, for unexplained reasons, the house was sold to ICI, and was leased to a textile manufacturer, R.H.Prestwich, who supplied waterproof yarn to Burberry. Prestwich eventually became chairman of Burberry. His family was able to move into Tirley Garth in the summer of 1912 and Mallows was recalled to complete what he had begun. Long discussions followed with the family as to the finishing of the house and the design of the garden.

The garden at Tirley Garth demonstrates two things: the close relationship between Mallows and Mawson, in terms of their skills in architecture and garden design, and how these flowed into one another so smoothly that at first it is not easy to distinguish the work of Mawson from Mallows. Both men had an instinctive feeling for craftsmanship, as shown in their approach to hard land-scaping, blending the vernacular sandstone for rubble

walls, the edging of paths, and sturdy balustrades, with York stone for steps and paving. Wood was used as skilfully in the buildings for the gardeners. Mallows would stay with Mawson at Hest Bank while they discussed their plans, and maybe partnership, which Mawson was pressing on Mallows in 1912. There is no record of Mallows' feelings on the offer, which was declined.

An early design by Mallows published in *The Studio* in 1908 shows a long, rectangular building with its entrance court on the west side, a garden entrance to the south, space for large lawns on the east from which extended a bastion with stonework like spokes of a wheel, a huge semicircular kitchen garden on the north and many smaller compartments for paved courts and flower beds matching the ground plan of the house.[10] In 1912, Mallows had taken the lead once again, with a simplified but similar plan for the gardens, but with a grass sward facing the south.[11] Mawson is likely to have suggested moving the entrance to the west, avoiding the windier, southern side of the house as Mallows had originally planned.

The front door opens to a surprise – a sunny cloister with a sunk pool, edged with brilliant blue mosaic small tiles, and a fountain in the centre, and beds for plants in the four corners. This is the 'garth' from which the house (earlier called Tirley Court) takes its name.

Mallows' architectural plan for the garden presented an impressive semicircular bastion with terraced geometric beds facing east and destined to become a rose garden, though the planting plan for this is not in Tirley Garth. It overlooked the course of a stream which did not appear on the 1908 map, and it is likely that Mawson encouraged Mallows to suggest the possibility of water gardens along the stream. Another characteristic Mawson feature is the strongly axial line from the gardeners' bothy, which threads through and connects the gardens on different levels. It begins on the north, through the now circular 'round acre' kitchen garden, down across grass with ornamental flowering trees, over the top of the bastion terraces and out to join the natural landscape surrounding Tirley Garth on its south side. A pleasing feature of the garden's layout is its acceptance of the sloping site, its progression from formal design near the house to natural landscaping as the land falls: from the rose garden on the bastion, paths overlook spring-flowering shrubs or autumn colours in the trees across the stream.

Planting plans made by Mawson & Sons (here calling themselves garden architects) for the beds on each side of the bastion show a colourful explosion from a central bed of rhododendron 'Pink Pearl', into masses, two clumps deep, whirling around its centre. There were white and mauve 'Sappho', crimson 'Earl of Shannon', rose-purple 'Lord Derby', salmon 'Mrs R.S.Holfold' among many others, and the outside of the whirl was planted with shorter masses of azalea such as the pale yellow 'Mr A. de Warreher', the alpine rhododendrons *praecox* and *ferrugineum*, and heathers such as *Erica veitchii* and *Erica vegans* which smoothed the boundary into the grass.

Plans for the planting of the terrace borders, though unsigned, are made on the same type of paper as the Mawson rhododendron plan, and are written in the same hand. Two borders, about 30 foot long, have a packing of clumps, one behind the other with slight asymmetry, of old-fashioned perennials such as peony 'Queen's Perfection' and 'A.M.Kelway', aster 'Elsie Perry' and *praecox*, gaillardia 'sunset', phlox *alata* and 'Mrs Jenkins', red and salmon pink hollyhocks, iris, delphiniums, pyrethrums, lupins, cheiranthus and many more.

LEFT A strong axis from north to south links different parts of the garden at Tirley Garth. This one, through the round kitchen garden, is entered through craft-worked semicircular gates, ending at the bothy.

ABOVE The magnificent
bothy at Tirley Garth, home
to the gardeners, which was
probably made by Mawson
Brothers. Mawson Brothers
demonstrated Arts and
Crafts skills in wood, as well
as brick, stone and metal,
as seen in the gates and the
bothy at Tirley.

Wall plants included roses such as white 'Dorothy Perkins', 'Jersey Beauty' and 'Alberic Barbier'; wisteria, ceanothus, berberis, jasmine and *Garrya elliptica*.

There are planting plans produced by Mawson & Partners for Tirley Garth for the drive curving to the south, with rhododendron and azalea in groups of thirty-six, twenty, eighteen or twelve, and with fifteen Japanese maples visible from the house. Andromedas and pernettyas were massed at the front of the shrubs, moving forward into the rough texture of the heather. These, planted on the southeastern side, were to hide the view of the tennis courts below, which only came into sight from the lower parts of the winding drive to Mallows' lodge by the exit.[12] By the lodge on the south-west side, a colourful massing of the same flowering evergreen shrubs enhanced privacy and gave the impression that the visitor was entering a well-stocked estate.

Tirley has the most comfortable bothy ever granted to Edwardian gardeners, even though they had to climb a ladder to get into the rooms above. It towers on the northern boundary with its dovecote, the path climbing

gently to it beyond a typical Mawson gate with its half-moon shape. Through the archway under the bothy entrance, cold frames and greenhouses are laid out.

Tirley Garth is a remarkable example of an Arts and Crafts garden, surprisingly undisturbed. It continued to be rented by the Prestwich family – the last payment made by them to Mawson was on 12 June 1914, for £87 7s. 2d. – until 1949, when a trust was set up that bought the house from ICI. It was used as a centre for the Moral Rearmament movement until it was sold in 2002.

In 1913, Thomas and his son Edward Prentice worked together on Lord St Cyres' large house, Walhampton, on the edge of the New Forest in Hampshire. The house and estate had been bought in 1911 by Dorothy Morrison, whose family came from Fonthill House in Wiltshire; she married Stafford H. Northcote (1869–1926) in 1912. Thus two sets of 'old money', with shared interests in horticulture (both were Fellows of the Royal Horticultural Society), set about making improvements to their red brick Georgian house and its gardens, with their rolling grounds dropping to

lakes on the western side of the estate and long walks through the woodlands which surrounded the house. A large greensward faced the house on its southern aspect. All typical environs, it would have seemed, for Mawson's landscaping art.

Walhampton had been altered already by Norman Shaw and Edmund Fisher, FRIBA, before the arrival of the St Cyres family. After 1912, and using plans made by Fisher, the south front was substantially changed by raising its centre, balancing two octagonal towers by adding a storey to the one on the west, and realigning all the windows. To make this front even longer, and to give a sheltered outdoor place to sit, a colonnaded loggia was added. The north side of the house was moved forward to even up its frontage. It was Edward Prentice's work to put Fisher's plans into action.

However, the Mawsons also planned three of the exterior features close to the house. On the north front, plans for the walls and wrought-iron entrance gates for the carriage court were drawn up by Mawson & Sons in August and September 1913. A new north drive was made. There are also detailed plans for the loggia and its semi-domes (half-domes at the ends). This had a central closed space under the colonnades for a dining room flanked by open access between the pillars to the north front, also made in August and September 1913.[13] The loggia roof was edged with a mix of flat-topped, open balustrades and a network of half-circular terracotta tiled balustrades, their colour blending with the red brick of the building and the brick paving. Facing the loggia was a paved, sunk court, which eventually housed an oval pool and a fountain, statuary and planting; photographs of the winter of 1915–16 show it to be all but complete. The plans were made by Edward Prentice Mawson. But originally the loggia was to have been closed all round, as a cloister; opening it to the north created the need for another garden on the north side, which may have been that illustrated by a painting of a garden court in the *Builder* in November 1916.[14] However, this is very unlike the loggia on the south. The Mawsons' preoccupation with the Georgian style of the architecture of the house may have been watered down by Lady St Cyres, who liked Roman colonnades and Italianate design, but in the end the north garden seems to have looked very much like its counterpart. No plans of the garden have been found and a house has been built partly into the space it once occupied.

A simple terrace was made by the Mawsons along the south front, with red brick paving. There was no attempt to marry it to another terrace at the end of the lawn, made in an Italianate style before the Mawsons arrived, and just possibly by Harold Peto. However Mawson did place a curved stone seat facing the end of this terrace.

In front of the south terrace on the eastern side Mawson made a round pool with a statue of Mercury in its centre. It was eventually planted with roses and surrounded by stone benches.

It seems that Mawson did not return after the war; the accounts show payments for 23 April 1914, June and August 1914 – the first for £654 4s. 6d. – and the final £399 12s. 11d. 'to the end of December 1915'. Mawson had other, larger concerns at home and abroad and

the garden was taken on by Edward White, a landscape designer from the firm of Milner-White. A *Gardeners' Chronicle* report in June 1924 described Walhampton's garden burgeoning with flowers and shrubs.[15] But with this commission the tables had been turned in favour of architecture: the house fronts were straightened and formality reigned, but it was left to others to arrange the gardens beyond. The house and grounds were sold to a school in 1948; the loggia, colonnade and north garden have been considerably altered.

After the First World War Edward Prentice Mawson took on more of Mawson & Sons' work for gardens. His brother, James Radcliffe ('Cliffe'), who was to have been the horticulturist of the firm, had been killed in action in 1915. His father, approaching sixty, and sometimes unwell, discovered without surprise that there were fewer commissions for large gardens, though he had always spread his work into other spheres, including that of 'civic art'. There was much need for homes for disabled soldiers; there were large schemes for

BELOW Edward Prentice Mawson's loggia and half-dome, linking two sides of a colonnaded space, made in 1914 at Walhampton.

Lord Leverhulme which involved time and total commitment; there were lectures to be given at Liverpool University, and there was continuing involvement with schemes in Canada and Greece. Much of the labour force of large estates had been killed in the war, large gardens were labour-intensive and many agricultural estate owners lacked resources. The emphasis for landscape architects was slowly shifting towards public works. But Mawson's declaration in his autobiography that his old clients had begun to return (as had his own labour force to the Lancaster office by 1920), reinforces the optimism and determination of the public face of Mawson & Sons.[16] Assisted by Lakeland Nurseries in Windermere, the staff – Harry Pierce, James Walker and Alec Mawson – continued to manage and design smaller gardens all over the country.[17]

In 1920, two 'most attractive' schemes arrived, one from east Dorset and the other from Perth in Scotland. With his usual ebullience and the help of Edward Prentice, Mawson prepared to do business with the two shipowners who had simultaneously commissioned him. They were Charles W.Gordon of Boveridge Park,

near Cranborne, and W.Gilchrist Macbeth, of Dunira, in Perthshire.

Boveridge Park, a Georgian house which had been recently altered by architect Guy Dawber, was admired by Mawson for its site in the middle of its parkland and the beautiful landscape with which it was surrounded. Approached by two long drives through beech and pine to the house entrance on the west side, Boveridge had both an impressive carriage court and a porte cochère to greet the visitor. The house already had a formal garden, and a terrace on the eastern side, and Guy Dawber had made a garden loggia.[18] But to Mawson these features seemed to lack unity with the house. He confined his efforts on the east side to the original layout, making it compatible with his more extensive terracing on the south.

A plan of 7 February 1920 and Mawson's description of his work below the house on its south side can be followed today.[19] Beginning with stone terraces close to the house, next down was a grass terrace supported by a wall filled with alpines, then, eight feet lower, came another, planted with rose beds in panels. Most striking

ABOVE Charles Gordon's house, Boveridge Park, needed a garden appropriate to the site. Mawson was called in 1920 – and so was Gertrude Jekyll. Mawson's pool in the foreground is in full view from the back of the house; on the left a canal leads to the garden house.

RIGHT A garden house ends a long canal at Boveridge Park.

was the long stone canal for water lilies made across the lawn, parallel with the terraces – a much smaller version of Dyffryn. The western vista, along the canal, was closed by a garden pavilion, though this does not appear on the plan. Below the lawn, down steps through a low stone wall was a bowling green, and down yet again lay space for two tennis courts.

However, what Mawson did not tell readers of his autobiography was that the planting was to be done by Gertrude Jekyll. He made comments about the difficulty of the soil, which was a thin layer over chalk. 'No other garden is so trying to the men who construct it, as a garden on a chalky base,' Mawson rightly maintained, while agreeing that 'the results attained'…were…'a credit to the firm responsible for its execution'.[20] Once again there are no records of discussion between the two garden makers, but, of course, in later life Jekyll rarely visited her sites, and there may have been lingering memories for Mawson of his menial position replying to correspondence

at Hale Farm Nurseries thirty years before, when he was employed to answer Miss Jekyll's questions.

Jekyll's planting plans are dated February and March 1920 and, as at Lees Court, she was given Edward Mawson's neatly executed plans while she was making up planting schedules. A copy plan of Edward's of 7 February 1920 reveals three garden parts: the original eastern formal garden, Mawson's architectural garden to the south and an indeterminate southeastern corner which could be a mix of Mawson's plan and Jekyll's planting arrangements superimposed. There are Jekyll's irritable pencil rearrangements of paths and beds.[21] The Mawsons were clearly only briefly involved with the structure of the garden and payments in June and December 1920 amounted to £394.

'The landscape architect is constantly engaged upon schemes leagues apart, and under totally different conditions of climate, soils and local tradition,' Mawson's autobiography related, but this could be handled 'when

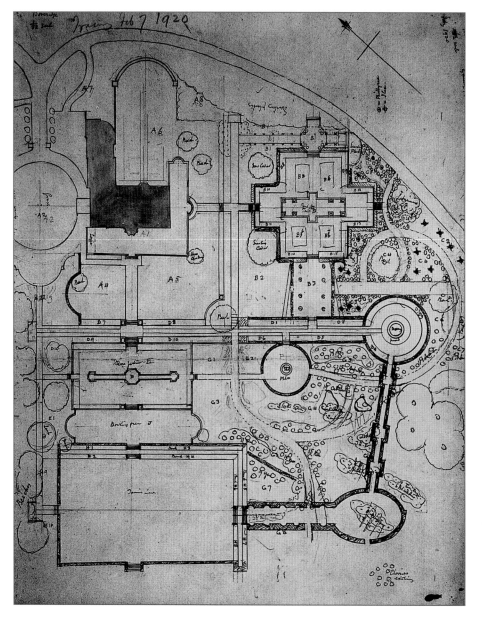

LEFT The plan for the garden at Boveridge Park was made by Edward Prentice Mawson, and Jekyll had a copy for annotation. Her pencil scribbling over the paths in the right-hand lower corner can just be seen.

the architect is given to enthusiasm and absorption in his work'. The journey from Dorset to Perthshire was no mean distance, but Mawson's enthusiasm for the Dunira commission shone through his account. The Glasgow architects Clifford and Lunan were responsible for introducing him in 1920 to Dunira's owner, W.G.Macbeth, who had employed them to make alterations to his Scottish baronial home near Comrie in Perthshire. Placed on a broad platform with its back to the rocky hills of Creag Liath, the house looked across the wide and gentle strath of the River Earn to the Aberuchill Hills beyond, with grand and glorious views of river, mountain, pine forest and pasture below. A long drive with two exits gave views of the plantations of oak, larch and spruce on the lower hillslopes around the house. 'Dunira is one of the most beautiful estates it has ever been my pleasure to study,' said Mawson, who was reminded of Grasmere and Windermere in the Lake

District. He was anxious to repair 'what passed for the gardens…to all appearances arranged by a waterworks engineer with railway experience'.[22]

Dunira was the third house to be constructed on the site; the original house, built further down the slope by Henry Holland (the son-in-law of 'Capability' Brown) for the first Viscount Melville in 1798, flooded, and so did its replacement. William Burn was the architect for the third house for Sir David Dundas. By the time that W.G.Macbeth bought the estate just before 1920 it had shrunk to a little under 6,000 acres. Macbeth then asked Mawson to design the gardens as he (Mawson) would like to see them. These were later described in the last edition of *The Art and Craft of Garden Making*.[23] He recognised that the house was placed on the edge of a spur as 'a foothill seemingly slidden from the mountains'. On the west side the grass banks that acted as levels below the house would need to be replaced with stone terraces.

The top one, balustraded and with flat coping stones, was partially hidden by flowering shrubs such as cotoneaster, ceanothus and escallonia. Stone steps led down past walls made of black whinstone with balusters, the gaps in the stones crammed with rock plants. Below the top terrace the surface dropped to a semicircular, grassed space, the introduction to a bastion – a viewing balcony over the landscape beyond. But immediately below this was a surprise: an arched roof to a pool held a fountain which spilled water first into the oval basin of the pool and then into a rill with insets planted with iris and reeds, which continued down towards a round lily pool with a fountain. The rill garden was set with rose beds; there were borders along the lawn edges which climbed to flagged paths, from where the rose garden could be admired. This floral spur ended in a semicircle, which completed the elliptical garden, though Mawson felt that this end needed further definition.

BELOW The magnificent early view to the hill, forest and meadows from a terrace at Dunira. Below the terraces a wall fountain fills the canal which divided the rose garden. The photograph was reproduced in the 5th edition of *The Art and Craft of Garden Making*, fig. 487.

RIGHT A plan for part of the garden at Dunira, Perthshire. From *The Art and Craft of Garden Making*, 5th edition, fig. 485.

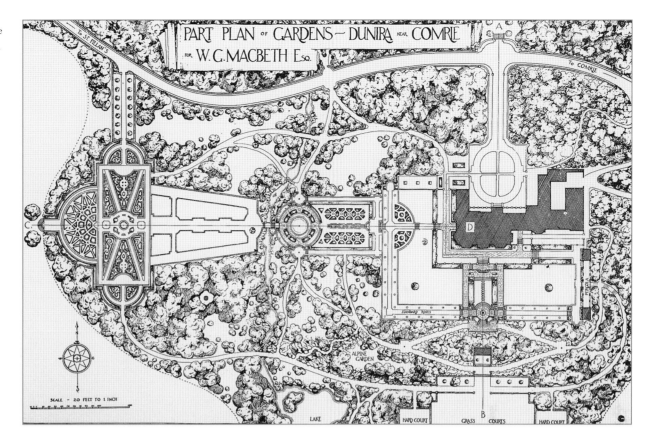

A similarly eye-catching garden was laid out on the southern side of the house. Again, Mawson used the slope to his advantage, this time opening a viewing balcony with its flat-topped, simple balustrading above a wide, peaceful view down the strath. Flagged paths and steps dropped to this balcony, with its roundel in which sat a sundial and beds of lavender, square stone beds containing box, and pots of rhododendron. In the middle distance, at the level of the parkland, opened another picturesque garden. This was contained between clipped beech hedges and defined by parallel lines of pergolas, made of metal hoops draped with clematis and held by yew pillars. By 1931 there were semicircular beds of salvia, heliotrope, ageratum and larkspur, and in the middle there was the ubiquitous wellhead with its lacy metal arch.[24] Below the steep incline on the south side and out of sight of the view from the balcony there were four grass and two hard tennis courts, with a teahouse, which presumably offered changing-room space.

Macbeth's favourite part of the garden was constructed by James Pulham, who built a water garden on the Allt Eas an Ion, a stream which came in from the north to a small loch below the rose garden on the west.[25] Using the boulders from the stream bed and nearby, Pulham created cascades, waterfalls and rock pools. The stream edges were later planted with candelabra primula and iris in their vigorous upper stretches,

loosestrife, ferns and rodgersias for their colour and foliage. The pools below were framed with bamboo, weeping willow and weeping birch.[26]

The garden was made by Edward Prentice, while his father went back to Greece. It had taken three years to construct and had cost its owner over £3,000 – money which he must have considered well spent.[27] But all this lush glory was short-lived; in 1948 the house burned down, leaving only the east side and office court. For a while the latter was occupied, but in 2006 the remaining structure was pulled down, leaving a ghostly, stranded terrace with steps leading down into a melancholy forest of foliage. For an instant a television series revived the rose garden and its rill in the 1990s. They left, and the garden sank back into its quiet and sad decay. The yew pergolas on the parkland now make silent walls, overlooked by a blind-windowed teahouse. The water garden has vanished underneath a sea of leaves.

Elm Court was built in about 1907 in a high-class residential part of the dignified spa town of Harrogate. Spacious development has given the house all the characteristics of the mansion of the large estate, but on a smaller scale. Approached by a carriage drive, the front of the house, made of good class brick and rough casting with a Westmorland slate roof, faced south and at the time of building its back garden looked on to magnificent views over Nidderdale and the Yorkshire Moors. It had the Edwardian idea of an Italian garden, but

the half-acre site was insufficient on which to make any additional designs.

The house was bought and altered by a Mexican businessman, Luis Guevara, whose work, which was probably in the textile business, took him to Bradford and Leeds. Inside there were panelled rooms – oak in the dining room and walnut in the morning room – Italian marble fireplaces and a marble bathroom, William and Mary tapestry and ceiling relief, and a grand drawing room overlooking the Nidd valley with Louis XV wall and ceiling decorations. The owner boasted that 'Every known modern improvement has been installed regardless of expense.'[28] Small wonder that Guevara asked Thomas Mawson to bring the gardens up to the standard of its interior.

The garden, 300 feet long, and with a drop of 11 feet from south to north, allowed the making of two shallow terraces. The first terrace, next to the house, formed a rose garden set in a pattern of beds, which ended at a pergola at the west end; next to it was a centrally-heated

ABOVE The garden, with its shallow terraces and pool in its centre, has two garden houses on the sides nearest the house at Elm Court, and an open pavilion at its far end.

LEFT Cupid with a fish in the pool at Elm Court.

garden room 'decorated in the Oriental taste' – for writing letters, reading, and playing indoor games. (Mawson had intended this to be a pergola pavilion marking the west end of the next terrace). But the main aspect was down the garden from the house terrace. From the steps, the eye went first to the garden pavilion with its four classical pillars which ended the view – and the axis – to the north; next, to the fan of raised beds of single varieties of hybrid tea roses and then the lily pool below with its fountains and statuary. The garden was wide enough to accommodate more flower beds on each side of the lily pool, and the whole was set into York stone paving

which gave warmth – and width – to the scene. Trellises took swathes of honeysuckle, briar roses, clematis and ceanothus along the sides of the garden, and alpines and wall plants were tucked into the cracks and crannies in the stonework. Behind the pavilion, for privacy, Mawson had suggested planting 'trees of a towering upright nature' and shrubs and semicircular yew hedges. But contemporary photographs show the encroaching houses in the road behind, which may have led Guevara to put the house up for auction in 1927.

How much was Thomas Mawson involved with Elm Court? In 1923 he had been diagnosed with Parkinson's disease and, though mentally alert, his activities had to be diverted into less physically challenging channels, with less travelling and much more writing, as the last chapter will tell: Elm Court becomes a metaphor for the winding down of a career in making gardens. The plans were drawn up in the Mawson manner, and the blueprint of the layout carries a note in Mawson's handwriting. It is impossible to tell whether this commission was surveyed by Mawson – if so, it must have been his last. A drawing of the garden in the fifth edition of *The Art and Craft of Garden Making* was made by E.L.Spivey, one of Mawson's pupils and probably attached to Lakeland Nurseries, which drew up the working plans and put the garden into place.[29]

Elm Court was the last garden that Thomas Mawson included in the last edition of *The Art and Craft of Garden Making*, in 1926, but there was a third Yorkshire garden made in the late 1920s for Mrs Alfred Chaytor at Croft Hall, Croft-on-Tees. Both pond and Italian gardens were completed in a design which was almost certainly the work of Edward Prentice Mawson and which marked the point at which father turned the leadership of Mawson & Son to the son. Nevertheless there is no doubt that Thomas Mawson remained capable of inspecting and approving every plan into the late 1920s, and he continued to do this as long as he was mentally capable in the early 1930s.

CHAPTER FIVE

The New World and the City Beautiful 1905–1914

THOMAS MAWSON'S first commission in North America in 1905 was to make a garden, but his work in this continent rapidly turned towards larger commissions for the beautification of cities.

Theodore Marburg, President of Baltimore's Municipal Art Society, had been holidaying in the Lake District in early 1905 and made a preliminary – and unexpected – call on the well-known local landscape architect. They spent several evenings discussing Marburg's interest in urban improvement in his home town, which confirmed Mawson's ideas of the moral benefit of beautiful surroundings. Through this visit, Mawson was recommended to Baltimore businessman H.Carroll Brown and his wife. The Carroll Browns met Mawson at Claridge's Hotel in London to ask him to work on the gardens of their holiday home on their estate at Green Spring Valley, Massachusetts, where they entertained their friends and business colleagues. They had

a 'hair-raising' afternoon's car ride (presumably Carroll Brown was at the wheel, as Mawson did not drive) around Kent and Surrey. His clients had ambitions to have an English garden, and the country houses of the Home Counties offered some excellent examples. Then Mawson prepared to sail for New York on 26 September 1905 with his twenty-year-old eldest son.

On a 'dreamy autumn day of the New England Indian summer' Thomas and Edward Prentice Mawson took a train from New York to Brooklands, near Baltimore, relishing the landscape and the colours of the sumach, hickory and red-leaved American oak. They stayed three weeks with the Carroll Browns at Brooklandwood, making surveys and plans which were later completed in England. The Georgian-style house, built with small plum-coloured bricks, was set in long lawns. Mawson cut some trees to open a drive on the front, leaving other established red oaks and hickories

LEFT The Parliament Building, Regina, 2005.

RIGHT The garden plan for Brooklandwood, Baltimore, was drawn in England after Thomas and Edward Mawson had visited the Carroll Brown family in 1905. The garden (right) appears to have been somewhat glamorised by its owners.

ENTRANCE TO BROOKLANDWOOD HOUSE, BALTIMORE USA
THE RESIDENCE OF H. CARROLL-BROWN ESQ

to frame the house and make an avenue, and, with Dan Gibson, planned twin lodges and a gateway at the entrance to the drive. The illustration of the lodges, drawn by Robert Atkinson after Dan Gibson's death in 1907, featured in *The Studio* in the same year. Mawson planned an enclosed garden on the east with greenhouses and conservatories, and an irregularly-shaped fruit and vegetable garden on the west with rows of standard *Magnolia grandiflora* and espaliers of American blackberry canes. The site fell towards a stream and Mawson suggested terracing to set off the historic house. As with so many of his designs, there are no further references to Brooklandwood apart from some photographs in Kendal Record Office.[1]

But there was another garden commission, probably in 1908, from New York, for which the archives hold only a garden plan and no date, and no hint of where Mawson found his client. She was a Mrs George Rose, from Old Westbury, New York; perhaps her husband had attended one of Mawson's New York lectures. The village is on the North Shore of Long Island, once an isolated Quaker settlement that only began to expand after the arrival of the railway in 1836. Eventually the rich New Yorkers descended, with money from industry and transport, and very grand homes went up – the equivalent to the English country house, but much larger, and called 'cottages'. Bennett Cottage (later renamed Overland) was built by New York based architect Frank Hoppin, set in 56 acres of land at the top of a hill, and completed in 1909. Hoppin, with his business partner Terrence Koen,

had completed his apprenticeship with the well-known American firm of architects, McKim, Mead and White; Hoppin had built The Mount at Lenox, Massachusetts, for Edith Wharton. The Rose family of six, photographed in 1908 on a garden terrace, was two boys and a girl and a baby, held, strangely, by his businessman father who is seated. The well-dressed mother looks expressionlessly to the foreground, the boys in new country suits and boots and ties posed appropriately for the camera.

The house, an imposing rectangular three-storeyed 'Georgian' colonnaded mansion with its pedimented sides standing forward from the colonnade, had a first floor balcony overlooking the garden. Inside there were eleven main bedrooms, six bathrooms, ten servants' bedrooms and two bathrooms, and a separate servants' dining room. Outside were a tennis court, kennels for a pack of beagles, a four-car garage and a gardener's cottage, rented stables and a coachman's house. Mawson was moving in affluent circles.

An open tiled porch led on to a terrace and then down steps to a garden with a lily pond. Further steps through terraces on another side of the house led to the tennis court, and a walk through woodland to the kennels and garage. The undated aerial photograph shows the imposing carriage court joined by the drive, with hay meadows beyond. Designed metal gates with stone pillars stood at the entrance to the drive. Another, service road, came to the side entrance. The garden, by this time well established, was divided into formal separate, hedged compartments near the house on one

ABOVE The illustration of Dan Gibson's lodges at Brooklandwood, drawn by Robert Atkinson after Gibson's death in 1907, featured in *The Studio* in the same year. It was a chapter opener in the 5th edition of *The Art and Craft of Garden Making*, p.69.

side and, beyond a long rectangular lawn, was another separate square garden contained by hedges, and probably planted with fruit bushes or flowering shrubs. All the planting of the gardens was done by Mr Hicks of Westbury. Mawson's cash book records charges and expenses for £104 3s. 4d. on 11 October 1912, confirming that he was employed only to supply the plan of the landscaping, and the pictures show this was adopted.[2]

There are no further firm references to the making of individual gardens in North America, though Mawson continued to lecture on garden making throughout his tours. 'Work designed in this country [England] and executed across the Atlantic by a foreign mind, from a garden standpoint never struck me as satisfactory,' he said.[3] From these commissions and with useful contacts, Mawson turned his attention to larger landscape and urban commissions.

The New World was experiencing rapid change as industrialisation and the building of the railroads encouraged massive immigration from the Old World, with its inevitable accompaniment of overcrowded, unsanitary conditions and social unrest. In America the City Beautiful Movement arrived with the World's Columbian Exposition in Chicago in 1893. Expecting moral regeneration to follow, the landscape architects Frederick Law Olmsted and Daniel Burnham and journalist Charles Mulford Robinson (1869–1917) believed that improvement to the landscape and the construction of a beautiful city would reform the antisocial elements within it. Olmsted and Burnham built a Beaux-Arts, classical-style settlement with a monumental civic centre in Chicago. This 'White City' was said to have introduced order and harmony at an unsettled time in American history.

BELOW Bennett Cottage from the air, c.1909.

In 1899 Robinson wrote the first of a series of articles and books on the problems of urbanisation and how to deal with them. *The Improvement of Towns and Cities; or, The Practical Basis of Civic Aesthetics*, published in 1899 followed in 1903 by *Modern Civic Art, or, The City Made Beautiful*, offered ways in which a city could be made visually pleasurable and which would encourage civic pride and good behaviour. Many of his examples were attributed to the Belgians and French. However it was not until the first two decades of the twentieth century that Americans turned their attention from beautification to the practicalities of the structure of the city: transport, streets, water, sewerage, housing for the working classes, and above all, the need for a city plan. Mawson was a passionate believer in town planning, and campaigned for the need for beautiful cities which fostered civic dignity and respect, and also catered for their practical requirements. It is clear that he had read Charles Mulford Robinson's books and adopted many of Robinson's ideas – especially in North America.

Mawson's second son, John William, was destined to be the planner and he blazed a survey trail for his father to follow in Canada. Trained by the architect Dan Gibson, John then took the Diploma course in Civic Design at Liverpool University. In his early twenties he shouldered the responsibility of managing the Vancouver office of Mawson & Sons. As the staff in the Lancaster office built up from twenty-five in 1908 to thirty in 1912, the firm could confidently take on ambitious commissions abroad. While John took charge in Canada, Edward Prentice, Mawson's eldest son, was to be involved more closely with the firm's work in Greece.[4]

Mawson spent the summer of 1910 at the National Housing and Town Planning Conference in Vienna, where he noted that the British delegates were not alive to serious town planning problems. Despite the conference's emphasis on town planning, privately there may have been requests for garden work, including one from Baron von Boeslager; Mawson redesigned his overgrown garden at Schloss Hessen near Hamm in Prussia, neglected while the baron had been exiled to England.[5]

The RIBA organised the first British conference of town planning to be held in Great Britain in October 1910, and facilitated meetings from 1913 for a group of architects, surveyors, lawyers and engineers who professed an interest in the subject. Its committee was chaired by Thomas Adams, of the Local Government Board in London, who had worked briefly with Mawson (as Mawson and Partners) before leaving to work in Canada.[6] The group from 1913 became the Town Planning

Institute, formally recognised in 1914, and Mawson was to become its president between 1923 and 1924.[7]

By 1910 the first three editions of *The Art and Craft of Garden Making* (1900, 1901 and 1907) had been published both by Batsford in London and by Scribners in the United States and this had led to an invitation to come to speak to the professors of landscape architecture, horticulturists and architects with whom Mawson had been corresponding. On 26 September 1910 he left Liverpool on the SS *Celtic* for an American lecture tour, which was organised by an American landscape architect, Robert Anderson Pope, who became Mawson's agent.[8] He had offices in Fifth Avenue, New York, and wrote about Mawson's work in *Architectural Record*.[9]

Mawson spoke at the prestigious universities of Harvard, Cornell and Yale, and went on to New York, Richmond, Virginia, Philadelphia, Washington and Chicago, dividing his lecture subjects between landscape architecture and civic art. The useful contacts and lasting friendships which this gregarious and lively man was to make were just as significant as the impact of his lectures. Harvard had introduced the first degree course in landscape architecture in 1900 and in city planning in 1909. By 1914 the university was recommending Mawson's fourth edition of *The Art and Craft of Garden Making* on the reading list from the School of Landscape Architecture Library. At Harvard Mawson met Frederick Law Olmsted junior (1870–1957) and his stepbrother John Charles (1852–1920), who had founded the American Society of Landscape Architects in 1899. Their father (John's stepfather), Frederick Law Olmsted (1822–1903), had begun the family firm of landscape architects, establishing the firm's competence and importance in many fields, including (with Calvert Vaux) the making of Central Park in New York and Stanford University campus. At the Olmsteds' office in Brookline, near Boston, Mawson explored the firm's offices, noting the importance given to drawings and photographs at all stages of the development of the plans in progress. Photography rapidly found Mawson's favour as a method of recording sites as well as illustrating lectures with glass slides. He admired the businesslike organisation of the firm, but felt his own introduction of foremen, well trained in planting and design, helped the running of many commissions in his absence.[10]

Mawson's lecture material covered designs in gardens which he had undertaken in Great Britain and the Peace Palace at The Hague, and landscape studies of English villages, Italian and Renaissance gardens; he also spoke about town planning. The lectures were well received at

Harvard, at Cornell's School of Landscape Architecture, where the presiding academic was Dr Andrew Dickson White, and at the School of Architecture in Columbia. In Chicago he met Daniel Hudson Burnham (1846–1912) who had progressed through an architectural apprenticeship to become manager of a firm which had a national market to build skyscrapers. It was responsible for city plans such as San Francisco and Cleveland. Mawson was impressed with the spacious boulevards of Chicago and from regarding skyscrapers as 'monstrosities' he began to accept them as a 'new and necessary phase of construction'. But it was not until his visit to America in 1917–18 that Mawson was to meet Charles Mulford Robinson with whom he had only exchanged letters. Robinson, who had promoted landscape architecture as the keystone of town design, became the first American Professor of Civic Design, at the University of Illinois in 1913.

In 1911 Mawson had returned to America, this time to attend the third National Conference on City Planning at Philadelphia between 15 and 17 May. In the chair was Frederick Law Olmsted junior, whose expansive introductory speech dealt with the problems of congestion in cities and the need for legislation to control growth. In America one of the most serious difficulties standing in the way of change, claimed Olmsted, was the gridiron plan with diagonals, which had been used to design cities. Raymond Unwin, representing the RIBA, also condemned the grid system, urging low-rise garden cities and suburbs rather than large, unhealthy tenement blocks for housing the overcrowded American cities. Better planning could only be achieved by a comprehensive plan, he stated, which would encompass social conditions, site and beautiful design.[11] Mawson agreed with these summaries of North American city planning problems and their 'monotonous gridiron plan, which ignores topographical conditions and internal circulation of traffic, along with an utter neglect of zoning for specific needs of a modern, well-equipped city.'[12]

Mawson's visits to North America followed a pattern, with spring and autumn tours, interspersed by attendance at the springtime National Conference on City Planning, lectures in universities, private clubs and civic halls, seeking commissions and covering expenses with his commission and lecture fees, and advertising further lectures. On 4 November 1911, *Varsity,* Toronto University's student newspaper, announced that 'Mr. Thomas H. Mawson, the noted landscape architect of Liverpool, will give a series of six lectures on Town Planning in the University in the first week of November.'

Mawson welcomed the break from home and fresh experiences, though he travelled continuously and worked on his lectures and reports in trains, on liners and in hotels. His staff in Lancaster coped with the constant pressure, drawing up plans from surveys in Britain and abroad; but his absences caused discontent at home about the work of the practice, which Mawson chose to ignore, believing such endeavour was good experience for the staff in England. More dangerous was that some of Mawson's clients became restive, wanting the attention of the head of the firm, not his staff. Such a man was Sir William Lever, for whom work was presently in hand at The Hill, Hampstead. Lever fired Mawson as he was about to set off for America with his wife and sons. This was a client Mawson could not afford to lose – for financial and prestigious reasons. It was after a well-crafted letter stressing the need to give experience to his sons by taking them to his clients and setting them to work across the Atlantic that Lever relented.[13]

Mawson had accepted an invitation earlier on from Earl Grey, the Governor General of Canada, briefly to visit Ottawa and 'stir up an interest in civic betterment'. A chance to work on the Niagara Falls Victoria Park was dashed as the commission decided they could not afford professional advice. But there was a better chance that Mawson would be backed, especially by Sir Robert Laird Borden (1854–1937), prime minister of the Dominion of Canada from 1911–1920 and the Canadian Society of Architects, if he put in a design to replan the capital, Ottawa.

Four provinces of Canada had been united in one dominion in 1867 by the British North America Act; other provinces were constituted and joined the dominion, partly as a response to the need for agreement between the French and the British. In 1857 Queen Victoria had chosen Ottawa as the capital, between the French-speaking town of Montreal and the English-speaking town of Toronto. The provinces had been growing fast enough to need capital cities of their own. Towns were becoming more conscious of their identities; civic authorities needed landscaped, dignified legislative buildings to replace their small nineteenth-century establishments, sometimes no more than wooden huts; the growing towns needed new street layouts. This could be the opportunity for which Mawson had been waiting, to beautify the new settlements of part of the British Empire, with the backing of its pro-British dignitaries. But there were two obstacles that Mawson had not realised: the power of the railway companies was stronger than the support of British dignitaries and Canadian nationalism was taking root.

For some time the capital had been neglected. In the late nineteenth century Ottawa had no sewerage, no lighting, no water supplies and no paved streets. Wooden buildings reminded inhabitants of the timber industry, whose lumber yards and central activities helped to make Ottawa a dismal town. Little had been spent on the new parliament buildings; the Ottawa Improvement Commission had been set up in 1899 but ignored early plans and the advice of landscape architects. After the end of Sir Wilfrid Laurier's premiership in 1911, Sir Robert Borden renewed the attempt to start work on improving Ottawa's townscape.

But the state government was wary of Borden's desire to control the process. There was political manoeuvring among some businessmen who favoured Edward H.Bennett (who had worked with Daniel Burnham on Chicago) and his Ottawa plan for a City Beautiful Municipal Plaza with stately buildings and tall spires, a large railway presence lying below the city but open to it and crossed by wide bridges leading to the Ottawa river.[14] Mawson had asked Sir Robert to send to the RIBA for further recommendation for himself. Instead, the RIBA submitted an alternative plan for Ottawa by Raymond Unwin, and the directors of the Canadian Pacific Railway (CPR) backed Edward H.Bennett.[15] In fact this plan was not implemented either, as a fire in the government buildings depleted their finances and the First World War stopped any further action. It was many

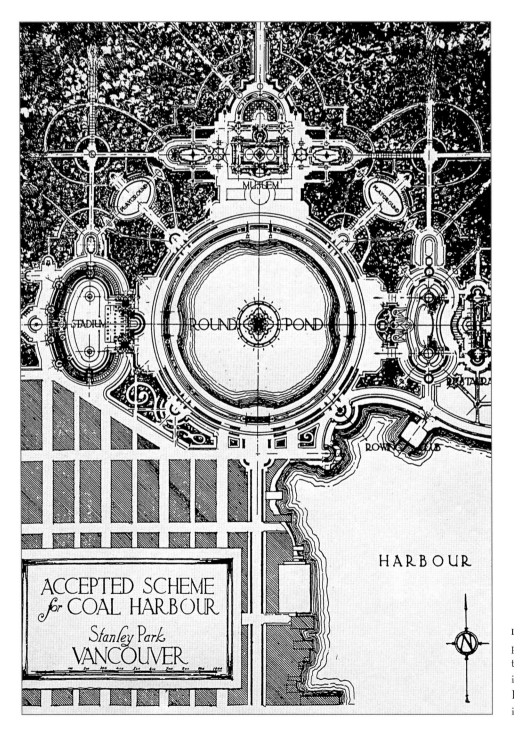

LEFT The final Mawson plan for Stanley Park aimed to make Vancouver consider itself an international 'City Beautiful'. The plan appeared in *Life and Work*, fig. 41.

decades before premier Wilfrid Laurier's dream that Ottawa should be remodelled as 'the Washington of the North' came anywhere near fulfilment.

In the spring of 1912 Mawson arrived in Vancouver to John's manager's office on the eleventh floor of the Rogers building in the centre of the town. This had long views past the nineteenth-century office blocks and steam boats on the Burrard Inlet to the mountains of North Vancouver. Later they occupied a less expensive site in Mawson's weatherboarded house in Maple Street.[16] Today Vancouver straddles the lazily winding distributaries of the Fraser river towards English Bay; the early city was more confined around a promontory butting into the Pacific, with False Creek and English Bay on the south and west and Coal Harbour on the north. Topping this promontory was a large forested area which had become Stanley Park in 1889, named after Lord Stanley of Preston, Governor General of Canada; the future of the park and its adjoining Coal Harbour was to absorb Mawson for the next few months.

Mawson gave a lecture to the Vancouver architects that was reported in the *World Vancouver* on 30 March

1912: 'Long ago Vancouver made up its mind that something must be done to conserve the natural beauties of this wonderful city... May we hope that Mr Mawson is the man who can tell Vancouver what shall be done – and persuade Vancouver to do it.'

Stanley Park, a military reserve leased to the city of Vancouver in 1908 by the dominion government, had become an undisturbed woodland. Mawson was commissioned by the Board of Parks Commissioners to reclaim the shallow Coal Harbour from its mud flats on the southern edge of the woodland and improve the park to make it more accessible.

Mawson made three alternative schemes for Coal Harbour for the board to discuss. The first was to leave it as it was with minor adaptations for its use as a public park; the second was to fill it in and devote the area to a series of playing fields; and the third was to 'partly fill in Coal Harbour and redesign the whole area as an ornamental fore-ground to Stanley Park'. Mawson, somewhat dissatisfied with his first three plans, then submitted a fourth, 'a rather audacious enterprise', which the board accepted.[17] This sought to connect the town with the

ABOVE The Georgia Street
axis which was intended
to link a museum with the
centre of Vancouver.

park by making Georgia Street the main axis of the grid on which the town was designed. It would join the heart of Vancouver to a new and magnificent building for the Museum of the Natural History of British Columbia.[18] Coal Harbour was to be turned into 'a great round pond, with a central monumental shaft surmounted by a statue of Captains Cook or Vancouver'.[19] There would be a stadium, a restaurant, a kursaal (a social centre) and an ornamental garden with American plants. Beyond the stadium, playing fields would be screened by young plantations; playgrounds were to be sited between the museum and the main buildings, and a 'fine park entrance' would be built leading to a granite-edged causeway with a central avenue of red-twigged lime trees, grown by a nursery, and pleached or trimmed to twenty feet.

To convince Vancouver that it had the potential to be a great international city, Mawson assured the commissioners that the Georgia Street axis, new civic centre and finally a new enlarged Union railway station would create a boulevard which:

would secure the 'grand expression' to your city as surely as the main axis from The Louvre to the Arc de Triomphe secures to Paris the expression of the 'grand manner'... In considering my scheme I would like you to think along the lines of the Paris model... regarding your Civic Centre as the Arc de Triomphe, Georgia Street as the Champs Elysées, the Coal Harbour as the Place de la Concorde and the Tuileries Gardens, and the Museum of the Natural History of British Columbia as the Louvre.[20]

He had already admitted that the scheme might be regarded as 'too imaginative' and 'financially unattainable', but asked the commissioners 'not to be appalled by the comprehensiveness of any of the schemes, but to regard them as suggestive policies of development, any one of which may require twenty years or more for its realisation'.[21]

Stanley Park, a 'wild impenetrable jungle' of some 750 acres was aloof – 'apart from rather than a part of Vancouver City'.[22] Mawson suggested that streetcars should circulate round the existing road on the edge of the forest and that separate provision should be made for cars, horses and pedestrians with roads and walks following the contours. The commissioners' nervous anxiety to preserve every natural feature had sometimes resulted in its destruction, Mawson claimed, and he urged the clearing of dead trees, some judicious trimming to display their spectacular trunks and the planting of native species only. Conversely, he urged the copying of nature in the development of a stream course from Seal Pool, with cascades and pools planted with

BELOW Totem poles of the American Indians seemed more appropriate than a massive museum to mark the end of an axis which led back into town.

sedges and reeds. He praised the commissioners' consideration of a plan to naturalise the shrubs and flowers of British Columbia within the park, reserving the use of decorative plants to the edge of Coal Harbour.

Mawson's general survey and propositions of what was possible for Coal Harbour and Stanley Park showed 'the importance of working towards a great ideal which shall have as its "raison d'être" the perfect blending of Art with Nature, Forest with City: the entire scheme is conceived as a great composition in which ordered balance and symmetry predominate'.[23]

Such sentiments were aimed to rouse patriotism and pride. The *Daily Province* of 20 December 1912, however, recorded strong dissenting voices in 'Hands Off Stanley Park', a report of a meeting of the City Beautiful Association which 'very strongly opposes the Mawson Plan and Stadium' and would take 'legal action to prevent building a Stadium in Stanley Park'. Mawson's Plan Four was a 'proposed vulgarisation and desecration'; chairman F.C.Wade likened the Coal Harbour pond to 'an immense manhole'. And here a spurt of Canadian nationalism surfaced: 'it was fundamentally impossible for the Mawsons with their English training, English ideas and English experience, to know what was best to do with Stanley Park... It is art from end to end – do you want it?'[24]

Despite Thomas Mawson's persuasive, sometimes eloquent, always lively, direct communication whether on paper or in the lecture hall, that Vancouver could be possessed of a remarkable piece of civic art in his plan for their town, his scheme was rejected. Vancouver was not ready for such highfalutin ideas. Instead the approach to the park became a low key affair with some balustrading and trees and a wider path with designated space for walkers, cyclists and cars. The proposed museum 'eye-catcher' at the top of the Georgia Street axis was replaced by a more appropriate display of the totem poles of American Indians.

Brushing off the lack of success, Mawson announced: 'Vancouver settled.' There were other, less attention demanding or controversial tasks.[25] On Vancouver Island Mawson was asked to set out two model estates as suburbs for the city of Victoria by the B.C.Electric Railway Company in 1912. The first, the James Estate, designed as a suburb on the steep and rocky east coast, was closer to Victoria than the second, the Meadlands Estate. Set behind the less rugged western coastline with its white sandy beaches, Meadlands suggested a resort rather than a suburb. It was planned with flowing road systems following the contours, not Mawson's detested grid system, and with more formality in the centre of the settlement. The map was drawn with English cottages, presumed to be the desired form of accommodation, at the top of the plan. Mawson left, satisfied that Meadlands was an acceptable proposition; he does not comment on the James Estate.

During 1912 Mawson took up the invitation to join a commission which reported on 10 November 1913 to the Board of Governors of the University of British Columbia on the preparatory work done by the architects Sharp and Thompson on the general design for the university. This was to be sited overlooking English Bay, to the west of the city, on a wide plateau surrounded by forests. There were four others in the commission, including Professors Laird of Philadelphia and Darley of McGill, who agreed that the style of the buildings should be 'Modern Tudor. As a phase of English Gothic architecture, and better than any period of the Renaissance, does it express and perpetuate the traditions of British scholastic life'.[26] It is likely that Mawson would have had most to contribute on the layout of roads, lawns, recreation grounds and plantations, and to have advised the establishment of a home nursery as a preliminary to laying out and planting. The collection of gaultheria, berberis, cedars and pines on site with other serviceable native trees was close to Mawson's planting palette, but he would not have agreed with the commission's advice to hold back from cutting further trees to create vistas.[27]

At this time Mawson was appointed as landscape architect for Saskatoon University campus on 21 October 1912.[28] The correspondence between Thomas and John Mawson and Professor Walter C.Murray reveals an uneasy relationship between the landscape architects and the university, beginning with a dispute concerning the Mawsons' use of Malcolm Ross to provide arboricultural expertise on the campus plan. Ross explained that Mawson & Sons 'do not themselves, profess to be personally familiar with the planting material suitable for this country'. He also advised the university to start a tree nursery in order to furnish its grounds, offering his help. Both suggestions were refused.[29]

John Mawson found the survey material given to him by the university was inaccurate, and the grounds were resurveyed. Plans were lost. Thomas Mawson delayed producing his plans for landscaping the campus. This was to expand into indignant exchanges, with Professor Murray claiming that the layout round the faculty buildings was both inefficient for the movement of students and that the campus layout had to be seen as a whole.

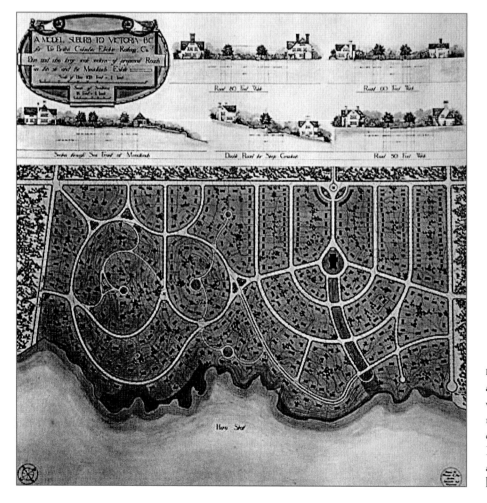

UNIVERSITY OF SASKATCHEWAN

Soon the university architects, Brown and Vallance of Montreal, took over the landscaping. By July 1913, having lost his authority, Mawson decided to cut his links with Saskatoon. He wrote politely to Professor Murray: 'I have been asked to undertake so much new work lately...Mrs Mawson and I sail on Tuesday on the *Laurentic* from Montreal and we are both looking forward very much to seeing the young people at home again'.[30] A letter from John to the Bursar in August 1914 required the settlement of the account, as, due to 'the suspension of all finance between England and Canada...I am faced with the prospect of having to dismiss my Canadian staff and of closing the office'.[31]

But there was one more commission to be done for the Board of Park Commissioners within Stanley Park, on Brockton Point, on the promontory pointing east. John Mawson's name is on a series of drawings made between May and December 1914 to rebuild a lighthouse here and to plan a park beside the lighthouse. The position commanded magnificent views along the wide Burrard Inlet leading upstream to Port Moody, to the timbered slopes on the north shore of the Inlet and down below the lighthouse to the stony beach stretching endlessly along the shore. Two promenades were designed: the upper one, with a teahouse and pergola, intended for circulating the horseshoe-shaped park, and divided by a grassy slope from the lower promenade which joined a trail leading westwards around Stanley Park. Between them was the lighthouse keeper's house and kitchen gardens. But there is no evidence that the promontory was ever developed in this way, except for the rebuilding of the lighthouse.[32]

After his customary round of lectures and planning work in 1913, Mawson had returned to Ottawa to take up another commission, to develop a suburb for the capital on behalf of the Great Eastern Realty Company on the shore of Lake Deschenes. The report on this 600-acre estate, to be called Borden Park, was published in 1914. An electric railway was to be built out to the suburb 'with enough space between the two to allow urban development without swallowing Borden'; there was already an electric tramway and access to transcontinental railway lines. It was clearly intended that Borden Park was to be for the well-off resident, with a zoning of functions and housing. The design of the houses was to be controlled from the beginning, though there was to be no restriction on architectural styles or types of material used.

Next to a lake and a golf course would be built the best class of property – the 'country homes of wealthy people' with some of the characteristics of the 'picturesque English village or Market Town'. There would be a country club, garages, golf course, tennis lawn and a garden. A teahouse, said the report, would be an ornament to the estate. Borden Park's boating lagoon would have a wharf and piers for all classes of yacht, launch, skiff or canoe. The business centre of the estate, within easy access of the tram, would attract the next class of housing. Here would be dignified buildings, up-to-date stores on American lines, and an hotel for boating and golfing weekenders. There would be artisans' dwellings and a manufacturing zone on the most detached portion of the estate which adjoined the railway.

Perhaps the most important departure from North American plans (apart from the English colonial flavour which pervaded throughout) was the refusal to design on the grid. Roads which were guided by contours encouraged the making of both a lakeside promenade and a lakeside drive which went all the way to Ottawa. Roads were of three sizes: the wide promenade, those for access to shops and houses which carried no through traffic (and gave greater space for gardens) and those for pedestrian access only. The landscaping paid considerable attention to trees, suggesting the grouping of one sort of tree next to a mass of another, though not using exotics.

And here the report, possibly anticipating events to follow, moved into advertising, offering the help of Thomas H.Mawson & Sons, of London, Lancaster, Vancouver and New York, as capable landscape architects conversant with the aesthetics of their profession, as well as the practical details of arboriculture.[33]

But, like so many other commissions, this one, with its mix of English garden suburb and English lake resort, foundered on financial insecurity. Sensing the railway company's uncertain position, Mawson claimed £500 of his £1,800 fee before he began; the rest was never paid as the value of land went down and the railway company suffered heavy losses on its investments.

Eastern Canada offered the encouragement of prestigious connections such as the Governor General, HRH the Duke of Connaught (to whom Mawson dedicated the fourth edition of *The Art and Craft of Garden Making* in 1912) and Sir Robert Borden. Mawson continued to

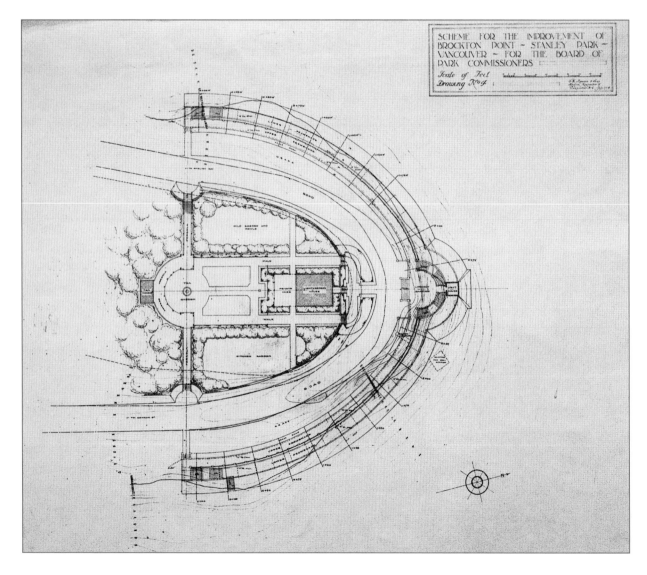

LEFT John Mawson's design for the gardens on Brockton Point, 1914.

ABOVE A perspective drawing
of part of Borden Park,
looking towards the harbour.

lecture at universities such as Toronto and McGill in Montreal, and was persuaded to venture northwards to Halifax, Nova Scotia, where the Canadian architect Frank Darling (1850–1923) wanted him to assist in planning the campus of Dalhousie University (as he had done for the University of British Columbia). Mawson accepted, made surveys and contributed to three of the four sets of drawings for the campus, encouraging the planting of a double avenue of trees lining the boulevard from the campus along Morris Street. This enhanced the feeling of civic consciousness given by its cathedral, two hospitals and schools, and provided the main entrance to Dalhousie University.[34]

As Mawson travelled westwards in 1913, his train moving slowly across the endless, treeless, wide, flat plains of the prairies, his luck began to change for the better. Saskatchewan had become a province in 1905, with Regina confirmed as the capital the following year. The CPR had driven its lines across the south of the (then) Northwest Territories in 1882, looking to challenge the

American railway which had reached the Pacific coast in the same year. The CPR had been given tracts of land by the dominion government, which put them in a powerful position – they sold land for farming and building. They also encouraged tree and flower cultivation in newly settled areas, opening two nurseries in 1907 for ornamental plants at Springfield, Manitoba, and for trees and shrubs at Wolseley, Saskatchewan, followed by experimental tree farms in Alberta.[35] The capital's site had been determined by the CPR's decision to place its station in the town centre. However this was three miles away from the Wascana plain, on which the dominion government wanted to place Regina's new legislative building.

In Montreal the architect brothers William Sutherland Maxwell (1874–1952) and Edward Maxwell (1867–1923) had won the competition to design the building. William Maxwell had been educated at the Ecole des Beaux-Arts in Paris, Edward in Montreal and Boston. They recognised that the architecture of such a building would require a certain symbolism since, as Percy Erskine Nobbs,

ABOVE Ice hockey on Lake Wascana, c.1919. This bleak, winter view of the exposed site of the new parliamentary buildings in Regina in 1912 underlines the need felt by Mawson's team to design and plant appropriately to remove 'the reproach of the treelessness of the plain'. Trees and shrubs gave shelter around a lawn and bright bedding cheered the front of the buildings in summer.

the Macdonald Professor of Architecture at McGill University had made plain, 'the province is politically within the British Empire, and this fact should be expressed in its public building'.[36] As the site of the legislative building was some distance from the centre, Nobbs urged that it should be topped by a dome, perhaps reminiscent of St Paul's Cathedral, which would be widely visible across the plain and from the end of many streets in the capital. The Maxwells later described the style of their rectangular building with its four wings and octagonal dome crowning the pillared entrance, as a:

> free adaptation of English Renaissance work... being best suited to the requirements... representative of British sovereignty, under which the province is governed...To this end, dignity, simplicity and purity of style have been combined with a monumental treatment of the best period of British architecture.[37]

On 30 June a twisting, destructive funnel of rising air created by the heat of the flat plain swept its way through Regina at 500 miles per hour. This tornado, the worst in Canadian history, hit the downtown region, wrecking houses and town landmarks, leaving 2,500 homeless, destroying the telephone exchange, library, churches and the YMCA and YWCA. The new legislative building, three miles from the eye of the twister, was relatively unhurt, apart from its library, and – its white Tyndal limestone shining – it was opened in October 1912.

The effects of the tornado may not have led directly to the commissioning of Thomas Mawson & Sons as town planners and landscape architects in 1913, although for some time Regina had been considering how best to shape its city, which was fast becoming a straggling settlement joining the downtown and the Wascana plain. The Lieutenant Governor required an official residence, and the legislative building needed dignified landscaping. The Maxwells had already begun some work assisted by the province's gardener, George Watt, based on the 1907 plan prepared by Frederick Todd. However it was realised that these tasks required more 'English' skills than were available locally. Thomas Mawson had visited Regina and Winnipeg, in southern Manitoba, before: many had heard him speak. Winnipeg had become a prairie pioneer of civic beautification, but Mawson had realised that the land boom there had made city planning far too expensive. Already space dedicated for parks had been pounced upon by developers who divided the plots for residential construction.[38] Mawson was commissioned at Regina, and work was begun to design the landscaping of the Wascana plain and the Lieutenant Governor's residence.

The plain at Wascana (the name derives from a Cree word for a pile of bones, from the Indian use of the place for drying buffalo flesh) which surrounds the legislative building is crossed from the east by a wandering stream, the Wascana creek. The CPR made a temporary dam across the creek in 1882 for water for the locomotives. As a more permanent dam was constructed to contain the flood of spring meltwater to supply the city, so a large lake appeared which was to become the focus for outdoor leisure, with duck shooting in the autumn, winter skating and ice hockey, and swimming, boating, and picnicking by the waterside in summer.[39]

Mawson's vision for the plain, though partly based on work done earlier by the Maxwells, Frederick Todd and Malcolm Ross (the superintendent of parks from 1911), tied the legislative building site and the Lieutenant Governor's house together. The legislative building faced north, across a bend in the lake. To its east was to be placed the official residence, designed by the Maxwell brothers. Mawson decided that two islands were to be constructed, flanking the jetty from which the Lieutenant Governor's boat could set out, in ceremonial magnificence, towards the parliament building. A bridge across the lake gave access to a drive which curved round the lake to the parliamentary buildings; not only did this give a leisurely approach to parliament, it could be used when the lake was frozen. Substantial shelter was provided from the lake by trees; the residence was flanked by formal gardens.

Todd and the Maxwells considered that the space between the parliament buildings and the lake should be treated formally, with driveways, a wide lawn and fountains, all contained by hedges. The government had bought parcels of land around the lake, with which to enlarge the 600-acre park, and sold land to buyers who would dignify the area with good buildings, such as Regina College, later (in 1959) Regina University.

BELOW The dam on the Wascana creek which created the lake.

John Mawson managed the work from his office in Vancouver, corresponding with Malcolm Ross, who had made his own plans for the layout of Wascana. He and his brother Norman M.Ross managed a forestry nursery at Indian Head which had been set up by the dominion government in 1903 for experimentation with indigenous trees, shrubs and flowers, and which Mawson eagerly visited.[40]

Apart from the two Mawsons (John had been made a junior partner in Mawson & Sons and directed the Vancouver office), there was Thomas' nephew Robert H.Mattocks who had been at school in Windermere and at Liverpool University at the same time as his cousin John and was chief of staff. Mattocks was holder of the civic design diploma and the Sir William Lever student's

prize of the University of Liverpool; Richard Ellison, an engineering graduate from Liverpool; Alexander Cameron, an urban district surveyor; John Giles, who

PROPOSED·SUBDIVISION·OF·
PROPERTY·NEAR·WASCANA·LAKE·
REGINA·
FOR·THE·GOVERNMENT·OF·
SASKATCHEWAN·

SCALE·200·FEET·TO·1·INCH·

DRAWING·Nº   REGISTERED·Nº

PROPOSED SVBDIVISION of PROPERTY and LAY OVT of GROVNDS to
LIEVTENANT GOVERNORS RESIDENCE   REGINA   SASKATCHEWAN

had worked in great estate gardens in England before training at Kew; Thomas Korner, a Canadian architect; John Blamire Shaw, head draughtsman; and James Crossland, a manager and secretary of Thomas Mawson & Sons, a licentiate of the RIBA and gold medallist of the National Housing and Town Planning Council – all men of considerable expertise.[41] Crossland was frequently 'on the road', travelling with Thomas Mawson, deputising for him, sometimes going ahead to prepare the way and to collect data and take slides which Mawson could use in his lectures.

Robert Mattocks was also out and about with his camera, capturing the winter stillness of conifers in snowbound forests; a train winding through smoke and piled ice banks and the silent wildness of the lakes in Stanley Park. The two young men had played in Liverpool University's hockey team, when John was captain, and had swum and played tennis together. In Vancouver they explored on horseback and walked in the mountains with their colleagues.

Thomas Mawson soon recognised the worth of Malcolm Ross, whose comments he sought in 1912 on the present state of the parliament grounds. In a letter to John Mawson on 3 December 1912, Ross commented unfavourably on work already done in front of the parliament building with 'inappropriate' fountains and shrubs which collapsed under the weight of snow.[42] Ross criticised the plan for the terrace and entrance to

the Normal School and other buildings along Sixteenth Avenue for which John Mawson was responsible, pointing out the 'depressing and gloomy' effect of too much shadow on the north side of the buildings. He suggested flower beds to 'enliven it as much as possible'.[43]

Thomas Mawson & Sons had submitted their schemes and plans and quoted their fees on 17 February 1913. In addition to plans for the new government house, the Mawsons were also landscaping other buildings on the Wascana site, among them schools, the Anglican cathedral and Catholic churches. The original intention to build a high-class residential area mentioned in Ross' request for plans on 11 April appeared

later in Mawson's report on Regina.[44] But a long delay in the return of plans which had been drawn up in the Lancaster office hindered the start of the work. In October John admitted to Ross that he was 'nearly worried to death over it' before the plans were left for him by his father with the station agent at Regina on 4 November.[45] Thomas Mawson, as usual, was hurtling between engagements; John's letters show that between May 1913 and February 1914 Thomas had been to Regina, Calgary, Winnipeg, New York, to England and back, and to Athens and back. This put a huge strain on timetables, and on those trying to work with him. John was pleased to inform Ross

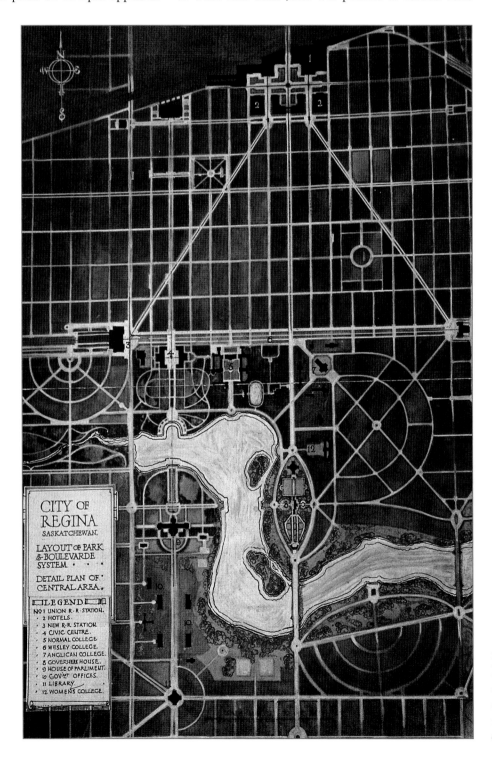

LEFT Mawson's plan for Regina, 1914, was placed over his disliked Canadian grid system of streets. The plan was reproduced in *Life and Work*, fig. 39.

RIGHT The flower garden in
front of the Parliament
Building, Regina, 1919.

that he had helped his father improve the plans 'enormously', and that Ross should go ahead with work on the plantations and 'provisions for big Herbaceous borders'. Mawson's plans thereafter named his collaboration with Ross.[46]

In the end, the Maxwell brothers' lawn was jettisoned for an intricate pattern of colourful bedding in front of the parliament building. There were no fountains and no hedges along the paths. The building was centred among green lawns, trees and shrubs, all within paths which followed the lake on its north and south banks.

Mawson's *Regina: A Preliminary Report on the Development of the City*, in which he repeated his recommendations to ease grid-planned roads, place factories together away from housing and create a model suburb for workmen, was delivered in 1914. The problem of railway lines at street level in the city could only be dealt with by insisting on bridges over the rails or getting the Grand Trunk Railway to depress its lines under the roads. Mawson felt that the city centre lacked an expression of civic pride, which could be provided by a grand entrance near a railway station, and attention to a common grouping of facades. There should be vistas and street pictures – especially that formed by the view of the new parliament – and the careful placing of buildings such as a municipal theatre or opera house (which he suggested locating on an island). The civic centre, he announced,

should be moved to the axis of Smith Street, between Sixteenth Avenue and the lake.

Mawson left the discussion on the park system to the end of the report, because 'it is the chain which binds the City into one unified system and combines together all the features mentioned in the earlier chapters'. It would 'raise Regina from its present treeless condition and so adorn it with sylvan beauty that it will become the Garden City of the Prairies'. Mawson envisaged protective belts of plantations, linked by the Wascana parkway. Trees should enhance the edges of Wascana Lake, the boulevards and a parkway into Regina. An exhibition site which was an all-year park, beautified cemeteries and recreation grounds should be made and school gardens encouraged. A country club was recommended near the city because of the 'immense popularity and importance... these clubs have gained in Canadian cities'. This closed the plan, which was completed and accepted in January 1915.[47]

All of this was soon after the outbreak of war. The government had decided that the Lieutenant Governor's residence was too costly to build almost as soon as the ink had dried on the plan. Property prices dropped sharply and Mawson's design for Regina was put on one side. The Grand Trunk Pacific Railway, which had begun to build an enormous chateau-style hotel in Wascana Park, went bankrupt, the steel girders for its framework standing useless until they were dismantled in the 1920s.[48] Malcolm Ross joined the Canadian Expeditionary Force; three members of the Canadian office of Thomas Mawson & Sons, engineers who were responsible for much of the Regina plan, were killed in action in France.[49]

After the First World War Regina was unwilling to accept a 'City Beautiful' plan which it could not afford. A sour note was introduced as John Mawson questioned the five-and-a-half-year delay in settling the incomplete payment of accounts relating to the laying out of the grounds around the parliament, which had been rejected by the Canadian Department of Works on what seemed like spurious grounds. Correspondence begun in the autumn of 1920 rumbled on into the summer of 1921 about inaccurate Canadian surveys and who was responsible and lost plans. Mawson and his colleagues had worked to provide detailed layouts on college grounds for which they had not charged. 'It really is not necessary to point out to you', Mawson wrote to the deputy minister of public works on 21 May 1921, 'that if we had carried out the construction work in the usual manner employed by architects, the whole of our fees would have been more than absorbed in travelling expenses.'[50]

Despite the arguments, trees and shrubs continued to be planted around the parliament building, and a pattern of flower beds was made in front of it in 1920.

Mawson was asked to submit a further report, though the financial downturn of 1920–21 had much to do with the lack of Regina's response to costly innovation.

But Mawson has remained on the edge of the picture. In 1929 two islands were made using material from dredging the lake. After Regina College had been granted university status in 1959 a large area of land around the parliament building was designated as the Wascana Centre, coordinating teaching and recreational facilities and encouraging the continuation of the beautification of the park. The architect Minoru Yamasaki, designer of the twin-towered World Trade Centre, New York, worked with landscape architect Thomas Church on a new master plan for the Wascana Centre, resurrecting Mawson's proposals for a tree-lined mall running south from the parliament building. These suggestions were confirmed in government policy in the master plans for 1982 and 1992.[51] Trees, shrubs, lawns and flower beds now occupy space once windswept and featureless, as 'by a determined effort to remove for ever the reproach of treelessness from Regina'.[52] This, more than any other town in Canada for which Mawson had made plans, was to be the one which achieved his ideas most closely.

The railway from Regina climbs westwards, into the foothills of the Rocky Mountains. Alberta begins where the South Saskatchewan river is joined by the Bow river

ABOVE Prince's Island, Calgary, with children's playground photographed by Mawson, 1912.

Seventh Avenue and Second Street sold for $150 in 1895 and $300,000 in 1912.[54]

Here, thought Mawson, as he walked over the river bluffs on the north shore, was an ideal place for long drives or boulevards which would look down on a newly planned city, but its expansion needed to be controlled. Below were water meadows and rough grassland which, if purchased, could later become public parkland, and the larger islands could have children's playgrounds like the Prince's Island collection of slides, seesaws, swings and climbing frames he had photographed. There were three sets of railroad track cutting uncomfortably through the city centre – the Canadian Pacific, the Grand Trunk Pacific and the Canadian Northern. They crossed main roads, bisecting built-up areas and making their way past lumber yards, rubbish tips, isolated farms and storage barns as they moved out to the country. How could a dignified civic centre be created in the midst of unfettered development? There were, already, solid and sensible buildings: the spacious Central Park library, its pillared entrance set back from the street behind a tree-planted lawn, the classical Molsons Bank, the Dominion Bank and the Victorian Presbyterian Knox Church in its tree-lined street. Mawson had taken pictures of houses built from local sandstone and of wooden huts because, as a lover of arts and crafts, he was interested in the way materials had been used. There were pictures of middle-class housing with shingle-style towers, gables and porches, and ten-storey stores under construction, as well as streetcars and the occasional automobile.[55]

Mawson returned to Calgary in 1912 to stir up awareness of the dangers of allowing a town to develop without check and to encourage the newly established town planning commission to put their ideas into action. He gave a lecture to the Canadian Club on 9 April entitled 'The City of the Plain, and How To Make it Beautiful'. This related to 'convenient transit… controlling [the] density of population, provision of ample open spaces for physical recreation and especially playgrounds for the children, water, and perfect sanitation' and the beautification of the city's features.[57] The audience applauded, roused by his direct and forceful delivery. He later spoke at the Central High School on 4 October. The secretary of the city planning commission, G.Wray Lemon, invited the mayor and the council to come to hear the lecture 'to promote the well fare [sic] and solid development of our city along the lines of utility, health and beauty'. Aware of the fact that Vancouver, Winnipeg, Saskatoon, Edmonton and Lethbridge had moved towards city planning, Calgary accepted the need for a

and the train turns northwest towards Calgary. Mawson had earlier explored the hills and valleys round the city, with a camera and its stand, in the expectation of a commission to plan Calgary, discovering it to be very different from the flat prairie to the east. The Bow river cut a wide valley to the north of the city through a range of hills, on which the town proposed to build its university. There was no railway joining the site to the city, which was several miles away. Mawson, who had been asked to prepare a plan for the campus, thought that it was 'a scheme…exploited in the interests of real estates', and drew it up rather reluctantly, though he was never paid for the plan or his week's expenses.[53]

His pictures, taken early in the year, showed a fast-flowing, willow-hung river with dark conifers on the hills behind. Prince's Island and its bridge was close to the south shore of the Bow, where it formed a natural extension to Centre Street, the main route through the city's heart. The most direct route for the proposed university and the expected expansion of population would be by bridging the island and the north shore of the Bow, if some way could be found to offset the steepening of the slope on its north side.

Calgary had become the fastest growing town in Canada: from 4,000 people in 1900 it had jumped to 12,000 in 1906 and by 1911, the year of Mawson's first visit, the figure stood at 44,000. By 1913 it was 80,000 spread over 26,000 acres. Land prices exploded: a plot on plan of its own and wanted 'the best man for the job…at the top of his profession… and an expert of world-wide repute' who would lead them into the future.[58] On 4 February 1913, Mawson was informed that he had been approved as an adviser and asked to draw up a report on the future development of Calgary.[59]

Mawson returned to England in June 1913, where the report later named *Calgary, Past, Present and Future* was written. The best presented of Mawson's many reports, 1,000 copies were printed by Tillotsons in Bolton, with coloured plates illustrating the plans. The most striking was the frontispiece, but its proposed civic centre with buildings reminiscent of nineteenth-century revivalist London may have startled, perhaps shocked, those who looked for skyscrapers and a modern Canadian town. No doubt Mawson had realised that the councillors with whom he was dealing had little idea of what they wanted in their city plan and felt that this might inspire them.

The most controversial piece of planning involved the making of the low level bridge from Centre Street across the Bow river, in order to keep the street pictures of the civic centre and the suggested architectural feature at the end of the bridge. Mawson had corresponded with Otis in Victoria Street, London, about the possibility of lifting automobiles and streetcars in a tower made for the purpose at the far end of the bridge, to take traffic up to the top of the hill on the north side of the Bow river. Maybe he had in mind comparable hydraulic methods of raising barges on canals. The alternative, a high incline bridge, would mean forfeiting his architectural panorama.

But on 21 July 1913, the City Planning Commission resolved that 'sufficient consideration has not been given to the Mawson plan for the proposed bridge crossing the Bow river at Centre Street, and that the city council be asked to submit the plan, and the alternative, high incline bridge, to the ratepayers in the form of a plebiscite to be voted upon before the money by-law is submitted'.[60] And the cost and associated engineering difficulties ended the dream of a low level bridge.

Mawson's *Report on Calgary* repeated his heartfelt objections to the monotony of the grid system and its

LEFT Mawson's observation of dignity – Molson's Bank, Calgary, 1912.

ABOVE RIGHT Calgary slum, photographed by Mawson.

BELOW RIGHT Skyscraper, Calgary, 1912.

suggested remedies, including placing parks rather than buildings at the intersection of blocks. Street widening was needed, as was more space on sidewalks and shelter in bad weather, given by setting shop fronts back under arcades. Such a move was now possible with the introduction of steel frames in the construction of large stores; and Mawson often cited the example of arcades in the Rue de Rivoli in Paris. He hoped that the opportunity for grouping fine buildings for the CPR station, the CN depot and the market – the centre of commercial interest – would not be lost. Often the railway station was the only large building in a new settlement and railway hotels clustered round. Mawson foresaw that much of the present infrastructure would need to be replaced as Calgary grew. The time for designing a great city of the future should not be missed.

Industry should be sited together near the railway, away from housing. The workmen's housing of Manchester and Connaught was designed to replicate garden suburbs, with grouped detached cottages with gardens and allotments. In their depiction on the coloured illustration they look like their British or German counterparts. Connaught had a school sports ground shared with other community uses. Both settlements were surrounded by trees – on slopes, along roads and in empty spaces.

Mawson got into his stride with his description of a park system. Calgary was poorly supplied with open spaces, he decided, and it needed riverside boulevards and children's parks. No work had been done on the suitability of the trees, shrubs and flowers which were planted in public places. The cemetery was full of rhododendrons, azaleas and tender roses which were unsuited to the area. He suggested the park superintendent should start another experimental centre and nursery, like that of the Ross brothers in Saskatchewan, and propagate indigenous trees and shrubs.[61]

To stir the town into action, Mawson invited the entire Calgary city planning commission to lunch at Cronn's Rathskeller on 29 November, as he returned to Canada in 1913 for his autumn round of visiting clients. The Rathskeller lunch was undoubtedly an opportunity to rouse the members and enthuse them with the city plan. The council and its commission were made up of businessmen, brokers and financial agents with reactive responses to present requirements and no long-term view.[62] Mawson had sensed the absence of commitment to the plan and advance copies of the report, 'with a view to interesting influential people in your city and your scheme' were circulated in Calgary and London.[63]

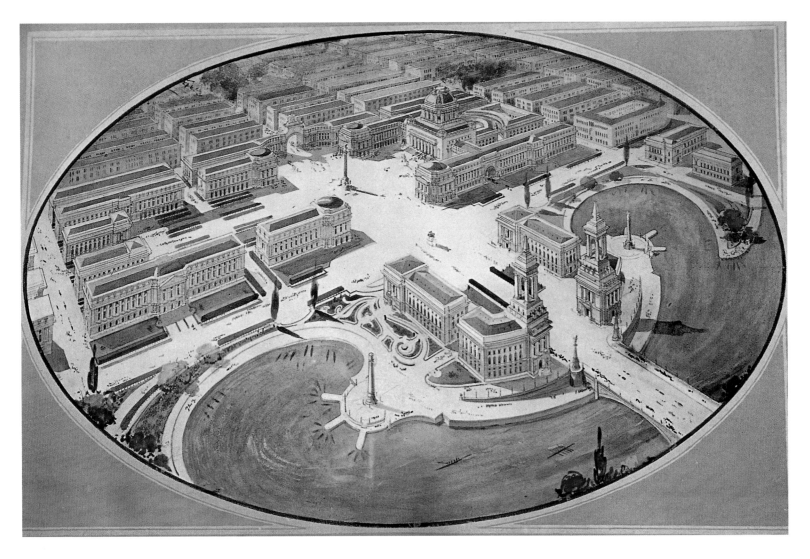

Mawson had asked for the printing to be done in England, where there were better facilities for using colour, and a sum was agreed towards this by the commission on 23 December 1913.[64] Mawson saw these reports as sound advertising for his firm as well as for the city and its scheme ('copies knocking about are bound to do us good', as James Crossland remarked in a letter to T.T.Johns, secretary of the City Planning Commission, Alberta, on 6 August 1914). John Mawson collected Calgary's spare advance copies and took them on to the town planning conference in Toronto. Tillotsons had shipped the rest of the insured reports on the SS *Tunisia* on 29 April 1914 to travel from Liverpool to Montreal, whence they were to trundle on slowly by rail to Calgary.

The excitement and anticipation of the early summer after the months of planning came to a sickening halt in August 1914 with the outbreak of war, and an anguished letter was sent from John Mawson in the Vancouver office to T.T.Johns, urgently requesting the payment of Thomas Mawson & Sons' outstanding account: 'To be quite frank the situation which has arisen over the war has left us badly stranded in the Canadian office and

with the shutting off of communication with the head office I am faced with the prospect of having to close down the office if I cannot get in some money before the end of the month.'[65]

The pre-war financial depression had hit the printers as the report arrived and they were unable to sell many books. Drawings of the bridge over the Bow river which had been dispatched to Canada via SS *Tunisia* had disappeared, and copies of the reports, sent by SS *Grampian*, did not clear customs until January 1915. Some lost plans had to be redrawn. Accounts could not be settled as it was forbidden to send money out of the country. 'Let us hope that this disastrous war, which is holding up so many excellent schemes may very soon be brought to a close,' Thomas Mawson wrote to Alexander Calhoun, who had replaced T.T.Johns.[66]

Despite the approval in principle of many individuals and the newspaper the *Albertan* of 8 May 1914, councillor James Garden's half-hearted comment in the *Albertan* of 1 May was: 'it is well to have the plan for when the time comes we can take advantage of it'. Calgary was broke: in 1914 the city had outstanding taxes of half a million dollars, rising to $2.8 million in

ABOVE Mawson's City Beautiful plan for the centre of Calgary, 1913, dazzled or puzzled the city authorities. In particular, they could not appreciate his attempts to provide a fitting architectural approach for a crossing of the Bow river. The plan was used as the frontispiece to *Calgary*.

1915 and $3.6 million in 1916, coinciding with the end of a shortlived (1913–16) oil boom in the Turner Valley to the south of Calgary.[67]

Mawson's suggested procedures were exceedingly costly, and the councillors whom Mawson was attempting to win over were not persuaded by the illustrations made in the Lancaster office by staff who had not been to Canada. Finally, there was insufficient local expertise among the council to understand either what was needed in terms of city planning, or to assess what they were given and how to respond in practical terms. The report was soon dropped from the programme.

RIGHT Mawson's drawings for the dignified Canadian Pacific Railway plaza (top), and Market place for Calgary in 1913. They were figs 34 and 35 in the published report *Calgary*.

Fig. 34.

·THE· C.P.R. STATION PLAZA·

· THE· MARKET· PLACE·

Fig. 35.

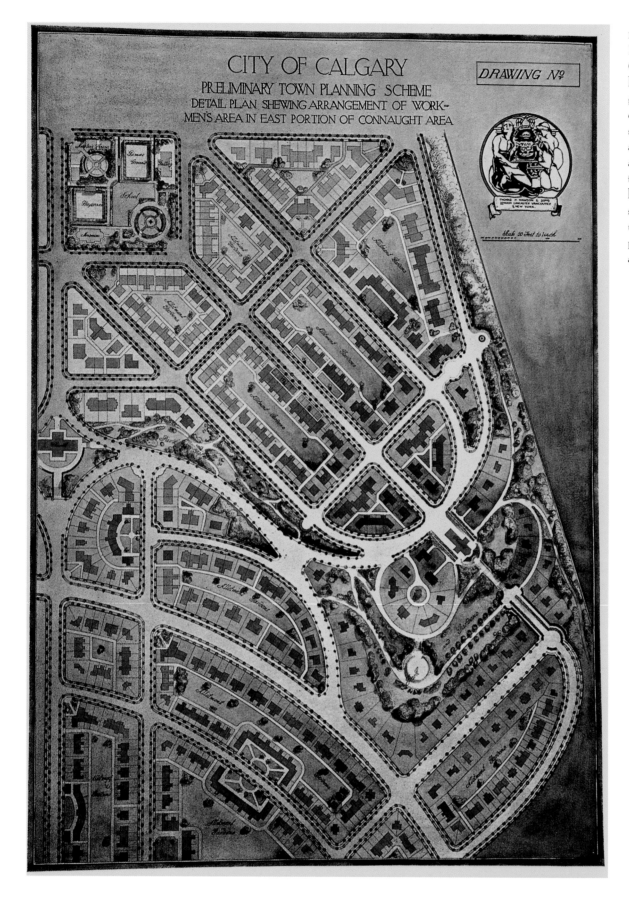

CITY OF CALGARY
PRELIMINARY TOWN PLANNING SCHEME
DETAIL PLAN SHEWING ARRANGEMENT OF WORK-
MEN'S AREA IN EAST PORTION OF CONNAUGHT AREA

DRAWING Nº

THOMAS H. MAWSON & SONS
LONDON LANCASTER VANCOUVER
& NEW YORK.

Scale 50 Feet to Inch

The original large illustrations for the report, having remained uncollected from a CPR Express freight warehouse in Calgary in 1931, were bought as scrap when the warehouse sold off its uncollected materials and used to back wallboard in a garage in Hillhurst, Calgary, where Mawson's maps, diagrams and pictures were rediscovered in 1977. After conservation in Ottawa, they are now carefully stored in the University of Calgary.

At the time of their rescue, Mawson's plans were criticised scathingly as colonialist and imperialist. More recent appraisals have shown how the concepts of the parklands, river banks and the children's playgrounds have influenced

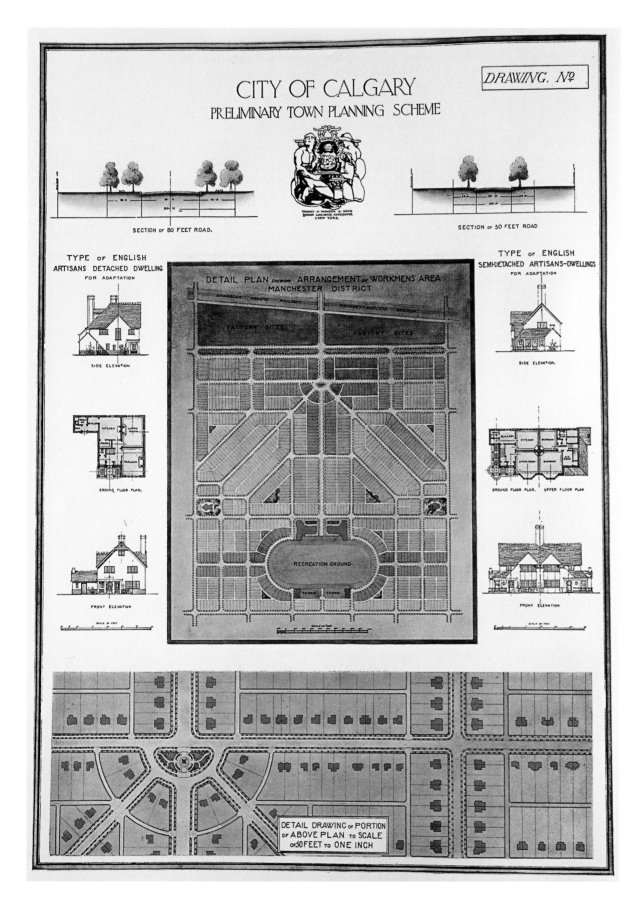

CITY OF CALGARY
PRELIMINARY TOWN PLANNING SCHEME

DRAWING. Nº

SECTION of 80 FEET ROAD.

SECTION of 50 FEET ROAD

TYPE of ENGLISH
ARTISANS DETACHED DWELLING
FOR ADAPTATION

SIDE ELEVATION

GROUND FLOOR PLAN.

FRONT ELEVATION

TYPE of ENGLISH
SEMI-DETACHED ARTISANS-DWELLINGS
FOR ADAPTATION

SIDE ELEVATION

GROUND FLOOR PLAN.   UPPER FLOOR PLAN

FRONT ELEVATION

DETAIL PLAN showing ARRANGEMENT of WORKMENS AREA
MANCHESTER DISTRICT

FACTORY SITES   FACTORY SITES

RECREATION GROUND

DETAIL DRAWING of PORTION
of ABOVE PLAN TO SCALE
of 50 FEET TO ONE INCH

LEFT Mawson's plan for the workmen's district of Manchester, Calgary, shows factory sites set beside the Canadian Pacific Railway tracks, and artisans' housing which could have come straight from English cottage estates of the time. Different road widths are shown at the top of the plan, for different vehicle usage. *Calgary*, fig. 30.

the planning of parts of Calgary. Memorial Drive, a boulevard on the north bank of the Bow with trees planted for each of the casualties of the Second World War, and the informal park and play area of Prince's Island have consciously adopted the thinking behind a small part of Mawson's report: *Calgary: Past, Present and Future*.

When Mawson lost the contract for Ottawa in 1914, Sir Robert Borden sought to temper his disappointment by giving him the contract to make Banff, on the east side of the Rocky Mountains in the valley of the Bow river, more attractive to tourists. The Dominion Parks Department had already encouraged trails into the mountains and motor roads. The premier thus reversed the policy which had encouraged settlement for agriculture only to one which would cater for the visitors as well. Banff was the next important stop from Calgary on the CPR's route through British Columbia and the CPR had built the chateau-styled, 'million dollar' Banff Springs Hotel. The town had been set out in 1888 by George Alexander Stewart, Dominion Land Surveyor and First Superintendent of Rocky Mountain Park. Its population had rapidly expanded and Mawson's task was to 'study, report upon, and plan out the town as a tourist resort on a great scale'.[68] He spent five days surveying the site and its environs, collecting material and considering how Stewart's town, with its incipient shopping centre, hotels, museums, clubs and zoo, could be best arranged. He planned to join the CPR's station to the civic centre via a boulevard and to close the vistas leading off the main Banff Mall with suitable buildings. The report was to be written on the train to his next destination, Vancouver.

But this time, delighted and yet awestruck by the beauty of the journey through 'Nature at her grandest, aloof, austere, inexplicable, and incomparable,' he put down his pen and gazed out as the train wound slowly through the ranges of peaks, entering tunnels, sounding its mournful warning, then moving out beside dazzling glaciers and lofty rock faces. Mawson looked out over pine forests, lakes and waterfalls. 'O for a modicum of John Ruskin's powers of description!'[69]

Mawson began his assessment with a concern 'to open nature's storehouse and yet not to spoil it,' while making provision for visitors.[70] Encouragement should be given to all sorts of outdoor sports, from ice hockey to tennis. More hotels were needed, and better access. Carried away by enthusiasm he suggested five bridges over the Bow river. Once again, the aim to make Banff a work of art fell on deaf ears, the plans were not implemented, and the report was thrown away by the park staff.[71] Only a few small illustrations remain in the archives.

In 1912 Thomas Mawson announced triumphantly in his autobiography, 'I had now metaphorically speaking, annexed America, and made this vast continent a part of my sphere of influence.'[72] But by 1914 it seems that very little was accomplished in Canada, despite the optimistic tone of Mawson's reports and autobiography. From 1905 he had travelled incessantly, covering some 30,000 miles per year, consulting, designing and lecturing. But he arrived in Canada just too late to achieve any large-scale scheme, had it been approved, and the backing of the powerful railroad companies carried

more weight than that of pro-British dignitaries. The First World War was undoubtedly the greatest factor in halting activity, combined with the economic depression in the approach to war and subsequent downturn in 1920-21. Mawson's inability to recognise that the majority of townsmen were neither ready for grandiose schemes nor had the skills to implement them led to the demise of many of his efforts. In his speech to Calgary in the autumn of 1912 he told his audience: 'City planning is not the attempt to pull down your city and rebuild it at ruinous expense. It is merely deciding what you would like to have done when you get the chance, so that when the chance does come, little by little you may make the city plan conform to your ideals.'[73]

But his words were apparently not comprehended. As Frederick Olmsted found when his plans for Central Park in New York were challenged, his clients 'were simply not willing to make the sort of long-term public investments required by city planning'.[74]

Mawson's works of civic art were understood and approved in principle by the leaders of society and higher education, Earl Grey, Sir Robert Borden, Professors Darley and Laird from McGill and Philadelphia, Bryant Fleming from Cornell. These men either admired or were intensely patriotic to Empire and its roots in the Crown. Mawson could write of the malls he planned for Vancouver that these were places for viewing royal processions, without a flicker of doubt that this might not be appropriate. References to chrysanthemum shows in Stanley Park and English cottages on plans for Calgary might have been dismissed as comic aberration, or wishful imperial thinking. But the Canadian Maxwell brothers and the Canadian Board of Commissioners of the University of British Columbia had made plain the general approval of an imperial Canada by referring to a preferably British style of building. There was nationalistic criticism of Mawson in the 1970s after the discovery of the lost Calgary plans, including a strong but poorly argued attack by John Crosby Freeman in the *Canadian Art Review*, vol.2, no.2, 1975. E.Joyce Morrow commenting in 1979 on *Calgary, Past, Present and Future* said: 'The Mawson Report expressed the aspirations of a staunch British Imperialist who believed that civic architecture should be designed in the Edwardian Grand Manner to proclaim to the world Britain's sovereignty over her Canadian Dominion.'[75]

The outburst in Vancouver's City Beautiful group demonstrates that there was the beginning of a Canadian national consciousness, and a need to forge their own style. But they had not discovered what this style was to be. By contrast Regina's concern to change the flat bleakness of the plain coincided with Mawson's vision of a beautiful city. Calgary's children's playgrounds and riverside parks are acknowledged to be Mawson's original ideas. There are fleeting traces of Mawson in Stanley Park, Vancouver. Mawson was best adopted where he planned for parks and boulevards.

North America had beguiled and engulfed him, for the American City Beautiful movement and its architectural form, the Beaux-Arts style, influenced much of his urban design in his new role as a city planner.

He was generally welcomed wherever he went, and found the American architects' attitude to landscape architects such as himself 'distinctly friendly and helpful; in England, with rare exceptions, it is frankly resentful and unsympathetic'.[76]

Mawson was not recalled after the war because City Beautiful and nineteenth-century Beaux-Arts ornamentation were considered passé. However, though Mawson's plans were rejected or laid on dusty shelves in Ottawa, Calgary, Banff and Vancouver, no other landscape architect or planner was awarded the work at the time, either.

RIGHT The flower garden in front of Regina's parliament buildings, with a statue of Queen Elizabeth II in the year of her visit to Canada, 2005. Here, at least, the imperial argument has been laid to rest.

CHAPTER SIX

The bittersweet adventure: Greece 1913–1920

LEFT The church garden of the Panagia Chalkeon in Thessaloniki, with its garden reflecting Mawson's suggestion that churchyards should be made into city gardens.

AT THE AGE of 51 Mawson was a seasoned traveller, eager for new challenges, optimistically excited by each new commission, and – if it only brought payment for the design – moving swiftly and expectantly to the next. He had made himself a name as a landscape architect in the northern hemisphere and was well considered across the Empire. On 24 September 1912 the University of Sydney had led Australian universities in an invitation to 'Professor Thomas H.Mawson… to deliver a course of Extension Lectures in the chief centres of Australia'. Mawson was attracted by this youthful and developing colonial territory. He had a burning desire to 'contribute my quota to town planning propaganda'.

First, in January 1913, there had to be some haggling over his 'honorarium of £450 [which] will entail a very considerable loss on my average earnings' and he asked that he might be employed by city councils to make up the shortfall, though he realised 'the difficulty in persuading the average town council to take advantage of the visit of an expert but I am quite sure it will pay them to do so'. By the spring of 1913 he had made arrangements for a lecture tour including the universities of Melbourne, Brisbane, Perth, Sydney and Adelaide, in which he could 'give to Australian civic art something of the force and directness of English ideals'. He would tell them about city building, civic surveys, street planning, park systems, street equipment, model suburbs and villages and the housing of the industrial classes, and also give two lectures to the National Council of Women on 'English Homes and Gardens' and 'City Playgrounds, their maintenance and upkeep'.[1]

Mawson intended to move on to Australia later in 1913, after he had finished work in Calgary. But Australia was to slip from the horizon, for in mid journey in Canada he was summoned by cable by Constantine (1868–1923), the new King of Greece, to come to Athens to discuss work for the palace gardens and a park system; in addition, Mawson was to be asked to create a new city plan. 'The possibility of working in this world-famous city under royal patronage was irresistible', he claimed.[2] Believing that he could manage both commissions, he left the Australians hanging. In August 1913 the University of Melbourne's registrar received a cable to say that Mawson intended to come in March 1914. But on 4 March 1914 Mawson cabled again, asking for a postponement and offering his son in his stead; Mawson was sure the Australians would understand the Greek commission was 'one of the greatest compliments which could be paid to British art', and, of course, to himself. But the University of Sydney immediately cancelled the invitation.[3]

Edward Prentice, a fluent French speaker (French being the language used in official circles in Greece), was dispatched to Athens. He took with him staff to collect material for surveys, while Mawson finished his business in Canada. In Greece, the king took Edward out by car to Tatoi, to the north of Athens, where there was a royal villa, and later granted almost daily interviews to discuss his plans for the palace gardens.

It was surprising that Mawson was prepared to leap towards commissions in a country in a territorially fragile political situation, in which his projects might never materialise. He had, so far, been involved with a broadly anglophile and peaceful Canada and with the Netherlands, Denmark, France and Germany. The Greek kingdom was established as recently as 1829 and Athens as its capital only in 1834. England, France and Russia, the *Entente cordiale* powers, watched over Greek affairs keenly, each having interests of its own. For five centuries the land which is now known as Greece, together with land settled by Serbs, Albanians, Rumanians and Bulgarians, had been controlled by the Ottoman Empire and this empire was beginning to fracture. Thanks to the strong leadership after 1909 of the Cretan Eleanthérios Venizélos (1864–1936), a new nationalism emerged in Greece which became known as 'The Great Idea' (*Megali Idea*). This irredentist policy, beginning with the absorption of Macedonia in 1912 and the linking of Crete and Greece in December 1913, sought to bring together all the scattered territories in which Greeks lived, from Anatolia on the west coast of Turkey to the Mediterranean islands, and to combine them under Constantinople as the capital. The dream of a Byzantine reawakening was dear to the heart of Venizélos, who was to be Constantine's prime minister, but not to the king himself, who was more concerned to create a smaller kingdom based on the classical connections with Athens. This was to lead to tension between the two men and changes in leadership in Greece which eventually affected Mawson's presence in the country.

As the Ottoman Empire's economic and cultural strength began to collapse, the Turks were expelled from Greek territories in a series of battles. Two Balkan Wars in 1912 and 1913, backed by Venizélos, and led by the then Crown Prince Constantine, released parts of Macedonia and Thrace to Greek rule, and increased Greek territory by some seventy per cent. In March 1913 Constantine's father, King George, was assassinated by a madman in the town of Thessaloniki (Salonika) and Constantine became king.

The speed with which Mawson was invited to Athens at the end of the conflict clearly demonstrated Constantine's wish to waste no time in making firm his own presence and standing in the capital. This would involve important changes to the structure and management of the city. Constantine confided that he had previously asked Kaiser Wilhelm II of Germany's architect Ludwig Hoffmann to provide a city plan, but Hoffmann had merely driven swiftly around Athens and had produced an elaborate and ill-conceived proposition which was promptly rejected.

Mawson does not reveal how Constantine chose him to be Athens' town planner. Mawson was confident

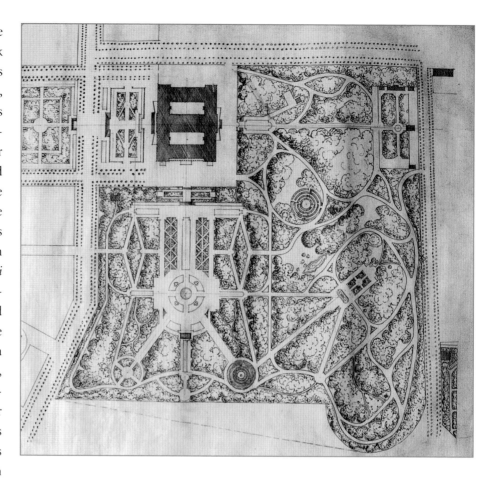

in his own international reputation and, in addition, Constantine was married to Sophia, whose mother, Victoria, was the sister of the British King Edward VII (1841–1910). As chapter two describes, Mawson had made a garden some four years before for Edward's wife, Queen Alexandra, at Hvidöre; and both Alexandra and Constantine were related through the Danish royal family. Although there is no evidence to confirm any connection, it is intriguing to note that Samuel Waring, the *éminence grise* who suggested Mawson to Alexandra and appeared to be on good terms with many of the branches of the royal families of Europe (including the Kaiser Wilhelm II, for whom he had furnished a yacht), also had business in Athens at this time.

Events proceeded quickly in 1913. In May both Thomas and Edward Prentice returned home, Thomas from Canada, and his son from Athens with completed designs for the palace gardens and holding additional requests that they should address the possibility of a new villa at Tatoi and landscaping for the nearby royal burial ground. The Greek royal family were to meet the Mawsons again in June as they visited the Grand Hotel at Eastbourne as part of their annual English summer holiday. Four of the six children – Princes George, Alexander and Paul and Princess Helen – were introduced to the Mawsons. Both George and Alexander were to become Greek kings during Mawson's lifetime.

ABOVE One of Edward Prentice Mawson's designs for the royal palace gardens in Athens, 1913-14. Reminiscent of the seventeenth century in England, there is a formal layout near the palace next to which the wandering paths of a wilderness enclose a maze.

During this short visit Constantine approved Edward Prentice's plans for the palace gardens and discussed in outline plans for Athens. Queen Sophia stressed her own concern for the need for working-class housing. The Mawsons were requested to come to Athens in September.

In August 1913 Mawson and his son Edward Prentice left for Europe, with a long and scenic journey ahead of them. After reaching Paris, they took a train south to Rome and then travelled across to Brindisi on the east coast of Italy where a boat was boarded for Corfu. The sea journey along the west coast of Greece brought the first physical evidence of the recent Balkan Wars to the eyes of father and son, as they saw the damaged buildings and settlements, and 'the once prosperous little seaport of Santa Quaranta in complete ruins' as a result of sea bombardment by the Greek fleet.

Corfu 'far surpassed in beauty and depth of colour what I had regarded as merely imaginative', wrote Mawson, describing the contrasts: squalor in the huddled buildings; the roofline of cupolas and belfries; the massive, horizontal fortifications broken by the dark green vertical shafts of the cypress trees.[4] Corfu also offered other commission opportunities; the royal family had a villa there, and so did Kaiser Wilhelm II, the German Emperor and King of Prussia. The brother of Queen Sophia, he also had landscaping requirements for his Villa Achilleon and gardens on the island. Edward had

already collected data in order to plan the restructuring of the town, of which the Kaiser was to express his approval in 1914.[5] Evidently the two men, Wilhelm and Constantine, worked closely together.

On reaching Athens, the king again proceeded rapidly with discussions. Edward Prentice's plans for the gardens of the palace, though approved, were to be handed on to the court architect and superintendent of the royal garden and presumably Edward would have no further hand in the project. A number of alternative plans and drawings remain; some may relate to separate parts of the garden. A sketch plan of 'the projected new Italian garden at Athens for the King of the Hellenes', dated 20 May 1913, shows a simple formal layout with two double avenues of trees below the palace, with other avenues opening on each side below the building. Other plans and drawings are dated 1914, including one which adds a double-arched loggia to the existing terrace wall. There is no list of plants, as this is a very arid site; but some planting is indicated on plans, including double avenues of orange trees beside a walk between three marble fountains, hedges of *Thuyopsis dolobrata* (from the *Cupressacea* family), and indications that flowers were intended to be planted by the fountains, and climbers on the terrace walls. The designs were meant to be seen from the *piano nobile*, or main floor, in common with most ornate plans for wealthy European clients dating from the seventeenth century onwards.

BELOW Mawson's perspective of a plan for the centre of Athens, with wide, tree-lined streets and squares.

LEFT Part of Edward Prentice
Mawson's illustration for a
collegiate school in Athens.

A well-defined plan, which combined most of the elements of the others, showed a paved terrace leading from the loggia with a divided rectangular space, where a fountain played in a white marble setting. There were semicircular steps down to another perhaps gravelled terrace, facing three axes. The first, placed straight ahead, led between a double avenue of trees to a rounded opening, possibly edged with low evergreens. It was joined on both sides by square beds, set diagonally, for ornamental plants or flowering shrubs. The other two axes proceeded diagonally through shrubberies to rounded meeting points, joining with narrower, closely planted avenues. Semicircular paths joined these avenues at the end of the site, perhaps at a garden pavilion. In between the axes led sinuous paths, enabling the royal family to prolong its stroll, gossip with guests, or just enjoy the shade.

On another side of the palace was a more natural, loosely designed garden. Though a straight axis led from the building past two ornate parterres to a circular central area in which there might be a fountain, the ground spread out to the back of the building with winding paths through shrubs and trees, and the odd surprise presented by a small parterre or a maze. These plans gave a picture of a shaded, elegant garden for Constantine, his family and guests, with paths and vistas, which would be a delight in spring and cool in the heat of summer. Steps led to the top of the terrace, and balustrades and ornate pots decorated the terrace walls, from which opened pavilions.[6]

However, the serious business of the meetings concerned the town. Mawson's first thoughts had been that 'The very idea of remodelling and replanning "Ancient Athens" seemed as out of place as the revision of the Bible did to our fathers when it was suggested', but new and productive territory had been added to Greece at the end of the Balkan Wars and Athens had grown from a dusty village of some 4,000 people when it had been made a capital, to some 200,000 in the second decade of the twentieth century. It was growing fast and there was no restriction on where and how buildings were erected.[7] Over the coming months the king expanded his plans, to which Mawson enthusiastically added. Recognising a need for a better designed city, worthy of its position as capital, Constantine proposed a boulevard leading west past the Kaiser's villa, a park system with large planted spaces, a new hotel and a casino (for rich tourists) and the improvement of the palace surroundings. New parliamentary buildings and government offices were needed; a well-built railway station would provide a dignified entry to the town; and there should be a new university. The port of Piraeus should be upgraded, and there should be a model workmen's suburb on garden city lines near the railway.[8] All main roads connecting with Athens needed attention, and Mawson foresaw the building of railways which would not only link Athens with Thessaloniki and the west, but would cross the Near East into India.

Tourism would be encouraged by clearing the shacks and hovels from around the foot of the Acropolis and obstructions from around ancient remains. Astonished at the companionable manner in which the king chose to walk with his planner through Constitution Square

(Syndagma) in the city's heart, Mawson applauded the decorative presence of orange trees. But there was, as he noted, great need for shade, and places for workers to retreat from the heat, and coffee shops where they could linger. He was also concerned that there were few open spaces accessible to the public: the royal gardens and the hilly landscapes of Zappion, Lycabettus, Mount Filopappou and Jupiter Olympus which ringed the Acropolis – itself part open space – were accessible only to tourists. Later Mawson was to take trouble to combine these sites in a green belt or park system in his city plan. This would be matched by Constantine's love for trees and his interest in reafforestation. Constantine wanted a forest fringe around the city, which he rightly understood as the means for making Athens' rivers flow once again. He took his landscape architect to the edge of the Acropolis

where he had arranged for waggonloads of thousands of young pines, cypresses and shrubs in pots to be on hand while he, encouraged by his wife Queen Sophia, directed men with picks and shovels to plant them.[9]

Prime Minister Venizélos and the mayor, M.Benachies, agreed with the king's proposals: Benachies also underlined the queen's request for working-class housing, and added his own for other facilities – a post office, an opera house and a town hall. Venizélos stressed the need for a chain of hotels for tourists, on which he placed great importance as the main source of wealth for the future of the city.

Mawson set about his various tasks with characteristic optimism: a civic survey (which, unexpectedly, was paid for by a Greek bank) and the single-minded assembly of all his data. His inspiration and great ideas for a noble

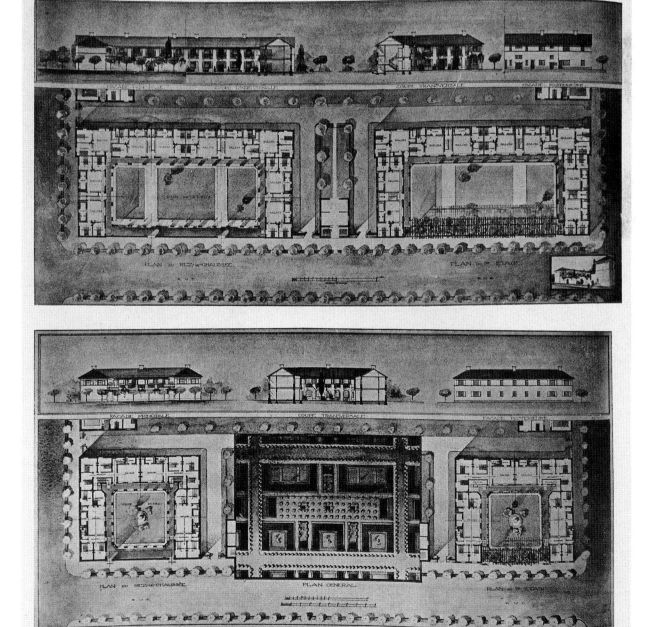

RIGHT Working-class housing designed for Athens, which Queen Sophia had requested. *Bolton*, slide 122.

city were tempered by the consideration of the means by which all this could be accomplished. 'We left Athens with our contract with the Council duly signed and delivered,' he wrote in the autumn of 1913.[10] Well pleased with his work, he would return in the spring of the following year.

But as 1914 advanced, Mawson began to perceive his work in Greece in a different light. He spent five weeks in Athens, Edward Prentice staying even longer. All the preliminary drawings and plans were placed with 'experts' by the town council. Delays began to rankle. Anxious to start work, Mawson sought guidance on significant sites from the head of the German School of Archaeology in Athens, Dr Karo, who gave him essential advice related to the city's historic structure. But Mawson had realised that nothing could be done without the provision of an adequate water supply, of which there was none. Before leaving for England he gave a lecture attended by heads of government departments, ministers and King Constantine, pointing out that the city had been discussing the need for water for forty years and had turned down every scheme for its introduction. 'They were always looking for something new and other experts,' concluded Mawson, realising that the audience at his lecture seemed unable to grasp that water shortage would jeopardise plans. Ten years later, as Mawson dictated his memoirs, there was still no start made on the supply of water for Athens.[11] And as the fires raged through the forests round Athens and elsewhere in Greece in the summer of 2007, Mawson's past unheeded warnings retained their dreadful significance.

King Constantine and Queen Sophia visited Eastbourne again in June 1914. They had a chance to consider the drawings for the tenements for the working classes on which the Mawsons had been working. Thomas Mawson invited the queen and her sister, the Grand Duchess of Hesse, to see gardens he had designed for Lord Brassey at Chelwood Manor and for Douglas

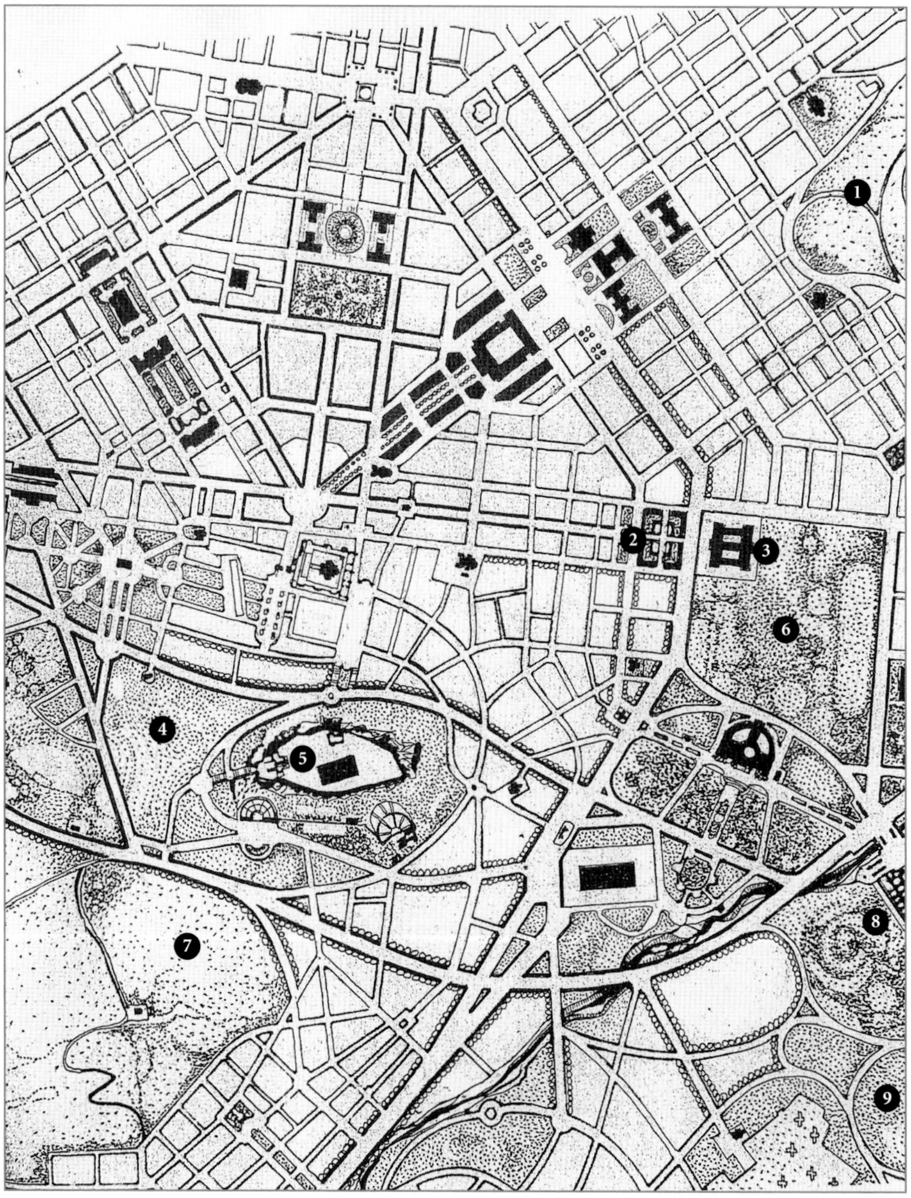

KEY:
1   Lycabettus
2   Sindagma
3   Parliament Building
4   Agora
5   Acropolis
6   The Royal Gardens
7   Filopappou Hill
8   Panathinaiko Stadium
9   Zappion

LEFT A part of the plan of the green spaces around Athens that Mawson planned to form a park system in Athens. Although this was never made, trees were planted around the hilltops of Lycabettus, the Acropolis, and Filopappou.

ABOVE A photograph taken by Mawson of the countryside in Thessaloniki.

Freshfield at Wych Cross in Sussex. The beauty of the planting, 'early roses, long glades of herbaceous borders,…and springy grass paths bordered by more and more roses, and then still more roses clambering over the pergolas', serene fields and woods gave little comfort, however, to those watching worsening affairs in Europe.[12] War between Germany and Britain seemed unavoidable. Set bizarrely against the news was the invitation the duchess extended to Mawson to visit her home in Prussia in August to meet the German crown prince, to plan the gardens of a new house he was building 'in the English style'. But that evening the Greek royal family were unexpectedly making plans for an immediate return to Athens; if war was inevitable, they wanted to be on home territory.

Later that year, with considerable misgivings, Mawson was making his way back to Athens. In Paris, he met Samuel Waring, also en route for Athens, where he had business to transact. Waring had arranged for them to visit the Kaiser at the Villa Achilleon on Corfu, but the Kaiser had been called back to Berlin by the time they arrived. Nevertheless they inspected the villa garden, which Mawson declared 'did not reach any high artistic level' with its lavish terraces decorated by 'ill chosen and badly placed sculptures'.[13] Waring gloomily assessed the political situation and retreated to England. Mawson could do little further: urged on by Constantine, he returned to North America in October, to lecture on 'Athens, Past, Present and Future' to American Greeks (migrants from political upheavals) and the universities of Columbia, Harvard and Toronto where he hoped to raise investment for the plans for Athens.

The declaration of war on 4 August 1914 precipitated a crisis of leadership in Greece. Venizélos believed the war would be won by the French and the English and wanted Greece to enter on the side of the *Entente Cordiale*. He still wanted to pursue the 'Great Idea', effectively eradicating the Ottoman Empire in order to unite the scattered Greeks and take Constantinople as its capital. King Constantine, closely linked with the royal families of Germany by marriage, and an honorary field marshal in the German army, was convinced of – and probably feared – the military superiority of the Germans, wanting Greece to remain neutral. There was still turmoil in Macedonia, where Thessaloniki's absorption by Greece in 1912 had given rein to the conflicting territorial aspirations of Serbs, Bulgarians, Romanians and Albanians. The entente powers, France, Britain and Russia, and the Central Powers, Germany and Austro-Hungary, had ambitions to take land in Bulgaria and to crush the Ottoman Turks. In addition, the British wanted to keep Greece neutral, to stop the Turks and the Bulgarians from joining the Central Powers.

Constantine, reluctantly agreeing to go to war, drew back again after the British had failed to organise a successful naval attack on the Dardanelles in 1915, in part to capture Constantinople. Venizélos resigned, but was returned to office with much public support. Great national and international political turbulence characterised the years that followed. In the summer of 1917 Constantine was asked to leave the country, though not deposed, and his second son Alexander briefly took the throne (1917–20). 'The Great Schism' had taken place, royalist against nationalist, 'German sympathiser' against entente supporter, Greek against Greek.

Where was this to leave Mawson and his two years' work for the capital? Respected by both king and prime minister, it appeared that the anti-royalist feeling of some of the Greeks in power would make it difficult for Mawson to continue, even if there had been no more conflict to follow. The only parts of the Mawson plan to be implemented were the reafforestation of the slopes of Filopappou and Lycabettus. There is no record of landscaping at the king's villa nor of the linking of the royal graveyard to a Byzantine chapel in Tatoi, which had been discussed with Edward Prentice; some afforestation but no further landscaping was accomplished in Corfu. As some acid-tongued wit remarked to Mawson, 'What a pity Willie did not get his august father to postpone his little war until you had laid his garden!'[14]

Despite his ignominious situation at the outbreak of war, Mawson was overjoyed to be recalled to Greece in 1917. He wrote little in his autobiography of the political situation which made the background to his recall to plan the rebuilding of Thessaloniki in 1917, except that:

King Constantine was no longer on the throne…M.Venizélos, after his successful revolution, was in control, and very popular with the people; whilst the young King, although popular, was entirely under the direction of his Prime Minister. 'I am merely a dummy figure-head exercising only the will of others,' he bitterly said to me later.[15]

On 18 August 1917 (or 5 August, according to the Orthodox calendar, changed in 1923), a fire broke out in the northwest of the oldest part of Thessaloniki, and, urged on by the violence of the southwesterly seasonal wind, the vardar, spread rapidly. The inhabitants had been subject to destruction by accidental inferno many times before, as the old town was packed tight with wooden buildings, the streets were narrow and the projecting upper storeys reached across to each other. There were larger, better constructed Macedonian houses on the fringes of the town, built of brick within a frame of wooden squares, set in small walled gardens; but even these were to be destroyed as the conflagration advanced. There was no efficient fire service and little water available; there were dangerous ammunition dumps in the town, awaiting use by the assembling armies.[16] Harry Pierce, a British soldier in Thessaloniki, who became a manager of the Lakeland Nurseries, described the panic as the inhabitants realised they had to run for their lives:

Slowly they came at first, but like a flood the volume increased rapidly, and soon the lower town was a seething mass of refugees…Anxious tradesmen locked their shops and put up their shutters as the crowd swarmed past, all carrying some treasure which they valued most. One woman pulled along a small child and her apron was filled with boots; an old man clutched a leg of mutton; another carried a live hen.

Pierce described soldiers and sailors in the town and on battleships in the harbour pumping water to the burning town from the harbour and blowing up buildings in the lower town in an attempt to halt the fire's advance.[17]

Mazower recounts the mayhem of the 'frantic throng of Muslims and *Ma'min,* elderly Jews wearing fezzes, slippers and their long gabardine *intari,*' and the release of 'veiled wives locked inside their *haremlik*' by their Turkish husbands. The military worked hard to persuade the inhabitants to leave the city, having to throw their belongings on to the boats before the people would budge.[18] It was all over by the following evening.

In the past the inhabitants would have returned as soon as they could, haphazardly rebuilding on the same sites. But once the damage could be assessed, it was clear that the old historic centre of Thessaloniki would have to be completely rebuilt. All the infrastructure of the city had been destroyed, together with the homes of 70,000 people; although, as Mawson later recounted in an article lauding the work of the British military during the fire, 'this large and congested population was removed without the loss of a single life'.[19] Temporary settlements would have to be made. Yet those in authority claimed that the fire had done the city a service. John Mawson, later in charge of rebuilding villages in eastern Macedonia, called the town 'an open sewer'.[20] He reported: 'Salonika [was the] breeding ground and starting point of every plague and pestilence known in Europe…[the fire] was literally an act of Good and was indeed a blessing in disguise.'[21] Feelings ran high: there was a strong sentiment abroad that all traces of settlement other than Greek should be eradicated and this was the time to do it.

Thessaloniki dates back to Hellenic times; even today, its city centre is dominated by a rectangular pattern of

saint of Thessaloniki, in the centre of the town. In 1423 the city was taken over by the Venetians; and then by the Turks in 1430, who made it part of the Ottoman Empire for nearly five centuries. Jewish migrants came following expulsion from Spain and Portugal in 1492 and, much later, as refugees from the Russian Revolution of 1917, helping to swell the city's numbers. Gradually differing ethnic and religious groups settled together in distinct areas in the city, with Turkish bazaars near the centre and a large Jewish cemetery to the east of the city walls. There was, however, very little to praise in the state of most of the housing, where there was no method of registering the ownership of the property, no rates or taxes to help pay for city infrastructure, 'water came from fountains scattered about the town, and sewers and drains, except the most primitive, did not exist'.[22]

Yerolympos plots the speed with which the national assembly decided to collect together a commission of engineers and architects on 12 August 1917 (Orthodox calendar), which could include foreigners, to Venizélos' announcement in the national assembly that it was his intention to nominate 'the celebrated English architect Mawson' to head the commission to replan the city. Eight days later Mawson was offered the position in a telegram from the Greek government. Eight days after that, Mawson accepted on the condition that 'he be allowed to work exclusively with English engineers'. By 8 September Mawson had agreed to collaborate with French and Greek members of the commission, and began preparations to find his team of English workers.[23]

It took twelve weeks before he could secure the release of his elder son Edward Prentice from statutory war duties on munitions work (he had been turned down from serving in the armed forces on health grounds), obtain passports, and, even then, he could not gain the release of any further staff.[24] The Greeks saw this as an unnecessary delay, and it appears that the lapse of twelve weeks cost Mawson the real leadership for the reconstruction of Thessaloniki.[25] Breaking his outward journey in Paris, where he met up with Venizélos, he was told that a team of eighteen under the direction of the French architect and planner Ernest Hébrard, trained at the Ecole des Beaux-Arts in Paris and in Rome, had already been at work making a survey of the town since 1 September.[26] Hébrard had been in Thessaloniki at the time of the fire, enrolled in the Armée de l'Orient and as head of the French army's archaeological service. He worked closely with the influential minister of communications, the socialist lawyer Alexander Papanastassiou, 'setting their own stamp on the whole scheme'. Mawson's

TOP Thomas Mawson and his son Edward Prentice in the back of a car driven by Greek soldiers, probably in Thessaloniki around 1917.

ABOVE Members of the International Commission for the replanning of Thessaloniki. From right to left: C.Kitsikis, J.Pleyber, E.Hébrard, Thomas Mawson, C.Angelakis, A Lefteriotis, Edward Prentice Mawson, John Mawson, X.Johnson and A.Zachos. The anger in Thomas Mawson's face reflects his feeling that he has been upstaged by the French.

straight streets. Its position at the head of a wide gulf in the northeast of mainland Greece has made it both a favoured Balkan port and a space for interaction for the many different nationalities on its borders – today's Albanians and Bulgarians, and those living in what used to be called Yugoslavia. Over the centuries the city has been subject to both domination and cooperation by many different groups. The Hellenic world of Thessaloniki became a regional then a provincial capital under the Romans from 168 BC, with its city walls, its forum including a semicircular odeon for musical performances for 400 people, Emperor Galerius' Rotunda (probably a mausoleum) and his archway nearby. The introduction of eastern orthodox Christianity brought monasteries and their churches such as the Agii Apostoli, on the west of the city, and Agios Dimitrios, the patron

SALONIQUE
ETUDE PRELIMINAIRE POUR
LA RECONSTRUCTION ET
DE L'EXTENSION
DE LA VILLE

summons by Venizélos was to 'counterbalance the French influence', but effectively he had already been marginalised.[27]

The commission of seven who began the work in Thessaloniki included Joseph Pleyber, a French military engineer, who planned the city infrastructure, and Aristotle Zachos, a Greek architect and planner, who headed the team and encouraged Byzantine revivalism. The Greek architect Constantin Kitsikis drew up the building regulations and favoured the concept of the garden city, and engineer Angelos Guinis made plans for the port and dock extensions. The commission was chaired by Thessaloniki's mayor, Constantin Angelakis.[28] Mawson arrived in Athens to confer with Papanastassiou, on his way by train to Thessaloniki, and, as the city survey seemed to be under way, asserted his wish to work 'as the director or senior member of a commission to include all the experts essential to the production of a development scheme in which every important factor should be correlated'.[29] All this appears to have been agreed, and Mawson was sufficiently relaxed to enjoy and recount the slow journey north through the fertile farmed areas growing cotton, tobacco and vines, with olives and sugar pine on the rougher terrain. He noted with admiration the majestic Mount Olympus rising from the plain and the rugged beauty of the Vale of Tempe.

Mawson's autobiography states his barely disguised displeasure with the situation he discovered on his arrival in November 1917; the tension shows in his face in the photographs taken at a dinner held for members of the commission. Hébrard had assumed himself to be the man in command. And though the commission of seven were supposed to be working together, in effect they were working in parallel. Two plans for Thessaloniki were to be made in 1918: one was Mawson's and the other was Hébrard's.

Mawson, still holding his ground, had to seek help from the Foreign Office and Sir George Milne, the British Commander-in-Chief, to find staff and accommodation, without which he would 'have had to return to England with our task unaccomplished'.[30] At the first meeting of all concerned, the French members disputed Mawson's position as leader of the commission, while the Greeks supported him. Despite the ability and skill of both groups, from now on Mawson was to work in complete cooperation with the Greeks and with growing disenchantment with the French. With this uncomfortable situation officially resolved, if not approved, the Mawson family's work in Macedonia began.[31]

Mawson left Greece in January 1918, leaving Edward Prentice and recently arrived John to carry on. Mawson's client numbers at home were beginning to rise again – he had fifteen in 1919 – and he expected to return later to Athens. Mawson had worked hard, producing an eighty page report in two months, as well as plans and diagrams, which were signed by members of the commission as a joint recommendation.[32] Unfortunately this report is nowhere to be found today in Greece or the United Kingdom; but Mawson wrote copiously of his suggestions in other contemporary publications.

There were three tasks which had to be addressed: the rebuilding of the old town of Thessaloniki, the planning of the wider environs of the town, and the associated work of reconstruction of the countryside of eastern Macedonia, to enable the agriculture which would support the population.

Yerolympos describes the mechanisms by which the rebuilding of Thessaloniki was to begin. Briefly, firm action to prevent piecemeal rebuilding was enabled by Law 823, passed by the national assembly within a fortnight of the fire, made possible because all planning powers had been given to the Ministry of Communications in 1914.[33] Some legal and financial framework was necessary in a town which, because of its Turkish precedents, had no rates and taxes, as the town's

BELOW Edward Prentice Mawson's drawing of church ruins, Thessaloniki.

income came from the port and customs duties.[34] For the first time a register of property was made. By setting up a Property Owners' Association in a law of 1918 of those who had held land before the fire, the whole area was then expropriated and the owners were granted shares as title deeds. The sites were then sold off, with owners able to surrender their deeds, and the government gave help to those building on their plots in the form of bank credit, tax cuts and cheap imported building materials. This took time, as there was much boycotting of the registration of land. Prices of land rose as speculation began, but the increase in price – the betterment – had to be returned to the Property Association for the good of the whole.

Amid the furore this caused, Venizélos was voted out of office in December 1920 and a conservative People's Party came to power. The rebuilding of Thessaloniki had barely begun by the end of 1920. It was not until changes had been made to the laws governing the auctioning of land and the size of the plots, that rebuilding began properly, and a new Thessaloniki began to emerge between 1921 and 1924. Two-storey houses were replaced by those of up to five storeys; flammable wood was replaced by concrete; instead of the traditional discrete zones which had grown up on their own relating to race and religion there were now areas of the city where groups of similar economic and social status settled.[35] The Jews were largely displaced. Thomas Mawson's plan for the environs of Thessaloniki, described and illustrated in the *Times Engineering Supplement* of May 1919, was not altogether dissimilar to Hébrard's. Both were dated January 1918, when Mawson left Greece. The first considerations had to be those connected with roads, drainage and water supplies; possible extensions to the railway system, and expansion of the docks. Mawson even suggested an underground railway between a new resort at Kalamaria and its link in town called Piccadilly Circus![36] – hardly a sound idea in a region prone to earthquakes. Both men enclosed the old town in a diamond-shaped street network, with central axes leading at right angles from the sea, and crossed by the main Egnatia highway and its parallel straight roads. The two outer axes were planned with radiating roads to help distribute traffic – a form much used by both Thomas and Edward Prentice Mawson. Both Hébrard and Mawson placed the industrial quarter behind and beyond expanded docks to the west, with Hébrard including a commercial section close to the old centre, and Mawson specifying factories and a workmen's quarter near the docks. Here also was the railway station,

LEFT The churchyard of
Panagia Chalkeon, its rose
pergola opening onto the
city square.

to which Mawson wanted a connecting highway to an oval garden exhibition centre. The southeastern side of the town, which had spread along the coast beyond the White Tower marking the boundary of old Thessaloniki, developed in the late nineteenth century and would remain as an upper-middle-class area with large houses with gardens set among parks, playgrounds and schools. Mawson saw the White Tower as the 'social centre' for theatres, concert halls and great cafes', to which today could be added museums.

It was the aim of the commission that there should be 'a certain aspect of beauty combined with comfort'.[37] Mawson, wanting small islands of colour and shade in churchyard gardens, suggested that of Agia Sofia, which survived the fire.[38] Today, well-kept gardens have grown up surrounding the church of the Panagia Chalkeon, in the city centre, and a quiet, understated garden at the back of Agios Dimitrios. The garden exhibition centre was made in a park to the east and is enjoyed by the population who stroll through the grounds between the trees, push children on swings, or buy plants from stalls. Egnatia Street was given single lines of trees for shade, instead of the original plan for a double avenue.

None of the garden city settlements lauded by Mawson and planned by Kitsikis and Hébrard, with front gardens and vegetable plots, set into the contours rather than a neo-classical grid, was built.[39]

The central axis of the old town, which crosses Egnatia Street on its way to the sea, was to have been developed as a civic centre, which would have been strongly approved by Mawson. Long afterwards a central paved square set with trees has developed between the dim and impressive arched interior of the Turkish bath of Bey Hamam and the rose garden of the church of the Panagia Chalkeon, beside which old men sit playing cards. Beyond, as the ground rises, the site of the proposed civic centre is occupied by the excavation of the Roman forum, unknown until it was revealed by the earthquake of 1978. The lower part of this axis, however, has become a focus for the town. Below Egnatia Street, central formal gardens which have a strong flavour of the Edwardian period in England, run down to a breezy piazzetta framed by hotels and shops, set back under arches to give shade, next to the sea.

Mawson wanted three large zones of parkland to divide the urban area and to act as firebreaks. The

BELOW The Garden
Exhibition Centre now
flourishes in Thessaloniki
on a site which was
suggested by Mawson.

central axis, though interrupted by the forum, had some claim to such a zone, though to complete it northwards would have meant disturbing the churches of Agia Sophia and Agios Dimitrios. Further east, the remaining parkland which divides the centre from the eastern urban area, now accommodates museums, theatres, military establishments and Mawson's garden exhibition area. Mawson pressed the Greeks to plant trees around the boundaries of the city for shelter. 'Never have I experienced a wind which could cause such suffering and discomfort as the Vardar winds in Macedonia,' he claimed.[40]

Clearly Hébrard and Mawson had very similar ideas which were combined on the final plan, from the layout of the old town to the zoning of the wider urban area. Many of these ideas have infiltrated the general layout and smaller landscapes within the city. Mawson respected the teaching of the Beaux-Arts school which had trained Hébrard. However, continued political turmoil in Greece throughout the twentieth century, a second world war, a major earthquake in 1978 and a vast expansion in population delayed the city's development. Today's Thessaloniki still retains a French formal street layout with its main axis composed of Aristotelous

Square, linked to Dikastirion Square, and with the Agora Dimitrios behind it. To the east is an axis centred on the Rotunda. Roads have different widths according to need, as Mawson constantly urged. The parkland further east now surrounds the museum and higher educational needs of the city. There are some radial routes remaining which lead away from the Agios Dimitrios, on a level with the forum. Few attempts have been made to develop the promenade along the sea. Outside the limits of the old city, routes become sinuous, and to the north, housing in the upper town is piecemeal and appears to be as low cost as possible.

To the north of Thessaloniki rise hills, wooded with deciduous trees, containing the city to the south in a wide bowl. On the far side, the road drops down to a bridge over the Strimonas river and continues over an extensive, fertile plain. Fragile scarlet poppies cluster along the field banks. Small villages, with one-storey, pantiled houses surrounded by small gardens and larger vegetable plots are scattered at intervals over the plain; where there are unoccupied houses, peasant farmers grow crops and raise chickens, turkeys, sheep and goats. To the northeast lie Lake Kirkini and the Bulgarian border, with unhurried fishermen along the jetty and a

ABOVE The axis from Thessaloniki's city centre to the coast, with Edwardian-style gardens.

riding school setting off with its horses in the woodland beyond the lake.

This was an area of devastation and under-development when John Mawson arrived in the spring of 1918 as an advisor to the Greek government on housing and town planning; the Bulgarians had entered the war on the German side in 1916, occupying Eastern Macedonia. In early 1919, based on the results of his investigations as housing advisor, John had been appointed head of the service for the reconstruction of 150 settlements and 12,000 houses in Eastern Macedonia – the villages caught up in the war. In a long address made at the end of May 1919 to the Greek council for refugees, John Mawson admitted that 'the situation is infinitely more serious than I had been led to believe…the key to the whole situation is Building Materials, and there is, to mention only one item, not sufficient timber left in the destroyed villages to repair a single house'.[41] Over 200 settlements had been wholly or partially destroyed in the Strimonas plain and along the Vardar valley which crossed the old border with Yugoslavia. The Bulgarians had captured Macedonians and taken them over the border, meanwhile destroying their houses. Thomas Mawson had experienced the 'whizzing sound of the shells passing over us, and

evidently not very high, followed by the explosions' while lecturing to the army in a YMCA tent at Langaza, before he returned with the officers to their dugouts in the hillside.[42]

After the war was over, John Mawson's difficulties included the inevitable confusion between centralised government direction and those on the spot. The Athens government's intention to separate the functions of the men designing the houses from those planning the villages, led John to complain that he wanted to be left to get on with a job he had been appointed to do. There were letters addressed to the minister of communications, Alexandros Papanastassiou, as to who should pay his staff (Edward Prentice had earlier solved the problem by having himself placed by the Greek army on their payroll).

There were fears that the returning prisoners of war would themselves mend their destroyed homes, and live in squalor: 'New villages and houses have to be planned and built according to the most modern and enlightened conception of convenience, efficiency, sanitation and comfort and that no compromise between the old insanitary dilapidated houses and villages and the new can be entertained for a moment', John insisted.[43] Some 5,000 people would be placed in 'conical tents' and 'wood and

BELOW Modern Thessaloniki, its central axis extending through the tree-lined square to the sea, and the Roman forum at the top of the picture. The plan followed much of its Roman footprint.

iron sheets' were purchased from outside Macedonia to provide roofs and patch up some bombed housing as an interim measure. Army huts would be assembled if they could be afforded. John recruited English members of the armed forces who were prepared to stay on and help, as there was a pressing need for architects, engineers, army transport officers and many others. In England, Thomas Mawson had also been recruiting men to help his son. In a letter to Papanastassiou on 24 June 1919 Mawson announced that he had received up to 500 applications, nearly all from 'English officers of good standing and good professional degrees'.[44]

The housing of thousands of refugees was associated with the need to drain the marshlands in the river valleys to create good farmland. This would bring millions of acres into cultivation,

> not, as in former times, by means of slow, oxen-drawn ploughs, but by the adoption of the most up-to-date agricultural machinery, including farm tractors…on the redeemed lands, almost anything can be grown – tobacco, cotton, currant-vines, raisins, oranges, figs, peaches, nectarines, olives, mangoes…the land…is admirably adapted for the cultivation of maize and most other cereals.

This would help to stem the drift of peasant workers from the countryside to the towns, as long as housing could be provided.[45]

The Ministry of Agriculture provided teams to survey land and eventually to drain it. It was John Mawson's job, with the help of the Ministry of Communications, to bring in materials, select new sites for housing, plan the infrastructure, lay out streets and build new houses. Village plans were prepared by British, Belgian and French architects. Many consciously adopted a garden village style, avoiding straight lines, and being led by the shape of the land. There was provision for gardens and public spaces. But, as Kafkoula relates, building, set to begin by the autumn of 1920, was halted by a series of disasters.[46] Money ran short because of the ill-fated Asia Minor campaign, one result of which was the inability to finish the construction of a water supply and road system; there was an influx of refugees from Russia, which created greater demand for housing than that already planned. But politics, once again, brought everything to a halt, as the Liberal government and Venizélos were removed in December 1920 and replaced by the republican People's party. The work of the reconstruction service was halted. John Mawson resigned in disgust and the other non-Greek architects left Greece. Perhaps, also, the Greeks were tired of comments such as John Mawson's 'we English have the gift of getting things done,' even if this was true.[47]

For a brief moment in 1920 a small flame of hope was ignited as Thomas Mawson's help in the development of the parks and boulevards of Athens was sought by the town planning commission, and Edward Prentice made a design for the 'Ionian bank in Salonika', but once again Mawson felt the French monopolised the work and appointed only a 'few Greeks in minor positions'.[48] Mawson enjoyed an expedition out into the hills below Mount Olympus, looking for a site for a proposed hotel. Finally the flame was extinguished, this time by a financial crisis which prevented any further development of the parks, boulevards, the bank or the hotel. Eventually Mawson's plan was dropped.

The departure from Athens, this time for the last time, was somewhat softened by Mawson's presentation by Papanastassiou of the Order of the Saviour for his 'work in Salonika and my preliminary scheme for the re-planning and extension of Athens', and for his son Edward the Order of King George 'as an appreciation of the splendid help he has given to us and to yourself in the working out of the Salonika plans'.[49]

A Liberal government was returned to power in the early 1930s, but only one of the original planned settlements was completed. This was a joint venture by Hébrard and the Belgian P. Deyong called Jumaya. Today this small town is called Iraklia, at the head of the Strimonas plain not far from the Bulgarian border. The geometrical plan has a central axis in which is sited its church, memorial and shopping area, and it reflects a return to the formality of the French Beaux-Arts settlement and not the looser pattern of the English garden city. Iraklia's streets are straight and rectangular, and its one-storey houses have their own small, well-kept gardens and vegetable plots. There is a sawmill, with piles of cut logs evocative of the wood shortages of 1918, and a cattle market, reflecting the recovery of agriculture. The other, smaller, settlements of the Strimonas plain are planned in a similarly compact manner. None had any connection with the Mawsons. However, Edward Prentice was designing a hotel, casino and bathing beach in 1932 for Loutraki, on the west coast of the Peloponnese, so the family's link with Greece had not been broken.[50]

How should Mawson's work in Greece be assessed? He stated his vision for the two most important Greek towns: 'while Athens is to strike the eyes of foreigners and locals alike as the seat of government…Salonica must on the contrary convey the character of a great port and centre of industrial and commercial activity'.[51] He praised Athens and urged the 'conservation of treasures bequeathed it by the past', and commended the beauty of Thessaloniki's great Byzantine churches, drawn by Edward Prentice, damaged by war and altered by the Muslims.

Mawson's town plans were always grand, costly, and sought uncompromisingly to demonstrate the very best for the site. 'Spaciousness and elegance are to be the trademarks of Athens,' he wrote in 1918.[52] In Greece any progress in Athens was impeded by the deposition of the king, the growth of nationalism and the financial problems of the 1920s. As for Thessaloniki, Mawson arrived too late on the scene and was upstaged by a determined team of French planners under Ernest Hébrard.

Were the Mawsons' requests for English staff in Thessaloniki simply a show of superiority over 'the procrastinating Greek'? It is notable that father and son worked well with the Greek engineers and surveyors and praised their skills, despite a shortage of engineers. But as Kafkoula points out: 'although connections with European planning thought were firmly rooted, they had not resulted in any updating of professional training. Drawing up plans "on garden city lines" was not included in the curriculum of the newly founded School of Architecture.' The design of the villages was therefore left to foreign architects, and both Mawsons wanted to employ English-speaking men on their teams, as the French had employed French speakers on theirs and with whom 'collaboration…became less and less effective'.[53]

Would Mawson's plans have succeeded if war and politics had not intervened? Greece was moving towards a more democratic approach to government and concern for the working classes, and though both Mawson and Hébrard designed workmen's housing and garden cities, Hébrard's known socialism linked him more closely to the left-wing Papanastassiou who wielded the most power. For Mawson, art mattered as much as politics, and his designs were more costly for this reason. Both Mawson and Hébrard designed formal, Beaux-Arts city centres, with reference to English and French architectural styles rather than traditional Greek, though the Byzantine churches were gathered into their plans. And there was little major difference between their designs for Thessaloniki. Mawson was too close to the royal family for acceptance by the socialists in Athens, and for that reason alone might have found himself barred from advancement in either city. So for both his royal client, King Constantine, and his prime minister, Elefthérios Venizélos, the 'greatest compliment to British art' remained on the drawing boards of the man they commissioned.

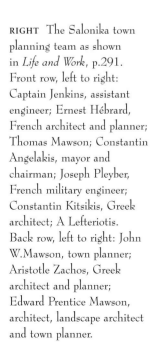

RIGHT The Salonika town planning team as shown in *Life and Work*, p.291. Front row, left to right: Captain Jenkins, assistant engineer; Ernest Hébrard, French architect and planner; Thomas Mawson; Constantin Angelakis, mayor and chairman; Joseph Pleyber, French military engineer; Constantin Kitsikis, Greek architect; A Lefteriotis. Back row, left to right: John W. Mawson, town planner; Aristotle Zachos, Greek architect and planner; Edward Prentice Mawson, architect, landscape architect and town planner.

CHAPTER SEVEN

Civic Art 1891–1931

LEFT Mawson's planning
for Haslam Park, Preston,
spilled over a long period
from 1911. He tried to
encourage civic pride by
planning a pavilion and a
boating lake, but the local
authorities were unwilling
to spend money on the park.
A drinking fountain had to
take the place of a pavilion.

THE RAPID CHANGES in population numbers during the lives of Thomas Mawson's parents, John and Jane Mawson, turned a country of rural dwellers into town dwellers – eighty per cent of the population lived in towns by 1911 and the number of people living in England had doubled. Those looking for jobs and housing in industrial towns found themselves subjected to long hours, dangerous working conditions, noxious fogs, outbreaks of cholera and typhoid, and high death rates. The workforce needed to be housed near their employment and all available space was occupied by houses, run up quickly by their employers and often sublet. Airless, gardenless courts containing outside privies formed the only spaces for children to play. One-family rooms were commonplace.

The housing in which workers were crammed, bereft of sanitation, light and space, was described by novelists of the time. Elizabeth Gaskell had written in the mid-nineteenth century about Manchester's slums, with unpaved streets and gutters taking all the effluent from the houses whose broken windows were stuffed with rags, and where visitors entering the cellar in which a family lived found 'the smell so foetid as almost to knock the two men down'. Here they discovered four small children, rolling on the wet brick floor, 'through which the stagnant, filthy moisture of the street oozed up'.[1] Investigations such as Henry Mayhew's *London Labour and the London Poor* (1861-2) informed the public who treated such matters as horror fiction, rather than as a spur for reform. It was not until the Reverend Andrew Mearns, Secretary of the London Congregational Union, published *The Bitter Cry of Outcast London* in 1883,

that the Victorian public awoke to the sexual immorality of one-room family housing and local authorities were shocked into the need for environmental reform.[2]

Mawson's awareness of poor housing would have accompanied his boyhood visits to the cotton towns of Lancashire. For him, the twin social problems of poor housing and a lack of green spaces swept clean by fresh air were to be solved by the umbrella craft of Civic Art – a mixture of town planning and park making. Mawson saw the design of both these public requirements governed by many of the same objectives as garden making. As he was to comment in the preface to *Civic Art* in 1911 (he had taken the name from Charles Mulford Robinson), he had intended to write about parks, gardens and boulevards, but he 'quickly recognised that these things, though intensely important, were merely parts of a larger whole, and that Civic Art must embrace town planning and a consideration of all those factors relating to civic design which bear upon it'.[3] There was no formal training for either town planning or park making, and so Mawson was able to help to pioneer the first and take up the second where others had left it.

Mawson's entry into the world of park making was first fuelled by the need to find work for his new firm. Five years after the foundation of Mawson Brothers, orders were coming in at speed, but most of the assets of the firm were tied up in stock, and all of Mawson's money was going into stocking the nursery. He needed larger enterprises and better pay, and decided to enter some of the many competitions to design public parks in the northwest.

Local authorities had edged slowly forwards from the 1830s as they considered the moral and social benefits they would give communities by providing open spaces for recreation. The Select Committee on Public Walks had voiced the necessity for a park in the East End of London in 1833; significantly, the first municipal park was made in the northwest, Preston's Moor Park, in the same year. Joseph Paxton, head gardener to the 6th Duke of Devonshire at Chatsworth, had made a commercially sound enterprise in Prince's Park, Liverpool, in 1842, where the sale of new housing round the edge of the park had helped to support the venture, which was for residents only. Local communities in Manchester had raised funds to make Philips Park and Queen's Park in 1846.

Birkenhead Park, which opened to the public in 1847, was a considerable step in the right direction in funding and design. Birkenhead's Improvement Commissioners, having applied to Parliament for permission to use public money, asked for Paxton's help. He helped to raise a boggy and flat site into an interesting landscape by creating lakes to drain the centre, and used the spoil to make scenic hillocks with rocky outcrops, all paid for by the housing he provided round the edge. Mawson went to see Birkenhead, and similar landscaping appeared in some of his commissions. An admirer of French design, he assessed the work of Edouard André (1840–1911), who had helped Jean-Charles-Adolphe Alphand (1817–91), landscape artist and engineer, to transform Paris' parks and boulevards. André won the competition for Sefton Park in Liverpool in 1867. Long vistas and elliptical paths were moulded around a central valley with cascades; local architect Lewis Hornblower was responsible for the park buildings which made terminal points for the vistas.

Mawson had high regard for the work of Edward Milner, who designed three parks for Preston, all of which used unemployed cotton workers to make the roads. Moor Park opened in 1833, and Avenham and Miller Parks in 1864, next to each other but divided by a railway which was carefully screened with trees and shrubs. So also admired was Edward Kemp (1817–91), who had worked under Paxton at Birkenhead, becoming head gardener there. He designed Hesketh Park, Southport and Stanley Park in Liverpool, which opened in 1868 and 1870 respectively. These parks from the 1860s had been designed by landscape architects, not the park superintendents and others put up for the job by borough engineers and surveyors, whom Mawson called 'amateurs' in an address to the Municipal County Engineers in 1890. Reports were made, partly as advertisement to those who read them, explaining propositions, what was done, and what could be achieved in the future.

As Mawson joined the park makers, Parliament had passed a number of Acts which encouraged progress. The Public Parks Act of 1871 aided the donation of land for use as a public park; the Public Health Act of 1875 enabled local authorities to acquire and maintain land for recreation and raise government loans to do so; the Open Spaces Act of 1881 and the Disused Burial Grounds Act of 1884 enabled the transformation of waste ground and defunct cemeteries for other uses. Mawson won the competition to design a public park for Hanley, near Stoke-on-Trent in the Potteries in 1891,

BELOW The plan for Hanley Park, 1898. Mawson shielded the park from the Cauldon Works on the west with trees. The industrial canal in the centre was bridged and embanked, which, with careful tree-planting in the north, made it invisible from both parts of the park. *Civic Art*, fig. 266.

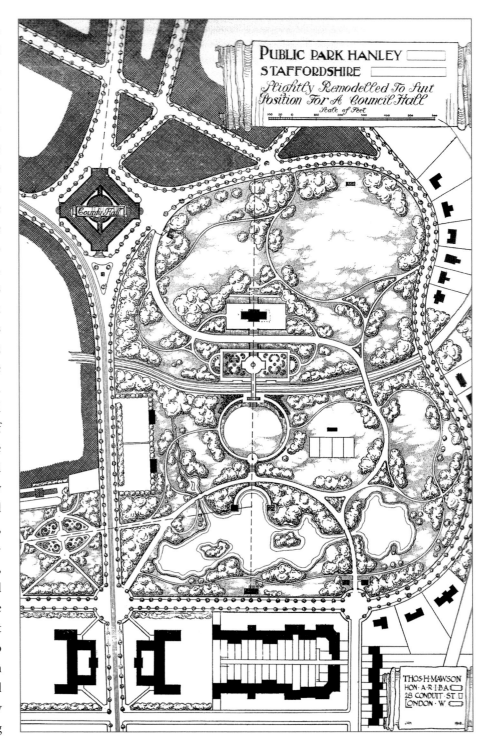

and the report he wrote in 1894, when the work was in progress, illuminated the problems he faced on this bleak 125-acre site. There were the unsightly Cauldon Works on the west, the area was cut in two by the North Stafford Canal, littered with spoil heaps and pock-marked by disused pit shafts. Where clay had been dug out, the holes were filled with pottery debris.[4] Adding to the physical difficulties of the site were 'chemicals unit-ing with smoke to destroy all tree growth, and where everything is so quickly discoloured'. It was 'useless for the park architect to think of quaintly clipped yew, holly or box edged gardens' where only privet would with-stand such conditions; other things had to be introduced 'to compensate for the deficiency' such as 'lodges, entrances, a pavilion, boathouses, seats, shelters, terraces and a boundary fence'.[5]

The inhabitants of Hanley were congratulated by Mawson at the park's opening in 1898 for converting 'such a desolate wilderness into a green oasis'.[6] In order to fund the operation, 25 acres of land were sold for building good-sized housing along the east side of the park. Cauldon Works on the west were shielded by plantations made up of trees which would 'survive in the neighbourhood', in front of which was placed Dan Gibson's conservatory as a winter garden, 'good for

growing chrysanthemums'. Parkland stretched from the works to a pavilion on a terrace edged by formal flower beds; 'a pavilion occupies the centrepiece position in a park, as a house does in a garden'.[7] The canal was bridged, with an embanked descent to the lower park. Here was the provision for sport which had come to be recognised as essential for good health – tennis courts and bowling greens. There was boating, on a splendid lake with two islands, where skating could pull in the crowds in winter, and fishing afterwards, and which brought in revenue for the borough. The lake was fed by a stream in which James Pulham & Son constructed rockworks and cascades.

Mawson's overall design, with formality near the centre emphasised by an axis which cut through the 'pavilion, terrace, bandstand, bridge, bowling greens, drinking fountain, boat houses and shelter',[8] and its sin-uous paths around the perimeters, underlined how close his park design lay to the gardens he had made. But the type of work was different. 'Park construction is not like working on a cultivated garden', said Mawson, who took on hundreds of unemployed men to do 'heavy navvy work with pick and spade, requiring hardened hands and hard muscles'. The men who survived were taken on full time, and joined a pool of labour for outside work.[9]

The completed park was greeted with great enthusiasm and immense civic pride. Encouraged by his success at Hanley, he agreed to take on the construction of Burslem Park nearby, where the ground was in a worse state than Hanley's.

Belle Vue Park to the west of Newport, South Wales, was made on land given to the town by Lord Tredegar in 1891, overlooking the Bristol Channel. In the early 1890s Mawson had been working on Beechwood Park, to the east of Newport; here he may have used ideas which he was to repeat at Belle Vue. Recently restored, Beechwood House was built in the late 1870s for a tobacco manufacturer, George Fothergill; Mawson worked for several men in this industry. Mawson won the 1891 commission – his thirteenth and only successful competition entry since winning Hanley – with a design called 'Seabreeze'. The steeply sloping, open and exposed hillside called for considerable skill in arranging the landscape, which lent itself more to grass and trees than tennis courts and bowling greens. A stream wound down through a valley, and though the parks committee thought this should play host to a lake, Mawson disagreed, unwilling to fell a group of old elms in order to fill the valley with water.

In its stead Pulham & Son planned a rocky cascade with a bridge. The park's heart lay in an architectural triangle of buildings, all of which were examples of good craftsmanship. The peak of the triangle was formed by a steep-roofed pavilion of Gothic proportions, made of rose and grey Hereford sandstone with terracotta dressings, which sat on a balustraded terrace above arched walls. Next to it were conservatories whose gabled roof and patterned white wood detailing made a contrasting companion to the pavilion. They were intended for the chrysanthemum exhibitions and flower shows which were currently popular, and with the pavilion provided somewhere to shelter from the rain. The steepness of the site required two terraces and steps down, with banks of turf dropping to the main, gravelled terrace on which stood the bandstand; this and the conservatories were built by Richardson & Sons of Darlington. Flower borders edged the terraces on which a large number of people could be seated to hear the band and enjoy views south to the Bristol Channel. On the east side were the nurseries to stock the park.[10]

At the time of its opening in September 1894 Belle Vue remained open, windy and exposed, and Mawson

Belle Vue Park, Newport Mon. 7961

ABOVE Belle Vue Park in Newport, from an early postcard. The steeply sloping, open and exposed hillside called for considerable skill in arranging the landscape, which lent itself more to grass and trees than tennis courts and bowling greens.

RIGHT A bridge over the stream in Belle Vue Park, restored to its former style in 2006.

ABOVE The lacy metalwork of West Park's beautiful conservatory, Wolverhampton, designed by Dan Gibson in 1911 and restored in 2007.

LEFT Inside the restored conservatory at West Park.

provided shelter by planting trees around the triangular site, and along the winding outer paths. Some were supplied by Shaw of Abergavenny, but some may have come from Mawson's own nursery in Windermere. He massed them in groups, focusing attention on good specimens at the junctions of his walks, and made a small avenue at the northeast corner beyond the fountain. Rhododendrons had been supplied, but flowers were not mentioned. They needed labour, and the park (at £19,500) had been costly to make because of its difficult site; maintenance on Belle Vue was going to cost the taxpayer an extra rate of 2d. There were no facilities for sport, and local people appealed for bowling rinks in 1904 and tennis courts in 1907. In this way Belle Vue began to move from being a place to promenade and take the air, just as space for sport was beginning to take a more prominent role in park design generally. Recently Belle Vue was restored and opened two years after its hundredth anniversary on 8 September 2006.

Mawson was commissioned for two Wolverhampton public parks: East Park – where his plan was partly utilised from 1896, and where Dan Gibson built the entrances and lodges – and West Park, commissioned in 1911, whose conservatory, recently restored, was designed by Dan Gibson and built by Richardson & Sons of Darlington, reputedly from the proceeds of the town's Floral Fêtes.

In 1902 Mawson went to Southgate, in north London, where the urban district council had bought a house and 54 acres of its grounds for development as a public park which opened in 1903. Broomfield's

sixteenth-century timber-framed house was owned by successive city merchants. The estate was let to tenants by the Powys family in the nineteenth century and the last tenant, barrister Ralph Littler, moved out in 1901. The local authority then asked Mawson, no doubt intrigued by the existence of a baroque water garden, to come and landscape the grounds. The house, which was to be badly damaged by fire in 1984, stood close to the second of three fish ponds and facing a double elm avenue. The Long Walk, a walled promenade now edged with flower beds, lay horizontally across the avenue, and was preserved by Mawson, with the ponds and avenue. He planned sports facilities – cricket and hockey grounds, tennis lawns, bowling greens, space for archery, and a gymnasium and separate swimming baths for men and women near the house. But he gave pride of place to the elm avenue at the front, and added two more lime avenues as wings on the diagonal from the Long Walk. An avenue of chestnuts led from the entrance on Alderman's Hill. The three fish ponds were left intact, but a fourth, close to the boundary with Alderman's Hill, was to be a model yacht pond.

The shape of Broomfield Park remains clearly today, though the Elm Avenue with its diseased trees was removed in 1978 and their place has been taken by silver limes. Young trees have replaced the chestnut avenue. The spaces for swimming baths are now occupied by offices and few of the suggested sports on Mawson's plan take place. Broomfield Park remains a well used public space, with its reflecting ponds and its walks

RIGHT Formal planting at West Park, 1910.

LEFT The caretaker's lodge at East Park, Wolverhampton, built by Dan Gibson in the early 1890s for £500, with entrance gates and piers for £420.

BELOW A plan of Broomfield Park, Southgate, which opened in 1903. *Civic Art*, fig. 168.

ABOVE RIGHT The bandstand in East Park, Wolverhampton.

BELOW RIGHT Mawson's map of Pittencrief Park and the Bridge Street extension (top left) which lost him the commission.

under mature trees. More work was done by Mawson in Southgate at Grovelands in 1912, in parkland shaped by Humphry Repton adjoining a John Nash house. The landscape of lakes and surrounding woodland needed little intervention. But the local authority in Enfield needs to rescue Broomfield House. Damaged by fire over twenty years ago, it remains forlorn and unrestored.

So far Mawson's park making had been an expansion of his ability to landscape large estates, in which all of his garden-making skills could be used. Such work could be transferred, after Mawson had made the design, to his team of trained landscape gardeners, James Pulham & Son and local unemployed labour. But in 1903 Mawson found himself unexpectedly at the junction between park making and town planning, as he was asked, with Patrick Geddes, by the Carnegie Trust to prepare a plan for a competition between the two men for the making of a park at Pittencrieff, Dunfermline.

Dunfermline's handloom weavers had been replaced by the power looms of the textile factories, and smoking chimneys and cramped, poor housing created similar problems to those of the larger industrial towns. Andrew Carnegie had been able to buy land which had been taken from the Dunfermline commons during his childhood by the Hunt family, and from which Carnegie's family had been banned. This had effectively removed some of the space which would have given green parkland to the city. The Hunt family had run into debt; Carnegie reclaimed the space for the town: 'This Pittencrieff ownership is the sweetest event in my life in the way of material satisfaction,' he wrote to prime minister Henry Campbell-Bannerman. To his great friend, cabinet minister John Morley, he announced, 'I'm going to make

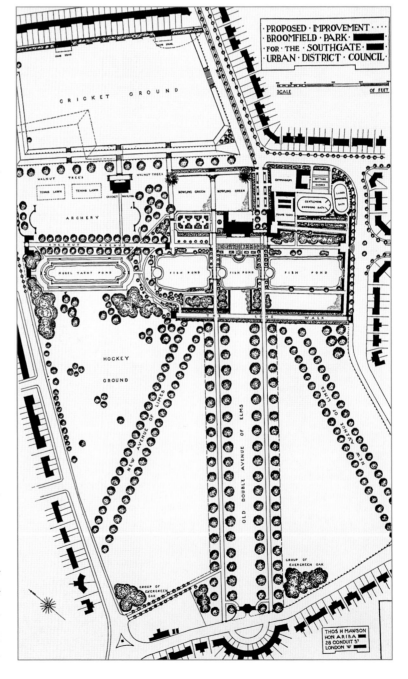

it a public park and present to Dunfermline.'[11] Carnegie wrote to the trustees, chaired by solicitor Dr Ross, that he wanted:

> to bring into the monotonous lives of the toiling masses of Dunfermline more of sweetness and light; to give to them – especially the young – some charm, some happiness, some elevating conditions of life…and the fortunate acquisition of Pittencrieff, with its lovely Glen, furnishes your work by making it a recreation park for the people…'[12]

The two men chosen for the preparation of competitive plans were utterly different. They were given a free hand to do what they saw best with the glen and its surroundings. Patrick Geddes (1854–1932) was a natural scientist and an evolutionist who wanted to apply his ideas to society; Pittencrieff Park was to be his entry into planning. Geddes was an assistant to the professor of botany and a part-time lecturer in natural sciences in the School of Medicine at the university in Edinburgh, where he lived. In 1889 he claimed his chair in botany at Dundee College, then affiliated to St Andrews, and for much of the next thirty years involved himself in town planning. Seemingly academics had neither the patience nor the inclination to study his complicated thoughts on the stages of human evolution, as Geddes himself found it difficult to express what he was trying, throughout his life, to apply. He believed that industrialisation and urbanisation had affected the evolutionary pattern of mankind, and this needed to be understood before town plans – or any part of a town plan such as a park – could be made. In order to understand, it was necessary to comprehend the history of the place and the relationships of all its parts.

Geddes set out to write his plan by asking over 200 people to give him advice, including such well-known names as Frederick Law Olmsted, Canon Barnett and Beatrice Webb. The report which emerged took him eight months to write instead of the three he was allowed, and spread itself over 232 pages. It explored each part of the space available, examining the history and geography and the social relationships with the buildings around it. His final plan dealt with the linkages which could be sought and introduced to what was already in place; for instance, reworking old stables by putting in an orangery and refreshment room, terracing and planting a gloomy slope by a church, and larger schemes such as the reworking of Bridge Street with an arena, music hall, improved tenement blocks and a new city plaza called Carnegie Place. There were lakes, a zoo, small lawns for games and places for tennis and bowls, rock gardens, bog gardens, a crafts village and many other delights; and yet apart from its many sensible and useful propositions and its sound concept of linkage, Geddes' drawn plan looked to be the work of an amateur, with inadequate space between the many activities, poor draughtsmanship and no concept of style.[13]

Mawson's report had also been the result of months of work in Scotland assessing the needs and possibilities for the making of the park in the glen, and its connections with the development of the city of Dunfermline. It was drawn by a draughtsman with knowledge of the land's shape and slope, gave adequate space to both landscaping and activities, and looked the work of a professional. The southern half of the design was strongly axial, with a double avenue leading to a round fountain garden contained by clipped hedges, from which straight paths radiated. From here Robert Atkinson had drawn an enticing vista towards the Scottish baronial Pittencrieff House, with topiary lining the path which was visible through a wrought-iron gate. Mawson wrote approvingly of the house, and took trouble over designing its gardens; Atkinson's illustration was placed as the frontispiece to Mawson's report.

To the north, around Bridge Street next to the town, Mawson placed a range of cultural assets – an art gallery, large and small concert halls, a museum, and a lecture hall. Finally in the north appeared a dominating new feature which would join the park to the town, a western extension of Bridge Street across Pittencrieff Park to allow the expansion of the residential area. Mawson saw the benefit of the town's cultural development, and with a characteristic flourish of salesmanship emphasised to the trust that Dunfermline had great possibilities for art industries, and teaching 'akin to the Boston School of Technology', and these would help to attract a more affluent population. Mawson felt that his report had 'surpassed anything I had previously done'.[14]

But what did the trustees think of these contrasting plans? Letters to the candidates from the secretary to the trust, J.Howard Whitehead, and trustee Henry Beveridge, were lacking in enthusiasm. Whitehead told Geddes that his report was 'too long and of such magnitude…proposals to use the stables as a refreshment room did not meet with approval'.[15] Beveridge wrote to Geddes: 'It must not come to the public…that he [Mawson] has sent in a plan for driving new streets right through the town and destroying nearly half the buildings including

the new baths…[and] Dr Ross's house! He has no shadow of justification to do this.'

But Beveridge went on: 'Dr Ross is very serious about the stables proposal. He considers it quite absurd…I am afraid your recommendations might not be acceptable or at any rate not sufficient.' Beveridge continued in this confidential tone, telling Geddes of his approval of the formal parts of Mawson's plan.

He has some good ideas in the most elaborate parts. He thinks the only suitable garden for a town with its straight streets such as he makes for us is one which reproduces the same character… The Glen is abruptly naturalistic. The old garden [Pittencrief House] is the site of the best part of the whole design I think – hedges clipped yews a square water basin, herbaceous flowers, walls, steps etc. Two nice perspectives of these.[16]

ABOVE Robert Atkinson's drawing of Pittencrieff House, 1909. *Civic Art*, fig. 252.

But by May 1904 it was clear that neither candidate had won the commission. Following a visit from Carnegie a meeting of the parks committee conveyed the message on 21 May that 'Carnegie has expressed a very decided opinion that the Park should be left as much as possible in its present entirety'. And on 23 June this was confirmed by Whitehouse.

According to Mawson, it was the bridge extension which sank his plan. 'The Chairman of the Trust told me that if I would reconsider my scheme and remodel it so as to eliminate the extension of Bridge Street across

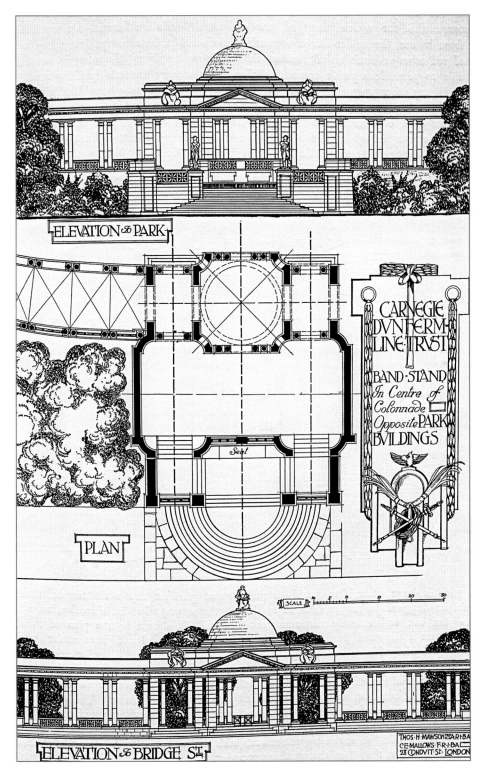

BELOW Mawson's plans for park buildings in Pittencrieff Glen. *Civic Art*, fig. 181.

Pittencrieff, he would propose my retention as landscape expert to the Trust.' Hardly surprising, since it would demolish his house. Mawson refused, seeing his proposal as 'so obvious, so practical, and so essentially logical' that he could not delete it – and lost the commission. Had nobody told Mawson of Dr Ross' house?

But neither did Geddes win the competition, and both men found that their expenses on researching and producing their reports were considerably underpaid. Mawson vented his spleen in a series of letters to Geddes, the two men comparing their financial ill-treatment, Whitehouse's support for them, Ross' opposition and Mawson's threatened legal action against the trust. The competition revealed Mawson as a man prepared to superimpose his views on the general good, and Geddes as researching the general good in such a detailed manner that he was unable to make a simplified version for the trust to read. Pittencrief Park was eventually laid out by a gardener from the Glasgow Botanic Gardens, James Whitton.[17]

There were, however, unexpected results. As described in previous chapters, Andrew Carnegie immediately asked Mawson to work on the gardens at Skibo Castle (see pp. 59–62), and his published report on Pittencrieff won him a new adventure designing parks and settlements across Canada. Mawson's developing interest in town planning and his strong colonialist sympathies led to conversations with Geddes about the possibilities of working with him:

Many thanks for your letter to hand and the suggestion which it offers, that at some future time co-operation between us may be possible. I think your suggestion of working with a number of colleagues, each with an expert knowledge of some important branch of city planning is not only wise, but most important if the best result is to be attained, and it will give me the greatest pleasure if the opportunity occurs of working out with you park and garden schemes for other cities in which you are interested, either in this country or in India.[18]

Though no further cooperative ventures between Mawson and Geddes were to follow, it is astonishing to see that on the bottom of the Canadian Report on Regina, Mawson lists the offices of T.H.Mawson & Sons, City Planners, as London, Lancaster and Calcutta.

Six years were to elapse before Mawson began to work in North America, and in this time more parks were made, mainly in the north of England. But a design for a park in Berlin in the archive dated 1901 suggests that Mawson was beginning to make contacts in Europe.[19]

In 1905 and 1906 Mawson was employed on contrasting commissions for Cleethorpes on Humberside and Rochdale in Greater Manchester. In Cleethorpes, south of Grimsby, a 12-acre site donated by the Wardens of Sidney Sussex College, Cambridge, was entirely devoted to sports. This was not what Mawson wanted to design, but health and sport were to be linked irrevocably together, especially by the Public Health Amendment Act of 1907, which gave local authorities the power to set land aside for sport and charge for the use of facilities such as bowling greens and tennis courts. In Rochdale, the Mount Falinge estate with its mansion had been saved from development in 1902, and 18 acres donated to the town by Alderman Samuel Turner to commemorate the coronation of Edward VII. Mawson was asked to design a highly formal Sun Garden.[20]

The making of Haslam Park in Preston was to struggle over the beginning of the First World War. The pastureland site was given to the borough in 1910 by Mary Haslam, who wanted it transformed into a public park in memory of her father, John Haslam, a cotton mill owner in Preston. Commissioned in 1911, Mawson requested that a foreman trained by his firm should be in charge; he was in the midst of a period of travelling to and from North America. Mary Haslam's main concern was for the provision of facilities for children.

Mawson took this into account by planning children's playgrounds as well as other sporting facilities. The triangular park was bounded on the north by a loop of the Lancashire Canal, and on the south by the railway line to Blackpool. Cosmetic requirements included the planting of a double avenue of limes to shield the park from the railway line, and a pavilion was to be placed midway along the avenue. Mawson planned to utilise the meandering Savick Brook, with Pulham & Son's assistance, to make cascades and a boating lake. A carriage drive was to cross the park, the lake and the canal by a bridge, to join the northwestern boundary of Preston. The main entrance on the south would have a wrought-iron gate and a bandstand with a formal garden.

But a typewritten review of Haslam Park by Mawson, dated March 1915, suggests that only the bare outline had been made by then, that the councillors were unwilling to spend money on the park, and they required an amended scheme omitting the lake and the pavilion, and the bandstand and its formal surroundings. Mawson remarked on the 'poverty stricken appearance' of the park, and promised another plan. Surprisingly little attention was paid by Mawson to wartime, and the fact that money was short. Drawn up by the Lancaster office, the 'amended' plan for the future put back the bandstand and pavilion and introduced an open air swimming bath, adding 'open air bathing is such an essential part of the fresh air movement of the present day that such a feature is certain to be appreciated throughout the summer'.

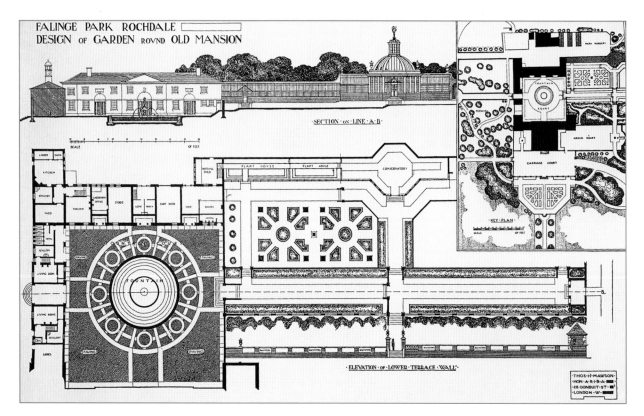

LEFT Falinge Park, Rochdale, where Mawson was asked to design a highly formal Sun Garden. *Civic Art,* fig. 184.

However this was not introduced until 1932, when money was donated, and neither bandstand nor pavilion was built, nor any other of the suggested extras such as a flagstaff, sundial, pergolas and statuary which would have provided a formal core. The boating lake and cascades were made and were filled by water from the Lancashire Canal, even though this required moving the boundary of the park northwards to take account of the spreading sheet of water.[21]

From 1905 Mawson had made several visits to North America, and had taken note of the way in which American towns were laid out. From the early part of the century he had built houses in Windermere as well as small estates, and had taken on larger enterprises such as the planning of a model village called Coryndon (Glyn Cory) near Cardiff, for John Cory, the owner of Dyffryn.[22] William Lever's association with Mawson from 1905 had given him work at Port Sunlight, where Lever had made a model village for his workforce. Mawson had made plans suggesting alterations to the layout, including a hospital site, public library, museum and central boulevard. It was becoming obvious that work on parks flowed easily into work planning settlements,

and that there was a new discipline called town planning (though nobody defined it) and it needed a centre for its instruction.[23]

In 1908 Lever won substantial damages from an action against some newspapers, which he gave to Liverpool University in part to found a new department for town planning. This opened in 1909 under Stanley Davenport Adshead (1868–1946) 'at a time of exuberance among town planners', who were delighted at the new Town Planning Act which had just been passed.[24] To prevent the further extension of slums, the Act permitted local authorities, with the consent of the Local Government Board, 'to prepare town-planning schemes, but only for land about to be developed'. The scheme had to be preceded by a survey of streets, buildings, public and private open spaces, objects of historical or natural interest, sewerage, drainage, lighting and water supplies, and gave local authorities powers to make by-laws to deal with these features. As parliamentary sources envisaged: 'The bill aims in broad outline at, and hopes to secure, the home healthy, the house beautiful, the town pleasant, the city dignified and the suburb salubrious'. However, there was still no definition

ABOVE The Lancashire Canal was used to make the lake in Haslam Park, and marks the northern boundary of the park.

RIGHT Coryndon (Glyn Cory), a garden village laid out by Mawson for John Cory near Cardiff, but never built. *Civic Art*, fig. 242.

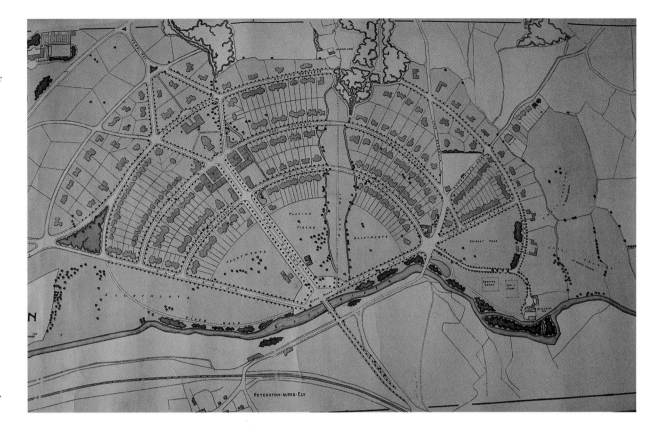

BELOW The Mawson plan for the model village for the workforce at Port Sunlight for Sir William Lever, with its large gardens and allotments for food growing. *Civic Art*, fig. 239.

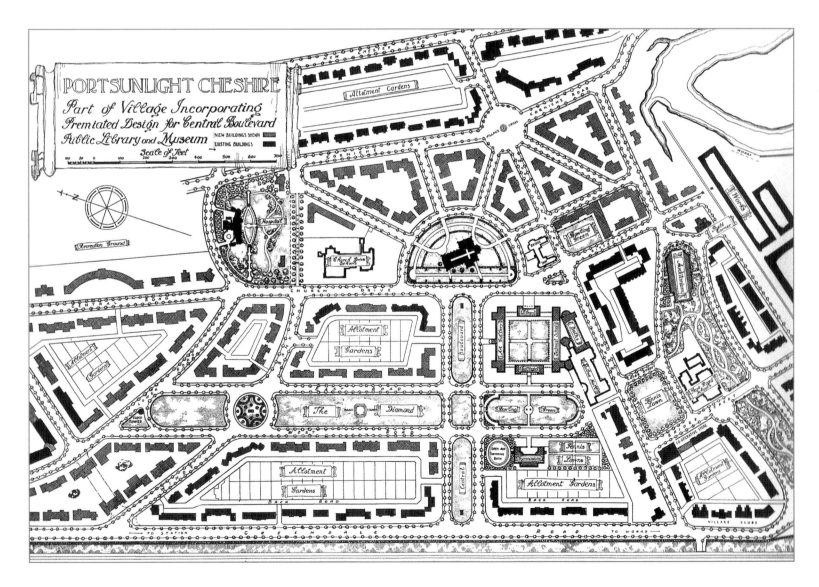

of 'Town Planning'.[25] But the preparation of new housing areas could provide work for landscape architects, hence the excitement in Liverpool University.

The exuberance was shared by Mawson, who was asked to lecture on the course. He claimed 'it added a new zest to my life' even though his busy timetable gave him space only to lecture on 'landscape design applied to park systems, boulevards, town gardens, and recreation grounds' amongst other relevant subjects.[26] Part of the School of Architecture, its teaching system based on the Ecole des Beaux-Arts pleased Mawson. As chapter four describes, Mawson had chosen the Parisian school for his son Edward (and later for James Radcliffe) because of its emphasis on the teaching of draughtsmanship and classical drawing. Adshead began the successful *Town Planning Review* with Patrick Abercrombie (1879–1957), which gave him his chair, and a department of civic design.[27] There were two options: a certificate course for two terms per year for two years or a diploma course for graduate students, but, as in architectural courses in other institutions of the time, there were never very many students. The largest number was five for the certificate course and three for the diploma. One of the students was Mawson's son John, who took the certificate and diploma in civic design in 1911 and 1912. Though at first he joined the family firm, managing the Canadian office and taking an important share of the work in Greece, he eventually went to New Zealand, where he became its second Director of Town Planning.

Mawson wrote articles for the *Town Planning Review* and between 1910 and 1924 lectured on the Landscape Design course on alternate Friday evenings on 'the arrangement, construction, and planting of parks, parkways, boulevards and open spaces with special reference to the kind of trees, shrubs, and plants best suited to particular localities…their cultures and the art of pleaching, pollarding and plashing' as well as 'the laying out of parks and gardens in connection with suburban and country residences'. His nephew, Robert Mattocks, took over from him in 1924 and introduced lectures on the historical development of gardens.[28]

Mawson attended the National Housing and Town Planning summer conference in Vienna in 1910, and travelled back through Dresden, Berlin and Hamburg; German settlements were in the minds of town planners at this time. Mawson searched for his own, pragmatic position among different schools of thought. He owed the greater part of his inspiration on the City Beautiful to Charles Mulford Robinson. There was the utopian Ebenezer Howard, whose policy on an ideal community was expressed from 1898 in his book *To-morrow; A Peaceful Path to Real Reform*, and was reprinted from 1902 as *Garden Cities of To-morrow*. The Garden City, part of a set of linked 'social' cities, was to be built on cheap agricultural land outside a metropolis, by investors who would benefit from the rising value of the land. The spacious, low density housing they built would be leased, and have sufficient garden space and allotments for the owner to grow food which would help to cut his living costs so that he could better afford the rent. Large boulevards around the city gave it dignity and echoed what Howard had seen in his recent visit to Chicago.

Then there was the architect Raymond Unwin, who had published his book *Town Planning in Practice: An Introduction to the Art of Designing Cities and Suburbs* in 1909. Unwin was strongly influenced by the history and appearance of European towns, especially German medieval settlements, and a book by the Viennese Camillo Sitte, *City Planning according to Artistic Principles*, published in 1889. Town planners spent most time considering the appearance and arrangement of buildings – it was the local authority's job to take care of the water supplies, sewerage and electricity.

Unwin's first chapter was called 'Of Civic Art as the Expression of Civic Life', but throughout the book he made no reference to parks, and few to open green spaces. Architect and garden maker Harry Inigo Triggs' (1876–1923) work for the RIBA's Godwin Bursary in 1906 had shown his interest in town planning, recording the practical and aesthetic aspects of parks, squares and open spaces in Paris, Berlin, Vienna and Munich with photographs, neat drawings and thoughtful analysis. Published in 1909 with American additions in *Town Planning, Past, Present and Possible*, Triggs referred to the cavalier fashion of the removal of trees, grass and shrubs by speculative builders in the suburbs. Future dictionaries, he suggested, might redefine 'park' as 'a district closely covered with houses but without either grass or trees'; 'grove' as 'a street of shops with plenty of flaring gas-lights'; 'garden' as 'a collection of houses without a scrap of ground attached to them', and an 'avenue' as 'two rows of houses opposite each other with lamp-posts planted at intervals'. In 1911 Mawson published *Civic Art*, which he claimed in the preface to be 'my contribution to the literature of civic art, which may be described as the aesthetics of town planning, the department which I seek to emphasise' and dedicated it to the Labour politician John Burns, who was also the President of the Local Government Board.[29]

Many of the principles on which Mawson was to base a sheaf of town plans related to one rule that echoed

William Morris: everything planned in a city should be beautiful as well as useful. Of the important factors governing planning:

> The foremost of these are the centralization and convenient grouping of the town's municipal or commercial activities, its development and expansion on a convenient traffic and economic basis, the attainment of perfect hygienic conditions and a beautiful collective presentment, the simplification of its plan and restraint in its adornments, and the power to retain and enhance its individuality.[30]

Centralisation ensured that all public buildings – library, museum, school and workplaces – would be reached quickly. Street perspectives and architectural façades needed to be part of a whole, and monuments, fountains and statuary in town squares and open spaces should be appropriately placed. Vistas along roads should end with dignified public buildings. Though Mawson did not use the term 'street picture', that is what he meant. Traffic around towns could move faster if gyratory systems were used, with vehicles moving along circular routes, and using roads with widths adjusted to needs: pictures of vehicles moving along different sized roads appeared in all the manuals. A system or chain of parks, gardens, open and tree-planted spaces connected by boulevards or parkways should extend into the country-side. The new Town Planning Act would ensure that 'dirtless and dustless' factories would be surrounded by enough space to build good housing for its workers, as Port Sunlight and Bournville had demonstrated. Mawson later believed in zoning different uses, so that all industrial activity would be together, and away from housing, which was itself zoned into high, middle and artisan class residential.

Many of these ideas had been shared by other town planners; Unwin's book, for instance, discusses the French gyratory traffic systems and the German use of different road widths, and Howard wanted to separate manufacturing from other functions in his garden cities. But from 1910, Mawson was thinking along garden city lines concerning the improvement of Bolton, the early home of William Lever, where he had been commissioned to prepare plans for the town.

BELOW Robert Atkinson's drawing of an arcaded boulevard joining town and countryside. *Bolton*, slide 16.

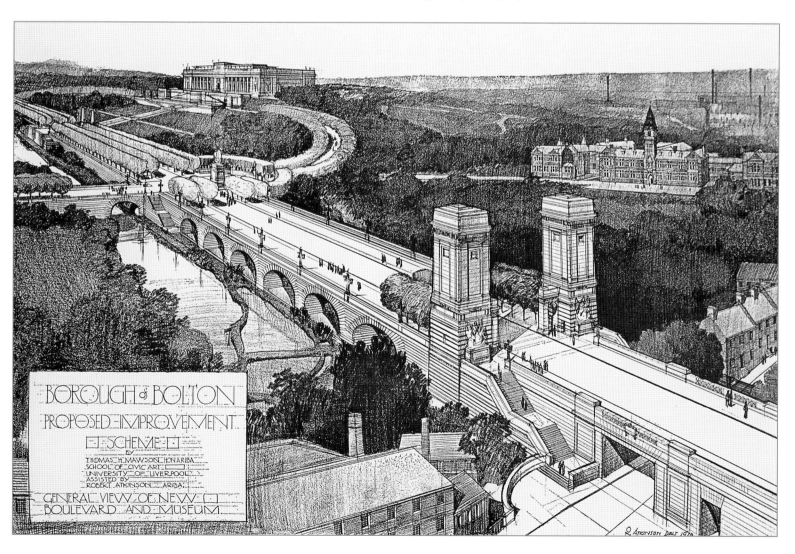

He 'tramped around' Bolton taking slides of 'the paramount evil' – back-to-back houses – for his report; it echoed the earlier writing of Elizabeth Gaskell. Here children played in doorless privies where the contents were strewn around outside; there were courts with no through ventilation not enough space to hang washing. He saw small efforts of self-respect, where one house in a row of back-to-backs had been pulled down to give light and air to the others, and another removal of a hovel where the space had been made into a garden. Mawson was appalled by the awful trap into which these people had fallen; but pulling down the slums – such a power was in local authority hands by 1890 – only added to overcrowding in the houses that were left, as there was no complementary directive to rehouse those whose homes had been demolished. New settlements were needed: Howard's Garden City had given rise to many smaller versions of the ideal – cottage-type homes built singly in garden villages and suburbs placed on greenfield sites. In order for the poor to be able to afford new homes in cleared or new areas Mawson urged the creation of cooperative building societies where the company owned the houses and sold shares to the buyers.[31]

Having visited Letchworth, Howard's first Garden City in 1905 (the only other was to be Welwyn Garden City), Mawson promoted the garden suburb, though it should not try to copy the city's spacious provision of land. The suburb's houses should be grouped in twos and threes or on short roads, and should be arranged around a green, or round a triangular space with gardens and allotments in the centre, not packed into a grid around a factory. The school site, as in America, should also be a civic centre with a library and a working men's institute. Recreational facilities such as tennis, croquet and bowls should be near the centre – as they were in Port Sunlight. Only then should houses be built, by the efforts of private enterprise and private philanthropy. Though the Town Planning Act of 1909 had given local authorities the right to prepare schemes for the development of housing, they were only for new areas; hence Mawson's gloomy but realistic assessment of Bolton's slums.

Ideally towns should have a mixture of two park systems: a radial plan of green fingers moving into the city from the countryside, allowing fresh air to blow in; but as there were factories in the way of continuous lines of green, Mawson added the Viennese concept of the Ringstrasse or ring road, which joined parks like a necklace on the outer edge. The town centre would have small gardens and squares; and as Parker and Unwin suggested in their plans for New Earswick in Yorkshire, there would be children's playgrounds within ten minutes' walk of every child's house, and no child would have to cross a main road. He continued to press for these features in his lectures to Liverpool University.

The boundaries of Bolton lent themselves to Mawson's imagination and his need to make a grand gesture to aid the town's civic pride. Once again he used Robert Atkinson's drawing skills to illustrate a great arcaded boulevard joining town and countryside, from which access could be made to a new museum on a hill overlooking the town and which diminished the scale of the factories in the distance. Certainly this lent itself to the City Beautiful school of thinking: but was it appropriate, or affordable?

All this advice for the future was given to the worthies of the Bolton Housing and Town Planning Society in 1916 in a series of lectures, the essence of reports made by Mawson and Sons to Bolton's town council from 1910 onwards, for which Mawson was paid £563 11s. The fear of Lloyd George's Incremental Value Duty and Undeveloped Land Duty in his budget of 1909, which set out to remove the unearned rise in the value of land from its owner, and later, the onset of war, held up implementation of this and many other town plans.

The town plan for Exeter was essentially an advisory document, published in 1913 as *Exeter of the Future, a policy of town improvement within a period of 100 years,* and shows how much American planning had made its mark on Mawson's imagination. If the town wanted to attract tourists, it was 'first impressions which count', and Exeter should consider building an impressive station front, 'a grand portal entrance to your city' as they had in Grand Central Station, New York. If they widened the railway bridge in Queen Street Station (now Exeter St David's) by three times, they could put the ticket office over the station, and make way for a wider concourse for vehicles to drop and collect passengers.

A civic centre was needed, with prominent buildings such as the guildhall, the town hall, a library, possibly an art gallery or a museum and an educational centre to reinforce the dignity of the core of the city, and vistas through to the cathedral and the guildhall should be kept clear. It was important to blend the many architectural styles of the past and build in a classical style so the shopping streets would avoid 'crude and bizarre business premises'. There was a short reference to Northernhay Gardens, which Mawson had written about before in *Civic Art,* but he did suggest the town should buy the grounds of Streatham Hall (now part of the University of Exeter) which would give an extra public park for the town, complete with terracing, planting,

pavilions, lodges and glasshouses. And it might help to attract American tourists!

The First World War brought heartbreak for the Mawson family. Their third son, James Radcliffe Mawson (Cliffe), a private in the 5th King's Own Royal Lancaster Regiment, died of wounds at Poperinge, to the west of Ypres in Belgium, on 23 April 1915. His cheerful letters home had told jokes about selling local young fir trees to his father's firm, and shown his admiration for the men with whom he would fight. To his mother he wrote: 'Whatever you and father can do for our wounded, I am sure you will do – nothing is too good for these brave fellows.'[32] James would have finished his studies at the Ecole des Beaux-Arts, and then joined Mawson & Sons as a horticultural expert. James' sister Dorothy also lost her sweetheart in the last months of the war, after nursing him back to health from injuries sustained earlier on.

After the immediate grief had subsided, Mawson set his mind and all his energy to honouring his son's wishes that something should be done for the wounded. The answer lay in the provision of industrial villages for disabled soldiers, not only to occupy them but to provide a future when the war was over. Attempting to gain government support, he lobbied Ministry of Pensions officials in December 1915 with a report and prospectus and urged that the work in such villages should be based on craft, such as woodwork, children's book illustration, or toy making. Other villages could be horticulturally based, growing trees, making baskets from osiers, and raising bulbs. This fell on deaf ears, and to silence him, Mawson was accused of 'segregating' wounded men from sound men.

He then set out his policy in greater detail in a book, adding illustrations and plans, and published it privately in February 1917 as *An Imperial Obligation: Industrial Villages for Partially Disabled Service Men.* He circulated it to the royal family, members of parliament, and leading names in the fields of culture, industry and the church, and foreign ambassadors in London. The book was well received and encouragement and some finance offered; a second edition was made, with a foreword from Field Marshal Sir Douglas Haig. Rent-free offices were provided by Gordon Selfridge in Orchard Street and they were furnished by Samuel Waring free of cost. Since there were so many wounded, and housing was an important part of domestic policy, Mawson suggested that a village could be peopled by men and their families and their occupations directed to crafts related to the building industry – plaster making, ornamental glazing, items for plumbers. The press took up the story, and a general committee was appointed to oversee village planning. But no ministerial support was forthcoming.[33]

Herbert Storey, a Lancastrian philanthropist whose family supported the foundation of Lancaster University, now wholeheartedly backed Mawson, donating the house of his father, 'the late Sir Thomas Storey, with 15 acres of excellent building land on which to erect cottages and workshops' on the understanding that they should be for disabled men of the 5th King's Own Regiment and for Lancastrian men. Storey's garden on the Bailrigg estate (later university land) had been redesigned by

Mawson in 1907, and both men had sons in the King's Own Regiment. A village was soon being built at Westfield, just outside Lancaster. Mawson and Storey, together with James Crossland, went searching for other sites for villages.[34]

The need for afforestation created another opportunity, this time for tree nurseries to be run as a form of therapy for men with shell shock, and those with tuberculosis. Money for land at Meathrop, near Grange-over-Sands, was donated by Lord Leverhulme; the Ministry of Agriculture agreed that this would raise good trees, but

LEFT The memorial to the fallen in the First World War, made by Jennifer Delahunt, in the centre of Westfield Village.

ABOVE Houses set back with green verges and trees in Westfield Village.

RIGHT Roads take the names of prominent soldiers, such as Field Marshal Sir Douglas Haig. Houses take the names of battles; 'St Julien' reminds the onlooker of the conflict in April 1915 near Passchendaele, where many Canadian as well as British soldiers died from gas poisoning.

once again the project was terminated by the beginning of Lloyd George's economy campaign. He had never offered any support for Mawson's projects, which were almost brought to a halt by the Ministry of Pensions' own drive to raise money for training centres for the disabled, which, as Mawson saw it, were short term only.[35]

But a final push from a group of men including Samuel Waring and Herbert Storey, and backed by Mawson though he had little to do with the project, raised enough money to buy Preston Hall, a mansion in 100 acres of parkland and gardens near Maidstone in Kent, which opened with sixty tubercular patients in 1920.

Westfield War Memorial Village, in Lancaster, was built and run on a smaller scale. At a public meeting in 1918 Mawson described the proposed village as a 'utilitarian kind of memorial [similar to] garden cities'.[36] It was opened officially in 1924 by Field Marshal Earl Haig, when there were thirty-five homes including eight bungalows, semi-detached and terraced houses for disabled ex-servicemen and their families. These grey stone cottages were named after battles, and were set back from the road by grass insets planted with trees. There was a strong concept of community in the layout planned by Mawson, which included wrought-iron gates through which the village was entered, open frontages to the cottages, and a large bowling green halfway down Storey Avenue, the central road. Allotments were planned for Haig and Storey Avenues. Mawson's church and a bandstand were never built. The war memorial in the village centre, a bronze configuration of two soldiers, one giving aid to his comrade, was made by Jennifer Delahunt; the council, in one of its sour moods, minuted that it would have preferred a sundial.[37]

Towards the end of the war Mawson was drawn into a town planning scheme by the mayor of Stepney, J.W.Kiley. 'Homes fit for heroes' had become a slogan of the wartime coalition government of Lloyd George for housing returning soldiers, and Stepney had urgent need for regeneration before its heroes returned to the parishes of Shadwell, Ratcliff, St George in the East and Wapping: here were squalid houses and high rates of tuberculosis, high infant mortality, and slum dwellers with both low physical and mental health. Why had these houses not been demolished and rebuilt?

Mawson believed it was because the London and Southend Railway Company owned the land, and the railway had been constructed on an embankment – 'a solid rampart' – across the centre of Stepney to its terminus at Fenchurch Street, blighting the area. In a brave move, he planned either to move the terminus, or to put the railway underground. The embankment would then feature as a new boulevard to be called Stepney Greeting, an American term for a wide public road, which would help to ease the flow of traffic. The slums would be demolished, and because there was no vacant surrounding land on which to put housing, he planned to build four-storey flats with garden and playground space around them. The high boulevard,

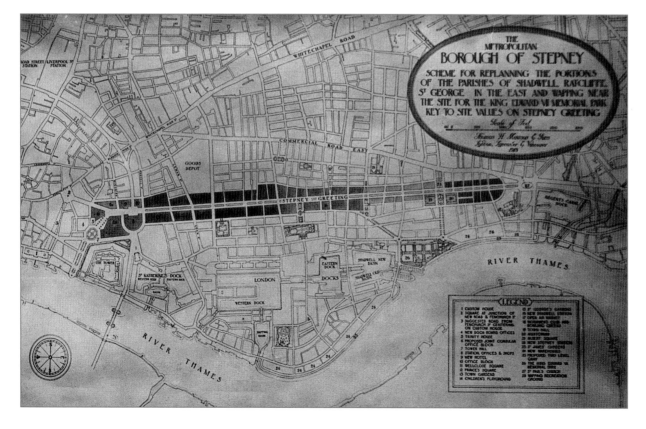

LEFT Stepney Greeting, a train embankment which Mawson wanted to turn into a boulevard by putting the London and Southend Railway underground.

RIGHT South of the
proposed Stepney Greeting,
Shadwell Park was planned
by Mawson as a green oasis
for slum dwellers. It was on
the site of the King Edward
Memorial Park overlooking
the Thames. The L.C.C.
who took charge of the park
in 1915 refused to accept
Mawson's plan and his
cooperation in the scheme.

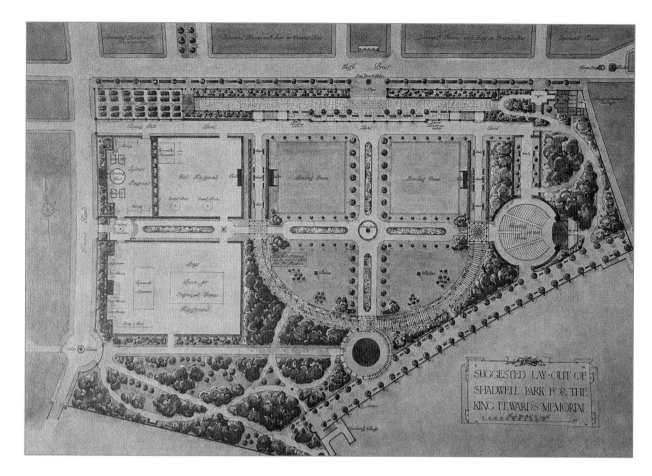

Mawson argued, would attract high commercial build-ings, especially as Stepney was so near central London and the docks. He planned a war memorial in the shape of a campanile high enough to be seen by shipping, and next to it would be a civic centre with a town hall and law courts. The river front would be opened up by setting back the warehouses. This was an extraordinarily forward-looking plan, and a very early example of high-rise planning for slum dwellers.

Mawson offered his plan in an advisory capacity, but it was considered 'too idealistic' by some critics. There were considerable obstacles in the competing plans to widen Cable Street, which ran alongside the railway, and the L.C.C. was unlikely to do battle with the railway

RIGHT Gordon Farrow's
depiction of the South
Shore improvement plan,
Lancashire, with its
promenade and gardens.

company. Mawson's homes were not to be built according to his heroic principles.[38]

After the First World War the Housing and Town Planning Act of 1919 made it obligatory for all towns with populations over 20,000 to submit town planning schemes and it recognised that there was a need for state subsidies for housing. The Tudor Walters Committee's report of 1918 laid down standards for working-class housing, and the density at which these houses were to be built. These factors together encouraged the construction of council estates, often referred to as 'cottage estates', as they attempted to borrow the perceived comfortable appearance of established village housing. These were usually built on the edges of towns, and developed beside private suburbs. Mawson & Sons were to be involved in just under twenty town plans before Thomas Mawson died.[39]

After the war the country began to look to its ability to attract visitors back to the seaside resorts. A Lancashire businessman reckoned that 'if it wasn't for Blackpool there'd be revolution in Lancashire', waving his hand in the direction of the smoke-filled mill towns. 'Men stick it as long as they can', he said to Mawson, 'and once a year they must either burst or go to Blackpool'.[40] From its beginnings as an upper to middle-class spa in the nineteenth century the town had expanded rapidly after the railway's arrival in 1846 and legislation gave mill workers paid holidays. An electric tram system, the first in the world, opened in 1885. There was talk of the population rising to one million from its figure in 1901 of 47,000; by the turn of the century Blackpool had three million visitors a year. The public wanted all the attractions expected of the seaside – Blackpool Promenade had opened in 1870, to be later extended; there were three

ABOVE RIGHT Stanley Park's Art Deco café, which evolved from Mawson's plan for a social centre, 2007.

BELOW RIGHT The revived Italian garden at Stanley Park, 2007.

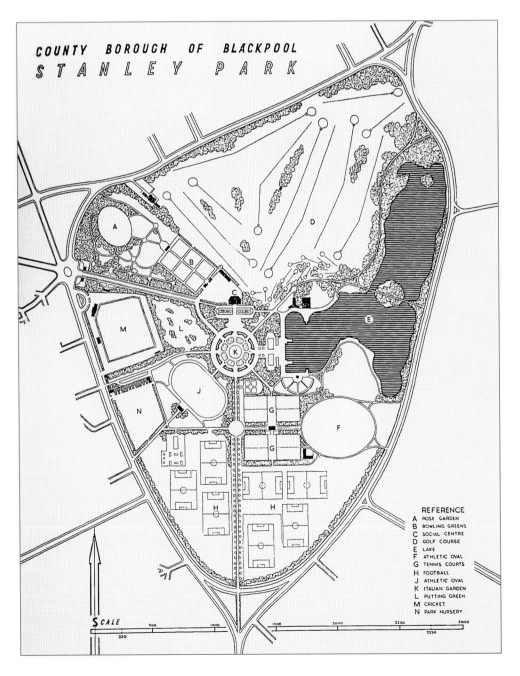

LEFT The plan for Stanley Park, made by Edward Prentice Mawson.

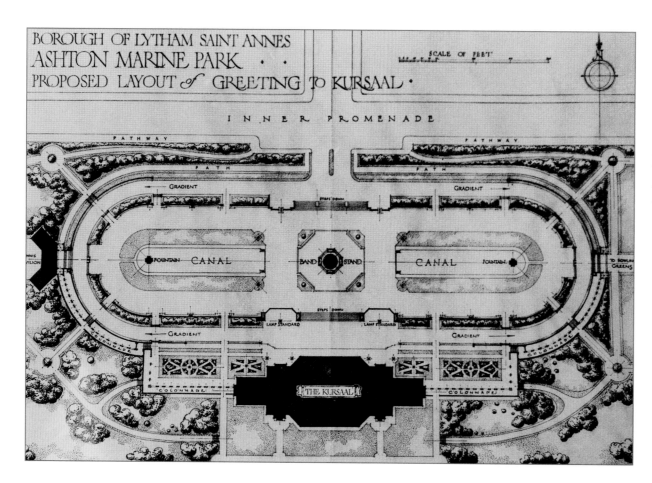

LEFT Ashton Marine Park's plan was made by Edward Prentice Mawson. To lend dignity to the site, he proposed a framework of formal flower beds in front of the kursaal, which looked across an ornamental canal. Winding walks led round the perimeter, much as they would have done in a garden.

piers by 1893, North Shore pier was a paying pier, and therefore staked its place in the more 'respectable' end of the town. Blackpool Tower, modelled on the Eiffel Tower, opened in 1894; there was a demand for parks, marine enterprises, pleasure grounds and children's playgrounds. The Winter Gardens, the Alhambra, the Grand Theatre and the Pleasure Beach, given electricity in 1906, the largest and most modern funfair park in Britain for which Blackpool came to be defined, 'responded dramatically to the surging demand for novelty and spectacle among the industrial working (and lower middle) classes of (mainly) northern England'.[41]

After the war, Mawson was approached by the town council with a view to his firm working on a very large site. Just under 280 acres had been bought by the council for use as a public park in 1922, and Mawson & Sons (Thomas, Edward and John) were to lay this out, but Mawson also looked for the possibilities for house building in the fast growing town. Park making in the northwest coastal towns was not a new venture for him. From 1906 Mawson and Charles Mallows had made designs for the Town Gardens, Lord Street, in upmarket Southport, across the Ribble to the south of Blackpool. Here Mawson had seen the need to combine the physically parallel attractions of Lord Street, the promenade and the Marine Park into a 'stately composition'. Robert Atkinson provided a drawing which gave the feeling of dignity and *gravitas* to the entrance to the Winter Garden, with its central domed pavilion and colonnaded wing walls. A campanile was suggested as an appropriate building to raise the eye above an architecturally uninteresting skyline. Mawson saw the whole as 'a scheme for the remodelling of Southport's famous street and the provision of a chain of parks and town gardens', and here, the formality of the geometric flower beds along the seafront as drawn by Edward Prentice Mawson, did not seem out of place.[42]

Mallows died in 1915, and Robert Atkinson, who had worked for Mallows as a perspective draughtsman, had set up his own practice in London. By 1913 he was Head Master of the Architectural Association School, and helped to move it from Tufton Street to Bedford Square. Later, as Principal of the AA, he lifted the syllabus from the past to the avant-garde position it has held ever since; too late, however, for the younger Edward Prentice Mawson. Postwar, therefore, the family had to provide all the skills needed by the firm.

A cluster of plans was made for gardens along Blackpool's Promenade in 1922 and for South Shore, to the south of Blackpool, at about the same time. In 1926 another batch of drawings introduced a new Marine Park at Lytham St Annes; this seemed to have moved slowly until 1937, after Thomas Mawson's death.[43]

Somehow during this period, Mawson needed to step back from his role as leader of the firm. While in Greece he had suffered a 'seizure', probably a slight heart attack, an affliction common to the men in his family. He found it difficult to take six months' rest, and though he would not admit it, he needed to do less. From 1908 the firm had absorbed another of its family members – the landscape architect Robert Mattocks. Robert was Thomas' nephew, and son of Richard Mattocks, who had married Thomas' sister Sarah. There was sufficient well-trained staffing for the firm to work without Mawson. So though the agreement signed by Thomas Mawson and John Dyer, his secretary, on 2 September 1924 was for Thomas Mawson & Sons of Lancaster to lay out and maintain the park at Blackpool, it was Edward Prentice who was the Architect for the Park, and his father was the Consulting Architect. As with garden commissions, the father was beginning to give his elder son greater control.[44]

The main entrances to the park on the south and west were to lead by tree-lined avenues to the social focus at the heart of the park, an Art Deco building which looks south to a massive and geometric Italian garden with its trellised classical colonnade (more French than Italian) as its outer wall. From the centre of the Italian garden, the view east is across a large boating lake, which occupies a natural declivity. To the north is a golf course on undulating ground; on its left are bowling greens (on an old brickworks site) leading to the rose garden. The rest of the space on the west side remains the province of the cricket and football grounds and the park nursery; to the east below the lake are tennis courts, an athletics oval and more football pitches. There were children's playgrounds, a model yachting pond, glasshouses for bedding plants and an impressive gated entrance from Mere Road.

With this scale of sporting space, the decorative aspects had to have a similarly significant impact, and the wide central avenue from the south edged by trees and then by herbaceous borders made a strong axis to the social centre on the north, past statuary in the Italian garden. A bandstand on the edge of the lake formed another focal point on a cross axis from the Italian garden. Perhaps to divest itself of the fact that Stanley Park was a muscular space for sport, and to attract a wider audience, E.A.Chadwick's illustrations in the souvenir programme for the opening gave a lot of attention to the rose garden and the Edwardian idea of the Italian Garden, and the flowers and fountain ponds of both gardens helped both to soften the image and reintroduce the formal core to the sporting surroundings.[45]

Stanley Park was a great commercial success, as the sale of plots for building covered the cost of the purchase of the ground. The costs of maintaining the grounds were met by the income from the hire of the public facilities. Mawson was anxious that the houses built overlooking the park, preferably detached, should face it, with no ugly back lanes in sight, and should be of a suitable design – 'nothing which is bizarre, eccentric or commonplace should be permitted'.[46] Recently restored, Stanley Park performs all the functions allotted by Mawson, and is a strong signifier of civic pride.

Both park and town needed to make Blackpool ready for its fast expanding influx of visitors, and in 1925 Mawson & Sons and the borough engineer, Francis Wood, were invited back to draw up a report on their town development schemes. 'Motor charabancs and motor omnibuses' were adding to traffic congestion and new national roads were needed into the Fylde before local improvements could be made, though a gyratory system would help; a new private aerodrome might be built near the golf course at North Shore (in addition to the municipal airport at Stanley Park); a new town hall was needed to try to place Blackpool as the capital of the North West. The team declared: 'The creation of a fine civic centre with imposing buildings, their architecture contrasting with tasteful town gardens and shown off by adequate promenading space, might do much for Blackpool and would appeal to exactly that class of visitor which it is most desirable to attract.' To give space and amenity to the town the market should be moved, and winter gardens should be built, and the market and arcades could connect both features with new picture houses and the tower. The aspirations of the cotton worker had moved on, and the team detected the development of a 'real aesthetic sense'.

But it was impossible to beautify the area except by artificial means: 'there is little natural beauty in Blackpool and its environs. It is treeless, flat inland, and on the coast devoid of natural stone cliffs on the grand scale.' It would be necessary to involve the powers under the Town Planning Acts which would improve the town's architecture, such as street façades, stopping the 'glaring combination of reddest of red pressed brick and whitest of glazed white terra cotta which offends the eye in many of the latest residential houses'; dealing with the 'higgledy piggledy architecture' on the promenade and preventing 'large and ugly signs' there. There should be 'large-scale use of trees, shrubs and flowers in tubs and plant boxes of neat and artistic design'. And to cap it all (referring to the Moorish Pavilion on the pier at Lytham St Annes), 'in the hands of an architectural genius, a Pavilion which like a fairy palace reflecting the blaze of light from the summer sea above which it stands poised should rival even the Taj Mahal itself'.

There was, however, praise for the 'continuous stretch of high class boarding houses and hotels along the whole length of the South Shore Promenade Extension [which] gives shelter to the houses and gardens behind, as well as adding greatly to Blackpool's accommodation for visitors and providing the opportunity for one of those dignified architectural façades for which the City of Bath is so justly famous.'[47]

The uncomfortable tone of the 1925 report and its embarrassed attempts at humour displayed an unwillingness to come to terms with the fact that Blackpool was 'the world's first working-class seaside resort' and would prefer to stay so, however much Mawson & Sons would attempt to change its culture.[48]

Mawson & Sons made other plans for and contributions to seaside resorts – a pergola-bounded water garden with a rotunda at Weston-super-Mare, a marine park with a Japanese lagoon for the borough of Lytham St Annes, town and seafront schemes for Southend-on-Sea, and general development plans for Hastings and Bridlington.[49]

In 1925, in collaboration with the London firm of Thomas Adams and Francis Longstreth Thompson, proposals for the development of Northampton concentrated attention on making sports grounds on the large area of low-lying land around the gasworks, tanneries and sawmills, a pleasure park with a lake on another open stretch near the railway, with another for the residents of the garden village of Delapre in north Northampton. And why should not the town create two 'productive' parks, similar to Howard's green belt, and Letchworth's permanent agricultural belt? Unsuitable for building, this land could have allotments, market gardens and grazing, and the other an exhibition ground (as in America) with annual flower shows like those of Wolverhampton.[50]

There were other town and park plans in the late 1920s and 1930s, but the plan for Plymouth's Central Park highlights the changes of design and usage which public demand and the cost of labour made necessary. The plans for Central Park were on the drawing board by 1928, as the minutes of the Plymouth Hoe and Parks Committee of 31 October show, when Mawson and Sons' report was approved and the committee set in motion an application to the Ministry of Health to borrow £92 6s. to start work on the park. Edward Prentice Mawson and

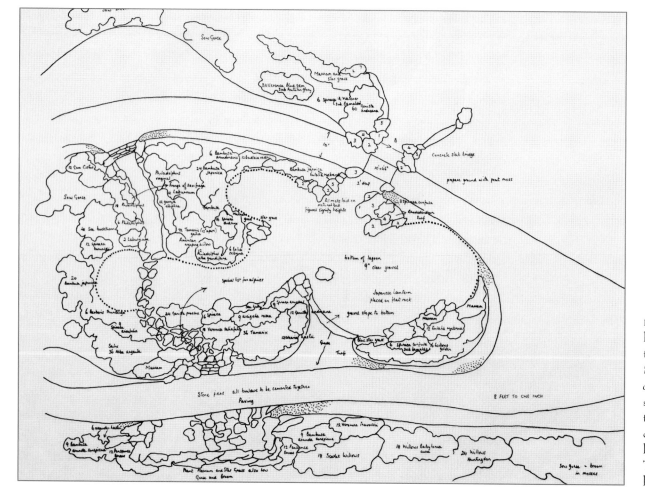

LEFT A plan for a 'Japanese' lagoon was drawn up for the Marine Park at Lytham St Annes by John Mawson, c. 1926. Though a pleasing shape, and beautifully drawn, there is little Japanese connection apart from the lantern placed on a flat rock. This does not appear to have been made.

the city engineer, J.Wibberley, were to be the men in charge. Thomas Mawson was beginning to lose his mobility at this point – he was in a wheelchair soon afterwards – but he wrote (or dictated) the report which accepted the changes. 'Lying as it does more or less in the centre of your large city,' he explained, 'it is practically certain to be put to greater use than many other parks in the country…Your Council have, in my opinion, very wisely decided that the recreational areas shall predominate. This is as it should be, and in accord with the modern trend of things.' And what was left unsaid was that here 'beautification' would no longer include the addition of formal geometric gardens, statuary and pavilions.

The park, on a sloping hillside, opened on 29 July 1931 with its landscape on the east still dominated by field boundaries and paths. There was little attempt to create a formal core, only two short tree-planted avenues along the main paths from the south and southwest, and a plan for a geometric garden near the northern entrance

from Peverell Road. The long Tavistock Road's west side was provided with all the sports facilities the town could create on its 234-acre site – cricket and football grounds, tennis courts, a running track and a swimming pool, which were serviced by a semicircular car park for 1,000 cars. There were children's playgrounds accessible from all entrances.[51]

By the mid 1920s there had been a change of focus in Mawson's long-established garden and landscape architecture firm. Due to the war and Lloyd George's income tax and death duties there were fewer men with money to spend on large gardens, fewer young men to make them and look after them, and public finances were channelled to making homes. Commissions for large gardens were rare, and decreasing in number for parks. Town planning schemes which embraced parks then made up the majority of the work taken on by the firm, which was organised almost entirely by Edward Prentice and John Mawson, under the watchful eye of their father.

Teacher, writer and campaigner

FOR A VERY BRIEF PERIOD in the 1920s, Thomas Mawson found himself to be the owner of a country house and so a member of the class he had served for most of his working life. Although his physical strength had waned – he had had much to endure in Greece – he stooped a little, his hair had become grey, his face had thinned and his eyes showed strain, yet there was no sign of his mind slowing down and a cigarette continued to appear in his mouth. Anna, keen to transport him to new surroundings which would give him horticultural things to do and possibly the opportunity to open a school for landscape architects after he returned from Greece, sold The Bungalow at Hest Bank – which was hers to sell – and bought Caton Hall, east of Lancaster. This was a large house standing in eleven acres at the edge of a village in the valley of the River Lune. The grounds were part garden, part timbered park, and Mawson was particularly pleased to discover that John Wesley had taught his flock from steps by a stream near the entrance to the hall.

Did Mawson see himself as a teacher? Certainly he was delighted to be asked to instruct the students of Liverpool University's new Department of Civic Design and to be able to continue there until the end of the session of 1923–24. He toured the lecture circuit of North American universities and also gave a series of lectures at Swanley College, for which he was paid £60 in 1922. This was the year in which Dr Kate Barrett, once a student at Swanley, became its principal. A woman of ambition for the college and for the role of women, she recognised in Mawson a campaigning zeal for the education of garden makers. Swanley College had begun in an old house in Hextable in Kent in 1889 as a horticultural college for

men and women. Soon the women outnumbered the men, and the men's department was closed in 1902. The teaching of two or three-year courses for certificates or diplomas in practical gardening was broadened by 1916 to include instruction towards the external degree of BSc Horticulture of the University of London. The college was a combination of the practical and the scientific, with laboratories balancing glasshouses and work in the propagating areas, gardens and orchards set against formal lectures.[1] Mawson was also approached by Reading University, but it was to be Edward Prentice who gave lectures there from 1933 to 1935.[2]

From 1912 Mawson had also taken on articled pupils, as was usual in the professions of architecture and law; each paid £105 for a year's tuition. There were more female than male students, possibly because men continued to work as gardeners and nurserymen; later the war was to have a strong negative effect on the recruitment of men. None of these students formed part of Mawson's plan to begin a school of landscape architecture in Caton Hall; he had 'hoped thereby to solve in some little measure the question of academic training, accompanied by a certain amount of practical training in horticulture'. A prospectus was published in 1921, to which there was 'a good response', but Mawson says no more about it in his autobiography.[3] The failure of the venture may have combined with a worsening of his illness, and the expense of running a large and old building precipitated another move, away from Caton Hall to a new home next to his son Edward Prentice.

Mawson had been spreading the word in favour of good garden making from 1900, when he published the

LEFT The Mawson family at Applegarth in 1932. Standing, from left to right: Dorothy Mawson (Dolly), John Mawson, Frances Marshall (Frankie), Edward Prentice Mawson, Millicent Mawson (Mint), Thomas Mawson junior (Tommy). Seated, from left to right: Helen Smethurst, Thomas Hayton Mawson and Anna Prentice Mawson.

first edition of *The Art and Craft of Garden Making*. The books were practical guides to the making of plans for large country estate gardens and smaller urban gardens, though these were still much larger than today's garden plots. The books used his own examples which were well illustrated with drawings by excellent draftsmen-artists, including Charles Mallows, his own son Edward Prentice Mawson and Robert Atkinson, and photography as it became practicable from the third edition in 1907. They explained Mawson's adherence to his 'composite' style of formal and informal, and the reason why he found the Renaissance garden, with its return to geometry, so important. The usefulness of these volumes to the gardeners and garden owners of the time cannot be underestimated, with their lists of plants, shrubs and trees for specified sites; their illustrations of suitable statuary and seats, pergolas, treillage and garden houses; their discussion of the importance of water, of the kitchen garden and its decorative effect, and their examples of both unexecuted and finished gardens to act as guidance. A review of the third edition for the *Architectural Review* claimed that:

> It is not often that a reviewer can give so hearty a welcome to a new edition as in the case of Mr.Mawson's book….Altogether, the increasing number of architects who attach great importance to garden design and equipment are thrown by this edition into deeper debt to Mr.Mawson, whose immense practical experience gives to his views a peculiar authority.

But there was a sting in the tail: 'If he would pay more attention to the literary side of book-making, the book would be greatly more readable.'[4] Mawson's high-flown phrases with many quotations from writers as diverse as Homer, Francis Bacon and the economist Walter Bagehot, often obscured the value of what he had to say. Although this was the style of the time, he eventually realised that rhetorical flourishes closed the ears of the audience.

He continued to write, contributing a chapter on 'The History of the English Garden' to Richard Sudell's *Landscape Gardening*, in 1933, the year that he died; it was short and did not use his own gardens as illustrations. It was probably dictated to his secretary John Dyer, who edited all his books for him and also acted as amanuensis for his autobiography.[5]

Using the same practical approach as for *The Art and Craft of Garden Making*, Mawson wrote about his own

contribution in plan and reality for park making and town planning in *Civic Art* in 1911. His park plans always had a formal core and adopted many of the same values as his garden making – the restfulness of beauty in the guise of greenswards with trees suited to the locality as shelter belts and avenues, and bandstands, pavilions and well-kept flower beds as centrepieces. Over thirty years, from Hanley and Belle Vue to Blackpool and Plymouth, he had to adapt the contents of the park to provide less for the promenader enjoying the air and the flowers – with perhaps a gentlemanly game of croquet or tennis – and more for the needs of those looking for a wider range of more active recreation, from football and swimming to running and golf, but with fewer flower beds.

Mawson's town planning was governed by aesthetics, although aesthetics were also to be governed by utility; beauty should accompany the setting of the town in the landscape which must also accommodate traffic; ordered street facades and the dignified architecture of its central core would also attract visitors. It was essential to look to the future and plan for the best arrangement of buildings, from the welcoming significance of the well-built railway station's entrance to the museum or art gallery in the town's centre. A bold approach was necessary with no half-measures as they would be regretted in the future; a town like Banff should build many bridges over the river Bow; Stepney should put its railway underground, and develop the embankment as a boulevard. A town should present civic pride.

Mawson was full of imaginative, far-reaching and exciting plans for the development of towns. On one

ABOVE Caton Hall, about 1921. Mawson's hopes of setting up a school for landscape architects were never realised, owing to the cost of maintaining such a building and his worsening health.

hand it could be argued that Mawson came to town planning too late to make much of an impact; the significant legislation which was to govern English town planning and the building of many estates was not set up until after the First World War. On the other hand, later planning legislation introduced curbs on imaginative and far-sighted development, and Mawson would not have flourished under its negative rules and regulations. In Greece and in Canada his grand schemes ran into trouble because of the war, because of the financial failure of those commissioning him, and because of his inability to get across the fact that a great scheme would need many years for development. Some of his plans in Britain suffered from the same problem. But also his plans for Greece saw competition from French architects who had more time to spend in Greece than Mawson did. In Canada many of his housing estates were based on English models with English cottages which would have graced English villages and cottage estates, but showed little attempt to discover a Canadian identity; small wonder that in Vancouver he was criticised for his 'colonialist' approach. Mawson was paid for the designs and the plans, so it was unsurprising that he could be both bold and outspoken, whether his ideas were adopted or not. But as he was to admit in his autobiography:

> Many of the commissions which I have undertaken have been sufficiently important to justify my throwing up all other work, had I had the courage to do so. My work in Canada or in Athens, or in Salonika, was quite sufficient to absorb my entire energies profitably.[6]

He was always a driven man, but this led to his doing too many things at once. However, many of his plans, including Regina's Wascana landscape and Exeter's city centre, have been taken into recent consideration, as cities reassess their surroundings and future possibilities and have taken inspiration from earlier thinking.

With the help of his sons, Mawson had worked on the reports of town plans, many of which were published, from Bolton and Calgary, to the large Amounderness – the old name for the Fylde – on which Thomas and Edward were engaged at the time of Thomas' death, and which was published by his preferred publisher, Batsford, in 1937.

Mawson wrote copious articles for the *Architectural Association Journal*, the *Architectural Record* and the *Architectural Review*, *The Builder*, the *Journal of the Town*

Planning Institute and many others – and most of these reciprocated by writing articles about his work. Many of the articles that appeared in professional journals began as papers read to audiences that Mawson wanted to influence. Though members of the Art Workers' Guild, to which Mawson belonged from 1905 to 1929, did not advertise, his papers campaigned elsewhere for his point of view, and used examples from his own work. These are useful in that they summarise his position, as it has emerged throughout this book. Writing on his long train journeys, Mawson was not afraid to take on his critics, especially on the issues which bitterly divided architects and landscape architects in the first decade of the twentieth century: whether the style should be formal or natural, and who should be in charge of making the garden.

'The Unity of the House and Garden,' given to the RIBA on 26 May 1902, accused the architects of using 'a plan prepared in the office, reminiscent of the latest sketching tour', rather than a proper preliminary survey. Site was about aspect, as well as the other factors such as shelter, local climate and soil: you should not build your house on the north, northwest or northeast sides of a hill. A house designed 'as a thing by itself, without reference to its setting or the special requirements of the individual site…. imposed upon the garden designer…[is]…a task which is well-nigh impossible', he claimed. To solve it by asking the architect to design the space close to the house…would suppose 'the architect to have the

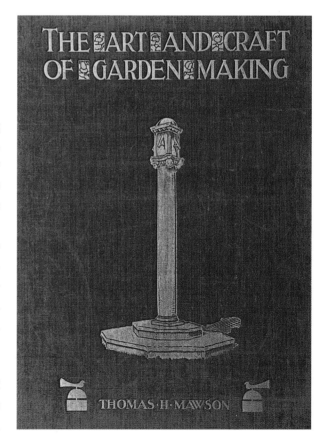

technical knowledge requisite for the successful accomplishment of his garden designs, which few possess'. One could almost sense the *frisson* which must have circulated at this statement; the Scottish architect Robert Lorimer's (1864–1929) comments after the paper, while polite, referred to the knowledge of horticulture 'about which no architect could possibly have a thorough knowledge' as 'a nurseryman's knowledge'. Lorimer, who had read Humanities, Greek and Fine Art at Edinburgh University before becoming an architect, underlined the current snobbish perception of the unlettered gardener and the educated architect.

Using examples from his own work, Mawson explained why the principal rooms for entertaining should overlook the garden, why the carriage court and main entrance should be on the other side of the house, and why the kitchen court and buildings should be screened from the house and served by the tradesmen's entrance. A garden 'depends in a large measure on its plan and connection with the house' and yet as a completed whole it partakes as much of the character of the landscape as of the house'. The walled kitchen garden should be close to the house, where sheltered walks would be possible in winter and where you could 'pluck your earliest flower and last rose of summer'.

Mawson would not be drawn on his position on the formal or the landscape school:

If you ask me to say to which I belong…show me your site and I will tell you; there is work in plenty for both; the help of all is needed. I believe if we could divest ourselves of some of the prejudices called schools…and devote that study to the perfection of our craft, [and] allow our professional jealousies to give place to a spirit of mutual helpfulness, we might yet do something to advance the peaceful arts of the little England we all love so well.[7]

In a lecture on garden architecture given to the Architectural Association at its home in 18 Tufton Street, Westminster, on 8 April 1908, Mawson again made his case for the harmonious combination of architecture and nature in the setting out of the garden. 'Architecture', he said, 'no matter how fine or impressive it may be in the abstract, if it not be in accord with and happy in its natural surroundings, had better be absent.' Both architect and garden maker needed to combine their ideas on the siting of the house, or 'the best made of a bad job'.[8] Edwin Lutyens, expecting to propose a vote of thanks, had to sum up the discussion. He told his wife afterwards of his attack of nerves. 'It was horrible!' he said, 'my hand shook!...and 'oh, it has made me ill…'.[9] But his summary was amicable and his views close to those of Mawson. Lutyens was most startled by the comments

RIGHT Edward Prentice Mawson, who was to inherit Mawson and Son, and who quietly supported his father's ventures as draughtsman, designer, and architect.

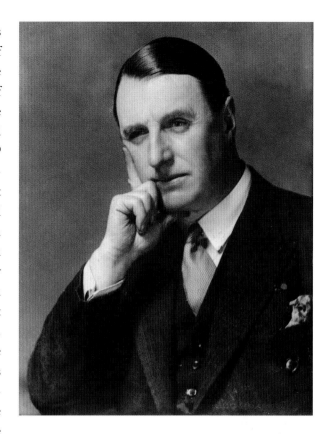

of Miss Iris Dunnington who sided with the architects (later she married Howard Grubb, an American pupil of Mawson's, and they founded a successful landscape architects' partnership in Canada). As Jane Ridley says of Lutyens, 'an outsider to the architectural profession, he was suspicious of his colleagues, from whom he learned little', and maybe he felt Mawson to be an outsider, too.[10]

Members of the RIBA continued to regard the relationship between architect and landscape gardener as that of the professional and the nurseryman amateur, until Mawson began his lectures at Liverpool University in 1909. Undoubtedly there was jealousy about the wealth and calibre of client Mawson was to attract; this may have worked to Mawson's benefit, for he was made an Honorary Associate of the RIBA in 1903: it was likely that the architects hoped to share some of Mawson's clients. Mawson's architect son, Edward Prentice, was well able to cope with the structural requirements of his father's commissions, though this did not stop the RIBA's accusation that Edward had had help from the staff of the Ecole des Beaux-Arts to prepare his submission for the Soane Medallion (a RIBA competition prize for an original architectural design) in 1910.[11] This was promptly countered by a denial from the principal of the Beaux-Arts school that any such assistance was given, and Edwin Lutyens, who knew of Edward's work, considered resignation from the RIBA in disgust at their treatment of a promising student.[12]

In February 1908, Mawson spoke to the Leeds and Yorkshire Architectural Association on the subject of English and Italian garden architecture, a paper which was later published in the RIBA journal. Italian gardens were very much in demand in Edwardian England; the Italian revival appealed to the richer landowner and aligned itself with the move to formality. Here Mawson makes the case against the Italianate house. 'The greater part of English mansions which have received their inspiration from the Italian Renaissance are not happy in their English settings', he stated, referring especially to the severe lines of Charles Barry's Trentham. Because the hot climate allowed few flowers to flourish, the Italian garden used 'the abundance of material' to build 'walls, balustrades, fountains and statuary, supplying the interest that grass and flowers yield in our own home gardens'.[13] This did not stop a large number of his clients from requiring such architectural magnificence for their gardens, whether at Dyffryn in South Wales or Rydal Hall in the Lake District.

Between 1908 and 1909, Mawson gave papers to the Royal Horticultural Society on 'Garden Designs –

Comparative, Historical and Ethical'. The last, read on 12 October 1909, was titled 'Renaissance Gardens'. It is the most important of the papers, because it discusses his position on formality, and, with the earlier paper on 'The Unity of the House and Garden', collects together most of the significant factors which informed his beliefs about garden making, and which stayed with him without alteration throughout his life.

Mawson appeared to base his interpretation of the Renaissance on a mixture of Italian and French forms. It was 'a form of art which is adapted to the expression of a considered scheme on a grand and stately scale' and 'the antithesis of the individualism and impressionism of the present day'. He realised that seventeenth-century French schemes such as Versailles were not to English taste, but he admired their 'logical and spacious planning'. By contrast, amateurs became confused when they attempted to lay out their gardens 'on the freer or landscape style'. Classical garden making was a form of discipline, of 'suppressing the individual for the common good'. It used geometry, axes, squares, circles and radiating avenues, canals, colonnades, fountains and garden houses. And it could use English equivalents of Mediterranean trees which would cope better in the English climate, such as the oak, the Wheatley elm, the Lombardy poplar, the evergreen oak, yew, box and cedar of Lebanon, cypress, Scots fir and stone pine.[14]

All Mawson gardens were made following a survey, with formality close to the house as the link between

or paths. But this did not matter to Mawson's clients, as in England the Edwardian country house garden held sway beyond the First World War, albeit in a reduced form and with fewer recruits to its ranks. These clients were not interested in asymmetry, freeform and greater simplicity in decorative stonework.

Mawson does not discuss the Edwardian interest in Japanese gardens, which had emerged strongly even before the Anglo-Japanese exhibition in London in 1910, though he appears to have found them beautiful. Perhaps he could not find a place for them in his very English overview of garden making, though he was prepared to ask his sons to design them for his clients, calling on James Pulham to construct the rock work, as at Rivington for Lord Leverhulme, or to make a design around water, as at Foots Cray in Kent.

Was Mawson a colonialist? He sought work in Canada and Australia, and had aspirations to work with Patrick Geddes in India. As a non-conformist Liberal it would be difficult to grow up in Victorian Britain without observing the approval of and pride in the Empire and the royal family with its European network of relatives which formed its centre; all this permeated the culture of the time. Joseph Chamberlain's views must have been known in Mawson's household. On his way to look at exhibits at South Kensington, the young Thomas would have passed museums built on the proceeds of the Great Exhibition, itself a celebration of the Empire, and the Albert Memorial, with its carved animals and figures representing the countries over which Victoria held control. It did not occur to him to question his firm's depiction of English buildings in Canada and Greece; and it was ironic that he was prepared to abandon his lecture tour in colonial Australia for the King of Greece. Mawson was a patriotic Englishman, who respected King and Country, and though he upheld British leadership of colonial countries, his patriotism did not lend itself to nationalism of the baser kind.

Mawson was a strong campaigner, especially for housing for disabled soldiers. A letter to George Bernard Shaw on 8 October 1917 took up the theme, and then expanded on their correspondence on garden cities and town planning.[15] As Mawson's mobility declined, a stream of short articles, reviews of books and lectures, and letters to *The Times* flowed from his pen, on everything from clearing litter and the reduction of the shrubberies in London's parks (23 August 1921), to the possibility of siting the new Covent Garden Market between Waterloo and Charing Cross bridges (21 October 1926), 'the lack of adequate educational

house and garden. The terrace, the bastion, and the flights of stairs were constructs to deal with slopes; statuary was placed where the eye would see it, and would add to the tone of the design. Garden houses were placed from which to admire the view, for the garden was part of the greater landscape. Informality was included around the core of his plans – the woodland walks, the lake at the bottom of the hill, the greensward above it. These were the links between the garden and the countryside. House and garden, formal and informal garden, countryside and informal garden, all had links between them, and were always there, in every plan except the very small urban garden, when informality was not possible. Not for him the abrupt halt between the formal garden and the countryside, as in Reginald Blomfield's Godinton in Kent, nor the plan drawn up in the studio without a visit, nor the plant list given without an inspection of the soil, as with some of Gertrude Jekyll's later work. At the end of his active career, Mawson was as widely known and respected as a landscape architect as any of the leading architects in their chosen profession.

Such gardens would not accommodate the new world of Modernism, which was very much about individualism. Mawson was prepared to adopt modern materials, such as asphalt, pre-stressed concrete and other forms of artificial stone, and these would be used in the making of balustrading, ornaments in traditional designs, pergolas

RIGHT The herbaceous border at Dyffryn owed some of its influence to Gertrude Jekyll, although it was not a copy of her work. Mawson had been in touch with her in his early horticultural training, but theirs was a distinctly chilly relationship. Mawson's concrete rose pillars with their metal hoops have recently been restored.

facilities in this country for the training of landscape architects, and the dissemination of knowledge upon which alone a sound and informed public opinion can be created' (6 December 1926) to the ugliness of unsightly petrol stations (25 April 1928) and the laudable proposal made by Labour politician George Lansbury to remove the railings around the Royal Parks (19 September 1929). He was particularly exercised about what he saw as the lack of educational training for landscape architects, fearing that the Americans would take the lead.

At a time when landscape architects and garden makers did not publicly praise or denigrate their colleagues, it is difficult to assess what Mawson thought of his contemporaries, or they of him. Approval could be gauged by the list of subscribers to a book; Mawson, Harold Peto, Edwin Lutyens and Charles Mallows all obtained copies of H.Inigo Triggs' first edition of *Formal Gardens in England and Scotland* in 1902; the first edition of Mawson's *The Art and Craft of Garden Making* in 1900 sold out in weeks after publication. Clients made plain that Mawson's work was in demand as he became the most sought-after international landscape architect of his time.

Gertrude Jekyll's distant and disapproving dealings with Mawson at Boveridge and Lees Court have been noted, in contrast with Lutyens' support of the Mawsons at the Architectural Association lecture in 1908 and the Soane Medallion in 1910. It would have been illuminating to know what Beatrix Farrand (1872–1959), the grande dame of landscape making in northeast America, thought of Mawson's stunning garden at Wych Cross in Sussex, as she observed it when staying there in the spring of 1933 before her return to the United States. With her connections to Edith Wharton and Mrs Humphry Ward, and her thorough knowledge of horticulture and landscape making, it is very likely that she knew Mawson's work, although there are no records in the Berkeley archives, University of California, which connect the two.

But as he grew older, Mawson feared that he had not been respected for his contribution to landscape architecture. Demand for country house gardens declined after the First World War. There were few written comments

RIGHT Thomas Mawson in his conservatory at Caton Hall. In a very short time he had developed a remarkable range of indoor plants. *Life and Work*, fig. 68.

amongst the garden makers of the time about each other's work, and even fewer from the industrialists who patronised Mawson. Maybe the anxiety which is caused by Parkinson's disease played on his self-confidence, for Liverpool University archives reveal that Mawson had written in 1919 to the Vice Chancellor, Dr J. G. Adami, asking if he could be awarded an honorary degree.[16] Such an act was unprecedented, as nominations for these awards could only be made by specified people. Not only was this request politely turned down, but – ironically – an award was bestowed upon Sir Reginald Blomfield. However, honours of a different kind were given to him in the 1920s from other directions. Recognition for his belief in landscape architecture as 'the master art' led to his nomination as a founder member of the Fine Arts Commission in 1924. (Blomfield, copying the Americans, had referred to architecture as the 'mistress art'! Mawson's was a sturdier description for a landscape maker.) Mawson was made President of the Town Planning Institute, 1923-24, and first President of the Institute of Landscape Architects in 1929, a position later taken temporarily by his son Edward Prentice after the death of his father. This seems to be the wrong way round, for Mawson was able to be more successful as a garden and park maker than as a town planner; but it took time for the ILA to establish itself. Although he was unable to attend many meetings he sent contributions related to the papers which were given. That he helped to build a

platform for urban planning is undisputed, and he saw that there were unnecessary boundaries around the disciplines of landscape making and town planning, which he preferred to call civic design. His planning was led by aesthetics, which he saw as the most important factor in building a city and improving the quality of life for its citizens, and in this he was no different from Inigo Triggs, Barry Parker and Raymond Unwin, or Edwin Lutyens, or Thomas Adams and Francis Longstreth Thompson.

Thomas Mawson's strengths lay in the commercial structure and enterprise of his firm with its nursery, its links with Garden Crafts in Staveley to make stone and wood accessories, its allies in the construction of water gardens under the Pulham family and its connections through Edward Prentice with London specialist businesses. The firm was made up from family members, educated as architects and town planners, whose specialisms were encouraged and skills employed in the British Isles, Europe and North America. Mawson's clients were often new industrialists who appreciated his energy, enthusiasm and optimism and became his friends – and recommended him to all of theirs – although he was proud and delighted to work for Queen Alexandra in Denmark and for the King of Greece. Though his ideas on style and design were not original, his gardens were just what the Edwardians wanted, and fitted the times; they had to reflect the taste of their owners, from the most monumental completed designs of Leverhulme's Rivington and the Hill at Hampstead, to the simplicity of Lethbridge's Wood House at South Tawton, or Bolitho's Hannaford in the southern folds of Dartmoor. His most significant ability lay in his use of the landscape, tailoring features to the lie of the land. He had the foresight to move beyond the garden to the making of parks, as the social order began to change after the First World War and the country house gently declined, giving way to smaller gentry houses, cottage estates built by public authorities, and suburban sprawl.

Caton Hall was to be home for two years only; here he took his little granddaughter Ursula for walks, to find the fairies she was convinced lived in the woodlands; here he enjoyed growing plants in the greenhouse. In 1913 Edward Prentice had married Hilda Bowhill, and built himself Bracondale in Lonsdale Road, Hest Bank. In 1921 a Georgian-style house called Applegarth was built by the Mawsons next door to Bracondale for Thomas and Anna. Here Thomas wrote his many short articles, put together the last of the five editions of *The Art and Craft of Garden Making*, and dictated his autobiography, *The Life and Work of an English Landscape*

Architect, to John Dyer, which was published in 1927. And it was between the two houses, Bracondale and Applegarth, that Mawson & Son was run, with the partners in the firm side by side.

As Parkinson's disease advanced, Mawson found difficulty in swallowing and speaking. But this did not destroy his ability to think and plan, and reading continued to give him pleasure. With the help of Edward Prentice, commissions could still be completed. Two late requests must have pleased him: one was for laying out the grounds of the first London mosque, and the other for making a cemetery at Saffron Hill, Leicester.

In 1920 an acre of land in Southfields, southwest London, was bought by the Ahmadiyya Community, a group of Muslims who wanted to build a mosque which would be the centre of their faith and activities. Five years later, construction began, and the Fazl Mosque (meaning Mosque of Grace) was completed in July 1926. Mawson & Son as landscape architects were assisted by the engineering firms of Moreland, Hayne & Co. from London and John Booth from Bolton.

Documents in the Mawson archive in Kendal Record Office dated April 1926 include a drawing of the plasterwork to the dome, details of the minaret, and a plan of the grounds surrounding the small mosque (which seated 150) with a site for a guesthouse. Around the mosque were a garden and an orchard – members today have memories of apple and pear trees. The garden was enclosed by privet hedges and fences. A contemporary photograph shows a formal design in front of the main entrance, with a pool in which there was a low fountain. Small conical bushes framed the space.[17] Today the gleaming white building with its green dome overlooks a lovingly tended garden, filled with bright impatiens, petunias, pelargoniums and roses which border an immaculate green lawn. The orchard and privet hedges have gone, the guesthouse has expanded to contain the mosque's many activities, and the fountain in its pool has been replaced with a tiled path to the entrance.

At about the same time, the City of Leicester had purchased 170 acres of land to build more houses, and a cemetery, for its expanding population. On 15 September 1926, Mawson & Sons won an 'architectural competition' from thirty-five other contenders, and planned a 'lawn cemetery' with formal open spaces, and vistas aligned on the chapel. Both men discussed the plans, but it was Edward who drew up the surrounding red brick walls with their wrought-iron railings and main gates, arched entrances and lodges, path layout and the chapel with its campanile. The City Corporation's Estates and City Cemetery Committee did not like the large, formal lawns, which were not implemented, though they put in the small lawns with surrounding rose beds that Edward Prentice had placed next to the chapel.

A local nursery, J.Coles of Thurnby, planted the trees and shrubs which Mawson & Sons had requested: around the boundaries and at the junctions of walks (as in Mawson's parks elsewhere) specimen trees were placed such as *Laburnum* 'Pendulum', *Tilia platyphyllos* and *Cedrus deodara* ; pleached limes and *Populus alba*, *nigra* and 'Serotina' along walks; and colourful shrubs such as hypericum, buddleia, berberis, eleagnus, ribes and *Rosa rugosa* in between.[18]

Mawson continued to inspect everything that was drawn up by his firm: his signature of approval is on plans as late as 1932 and his last article appeared in 1933. Thomas Mawson died at Applegarth on 14 November 1933 and was buried, 'a Lakelander by adoption', at Bowness cemetery, Windermere.

Mawson's legacy for his sons was the training in town planning which gave them work long after their father had gone, and for which he had pioneered; his will calls him only 'town planner'. But his lasting contribution in the eyes of those who appreciate landscapes remains the best of his private country house gardens, where each designed feature responds perfectly to the landscape for which it was made. Happily, both gardens and parks are now enjoying a revival of interest and receiving the attention they so deserve.

RIGHT This photograph of the Ahmaddiya Mosque, Southfields, in 1926, shows that the building was set in open land, enough for Mawson to suggest planting an orchard. By the entrance is a fountain in a pool, with small bushes at the corners. Both orchard and pool have now vanished.

Bibliography

PUBLISHED SOURCES OTHER THAN JOURNAL ARTICLES

Armstrong, Barrie and Armstrong, Wendy, *The Arts and Crafts Movement in the North West of England,* Oblong Creative Ltd, Wetherby, 2005.

Ashworth, William, *The Genesis of Modern British Town Planning*, Routledge and Kegan Paul, London, 1954.

Barnhart, Gordon L., *Building for the Future: a photo journal of Saskatchewan's Legislative Building,* Canadian Plains Research Center, University of Regina, 2002.

Bateman, John, *The Great Landowners of Great Britain*, 4th edition, Harrison, London, 1883.

Battiscombe, Georgina, *Queen Alexandra*, Constable & Company Ltd, London, 1969.

Beard, Geoffrey and Joan Wardman, *Thomas H.Mawson, A Northern Landscape Architect*, catalogue of an exhibition held in the Visual Arts Centre, University of Lancaster, 1976.

Blomfield, Reginald and Inigo Thomas, *The Formal Garden in England*, 1892.

Brunton, Jennie, *The Arts and Crafts Movement in the Lake District: A Social History,* Centre for North-West Regional Studies, University of Lancaster, 2001.

CADW/ICOMOS Register of Landscapes, Parks and Gardens of Special Interest in Wales, 1995.

Carnegie, Andrew, *Autobiography of Andrew Carnegie*, London, Constable & Co Ltd, 1920.

Chadwick, George F., *The Park and the Town, Public landscape in the 19th and 20th centuries,* The Architectural Press, London, 1966.

Cherry, Gordon, *Cities and Plans*, Edward Arnold, London, 1988.

Clogg, Richard, *A Concise History of Greece*, Cambridge University Press, 1995.

Colston Stone Practice, *Wood House, Historical Landscape Survey and Conservation Plan*, 2005.

Conway, Hazel, *People's Parks: The Design and Development of Victorian Parks in Britain,* Cambridge University Press, Cambridge, 1991.

Countryside Interpretation Team, *Lord Leverhulme*, West Pennine Moors Area Management Committee, Lancashire, 1999.

Cullingworth, J.B., *Town and Country Planning in Britain*, Unwin Hyman, London, 1988.

Desmond, Ray, *Dictionary of British and Irish Botanists and Horticulturists including Plant Collectors and Botanical Artists,* Taylor and Francis, London, 1977.

Eyffinger, Arthur, *The Peace Palace: Residence for Justice – Domicile of Learning,* Carnegie Foundation, The Hague, second impression 1992.

Ferguson, Niall, *Empire: How Britain Made the Modern World,* Penguin Allen Lane, 2003.

Gaskell, Elizabeth, *Mary Barton*, 1848, Panther edition 1966.

Geddes, Patrick, *City Development: A Study of Parks, Gardens and Culture-Institutes, A Report to the Carnegie Dunfermline Trust*, Geddes and Company, Edinburgh and Saint George Press, Bournville,1904.

Haslam, Sara E., *John Ruskin and the Lakeland Arts Revival, 1880–1920,* Merton, Cardiff, 2004.

Hay, Tempest, *Lees Court: an investigation into its history and architecture, Faversham Papers,* About Faversham, no.57, 1997.

Helmreich, Anne, *The English Garden and National Identity: The Competing Styles of Garden Design, 1870–1914,* Cambridge University Press, 2002.

Hendrick, Burton J., *The Life of Andrew Carnegie,* William Heinemann Ltd, London, 1933.

Honeycombe, Gordon, *Selfridges*, Selfridges Ltd, 1984.

Horticultural College for Women, Swanley College, Kent, Prospectus 1932–3.

Howard, Ebenezer, *Garden Cities of To-Morrow,* 1898, Attic Books, 1985.

Hunt, John Dixon, *The Wider Sea: A Life of John Ruskin,* J.M.Dent & Sons Ltd, London, 1982.

Jolly, W.P., *Lord Leverhulme*, Constable, London, 1976.

Kelly's Handbook to the Titled, Landed and Official Classes, Kelly's Directories Ltd, London.

Laird, Warren P., Thomas H.Mawson, Richard J.F.Darley, G.L.Thornton Sharp, Charles J.Thompson, *Report to the Board of Governors of the University of British Columbia,* 10 November 1913.

Lake District National Park Authority, *The House and Grounds of Brockhole: a Short History*, n.d; *Brockhole Windermere Restoration and Management Plan*, November 2002.

Land Use Consultants to the Countryside Commission for Scotland, *An Inventory of Gardens and Designed Landscapes in Scotland, vols 1–5.*

Lee, Hermione, *Edith Wharton*, Chatto & Windus, London, 2007.

Mackay, James, *Little Boss. A Life of Andrew Carnegie*, Mainstream Publishing, 1997.

Mawson Brothers', *Catalogue of Garden furniture*, n.d.

Mawson, Thomas H., *The Art and Craft of Garden Making*, B.T.Batsford, London, 1st edition 1900, 2nd edition 1901, 3rd edition 1907, 4th edition 1912, 5th edition 1926.

Mawson, Thomas H., *Civic Art: Studies in Town Planning, Parks, Boulevards and Open Spaces,* B.T.Batsford, London, 1911.

Mawson, Thomas H., *Bolton as it is and as it might be. Six lectures delivered under the auspices of the Bolton Housing and Town Planning Society,* Tillotson & Son Ltd. Bolton and B.J.Batsford, London, n.d.

Mawson,Thomas H. and Vivian, Henry, *Two Notable Addresses on Town Planning and Housing,* The Calgary City Planning Commission, c.1912.

Mawson & Sons, *Blackpool Promenade, South Shore, Blackpool Town Planning Scheme*, n.d., CCA Montreal.

Mawson & Sons, *The County Borough of Blackpool, The New Parks and Recreation Ground*, n.d., CCA Montreal.

Mawson, Thomas Hayton, *The City of the Plain and How to Make it Beautiful*, Calgary City Planning Commission, 9 April 1912.

Mawson, Thomas H, *Borden Park*, 1914, CCA Montreal.

Mawson, Thomas H. & Sons, *Calgary: A Preliminary Scheme for Controlling the Economic Growth of the City (The City of Calgary: Past, Present and Future)*, City Planning Commission of Calgary, 1914.

Mawson, Thomas H., 'Report of Proposed Artistic Lay-out of Banff', *Annual Report of the Department of the Interior*, Ottawa, 1914.

Mawson, Thomas H., *An Imperial Obligation: Industrial Villages for Partially Disabled Soldiers*, Grant Richards Ltd, London, 1917.

Mawson, Thomas H., *Afforestation and the Partially Disabled: A Sequel to An Imperial Obligation*, Grant Richards Ltd, London, 1917.

Mawson, Thomas H., *Athens of the Future and The Salonica of Tomorrow* (in Greek), National Printing Office, Athens, 1918, pp.1–16.

Mawson, Thomas H., *New Park and Recreation Centre for Blackpool,* 1922.

Mawson & Sons, *Agreement, Borough of Blackpool and Thomas Mawson & Sons*, 2 September 1924, Blackpool Central Library.

Mawson & Sons, *Opening of the Marine Promenade and Stanley Park, 1926, by the Right Honourable The Earl of Derby,* Blackpool Central Library.

Mawson, Thomas H., *The Life and Work of an English Landscape Architect*, Richards, Manchester, 1927.

Mazower, Mark, *Salonica: City of Ghosts. Christians, Muslims and Jews 1430–1950*, Harper Perennial, 2005.

Mearns, Andrew, *The Bitter Cry of Outcast London*, 1883; Leicester University Press, New York, 1970.

Meller, Helen, *Patrick Geddes, Social evolutionist and city planner*, Routledge, London and New York, 1990.

Morrow, E. Joyce, *'Calgary, Many Years Hence'*, City of Calgary/University of Calgary, 1979.

Nasaw, David, *Andrew Carnegie*, The Penguin Press, New York, 2006.

Ottewill, David, *The Edwardian Garden*, Yale University Press, New Haven and London, 1989.

Pearson, Graham S., *Hidcote: The Garden and Lawrence Johnston*, The National Trust, 2007.

Pearson Associates, Nicholas, *Rydal Hall, Historic Landscape Survey and Restoration Plan*, 2000.

Pearson Associates, Nicholas, *Wern Manor*, Historic Landscape Survey and Restoration Plan, November 2004.

Proceedings of the Third National Conference on City Planning, Philadelphia, Pennsylvania, May 15–17, 1911, Boston, 1911.

Rawnsley, Rev. H.D., *Ruskin and the English Lakes*, James Maclehose and Sons, Glasgow, 1902.

Reilly, C.H., *Scaffolding in the Sky*, George Routledge & Sons Ltd, London, 1938.

Ridley, Jane, *The Architect and his Wife: A Life of Edwin Lutyens*, Chatto & Windus, London, 2002.

Robinson, Charles Mulford, *Modern Civic Art, or, The City Made Beautiful*, 2nd edition, G.P.Putnam's Sons, New York and London, 1904.

Robinson, Charles Mulford, *The Improvement of Towns and Cities or the Practical Basis of Civic Aesthetics*, G.P.Putnam's Sons, New York and London, 4th edition 1901.

Robinson, William, *The Garden Beautiful Home Woods, Home Landscape,* John Murray, London, 1907.

Royal Academy of Arts, *Royal Academy Exhibitors, 1769–1970*.

Rybczynski, Witold, *A Clearing in the Distance: Frederick Law Olmsted*, Scribner, New York, 1999.

Sedding, John D., *Garden-Craft Old and New*, Kegan Paul, Trench, Trübner & Co. Ltd, London, 1895.

Simpson, Duncan, *C.F.A. Voysey: an architect of individuality*, Lund Humphries, London, 1979.

Sitte, Camillo, *City Planning according to Artistic Principles*, translated by G.R. and C.C.Collins, Random House, New York, 1965.

Smith, M.D., *Leverhulme's Rivington*, Wyre Publishing, Lancashire, 1998.

Spencer-Longhurst, Paul, ed., *Robert Atkinson 1883–1952*, Architectural Association, London, n.d.

Sudell, Richard, ed., *Landscape Gardening, Planning-Construction Planting*, Ward, Lock & Co. Ltd, London, 1933.

Sutcliffe, Anthony, ed., *The Rise of Modern Urban Planning 1800–1914*, Mansell, London, 1980.

Torode, Stephen, *Duffryn, an Edwardian Garden Designed by Thomas H. Mawson*, Glamorgan Record Office, 1993.

Triggs, Harry Inigo, *Town Planning, Past, Present and Possible*, Methuen & Co., London, 1909.

University of British Columbia, *Report of the General Design for the University of British Columbia*, 10 November 1913.

Unwin, Raymond, *Town Planning in Practice: An introduction to the Art of Designing Cities and Suburbs*, T.Fisher Unwin Ltd, London, 1909.

Vancouver City Archives, *Scheme for the Improvement of Brockton Point, Stanley Park, Vancouver, for the Board of Park Commissioners*, c.1914.

Walton, John K., *Riding on Rainbows, Blackpool Pleasure Beach and its Place in British Popular Culture*, Skelter Publishing, St Albans, 2007.

Wascana Centre Authority, *Wascana Centre 1999 Master Plan*, WCA and Du Toit Allsopp Hillier, 1999.

Westall, Oliver, ed., *Windermere in the Nineteenth Century,* Centre for North-West Regional Studies, University of Lancaster, Occasional Paper No. 20, new and revised edition, 1991.

Woodhead, Lindy, *Shopping, Seduction & Mr Selfridge*, Profile Books, London, 2007.

Wooller, Oliver, *The Great Estates: Six Country Houses in the London Borough of Bexley*, Bexley Council Directorate of Education and Leisure Services, 2002.

Yerolympos, Alexandra, *Urban Transformations in the Balkans (1820–1920): Aspects of Balkan Town Planning and the Remaking of Thessaloniki*, University Studio Press, Thessaloniki, 1996.

JOURNAL ARTICLES

Anon, 'Le Chateau d'Anglevillier', *Les Beaux Domaines*, vol. XIV, 1 December 1913, pp.320–7.

Anon (possibly Thomas H.Mawson), 'The Rebuilding of Salonika', in *The Times Engineering Supplement*, May 1919, pp.158–9.

Anon, 'Suggestions to the Promoters of Town Planning Schemes', in *JRIBA*, 3rd series, vol.xviii, p.662.

Brennan, J.William, '"Visions of a City Beautiful": The Origin and Impact of the Mawson Plans for Regina', *Saskatchewan History*, vol.46, 2, Fall 1994, pp.19–33.

Cherry, Gordon E., Harriet Jordan and Kiki Kafkoula, 'Gardens, civic art and town planning: the work of Thomas H.Mawson (1861–1933)', in *Planning Perspectives*, vol.8, 1993, pp.307–32.

Dick, Lyle, 'Greening of the West: horticulture on the Canadian prairies, 1870–1930', *Manitoba History*, Spring 1996 il3, pp.12–17.

Dowthwaite, Michael, 'The Lake District Defence Society in the Late Nineteenth Century', in Westall, Oliver, ed. (see Published sources).

Foran, Max, 'The Mawson Report in Historical Perspective', *Alberta History*, vol.27–28, Summer 1980, pp.31–9.

Freeman, John Crosby, 'Thomas Mawson: Imperial Missionary of British Town Planning', *Revue d'Art Canadienne*, vol.2, no. 2, 1975.

Gordon, David L.A., 'Ottawa-Hull and Canberra: Implementation of Capital City Plans', *Canadian Journal of Urban Research*, 11:2, Winter 2002, pp.179–211.

Hollingworth, G.H., 'Hartpury House', *Gardeners' Magazine*, 15 February 1913, pp.117–20.

Helmreich, Anne L., 'Re-presenting Nature: Ideology, Art and Science in William Robinson's "Wild Garden"', in Wolschke-Buhlmahn, Joachim, ed., *Nature and Ideology: Natural Garden Design in the Twentieth Century*, Dumbarton Oaks, Washington, 1997.

Hussey, Christopher, 'Lees Court, Kent', *Country Life*, 12 August 1922, pp.178–83.

Jordan, Harriet, 'Public Parks, 1885–1914', *Garden History*, vol.22, no.1, summer 1994, pp.85–113.

Journal of the Royal Institute of British Architects, 'Suggestions to the Promoters of Town Planning Schemes', *JRIBA*, 3rd series, vol.xviii, p.662.

Kafkoula, Kiki, 'The Replanning of the Destroyed Villages of Eastern Macedonia after World War I: the Influence of the Garden City tradition on an emerging programme', *Planning History*, vol.14, no.2, 1992, pp.4–11.

Leeuwin, Edward W., '"The Arts of Peace". De tuinen van het Vredespaleis in Den Haag naar ontwerp van Thomas Hayton Mawson', pp.121–49 in De Jong, Erik, ed., *Tuinkunst, 3, Nederlands Jaarboek voor de Geschiedenis van Tuin-en Landschapsarchitectuur*, Architectura & Natura, 1997; 'The Arts of Peace', in *Garden History*, 28:2 (2000), pp.262–76.

Mawson, Thomas H., 'Vancouver. A City of Optimists', *Town Planning Review*, vol.IV, no.1, MCMXIII, pp.7–12.

Mawson, T.H., 'Report of Proposed Artistic Layout of Banff', *Annual Report of Department of Interior*, Ottawa, 1914.

Mawson, Thomas H., 'Thornton Manor, Cheshire, England, The Home of Sir William H. Lever, Bart', *Architectural Record*, November 1917, pp.441–51.

Mawson, Thomas H., 'The British Soldier in Macedonia', *The Contemporary Review*, vol.CXIV, July–Dec. 1918, pp.1–16.

Mawson, Thomas H., 'The New Salonika', *Balkan News*, 29 January 1918.

Mawson, Thomas H., 'The Replanning of Athens', *Architectural Review*, vol.45, March 1919, pp.48–52.

Mawson, John W., 'The Future of Salonika', *Balkan News*, 21 and 22 May 1919.

Mawson, John, 'The Salonika Town Planning Act', *Town Planning Review*, vol.IX, 1921, p.148.

Mawson, Thomas H., & Sons and Thomas Adams and Longstreth Thompson, 'County Borough of Northampton, Proposals for Development and Reconstruction, 1925'.

Mawson, Edward Prentice, for Thomas H.Mawson & Sons, Thomas Adams and Longstreth Thompson, 'Borough of Hastings Town Planning Scheme', 1926.

Mawson, Thomas H. & Son, 'Bridlington of the Future: Being a Report on a Comprehensive Development Scheme for the Town and Sea Front', 1931.

Meller, Helen, 'Cities and evolution: Patrick Geddes as an international prophet of town planning before 1914', in Sutcliffe, Anthony, ed., *The Rise of Modern Urban Planning 1800–1914*, Mansell, London, 1980, pp.199–223.

Olmsted, Frederick Law, 'Reply on Behalf of the City Planning Conference', *Proceedings of the Third National Conference on City Planning*, University Press, Cambridge, Boston, 1911, pp.3–13.

Pope, Robert Anderson, 'Gardens as a Frame for the Country', *Architectural Record*, vol.30, 1911, pp.339–51.

Scott, M.H.Baillie, 'On the Characterisitics of Mr. C.H.Voysey's Architecture', *The Studio*, vol.42, 15 October 1907, no.175, pp.19–24.

Townsend, Horace, 'Notes on Country and Suburban Housing designed by C.F.A.Voysey', *The International Studio*, New York, vol.VII, May 1899, no.27, pp.157–64.

Walton, J.K., 'The Windermere Tourist Trade in the Age of the Railway, 1847–1912', in Westall, Oliver, ed., see Published sources.

Westall, Oliver, 'The Retreat to Arcadia: Windermere as a Select Residential Resort in the Late-nineteenth Century', in Westall, Oliver, see Published sources.

Yerolympos, Alexandra, 'Thessaloniki (Salonika) before and after 1917. Twentieth century planning versus 20 centuries of urban evolution', *Planning Perspectives*, vol.3, no. 2, May 1988, pp.141–66.

UNPUBLISHED SOURCES

Blackpool Town Planning Scheme: Blackpool Civic Survey and Development Scheme, 1952, Canadian Centre for Architecture (hereafter CCA Montreal).

Drury, Alexander, 'Environment and Community: Motive and Practice in the Case of Westfield War Memorial Village, 1918–39,' MA Lancaster University, 2004.

Dynevor, Lucy, 'A Dissertation on the Work of C.E.Mallows, Architectural Gardener and Illustrator', Post.Grad. Diploma, Conservation of Historic Parks and Gardens, Architectural Association, June 1993.

Jordan, Harriet, 'Thomas Hayton Mawson, The English Garden Designs of an Edwardian Landscape Architect', PhD University of London, 1988.

Kafkoula, Kiki, 'The Garden City Idea in Greek Inter-war Planning', PhD Aristotelian University of Thessaloniki, 1990.

Lutyens papers, RIBA.

Mawson, T.H, 'Hanley Park, Hanley', 1894, CROK.

Mawson, Thomas H. & Son, Cash Account January 1901–8 June 1901; then 30 June 1907–14 May 1936, CROK.

Mawson, Thomas H., 'Report on Alternative Schemes for the Improvement of Coal Harbour and Stanley Park, Vancouver, B.C.', 16 October 1912.

Mawson, T.H.& Sons, 'Calgary, A Preliminary Scheme for Controlling the Economic Growth of the City, Confidential Appendix to the Report', City Planning Commission of Calgary, n.d., c.1914.

Mawson, T.H, 'Haslam Park, Preston', March 1915, CROK.

Mawson and Partners, CROK WDB/76 132, Housing Scheme at Tarbert, Harris, Outer Hebrides; WDB/76 134, Circular Garden at Borve Lodge, Isle of Harris, Outer Hebrides; WDB/76 219, Planting plan for fruit trees, Borve Lodge, n.d., c.1917.

Mawson, T.H. & Sons, 'Regina: A Preliminary Report on the Development of the City', n.d., c.1920.

Mawson, Edward Prentice, 'Report on Squires Gate Holiday Camp, Lytham St Anne's', 1927, CCA Montreal.

Mawson, E.P., Blackpool Town Planning Scheme: Blackpool Civic Survey and Development Scheme, 1952 (typescript), CCA Montreal.

Mawson, Margaret and David, 'A Newsletter to Descendants of T.H.M: A Visit to Canada', September–October 1977.

Powers, A.A., 'Architectural Education in Britain 1880–1914', PhD University of Cambridge, 1982.

Sturgis, Tim, 'The Context around the building of Blackwell in 1898–1900', 1998.

Yerolympos, Alexandra, 'Ernest Hébrard en Grèce', mss.

References

Abbreviations used in the references

AAJ   *Architectural Association Journal*
AR   *Architectural Review*
BCL   Blackpool Central Library
BL   British Library
BN   *Balkan News*
CAA UCAL   Canadian Architectural
       Archive, University of Calgary
CCA   Canadian Centre for Architecture,
       Montreal
CDF   Carnegie Dunfermline Trust
CL   *Country Life*
CORA   City of Calgary Records, Archives
CROK   Cumbria Record Office, Kendal
GC   *Gardeners' Chronicle*
GH   *Garden History*
ISM   *International Studio Magazine*
JTPI *Journal of the Town Planning
       Institute*
LUL   Lancaster University Library
NLS   National Library of Scotland
PPA   Peace Palace Archives
PH   *Planning History*
PP   *Planning Perspectives*
SAB   Saskatchewan Archives Board
TB   *The Builder*
TBN   *The Building News*
TGM   *The Gardeners' Magazine*
TPR   *Town Planning Review*
TS   *The Studio*
USAS   University of Saskatchewan
       Archives

INTRODUCTION
pages 8–17

1. Mawson, *Life and Work*, pp.2–4.
2. ibid., p.4.
3. Jordan, 1988, p.15.
4. *Life and Work*, pp.6, 7.
5. ibid., p.6.
6. ibid., p.9.
7. ibid., p.10.
8. Jordan, p.16.
9. Desmond, p.665.
10. *Life and Work*, p.16.
11. ibid., p.18.
12. Bateman, *Acreocracy of England*, 1883.
13. Powers, pp.37, 38.
14. Sedding, preface, p.vi.
15. Blomfield, p.2.
16. Ottewill, *The Edwardian Garden*, p.8.
17. Robinson, *The Garden Beautiful*,
    passim.
18. Ferguson, *Empire*, p.247.

CHAPTER 1
pages 18–53

1. Thomas H.Mawson, *Life and Work*.
2. ibid., p.21.
3. Rawnsley, *Ruskin and the English Lakes*,
   pp.184–5.
4. Brunton, *The Arts & Crafts Movement
   in the Lake District*, p.132.
5. Walton, 'The Windermere Tourist
   Trade', in Westall, *Windermere*, p.20.

6. ibid., p.22.
7. Dowthwaite, 'The Lake District
   Defence Society Century', in Westall,
   Windermere, p.55.
8. Westall, 'The Retreat to Arcadia', in
   Westall, *Windermere*, p.36.
9. ibid., pp.34–5.
10. Cumbria Record Office, Kendal
    (hereafter CROK), WDB/76 44,
    *Proposed New Terrace at Belsfield,
    Bowness*, for H.Allen, 1912; WDB/76
    182, *Suggested Garden alterations,
    Belsfield*, for H.Allen, July 1922.
11. Brunton, p.14.
12. ibid., p.13.
13. Mawson Brothers catalogues for the
    Seed and Nursery Estabishment,
    Windermere; *Life and Work*, p.22.
14. *Life and Work*, p.353.
15. Family sources.
16. *Life and Work*, p.22.
17. Haslam, *John Ruskin*, 2004.
18. Dixon Hunt, *The Wider Sea*, p.396.
19. ibid., p.348.
20. Rawnsley, p.23.
21. *Life and Work*, pp.24, 64.
22. Anne L.Helmreich, 'Re-presenting
    Nature and Ideology, Art, and Science
    in William Robinson's "Wild Garden"',
    in Wolschke-Bulmahn, ed., *Nature
    and Ideology*, p.97.
23. Rawnsley, p.48.
24. Ottewill, *The Edwardian Garden*, p.30.
25. Thomas H.Mawson, *The Art and
    Craft of Garden Making*, B.T.Batsford,
    London, 1st edition, 1900, p.6
    (hereafter *Art and Craft*).
26. ibid., pp.1, 2.
27. ibid., p.6.
28. ibid., preface, p.xii.
29. *Life and Work*, pp.28–9.
30. *Art and Craft*, preface, p.xi.
31. CROK, WDB/76 49, *Plan of Gardens,
    Beechmount*, for Colonel Sandys, 1904.
32. Westall, pp.38, 42.
33. ibid., p.42.
34. CROK, WDB/86 M47, *Yews, Bowness,
    for Sir S. Scott* (c.1902).
35. CROK, WDB/76 27, *Layout of gardens,
    Provincial Insurance Co. Kendal* (no
    date).
36. CROK, WDB/76 108, *Suggestions for a
    Water Garden at Levens Hall* (no date).
37. *Life and Work*, p.41.
38. *Art and Craft*, 1st edition, 1900, p.211.
39. ibid., 1st edition, p.65.
40. CROK, WDB/86 L78, *Garden layout for
    Mr Sandys, Windermere*, 1912.
41. CROK, WDB/86 M4, *Trellis and bridge
    at Beechmount, Sawrey, for Col. Sandys,
    MP* (no date).
42. *Life and Work*, p.25.
43. CROK, WDB/76 49, *Plan of Gardens,
    Beechmount, Graythwaite Hall Estate,
    1904*.
44. *Life and Work*, p.25.
45. CROK, WDB/76 240, *Cottages at

Sawrey for Col. Sandys* (no date).
46. *Art and Craft*, 1st edition, 1900,
    pp.88–9.
47. CROK, WDB/133/2/67;
    WDB/133/2/163A, *Langdale Chase
    1880–1939 and estate of the late
    Mrs Edna Howarth*.
48. *Langdale Chase*, Designworks
    (unpaged).
49. ibid.
50. *Life and Work*, p.62.
51. *Art and Craft*, 1st edition, 1900, p.45.
52. Lake District National Park Authority,
    Brockhole, p.14.
53. ibid., p.15.
54. Townsend, 'Notes on Country and
    Suburban Houses', pp.157–64.
55. Baillie Scott, 'On the Characteristics
    of Mr C.F.A.Voysey's Architecture',
    TS, 15 October 1907, vol.42, no.175,
    pp.19–24.
56. Simpson, *C.F.A.Voysey*, 1979.
57. Haslam, p.145.
58. Baillie Scott, op.cit., p.20.
59. Simpson, op.cit., p.77.
60. *Life and Work*, pp.78–9.
61. *Art and Craft*, 1st edition, 1900, p.41.
62. *Life and Work*, p.79.
63. ibid., p.80.
64. *Art and Craft*, 1st edition, 1900, p.62.
65. Baillie Scott, *TS*, April 1897.
66. *Life and Work*, p.84.
67. *Westmorland Gazette*, 'The Old Halls
    of Westmorland', 31 December 1887.
68. O.S. 2nd edition, 1:2,500, 1898.
69. CROK, WDB/86 L68, *Survey at Rydal
    Hall; Proposed Alterations to Grounds,
    Rydal Hall; Proposed Alterations to
    Gardens at Rydal Hall for Stanley
    Le Fleming, Esq.* (c.1909).
70. My thanks are due to Simon
    Bonvoisin, of Nicholas Pearson
    Associates.
71. *Art and Craft*, 5th edition, 1926, p.419.
72. CROK, WDB/76 76, *Proposed Garden
    Far Park, Staveley, for Mrs Braithwaite*.

CHAPTER 2
pages 54–83

1. Family sources; *Life and Work*, p.67.
2. ibid., p.68.
3. T.H.Mawson, *Hanley Park, Hanley*,
   1894, p.7.
4. *Life and Work*, p.63.
5. ibid., p.69.
6. Pearson, *Hidcote*, p.16; *Life and Work*,
   pp.68–9.
7. Cash book.
8. *TS*, vol. XLIV, p.181; Lucy Dynevor, *A
   dissertation on the work of C.E.Mallows*,
   1993; Royal Academy of Arts, *Royal
   Academy Exhibitors*, 1769–1970.
9. Spencer-Longhurst, ed., *Robert
   Atkinson*, nd.
10. Carnegie, *Autobiography*, 1920, p.34.
11. Skibo Visitors' Book.

12. Nasaw, *Andrew Carnegie*, p.540.
13. *Life and Work*, p.102; Land Use
    Consultants, *An Inventory*, p.116.
14. *Art and Craft*, 5th edition, 1926, p.64,
    fig. 77.
15. Eyffinger, *The Peace Palace*, 1992,
    pp.58, 73.
16. Peace Palace Archives, unreferenced
    (PPA).
17. Thomas H.Mawson, *Civic Art*, 1911,
    p.308.
18. Leeuwin, 'The Arts of Peace:
    De tuin van het Vredespaleis', *Jaarboek
    voor de Geschiedenis van Tuin-en
    Landschapsarchitectuur*, Architectura
    & Natura, 3, 1997, p.142.
19. PPA; *Life and Work*, p.147.
20. PPA.
21. PPA, garden orders and receipts,
    15 December 1911, 1 May 1912,
    2 April 1912.
22. PPA; Eyffinger, p.102.
23. PPA; Leeuwin, 'The Arts of Peace',
    Garden History, 28:2 (2000),
    pp.262–76.
24. Honeycombe, *Selfridges*, 1984, pp.31,
    32, 33: *The Times*, 14 June 1909.
25. Wooller, *The Great Estate*, 2000, p.52.
26. Mawson, *Art and Craft*, 2nd edition,
    1901, p.236.
27. ibid., p.238.
28. Mawson, 'Proposed garden, Foots Cray
    Place, Sidcup, Kent, for S.J.Waring,
    Esq.', in *Art and Craft*, 2nd edition,
    1901, pp.236–40.
29. CROK, WDB/86 M66 d, Plan of
    plantations in the wild garden at Foots
    Cray, Sidcup, Kent.
30. CROK WDB/86 a, Plan of a Japanese
    garden, also The Park, Sidcup, for
    S.J.Waring.
31. *Life and Work*, p.148.
32. ibid., p.149.
33. *Art and Craft*, 4th edition, 1912,
    p.89, fig.107; *Life and Work*, p.149;
    WDB/86 L59.
34. 'Le Chateau d'Anglevillier' in *Les Beaux
    Domaines*, vol.XIV, I December 1913,
    pp.320–7.
35. ibid., p.320.
36. My thanks to Gay Daniels for her help
    with this information.
37. Battiscombe, *Queen Alexandra*, 1969,
    p.88.
38. ibid., p.263.
39. CROK WDB/86 M66 h, Flower border
    at Hvidöre, Copenhagen, for
    H.M.Queen; Gardens at Hvidöre,
    Copenhagen, for Her Majesty, Queen
    Alexandra; Royal Photographic
    Collection; Windsor.
40. Royal Photographic Collection;
    Battiscombe, p.263; my thanks are due
    to Dr Lulu Salto Stephensen for
    information concerning the fate of.
    Hvidöre.
41. *Life and Work*, p.115.

42. Thomas H.Mawson, 'Thornton Manor, Cheshire, England', in *AR*, November 1917, pp.442–9.

43. ibid., p.445.

44. *Life and Work*, p.117.

45. *Art and Craft*, 4th edition, 1912, p.247; *AR*, pp.441, 450.

46. Robert Atkinson drawing of Cricket Pavilion, *Civic Art*, p.40.

47. Robert Mattocks drawing of lake, canal etc, Thornton Manor, *Civic Art*, p.180.

48. West Pennines Moors Area Management Committee, Lord Leverhulme, 1999.

49. Prentice Mawson, drawing of shelter, *Civic Art*, p.189; *Art and Craft*, 5th edition, 1926, pp.374–80; *Life and Work*, p.129.

50. Robert Atkinson, drawing of look-out tower, *Civic Art*, facing p.342.

51. *Life and Work*, p.129.

52. *Art and Craft*, 5th edition, 1926, pp.374–80; *Life and Work*, p.129.

53. CROK. WDB/76 132, Mawson and Partners, Housing Scheme at Tarbert, Harris, Outer Hebrides; WDB/76 134, Circular garden at Borve Lodge, Isle of Harris, Outer Hebrides; WDB/76 219, Planting plan for fruit trees, Borve Lodge.

CHAPTER 3

pages 84–111

1. *Life and Work*, p.46.

2. Ottewill, *The Edwardian Garden*, 1989, pp.34, 36.

3. *Scottish Inventory*, vol. 4, pp.104–8.

4. *Art and Craft*, 2nd edition, 1901, p.216.

5. *Scottish Inventory*, vol. 2, pp.162–3.

6. *Art and Craft*, 1st edition, 1900, p.200.

7. *Life and Work*, p.152; Hermione Lee, *Edith Wharton*, pp.241, 462.

8. *Art and Craft*, 4th edition, 1912, p.363.

9. Cash book.

10. *Life and Work*, p.46.

11. *AR*, vol.27, February 1910, p.397.

12. *Art and Craft*, 5th edition, 1926, p.397.

13. *Art and Craft*, 4th edition, 1912, p.363.

14. Colston Stone Practice, *Wood House*, p.39.

15. *Art and Craft*, 5th edition, 1926, p.396.

16. ibid., p. 297.

17. *Art and Craft*, 4th edition, 1912, p.363.

18. *AR*, vol.28, August 1910, pp.70–72.

19. *Art and Craft*, 4th edition, 1912, pp.190–1.

20. *Life and Work*, p.95.

21. Gwynedd Archives Service, Caernarfon Record Office (CRO), CRO XD96/1/1.

22. CRO XD92/22, undated.

23. CRO XD92/23, undated; CRO XD92/35, undated; CRO XD92/36, 18 July 1902; CRO XD92/23, 29 September 1902.

24. Photograph of pavilion, 17 December 1901, Williams-Ellis collection.

25. CRO XD92/33, *c*.1901; CRO XD92/26, undated; *Register of Parks and Gardens in Wales, Conwy, Gwynedd and the Isle of Anglesey*: Wern, pp.309–14.

26. CROK WDB/86 A49, Details of proposed semi-detached houses in Roumania (sic), undated.

27. *Art and Craft*, 5th edition, 1926, p.387.

28. ibid., p.386.

29. ibid., p.387.

30. *Life and Work*, p.106.

31. *Art and Craft*, 5th edition, 1926, p.388.

32. *Art and Craft*, 4th edition, 1912, p.118.

33. *Art and Craft*, 5th edition, 1926, p.388.

34. ibid., p.389.

35. ibid., plan p.386.

36. Torode, *Duffryn*, p.27; CADW/ICOMOS *Register, Wales*.

37. *Life and Work*, pp.134–5.

38. CROK WDB/86 M37, Gardens at 'Hannah-Ford' for Major Bolitho, undated.

39. *Life and Work*, p.138.

40. CROK WDB/86 A5, Survey of house and garden for Mrs Gordon-Canning, Hartpury House, January 1907.

41. *Art and Craft*, 5th edition, 1926, p.63; *Life and Work*, p.139.

42. CROK WDB/76 138, Proposed additions and Improvements to the Gardens, Hartpury, Glos., undated.

43. CROK WDB/M66g, Arrangement of Flower Borders at Hartpury House for Mrs Gordon-Canning, undated.

44. CROK WDB/86 A 26, Survey of house and garden for Mrs Gordon-Canning, Glos., proposed additions and improvements to the garden, 1 August 1907.

45. G.H.Hollingworth, 'Hartpury House', *TGM*, 15 February 1913, p.118.

46. ibid., p.117.

47. Christopher Hussey, 'Lees Court, Kent', *Country Life*, 12 August 1922.

48. *Life and Work*, p.150; family sources.

49. Gertrude Jekyll, Reef Point Collection, Folder 80, Notebook, Lees Court, Godalming Museum Library.

50. Tempest Hay, 'Lees Court', 1997.

51. *Art and Craft*, 5th edition, 1926, pp. 267–8.

52. ibid., p.269.

53. ibid., p.100, fig. 133; p.101, fig. 34; p.42, fig. 27.

CHAPTER 4

pages 112–35

1. *Life and Work*, p.142. The 'London architect' is unknown.

2. ibid.

3. *TB*, XCI, 1906, p.249.

4. Kelly's Directories; CROK Box 55, photographs; Westminster City Archives, CD1 982, Air Raid Damage Report.

5. Family sources.

6. *Art and Craft*, 4th edition, 1912, p.115.

7. ibid., pp.114–18.

8. *Art and Craft*, 5th edition, 1926, p.268.

9. *Life and Work*, p.213; frontispiece. Acknowledgements to Kate Harwood and Fiona Leadley.

10. C.E.Mallows, Plan of Tirley Garth Court and Gardens, in Anne Helmreich, *The English Garden and National Identity*, p.152; Dynevor, p.32; Tirley Court Cheshire: East Side. Designed and drawn by C.E.Mallows, FRIBA, *TS*, vol.46, no. 192, 15 March 1909, p.127; Drawings of Tirley Court, *TS*, vol. XLII, pp.123, 124.

11. C.E.Mallows, 28 Conduit Street, Tirley Garth Cheshire, for R.H.Prestwich Esq., no date; Proposed Planting of Rhododendron Beds at Tirley Garth for R.H.Prestwich Esq., Thomas Mawson & Sons, no date; Terrace Borders, Tirley Garth, no date or signature. In hands of owners.

12. T.H.Mawson & Sons, Plan of House and Terrace, no date; CROK WDB/76, proposed planting at Tirley Garth for RH Prestwich, Esq.(undated).

13. CROK WDB/86 L55, Garden layout for Wall Hampton House (sic), Lymington, Hampshire, for Lord St. Cyres.

14. Enclosed Garden Court, Walhampton House, Lymington, Hampshire, *TB*, 3 November 1916, and Mawson's account, *Art and Craft*, 5th edition, 1926, p.276.

15. *GC*, vol.I, p.75, 21 June 1924.

16. *Life and Work*, p.321.

17. Lakeland Nurseries's mostly undated plans are filed at Kendal Record Office.

18. *TBN*, Garden Loggia at Boveridge Park, Dorsetshire, Mr E.Guy Dawber, FSA, FRIBA, Architect, 26 May 1922.

19. CROK WDB/86 113, Boveridge Park (undated); *Life and Work*, p.322.

20. *Life and Work*, p.322.

21. Jekyll, Reef Point collection, folder 136, Godalming Museum Library.

22. *Life and Work*, pp.153, 323.

23. *Art and Craft*, 5th edition, 1926, pp.400–3; *Life and Work*, p.324.

24. *CL*, 21 March 1931.

25. *Scottish Inventory*, vol.4, 00.104–8.

26. CROK WDB/86 M97A, proposed planting plan at Dunira, Comrie, for W.Gilchrist Macbeth Esq., November 1920; Detailed planting plan west and south terraces, Dunira, 3 March 1921; Box 3 photographs.

27. Accounts show last payment 10 January 1923.

28. Sale catalogue, Elm Court, Harrogate, 27 July 1927.

29. *Art and Craft*, 5th edition, 1926, p.373: CROK WDB/76 135 (undated): WDB/76 64, revised setting out plan for Elm Court, May 1924.

CHAPTER 5

pages 136–65

1. *Life and Work*, p.120; *The Studio*, 1907.

2. CROK WDB/86 L 69, Mrs Rose Old Westbury; my thanks to Richard Gachot, Westbury historian.

3. *Life and Work*, p.189.

4. See chapter 6.

5. *Life and Work*, p.113.

6. Cherry, *Cities and Plans*, p.73.

7. Landscape architects were slow to organise themselves into a professional body; the British Association of Garden Architects were established in December 1929, only to rename themselves the Institute of Landscape Architects in 1930.

8. *Life and Work*, p.160.

9. Pope, 'Gardens as a Frame for the Country', *AR*, vol.30, 1911, pp.339–51.

10. *Life and Work*, p.164; Official Register of Harvard University, vol.XI, no.III, part 7, 5 August 1914.

11. Frederick Law Olmsted, 'Reply on Behalf of the City Planning Conference', in *Proceedings of the Third National Conference on City Planning*, Boston, 1911, pp.3–13.

12. *Life and Work*, p.188.

13. ibid., pp.190–1.

14. David L.A.Gordon, 'Ottawa-Hull and Canberra: Implementation of Capital City Plans', *Canadian Journal of Urban Research*, 11:2, Winter 2002, pp.183–6.

15. *Life and Work*, pp.187–8.

16. David Mawson, *Newsletter*, 1977.

17. T.H.Mawson, *Report on Alternative Schemes for the Improvement of Coal Harbour and Stanley Park, Vancouver B.C*, 16 October 1912, pp.1–24; *Life and Work*, p.204.

18. Mawson, 'Vancouver: A City of Optimists', *TPR*, vol.iv, no.1, 1913, p.8.

19. Mawson, Alternative Schemes…Coal Harbour and Stanley Park, op.cit., p.3.

20. ibid., p.7.

21. ibid., p.3.

22. ibid., p.13.

23. ibid., p.17; 'Vancouver:A City of Optimists', op.cit., p.10.

24. *Daily Province*, 20 December 1912.

25. *Life and Work*, p.227.

26. Warren P.Laird, Thomas H.Mawson, Richard J.F.Darley, G.L.Thornton Sharp, Charles J.Thompson, *Report to the Board of Governors of the University of British Columbia*, 10 November 1913, pp.16, 32–3.

27. ibid.

28. USAS, Professor W.G.Murray to Thomas H.Mawson, 21 October 1912.

29. USAS, Ross to Murray, 20 December 1912.

30. USAS, Mawson to Murray, 3 July 1913.

31. USAS, John Mawson to the Bursar, 6 August 1914.

32. Vancouver City Archives, *Scheme for the Improvement of Brockton Point, Stanley Park, Vancouver, for the Board of Park Commissioners*, c.1914.

33. CCA, CAN NA44, Thomas H.Mawson, Borden Park, 1914.

34. Dalhousie University Archives; *Dalhousie Morning Chronicle* (undated).

35. Lyle Dick, 'Greening of the West: horticulture on the Canadian prairies, 1870–1930', *Manitoba History*, Spring 1996, i31, p.4.

36. J.William Brennan, 'Visions of a "City Beautiful": The Origins and Impact of the Mawson Plans for Regina', *Saskatchewan History*, vol.46, no.2, Fall 1994, p.23.

37. Barnhart, *Building for the Future*, p.36.

38. Lyle Dick, op.cit., p.2; *Life and Work*, p.198.

39. Brennan, op.cit., p.20.

40. Lyle Dick, op.cit., p.3.

41. SAB R.195.2 1.78, John Mawson to Malcolm Ross, 2 January 1913.

42. SAB R 192 1.78, M.Ross to J.Mawson, 3 December 1912.

43. SAB R 195.2 119G-1164/5, memo from M.Ross to J.Mawson, 2 January 1914.

44. SAB R 195.2 1.78, T.H.Mawson to M.Ross, 18 June 1913; SAB R-962 24n; T.H.Mawson, *Regina: A Preliminary Report on the Development of the City*, *c*.1914, p.44.

45. SAB R 195.2 1.78, J.Mawson to M.Ross, 14 October 1913.

46. SAB R 195.2, T.H.Mawson to John Mawson, 26 September 1913.

47. SAB R 195.2, J.Mawson to A.Mcleod, Minister of Public Works, 7 October 1920.

48. Brennan, op.cit., p.27.

49. SAB R 195.2-119G, J.Mawson to Deputy Minister of Public Works, 13 May 1921.

50. SAB R 195.2-119G-1229, J.Mawson to A.Macleod, 7 October 1920; SAB R 195.2-119G-1231/2, memo to Thomas Mawson & Sons from Minister of Public Works, 16 November 1920; SAB R 195.2-119G-1233/4; T.H.Mawson to Deputy Minister of Public Works, 14 December 1920; SAB 195.2-119G-1235-8, T.H.Mawson to Deputy Minister of Public Works, 13 May 1921.

51. *Wascana Centre Master Plan,* pp.10, 92.

52. *Regina:A Preliminary Report*, op.cit.,p.34.

53. *Life and Work*, p.200.

54. E.Joyce Morrow,'*Calgary, Many Years Hence*', City of Calgary/University of Calgary, 1979, unpaged.

55. CAA UCAL 59A/79.15, Inventory of prints made from original glass slides by T.H.Mawson, *c*.1912.

56. Max Foran, 'The Mawson Report in Historical Perspective', *Alberta History*, vol.27–8, 1979–80, Summer 1980, p.32.

57. Thomas Hayton Mawson, *The City of the Plain and How to make it Beautiful*, Calgary City Planning Commission, 9 April 1912, p.7.

58. CORA Town Planning Commission (Committee), RG 1501, Box 1, File*1, G.W.Lemon to Mayor and Council, 30 September 1912; Box 1 File*2, James Davidson, Chairman of the Executive Committee to Mayor and Council, 12 October 1912.

59. CORA City Clerk to Mawson, 4 February 1913.

60. CORA Box 1 File* 2, H.Waites, Acting Secretary to Mayor and Council, 21 July, 1913.

61. Foran, op.cit., p.37.

62. CORA Box 1 File* 2, H.Waites to members of the City Planning Commission (CPC), 20 November 1913.

63. CAA UCAL, MAW 180/A84.01, Mawson to William Pearce, President of Calgary CPC, 17 April 1914.

64. CORA Box 1 File*4, James Crossland to T.T.Johns, Alberta Town Planning and Housing Association, 6 August 1914.

65. CAA UCAL, 180A/84.01, J.Mawson to T.T.Johns, 6 August 1914.

66. CAA UCAL, T.H.Mawson to T.T.Johnson, 24 November 1914; T.H.Mawson to Alexander Calhoun, 7 January 1915.

67. Foran, op.cit., p.36, p.39 footnote 57.

68. *Life and Work*, p.203.

69. ibid.

70. T.H.Mawson, 'Report of Proposed Artistic Layout of Banff', in *Annual Report of Department of Interior*, Ottawa, 1914.

71. John Crosby Freeman, 'Thomas Mawson, Imperial Missionary of British Town Planning', *Revue d'Art Canadienne*, vol.2, no.2, 1975, pp.42–3.

72. *Life and Work*, p.187.

73. T.H.Mawson, *The City of Calgary*, Prologue, 1914.

74. Rybczynski, *A Clearing in the Distance*, p.344.

75. E.Joyce Morrow, '*Calgary, Many Years Hence*' unpaged.

76. *Life and Work*, p.197.

CHAPTER 6
pages 166-83

1. University of Melbourne Archive, File 1914–182, UM 312, Registrars' Correspondence (UM 312), Notice of Motion for Council; Mawson to Barff (Registrar, University of Sydney), 15 January 1913; *Life and Work*, p.211.

2. *Life and Work*, p.209.

3. UM 312, Dr Barrett, Melbourne, to J.P. Bainbridge, Registrar, Melbourne, 29 August 1913; Todd (Secretary, University of Sydney) to Vice Chancellor, University of Melbourne, 4 March 1914; *Life and Work*, p.213.

4. *Life and Work*, p.217.

5. ibid., p.219.

6. CROK, WGB/86 L6: *The projected new Italian garden at Athens for the King of the Hellenes*, 20 May 1913; *Proposed remodelling of Palace gardens layout Athens*, 1914; *Proposed remodelling of the King's palace gardens for His Majesty the King of the Hellenes,* 1914; *Suggestions for the remodelling of the Royal palace gardens for His Majesty the King of the Hellenes*, 1914.

7. Thomas H.Mawson, 'The replanning of Athens', in *AR*, 45, March 1919, p.48.

8. *Life and Work*, p.218; *AR,* pp.48–9.

9. *Life and Work*, pp.221–2.

10. ibid., p.226.

11. ibid., p.237.

12. ibid., p.239.

13. ibid., p.234.

14. ibid., p.317.

15. ibid., p.275.

16. Yerolympos, 'Thessaloniki (Salonika) before and after 1917', *PP*, May 1988, p.144.

17. *Life and Work*, p.281.

18. Mazower, *Salonica*, pp.318–20.

19. Thomas H. Mawson, 'The British Soldier in Macedonia', in *The Contemporary Review*, vol.CXIV, July–Dec. 1918, p.55.

20. John Mawson, 'The Future of Salonika', *Balkan News* (*BN*), 21 May 1919.

21. John Mawson, 'The Salonika Town Planning Act', *TPR*, vol.IX, 1921, p.148.

22. ibid., p.148.

23. *Proothos* (Progress): 12, 18, 20, 29 August, 9 September, in Yerolympos, ed., 'Ernest Hébrard en Grèce', unpublished.

24. *Life and Work*, pp.271–3.

25. Yerolympos, *Urban Transformations*, 1996, p.106.

26. ibid., p.92.

27. Yerolympos, *PP*, 1988, pp.152, 150.

28. Yerolympos, *Urban Transformations*, 1996, p.106.

29. *Life and Work*, p.276.

30. ibid., p.279.

31. ibid., pp.279–82.

32. *Life and Work*, p.284.

33. Yerolympos, *Urban Transformations*, 1996, p.103.

34. John Mawson, *BN*, 21 May 1919.

35. Yerolympos, *PP*, 1988, pp.158–63.

36. Thomas H. Mawson, *BN*, 30 January 1918.

37. Anon – probably Thomas Mawson – *Times Engineering Supplement*, May 1919.

38. Thomas H.Mawson, *BN*, 30 January 1918.

39. Yerolympos, *PP*, 1988, p.154.

40. *Life and Work,* p.288.

41. John Mawson, 'Address to Council for the Installation of Refugees in destroyed areas of Macedonia', *c*. end of May 1919, quoted in full in Kiki Kafkoula, 'The Garden City Idea in Greek Inter-war Planning', PhD, Aristotelian University of Thessaloniki, July 1990, pp.309–16.

42. *Life and Work*, p.286.

43. John Mawson, 'Address', op. cit., p.312.

44. Thomas H.Mawson to A.Papanastassiou, 24 June (11 June, orthodox calendar) in Kafkoula, pp.316–17.

45. *Times Engineering Supplement*, May 1919.

46. Kiki Kafkoula, 'The replanning of the destroyed villages of Eastern Macedonia', *PH*, vol.14, no.2.

47. John Mawson, 'Address', op.cit., p.312.

48. Royal Academy exhibit 1066, 1921; *Life and Work*, p.327.

49. *Life and Work*, p.333.

50. Yerolympos, see plan in *Urban Transformations*, 1996, p.30; RA exhibit 1256, 1932.

51. Thomas H.Mawson, *Athens of the Future and the Salonika of Tomorrow* (in Greek), National Printing Office, Athens, 1918.

52. ibid.

53. Kafkoula, 'The replanning of the destroyed villages of Eastern Macedonia', op.cit., p.8.

CHAPTER 7
pages 184–213

1. Gaskell, *Mary Barton*, pp.66–7.

2. Mearns, *The Bitter Cry of Outcast London*, 1883

3. Mawson, *Civic Art*, 1911, preface.

4. ibid., pp.337–8.

5. CROK, Thomas H.Mawson, *Hanley Park, Hanley*, 1894, p.9.

6. *Civic Art*, p.338.

7. *Hanley*, pp.13–14.

8. *Civic Art*, p.338.

9. *Life and Work*, p.36.

10. *South Wales Argus*, 8 September 1894.

11. Nasaw, *Andrew Carnegie*, pp.641–2.

12. ibid., p.642.

13. P.Geddes, *City Development*, 1904; Meller, *Cities and Evolution*, in Sutcliffe, ed., *The Rise of Modern Urban Planning*, Mansell, 1980.

14. *Life and Work*, p.100; *Civic Art*, pp.311–25; CROK WDB 86 M47, R.Mattock, Pittencrieff Park; WDB 86 M 174 CC D Pittencrieff House and Pond Garden, 1909.

15. NLS M 10536, letters to/from Sir Patrick Geddes, 25 February 1904.

16. NLS 10536, 26 July 1904.

17. *Life and Work*, p.101; NLS 10536 Mawson to Geddes, 3, 19, 29 August 1904.

18. NLS 10544, Mawson to Geddes, 16 October 1914.

19. CROK WDB 86/M66, L.Späth, Gartengestaltung, Berlin-baumschulenweg.

20. *Civic Art*, p.340; *Civic Art*, p.195; CROK WDB 86 L 89, Plan of terraces to east of Falinge, n.d.

21. CROK, T.H.Mawson, *Haslam Park*, *Preston*, March 1915, pp.12, 28; CROK WDB 86 Box 3, Haslam Park, n.d.

22. WDB 86 Cash book, 16 January 1908.

23. CROK, Port Sunlight, WDB 86 TP 12, October 1906.

24. JTPI, XXIV, p.191.

25. Ashworth, *The Genesis of Modern British Town Planning*, p.188; Parliamentary Debates, vol.188, col.949, 12 May 1908.

26. *Life and Work*, p.178; Cash book, December 1910, lectures for half of session, £30, examination fees, £1 15s.3d, March 1911.

27. Reilly, *Scaffolding in the Sky*, pp.128–9.

28. Jordan, 1988, pp.52–3.

29. Howard, *Garden Cities of To-Morrow*, 1898; Unwin, *Town Planning in Practice*, 1909; Sitte, *City Planning according to Artistic Principles*, translated by Collins, 1965; Triggs, *Town Planning, Past, Present and Possible*, Methuen & Co, London, 1909.

30. *Civic Art*, pp.14–15.

31. Thomas H.Mawson, *Bolton as it is and as it might be*, n.d.

32. *Life and Work*, p.245.

33. ibid., pp.262, 268; *An Imperial Obligation*, 1917.

34. *Life and Work*, p.264.

35. Thomas H.Mawson, *Afforestation*, 1917.

36. *Lancaster Guardian*, 'War Memorial: Westfield Industrial Village', 30 November 1918.

37. Alexander Drury, *Environment and Community: Motive and Practice in the Case of Westfield War Memorial Village, 1918–39*, Lancaster University unpublished MA, 2004, pp.38–40.

38. *Life and Work*, pp.291–6; CROK WDB 86 A216, The Metropolitan Borough of Stepney Scheme for Replanning, 20 September 1918.

39. *Tudor Walters Report of the Committee on Questions of Building Construction in Connection with the Provision of Dwellings for the Working Classes*, cd.9191, HMSO, 1918; Cullingworth, *Town and Country Planning in Britain*, p.4.

40. *Life and Work*, p.344.
41. Walton, *Riding on Rainbows*, p.4.
42. Thomas Mawson, 'Southport Improvement Scheme', *Civic Art*, pp.325–37; CROK WDB 86 Box 3 Southport, n.d.
43. CROK WDB 86 L18 *Blackpool Promenade, South Shore, Blackpool Town Planning Scheme*; CCA, *The County Borough of Blackpool, The New Parks and Recreation Ground*; WDB 86 M 174 and WDB 86 A2 *Marine Park Lytham St Anne's*, 1926; WDB 86 L110, *Lytham St Anne's seafront and layout and Japanese garden*, n.d.; CCA, *Report on Squires Gate Holiday Camp, Lytham St Anne's*, 1927.
44. BCL, *Agreement, Borough of Blackpool and Thomas Mawson & Sons*, 2 September 1924.
45. BCL, *Opening of the Marine Promenade and Stanley Park, 1926, by the Right Honourable The Earl of Derby*; CROK WDB 86 L81, *Stanley Park*, no date; WDB 86 A6, *County Borough of Blackpool, New Public Park and Recreation Centre, 1923*.
46. BCL, Thomas H.Mawson, *New Park and Recreation Centre for Blackpool*, 1922.
47. CCA, *Blackpool Town Planning Scheme: Blackpool Civic Survey and Development Scheme*, 1925 (typescript).
48. Walton, *Riding on Rainbows*, p.3.
49. *Life and Work*, Weston-super-Mare, p.346; CROK WDB/86 M 174, Town Planning, Southend on Sea, 19 August 1931; CCA, *Bridlington of the Future: Being a Report on a Comprehensive Development Scheme for the Town and Sea Front*, Thomas H.Mawson & Son, 1931; CROK WDB/86 TP4, Borough of Hastings Town Planning Scheme, Edward Prentice Mawson for Thomas H.Mawson & Sons, Adams and Thompson, September 1926.
50. CCA, *County Borough of Northampton, Proposals for Development and Reconstruction*, Thomas H.Mawson & Sons and Adams and Thompson, 1925.
51. Plymouth Central Library, Council Minutes, Hoe and Parks Committee including Mawson Report, 1927–8; Souvenir programme for the *Opening of The Central Park*, 29 July 1931; CROK WDB/86 L99, *Plymouth Central Park plan elevation and sections of winter gardens, potting sheds, offices, and range of glass*.

CONCLUSION
pages 214–23

1. The Horticultural College for Women, Swanley College, Kent, *Prospectus 1932–3*.
2. Cash book, 1933–5.
3. *Life and Work*, pp.335–6.
4. *AR*, vol.22, July–Dec 1907, p.156.
5. Thomas H.Mawson, 'The History of the English Garden' in Richard Sudell, ed., *Landscape Gardening, Planning-Construction Planting*, Ward, Lock & Co. Ltd, 1933, pp.13–20.
6. *Life and Work*, p.350.
7. Thomas H.Mawson, 'The Unity of the House and Garden', *JRIBA*, 3rd series, vol.IX, no.14, 31 May 1902, pp.357–75.
8. Thomas H.Mawson, 'Garden Architecture', *Architectural Association Journal*, vol.XXIII, Jan–Dec 1908, p.176.
9. Lutyens papers, Book 18, Lu/E/9/6/6 (i), Lu/E/9/6/7, April 8, 9, 1908, RIBA.
10. Ridley, Jane, *The Architect and his Wife: A Life of Edwin Lutyens*, Chatto & Windus, London, 2002, p.177.
11. An Entrance Gateway to a capital City – Design by Prentice Mawson, Soane Medallion Competition, 1911, *TBN*, 10 February 1911.
12. Family sources.
13. Thomas H.Mawson, 'English and Italian Garden Architecture', *JRIBA*, 3rd series, vol.XV, no.16, pp.485–96.
14. Thomas H.Mawson, 'Renaissance Gardens', *JRHS*, 12 October 1909, pp.335–41.
15. BL Add.63186 f.12, letter to George Bernard Shaw, 8 October 1917.
16. Liverpool University Archive, S.2363, pp.165,170; S.2363, p.396. My thanks are due to Adrian Allan, University Archivist.
17. WDB/86/A10: Ahmadiyya Mosque Southfields, January 1926; 19 April 1926.
18. WDB/86 M66 J,K: Saffron Hill Cemetery, no date.

Acknowledgements

In writing this book I discovered many people who were as enthusiastic about Thomas Mawson as myself, and I owe a great debt of gratitude to these relatives, colleagues, friends – including Pam and Mike Shafe – and private owners of gardens (whose privacy will be respected) who gave me access to their property. For illustrations I am indebted to Lancaster University's Librarian, Jacqueline Whiteside; Barbara Moth, Bronwen Williams-Ellis, David Williams-Ellis, Chris Jones, David Turner and Peter de Savary. Many weeks were spent in the Kendal Record Office, where staff nobly unearthed from the depths many plans and drawings. In Canada helpful city archivists in Vancouver, Calgary and Regina added to material found in the university archives of Vancouver, Calgary and Saskatoon. I am grateful for Kelly Casey's help in tracking down the campus plan of Dalhousie University. It was a unique experience to work in the Canadian Centre for Architecture in Montreal, and I thank Paul Chénier for his help. In Greece the kindness and assistance given by Alexandra Yerolympos and Kiki Kafkoula, both professors at the Aristotelian University in Thessaloniki, made unravelling the story of the Mawsons in Greece very much easier.

I would like to thank John Borron, Diana Matthews and Dr Jean Turnbull of Lancaster University, who helped to get things moving in the Lake District; Angus MacLaren, Alison Allighan and Christopher Dingwall, for their knowledge of Scottish gardens; Barbara Moth, for her advice on Midland parks and gardens; Kate Harwood and Fiona Leadley, for information on Bushey rose garden; Nasser Khan, for giving me access to the Fazl Mosque garden; Derek Woolerton, former landscape architect with Thomas H.Mawson and Son; Dr Paula Henderson, Magda Salvesen and Richard Gachot, for information on Long Island country houses; Claude Hitchens, for advice on Pulham & Son; Phillip Olterman for telling me about Kurt Schwitters; Professor Mark Mazower, for information about Thessaloniki; the Lake District National Park Authority, for access to Brockhole's archive; the Rt Rev. James Newcome and Christine Parker of Rydal Hall for access to the gardens and museum; Chris Crowder, the head gardener at Levens Hall, and the many members of the Association of Gardens Trusts who gave me leads to their treasures.

Simon Bonvoisin, of Nicholas Pearson Associates Ltd, Colson Stone Practice and Peter Atkinson, Hampshire County Council's historic gardens landscape architect, allowed me access to reports. Elisabeth King of the Royal Academy of Arts Archive, Frances Dimond, of the Royal Photographic Collection, Windsor, Olive Geddes, of the National Library of Scotland, Dick Lughthart, of the Peace Palace Archive, The Hague, and Adrian Allan, of Liverpool University, found me valuable material, as did the librarians of the Staveley and District Historical Society, the Imperial War Museum, the Landscape Institute, Godalming Museum Library, Plymouth Library, Blackpool Central Library; City of Westminster Archives; Aileen Smith, librarian at the Architectural Association and Bexley Council's Education Service. I thank The National Trust and Brantwood Trust for allowing me to take photographs on their land, and the archivists of Harvard, Toronto and Melbourne Universities.

I am grateful for translation from original material in Dutch by Trjntje Ytsma; from French by Gay Daniels; and from Greek by Mando and Philip Watson, and Panorea Alexandratos.

The wide spread of the Mawson family, each person with something new to add, gave much needed aspects to the Mawson story. My grateful thanks are extended to Ursula Brighouse, Ted Mawson, Andrea Rollins, Frances Hickman and Beverley Osborne, and extra specially to Christopher, David, Robert and Susan Mawson, and Thomas Mawson for all their help and encouragement and the loan of pictures and private archives.

To John Nicoll, Jane Crawley and Ian Hunt at Frances Lincoln I am indebted for their patience, support and kindness; to Philip Watson also, who, despite his own busy schedule, always found time to discuss progress on the book; but most of all to my husband Peter, who accompanied me on my travels and shared the delights of discovery, and encouraged me along the road to completion.

List of commissions

NOTE ON SOURCES FOR THE COMMISSIONS

The four lists of commissions have been gathered from a number of sources, the most important being the Cumbria Record Office in Kendal, under the references WDB/76 and WDB/86. Some of these records suffered variously from damp, when their previous home in a Lancaster Office sprung a leak in the roof; from Second World War bombing, when the Victoria Street Office in London was damaged by a direct hit next door; from storage, when many plans and drawings were rolled up together inside cardboard tubes with wooden bungs to seal the ends, and from dispersal, when the office of Mawson & Son was wound down in the late nineteen-seventies. Some records will always remain in the hands of their owners, and some have been lost, including the firm's ledgers. Only dated commissions have been included, as Mawson & Son continued as the name of the firm long after Thomas Mawson died in 1933, and the

Cumbria Record Office collection is not chronological. Mawson's many reports, listed in the bibliography, his five editions of *The Art and Craft of Garden Making,* his splendid book on town planning – *Civic Art* – and his autobiography have supplied valuable material. These document his attitudes to current garden and landscaping issues, and describe the vast spread of his achievements. However, with such a crowded life, perhaps Thomas Mawson can be forgiven for not concerning himself too much with the dates of his commissions, for which we hunt in his autobiography.

But thanks to Geoffrey Beard's pioneering exhibition catalogue of Mawson's works at Lancaster University in 1976, Harriet Jordan's London University PhD on Mawson's gardens in 1988, Jim Price's and Janet Thompson's gazetteer of 2007, and the Mattocks family's archive, it has been possible to check and add to the Kendal list.

T.H.Mawson's dated garden commissions

DATE	HOUSE NAME AND LOCATION	HOUSE ARCHITECT	GARDEN DESIGNER	COMMISSIONING
1887	**Birksey Brow**, Crook, Windermere			Sir H. Moore
1887	**Bryerswood**, Sawrey, Windermere	R. Knill Freeman	T.H.Mawson	Joseph Ridgway Bridson
1890	**Rivernook**, Staines, Middlesex	T.E.Colcutt	T.H.Mawson	George Gregory
1891	**Lowood Lodge**, Windermere (later Langdale Chase)	Joseph Pattinson	T.H.Mawson	Mrs Edna Howarth
1892	**The Grange**, Hoylake, Cheshire		T.H.Mawson	Thomas Pegram
1890s	**Little Onn**, Church Eaton, Staffs		T.H.Mawson	The Misses Ashton
1894	**Clevehowe**, Windermere		T.H.Mawson	A.R.Sladen
1894	**Langdale Chase**, Windermere	Grissenthwaite of Penrith	T.H.Mawson	Mrs. Edna Howarth
1894	**Redcourt**, Haslemere, Surrey		T.H.Mawson	Newton
1897	**Beechmount**, Graythwaite Estate, Windermere		T.H.Mawson	Colonel T.Myles Sandys, M.P.
1897	**Heathwaite**, Windermere (house and garden)	Mawson Brothers	Robert Mawson	Robert Mawson
1898	**Kincardine House**, Kincardine O'Neil, Aberdeenshire	Niven & Wigglesworth	T.H.Mawson (plans only)	Mrs Mary Grenville Pickering
1898	**The Corbels**, Heathwaite Estate, Windermere	Mawson & Gibson	T.H.Mawson	T.H.Mawson
1899	**The Flagstaff**, Colwyn Bay	Mawson and Gibson* (house never built)	Mawson & Gibson	Walter Whitehead (refused T.H.M. payment)
1898–1901	**Moor Crag** (late Gill Head)	C.F.A.Voysey	T.H.Mawson	J.W.Buckley
1901	**Storrs Estate**, Windermere			
1898	**Glen Tana House**, Aboyne Castle, Glen Tana, Aberdeenshire	Trufitt and Dan Gibson	T.H.Mawson	Sir William Cunliffe Brooks, M.P.
1898–1910?	**Wood**, South Tawton, Devon	Dan Gibson	Mawson & Gibson James Pulham	William Lethbridge
1898–1900	**Ormidale**, Glendurel, Argyll		T.H.Mawson	Col. Burnley Campbell
1899–1912	**Graythwaite Hall**, Sawrey, Lancashire	R.Knill Freeman and Dan Gibson	T.H.Mawson	Col. T.Myles Sandys, M.P.
1899	**Heathwaite Villas**	T.H.Mawson	T.H.Mawson & Dan Gibson	T.H.Mawson
1899	**Ballimore**, Otter Ferry, Loch Fyne, Lochgilphead, Argyll	Hamilton of Glasgow, designer, Wm. Leiper	T.H.Mawson James Pulham	Captain Macrae Gilstrap
1899	**The Grange**, Wraysbury, Middlesex		T.H.Mawson, James Pulham & Son	G.M.Freeman, Q.C.
1899–1900	**Brockhole**, Windermere	Mawson & Gibson	Mawson & Gibson	W. Gaddum
1899	**Mount Stuart**, Isle of Bute	Sir Rowan Anderson	Mawson & Gibson James Pulham & Son	3rd Marquis of Bute
1899–1912	**The Willows**, Ashton-on-Ribble, Preston, Lancashire		Mawson & Gibson	William C.Galloway

DATE	HOUSE NAME AND LOCATION	HOUSE ARCHITECT	GARDEN DESIGNER	COMMISSIONING
1900?	**Hampton Manor**, Hampton in Arden, West Midlands		W.A. & A.M. Nesfield; T.H.Mawson	Sir Frederick Peel
1900	**Brackley**, Glen Muick, Ballater, Aberdeenshire	Mawson & Gibson,	Mawson & Gibson	Sir Alan & Sir Victor Mackenzie
1900	**Broad Oaks**, Accrington, Lancashire	J.W.Watson, Glasgow	T.H.Mawson	George Macalpine
1900–06	**Greenwood**, Stock, Essex		T.H.Mawson	Richard Adam Ellis, J.P.
1900	**Slains Castle**, Cruden Bay, Peterhead		Mawson and Gibson	Lord Erroll
1900–08	**Cuerdon Hall**, Thelwall, Warrington, Lancashire	Wyatt	T.H.Mawson (plans not accepted)	R.A.Naylor
1900	**St Mary's Lodge**, Newport, Monmouth		T.H.Mawson	Sir Edward Watson, JP
1900	**Cleabarrow**, Windermere		T.H.Mawson	Mr. Long
1900	**Cringlemire**, Troutbeck, Cumbria	Pattinson ?	T.H and Robert Mawson Dan Gibson	Henry Martin
1901	**Kearsney Court**, Kent	Worsfold & Hayward	T.H.Mawson	Edmund Percy Barlow
1901?	**Walmer Place**, Kent		Mawson Bros., James Pulham	Albert Ochs
1901	**Hengrove**, Wendover, Buckinghamshire	P.Morley Horder	T.H.Mawson	Mr.Fletcher
1901	**Berkhamsted**		T.H.Mawson	C.J.Gilbert
1901	**Capernwray Hall**, Carnforth, North Lancashire	Sharpe 1844	T.H.Mawson (earlier, Edward Kemp)	Col. George Marton J.P., D.L.
1901	**Dalham Hall**, Newmarket	new wing Mallows; Lutyens	Mawson, Mallows (not accepted)	Sir Robert Affleck, then Rt Hon. Cecil Rhodes
1901	**Unnamed** marine villa, south coast		Mawson plans only	Abrahams (refused payment)
1901	**Haverbrack**, Lancaster		T.H.Mawson	E.P.Bulfield
1901–1911 1920	**Deoran**, St Ninians, Stirling and post WWI	W.Leiper	T.H.Mawson	Charles A.Buchanan
1901	**Fellside**, Bowness, Cumbria	Dan Gibson 1901	T.H.Mawson	T.D.Lingard
1901–04	**Foots Cray Place**, Kent		Mawson, Gibson, R.Atkinson	Lord Samuel Waring
1901	**The Krall**, Berkhamsted	Dan Gibson	T.H.Mawson	Samuel Rowland Timpson
1901	**Newlands Park**, Chalfont St Giles, Buckinghamshire		T.H.Mawson	Sir Henry A.Harben
1901	**Wych Cross Place**, Sussex	Edmund Fisher	T.H.Mawson	Douglas W.Freshfield
1901–04	**Wern**, Portmadog, Wales	John Douglas of Chester	T.H.Mawson, R.M.Greaves	Richard Methuen Greaves
1902	**Mar Gate**, Stirling	W.Leiper	T.H Mawson	W.Renwick
1902	**Shenstone Court**, Lichfield, Staffordshire		Mawson plans only	Sir Richard Powell Cooper, J.P.
1902	**Shrublands**, Windermere	Dan Gibson	Mawson Bros	Robert Mawson
1902	**Yews**, Storrs Estate, Windermere	W.T.Dolman	Mawson, Lakeland Nurseries, Avray Tipping 1911	Sir J.W.Scott
1902	**Moonhill Place**, Cuckfield, Sussex	P.M.Horder c.1898	T.H.Mawson	Walter Lloyd
1902	**Cripland Court**, Lindfield, Sussex	P.M.Horder additions	T.H.Mawson	Mrs Howarth
1902	**Pressridge**, Forest Row, Sussex	Edmund Fisher	T.H.Mawson	
1902	**Blackwell**, Storrs Estate, Windermere	H.M.Baillie Scott (1898–99)	T.H.Mawson	Sir Edward Holt
1902	**Holehird**, Windermere		T.H.Mawson	W.G.Groves
1902	**Hampton in Arden**, West Midlands		T.H.Mawson	F.R.M.Phelps
1902–07	**Madresfield Court**, Malvern, Worcestershire	Voysey lodges	T.H.Mawson, James Pulham	Lord Beauchamp
1903	**Newlands Park**, Chalfont St Giles, Buckinghamshire	Paul Waterhouse additions	T.H.Mawson	Sir Henry A.Harben
1903–04	**Chelwood Manor**, Sussex	Andrew Prentice	T.H.Mawson	Lady Brassey
1903	**Courtlands**, Goring		T.H.Mawson	
1904	**Walton Old Hall**, Warrington, Cheshire		T.H.Mawson	Frederick W.Monks, J.P. 1908
1904?	**Five Diamonds**, Chalfont St Giles, Buckinghamshire		T.H.Mawson	Dr M. Herringham
1904	**Athelhampton Hall**, Dorchester, Dorset		T.H.Mawson	A.C. de Lafontaine
1904	**White Hill**, Berkhamsted		T.H.Mawson	S.R.Timson
1904	**Wykeham Abbey**, Scarborough, N.Yorkshire		T.H.Mawson, plans only	Viscount Downe
1904	**Chapelwood Manor**, Chelwood Gate, Nutley, Sussex	Andrew Prentice	T.H.Mawson	Lord Brassey
1904	**Normanhurst**, Sussex, Dower House	Andrew Prentice	T.H.Mawson	Lord Brassey
1904	**Witham Hall**, Bourne, Lincolnshire	Andrew Prentice	T.H.Mawson	Walter Fenwick
1904–08	**Walton Old Hall**, Walton Superior, Warrington		T.H.Mawson	Frederick J.Monks, J.P.

DATE	HOUSE NAME AND LOCATION	HOUSE ARCHITECT	GARDEN DESIGNER	COMMISSIONING
1904	**Skibo Castle**, Sutherland	Ross & Macbeth 1900–05	T.H. Mawson	Andrew Carnegie
1904–14	**Dyffryn**, SouthWales	E.A.Landsowne, Newport	Mawson & Cory	John Cory J.P, D.L, then Reginald Cory
1905	**Budbrooke House**, Warwick		T.H.Mawson	Thomas Lloyd
1905	**Bracebridge Court**, Lincoln		T.H.Mawson	William Richardson
1905	**Keffolds**, Haslemere, Surrey	Hutchinson	T.H.Mawson	Commander Henderson
1905	**Friningham Lodge**, Maidstone, Kent	Farmhouse conversion	T.H.Mawson	Dr Edward Augustus Harboard
1905	**Burton Manor**, Burton,Wirral, Cheshire	Sir Charles Nicholson	T.H.Mawson, Beresford Pite	Henry Gladstone
1905	**Rushton Hall**, Kettering, Northamptonshire		T.H.Mawson	J.J.van Allen (refused payment for T.H.M)
1905	**The Shawms**, Radford, Staffordshire	Henry Sandy	T.H.Mawson	Henry James Bostock
1905	**Marden Park**, Godstone, Surrey		T.H.Mawson, plans only	Sir W.E Greenwell
1905	**Roynton Cottage**, Lancashire		Mawson & Lever	William Hesketh Lever
1905	**Rivington**		Mawson, Lever, James Pulham	William Hesketh Lever
1906	**Birch Grove House**, Sussex	since rebuilt	T.H.Mawson	Mrs. Macmillan
1906	**Maby Hall**, Cheshire, (did Mawson confuse this with the Manor House, Mobberley, Knutsford?		T.H.Mawson	Mrs Payne
1906	**Uplands**, Ben Rhydding, West Yorkshire		T.H.Mawson	Alexander Walker
1906	**Uplands**, Stoke Poges, Buckinghamshire		T.H.Mawson	Mrs. P.Lumby
1906, 1914–16	**Ribby Hall**, Kirkham, Yorkshire		T.H.Mawson	W.Duckworth
1906 1914	**The Hill**, Hampstead	E.A.Ould enlarged, Mawson & Leslie Mansfield	Thomas Mawson & Edward Prentice Mawson	William Hesketh Lever
1906	**Hall i' the Wood**, Bolton	Tudor, restored by Jonathan Simpson, Grayson & Ould	T.H.Mawson	William Hesketh Lever
1906–07	**Hannaford Manor**, Poundsgate, Devon	A.Wickham Jarvis 1900	T.H.Mawson	Major Bolitho
1906–14	**Thornton Manor**, Wirral, Cheshire	Douglas & Fordham Alterations from 1891	T.H.Mawson	William Hesketh Lever
1907	**Cross O'Cliff**, Bracebridge Heath, Lincolnshire		T.H.Mawson	Arthur C.Newsum
1907	**Detling Hill**, Maidstone, Kent		T.H.Mawson (not exec.)	Dr Augustus Harboard
1907	**Maesruddud**, Newport, Gwent	Edward P.Warren, enlarged and improved	T.H.Mawson	E.W.T.Llewellyn Brewer Williams
1907	**Farfield Hall**, Ilkeley, West Yorkshire		T.H.Mawson	George Douglas
1907	**New Place**, Botley, Hampshire	Lutyens, 1907	T.H.Mawson	Mrs A.C.Franklyn
1907	**Codford Manor**, Wiltshire		T.H.Mawson	H.C.Moffatt
1907	**Aston Lodge**, Derby		T.H.Mawson	R.S.Boden
1907?	**The Willows**, Ashton-on-Ribble, Preston, Lancashire		T.H.Mawson & Dan Gibson	W.W.Galloway
1907	**Bailrigg House**, Scotforth, Lancaster	Woodfall & Eccles	T.H.Mawson	Herbert L. Storey
1907	**Stonehurst**, Ardingly, Sussex		T.H.Mawson & Norman Searle	J.Stuart
1907	**Hartpury House**, Gloucestershire	Remodelled Guy Dawber	Alfred Parsons; Thomas Mawson	Mrs William Gordon-Canning
1907	**Place House**, Fowey, Cornwall		T.H.Mawson	C.G.Treffrey
1908	**Egmond Rectory**, Egmond, Newport, Shropshire		T.H. Mawson	Rev. Arthur Henry Talbot
1908	**Bryn-y-Mor**, Sutton Coldfield, Warwickshire		T.H.Mawson	William Henry Tonks
1908	**Braeside**, Prenton, Cheshire		T.H.Mawson (advised on gardens)	William Glen Dobie
1908	**Greenwoods**, Stock, Essex		T.H.Mawson	R.Adam Ellis
1908	**Raithwaite**, Penarth, S. Glamorgan		T.H.Mawson	John William Pyman
1908	**Bidston Priory**, Birkenhead, Cheshire		T.H.Mawson	Joseph Bibby
1908	**Fox How**, Loughrigg, Ambleside		T.H.Mawson	Miss Arnold
1908	**Rodborough Court**, Stroud, Gloucestershire	Alfred Bucknell, extended by P.Morley Horder	T.H.Mawson	Sir Alfred Apperly
1908	**Above Beck**, Grasmere	Stephen Healiss	T.H.Mawson	William H.Hoyle
1908–19	**Lees Court**, Faversham, Kent	rebuilt 1910 Edward Hoare & Montague Wheeler	T.H.Mawson, R.Atkinson, Gertrude Jekyll	Mrs Gerald Leigh, then Mrs Halsey to 1924
1909	**St Bernards**, Gerrards Cross, Buckinghamshire	P.Morley Horder	T.H.Mawson	Mrs and H.Prescott Moseley
1909	**Stocks**, Aldbury, Tring, Hertfordshire		T.H.Mawson	Humphrey Ward
1909	**Old Rectory House**, Kidlington		T.H.Mawson	Edward Whitnell

DATE	HOUSE NAME AND LOCATION	HOUSE ARCHITECT	GARDEN DESIGNER	COMMISSIONING
1909	**Skilts** (or Skells), Mappleborough Green, Redditch, Worcsestershire		T.H.Mawson	Sir William Jaffray
1909	**Dunchurch Lodge, Rugby**, Warwickshire	Gilbert Fraser of Liverpool	T.H.Mawson & Sons	John Lancaster
1909	**Bryn-y-Mor**, Sutton Coldfield, West Midlands		T.H.Mawson	W.H.Tonks
1909	**Rydal Hall**, Ambleside		T.H.Mawson	Stanley Hughes le Fleming
1909	**Holker Hall**, Grange-Over-Sands, Cumbria		T.H.Mawson	Lord Cavendish
1909	**The Priory**, Warwick		T.H.Mawson	Thomas Lloyd
1909	**The Cliff**, Warwick	extended by Voysey	T.H.Mawson	Sir Henry Lakin
1909	**Poundon**, Oxford		T.H.Mawson	J.Heywood Lonsdale
1909	**St Mary's Lodge**, Newport, Monmouthshire		T.H.Mawson	Sir Thomas E. Watson, J.P.
1909–10	**Perth and Kendal**		T.H.Mawson	Herbert S.Pullar and R.D.Pullar
1910	**Ashfield House**, Standith, Wigan, Lancs		T.H.Mawson	Harold Sumner
1910	**Kilfillan**, Berkhamsted, Bucks		T.H.Mawson	Harold de Boyd
1910	**Idsworth Park**, Horndean, Hampshire	W.Burn	T.H.Mawson	Sir E.Clarke Jervoise
1910	**Bodelwyddan Castle**, Clwyd, N.Wales		T.H.Mawson	Mrs Aitken
1910	**Holker Hall**, Grange-Over-Sands, Cumbria	Paley &Austin	T.H.Mawson	Lord Richard Cavendish
1910	**Newton Green Hall**, Leeds		T.H.Mawson	Sir Wilfred Hepton
1910	**Bowden Hill**, Laycock, Wiltshire		T.H.Mawson	Herbert Harris
1910	**Maer Hall**, Maer, Shropshire	Doyle of Liverpool	T.H.Mawson (plans made but not carried out)	Frederick James Harrison, JP
1910	**Breadsall Priory**, Derby		T.H.Mawson	Sir Alfred Haslam
1910	**Warren House**, Hayes, Kent	George Somers Leigh Clarke	T.H.Mawson	Sir Robert Laidlaw, M.P.
1910	**Wood Hall**, Cockermouth	C.Ferguson	T.H.Mawson	Sir Edward T.Tyson
1910	**Cragwood**, Windermere		T.H.Mawson	Arthur Warburton
1910	**Wightwick Manor**, Wolverhampton	Edward Ould	Alfred Parsons, then T.H.Mawson	Theodore Mander
1910	**Barwell Court**, Surbiton, Surrey		T.H.Mawson	Lord Erroll
1910?	**Moor Park**, Hertfordshire		T.H.Mawson	Lord Leverhulme
1910–11	**Leweston Manor**, Sherborne, Dorset		T.H.Mawson	Mrs George Hamilton Fletcher
1911	**Barley Wood**, Wrington, Avon	Ernest George additions	T.H.Mawson	Henry Herbert Wills, J.P.
1911	**Kirkby Lonsdale**, Cumbria		Lakeland Nurseries Ltd	Misses Wearing(Waring?)
1911?	**Dewbury House**, Newton Abbot, Devon		T.H.Mawson (not executed)	W.J.Curtis
1911–22	**Rufford Hall**, Rufford, Lancashire		T.H.Mawson	Thomas Fermer Hesketh
1911	**Liscard**, Merseyside		Mawson Brothers?	Captain Richards
1911–13	**Denbury House**, Newton Abbott, Devon		T.H.Mawson	W.J.Curtis
1912–14	**Belsfield**, Bowness, Windermere		Mawson Brothers	H.Allen
1912	**Bellevue House**, Lympne, Hythe, Kent		T.H.Mawson	Gerard W.Smith
1912	**North Cadbury Court**, Somerset		T.H.Mawson	A.L.Langmuir
1912	**Boyton Manor**, Upton Level, Wiltshire		T.H.Mawson	H.C.Moffatt (see also Hamptworth Lodge, Salisbury, Wilts Goodrich Court, all c.1912)
1912	**Briery Close**, Ambleside	Francis Whitwell	T.H.Mawson	O.W.E.Hedley
1912	**Graythwaite Estate**, Cumbria		T.H.Mawson (garden Layout)	Col. Sandys
1912	**Greenways**, Sunningdale, Berkshire		T.H.Mawson	William Marklaw Dean
1912	**Lindrick**, Worksop, Nottinghamshire		T.H.Mawson	J.F.Earley
1912	**Hatton House**, Hatton, Warks	Arkwright	T.H.Mawson	W.Arkwright
1912	**Hampworth Lodge**, Landford, Salisbury, Wiltshire	Dawber	T.H.Mawson	H.C.Moffatt
1912	**Higher Trapp**, Simonstone, Burnley, Lancashire		T.H.Mawson	Henry Noble
1912	**Greenthorne**, Edgworth, Bolton, Lancashire		T.H.Mawson	J.R.Barlow
1912	**Lululaund**, Bushey, Hertfordshire	H.H.Richardson	T.H.Mawson	Sir Hubert von Herkomer, CVO, MA, RA
1912	**Tirley Garth**, Tarporley, Cheshire	C.E.Mallows	C.E.Mallows & Mawson	R.A.Prestwich
1912	**Ashton Lodge**, Aston-on-Trent, Derbyshire		Mawson Brothers?	R.S.Boden
1913	**Walhampton House**, Lymington, Hampshire	Norman Shaw (east wing) E.P.Mawson (additions)	T.H.Mawson	Lord St Cyres
1913?	**Lacies**, Bath Road, Abingdon, Oxon		T.H.Mawson	Richard Chamberlain
1914–17	**Woolley Hall**, Maidenhead, Berkshire		T.H.Mawson	Walter Cottingham

DATE	HOUSE NAME AND LOCATION	HOUSE ARCHITECT	GARDEN DESIGNER	COMMISSIONING
1914	**Maiden Cross**, Hexham, Northumbria		Lakeland Nurseries Ltd	S.Salisbury
1914	**Dallas Road**, Lancaster		Lakeland Nurseries Ltd	Arthur G.Bradshaw
1914	**Ribby Hall**, Kirkham		T.H.Mawson	H.Noble
1915–16	**Hazelwood**, Silverdale, Lancashire	Edward Prentice Mawson (remodelled and extended)	T.H. & E.P.Mawson	W.J.Sharp
1915	**Grey Walls**, Silverdale	Edward Prentice Mawson	T.H. & E.P.Mawson?	W.J.Sharp
1915	**Keen Ground**, Hawkshead, Cumbria	James Jennings, ARIBA	T.H.Mawson & Lakeland Nurseries	Colonel Cowper Essex
1916	**Austby**, Middleton, Lancs		Lakeland Nurseries	J.W.Wilson
1917	**Borve Lodge**, Isle of Harris		Mawson & Partners	Leverhulme
1918	**Hengistbury Head**, High Head Castle, Bournemouth		Philip Tilden; T.H. and E.P. Mawson (plans for castle and gardens, separately. Not implemented)	Gordon Selfridge
1919	**Craigmore**, Colne, Lancs.		T.H. Mawson & Son	Mr Hyde
1919–20	**Thornton Hall**, Ulceby, South Humberside		T.H.and E.P.Mawson	Colonel Smethurst
1920	**Garrison Tower**, Wishaw		T.H. Mawson & Son	Captain Colville
1920	**Elmet Hall**, Leeds		T.H.Mawson	B.J.Redman
1920	**Sidegarth**, Staveley, Cumbria		Lakeland Nurseries Ltd	Mr Mather
1920, 1924–25	**Spinningdale**, Bonar Bridge, Creich, Sutherland		T.H.Mawson	A. Macomb Chance
1920	**Boveridge Park**, Cranborne, Dorset		T.H. & E.P.Mawson, Gertrude Jekyll	Charles W. Gordon
1920	**Dunira**, Perthshire	H.E.Clifford & Lunan	T.H. & E.P.Mawson, James Pulham	W.Gilchrist Macbeth
1920	**Aketon Close**, Spofforth, Harrogate		T.H.Mawson	Colonel Whitehead
1920?	**Ravenhurst**, Bolton, Lancashire		T.H.Mawson	Major Barber-Lomax
1921	**Ingleholme**, Prescot, Lancashire		Lakeland Nurseries Ltd	F.R.Dixon Nuttall
1921	**Russell Park**, Watford		T.H.Mawson	H.H.The Maharaja of Baroda
1921	**Aldworth**, Blackdown, Haslemere, Surrey		T.H.Mawson	H.H.The Maharaja of Baroda
1921	**Far Park**, Staveley, Cumbria		Harry Pierce, Lakeland Nurseries Ltd	Mrs Braithwaite
1922	**Curwen Woods**, Cumbria		T.H.Mawson & Son	Mrs Williamson
1922	**Low Borrons**, Windermere		Lakeland Nurseries Ltd	W.G.Groves, J.P.
1923	**Caldwell Hall**, Nuneaton		Lakeland Nurseries Ltd	A.C.Jones
1924	**Elm Court**, Harrogate, Yorkshire		T.H..Mawson & Sons	L.Guevara
late-1920s	**Croft Hall**, Croft-on-Tees, Yorkshire		T.H. Mawson & Son	Mrs Alfred Chaytor
1924	**Morley Cross**, Kendal		Lakeland Nurseries Ltd.	W.M.Harris
1925?	**Piper's Hill**, Bishopís Itchington, Warks		E.P.Mawson?	Mr Lakin
1925	**Grey Walls**, Silverdale, Lancashire	Edward Prentice Mawson	E.P.Mawson	W.J.Sharp
1927	**Thornton Hall**, Lincolnshire		T.H.Mawson & Son	Smethurst
1929	**Foxholes**, Bayhorse, Lancashire		Lakeland Nurseries	Mrs Barker
1929	**Manor House Estate**, Brightlingsea, Essex		Lakeland Nurseries Ltd	Captain Fenwick
1929	**Bowness-on-Windermere**		Lakeland Nurseries Ltd	E.C.Woods

SOME PARK COMMISSIONS IN THE BRITISH ISLES

DATE	COMMISSION
1891	**Hanley Park**, Staffordshire, Mawson and James Pulham & Son
1892	**Burslem Park**, Staffordshire, Mawson and James Pulham & Son
1892	**Bellevue Park**, Newport, South Wales, Mawson and James Pulham & Son
1896	**East Park**, Wolverhampton
1900?	**Beechwood Park**, Newport, South Wales
1902	**Abbey Road**, Barrow-in-Furness, Cumbria (work began 1907)
1902	**Hall-i'-the-Wood**, Bolton
1902	**Lever Park**, Bolton
1903	**Broomfield Park**, Southgate, London
1904	**Falinge Park**, Rochdale, Greater Manchester
1904	**Pittencrieff Park**, Dunfermline, Mawson & Partners, R.Mattocks
1905	**Sidney Park**, Cleethorpes, Humberside
1906	**Town gardens**, Lord Street, Southport (with C.E.Mallows)
1907	**Marine Lake, Park, and Promenade**, Southport, Lancashire (with C.E. Mallows)
1910	**Moor Park**, Herts, Thomas Mawson & Sons and Thomas Adams
1910	**Riverside Park and recreation ground**, Padiham, Burnley
1911–12	**Haslam Park**, Preston, Lancashire; further report 1915, Mawson and James Pulham & Son
1911	**West Park**, Wolverhampton
1912	**Grovelands Estate**, Southgate, London
1914	**King Edward Memorial Park**, Shadwell, London (not made)
1922	**Stanley Park**, Blackpool
1922–26	**Blackpool/Lytham/Lytham St Annes**: South Shore Extension, Ashton Marine Park, Mawson and James Pulham & Son
1923	**Marine garden**, Weston-super-Mare, Somerset
1931	**Plymouth Central Park**

Note: Pulham & Son may have been active in more of the sites than suggested here.

TOWN PLANNING COMMISSIONS – 1901–1933

DATE	COMMISSION
1901?	**Hest Bank**, Lancashire
1906	**Port Sunlight** for William Lever
1906 ?	**Chalfont St Giles**, Buckinghamshire, estate for Sir Henry Harben
1910/16	**Bolton**
1910	**Nelson**, Lancashire, design for a garden suburb on Haw Lea estate
1911	**Lakeside Improvement**, Windermere U.D.C, Mawson Brothers
1912	**Congleton**, Cheshire, estate for Union Bank, Manchester
1912	**Grovelands Estate**, town planning advisers for Southgate U.D.C.
1913/23	**Exeter of the Future**
1918	**Stepney Town Council** rehousing scheme and town development
1918	**Stornoway**, Isle of Lewis, designs for town, castle, factory
1919/25	**County Borough of Northampton**: Proposals for development and reconstruction
1922	**South Shore**, Blackpool, sea defences and town planning scheme; roads, golf course; Central Blackpool, T.H.Mawson & Son, Thomas Adams and Francis Wood
1922 /30	**Hastings and St Leonards**, Sussex, Thomas Mawson & Sons, Adams and Thompson
1924/5	**Weston-super-Mare**
1925	**Blackpool Town Planning Scheme**, T.H.Mawson & Sons
1927/37	**Report on Squires Gate holiday camp**, Lytham St Annes. Edward Prentice Mawson.

DATE	COMMISSION
1927	**Birmingham Civic Centre** competition
1927/31	**Southend-on-Sea**
1929	**Priory Estate**, Dudley
1931	**Bridlington of the Future**: Being a Report on a Comprehensive Development Scheme for the Town and Sea Front
1931	**Southend-on-Sea**, E.P.Mawson and Lakeland Nurseries Ltd.
1931	**Warberry Estate**, Torquay
1931	**Borough of Wood Green**
1932	**Kirkham Town Planning Scheme**
1932	**Ellesmere U.D.C.**, Port, Cheshire; drawn and checked by T.H.Mawson
1933	**Droitwich Development**
1933	**Leigh-on-Sea**

DATED FOREIGN COMMISSIONS: 1905-1932

DATE	COMMISSION	CLIENT
1905	**Brooklandwood**, Baltimore, USA (gardens)	H.Carroll Brown
1908	**The Peace Palace**, The Hague, Netherlands (landscape and gardens)	Andrew Carnegie
1908	**Angervilliers**, Paris (gardens)	Lazare Weiller
1908	**Hvidöre**, Copenhagen (gardens)	HM Queen Alexandra
1908	**Bennett Cottage**, Old Westbury, New York (gardens)	Mrs George Rose
1910	**Schloss Hessen**, Hamm, Prussia (gardens)	Baron von Boeslager
1912	**Coal Harbour**, Stanley Park, Vancouver (landscape)	Board of Parks Commissioners.
1912	**James Estate**, Victoria, B.Columbia (garden.suburb)	B.C. Electric Company
1912	**Meadlands Estate**, Victoria, B.Columbia (garden. suburb)	B.C.Electric Company
1912	**University of B.Columbia** (adviser on campus design)	Board of Governors, B.Columbia University
1912	**Saskatoon University** (campus and landscape)	Saskatoon University Board
1913	**Wascana plain and Lt-General's residence** (landscape)	City of Regina
1913	**Calgary** (town plan, university campus) Calgary (workers' suburbs Manchester & Connaught)	City of Calgary
1914	**Brockton Point, Vancouver** (park and lighthouse).	City of Vancouver
1914	**Borden Park** (suburb for Ottawa)	Great Eastern Realty Company
1914	**Dalhousie**, New Brunswick (university campus)	Dalhousie University
1914	**Banff** (as a tourist resort)	Dominion Parks Dept.
1913/14	**Athens**, new city plan, (park system, palace gardens, villa at Tatoi)	King Constantine of Greece
1914	**Corfu**, Villa Achilleon (garden) Corfu (afforestation	Kaiser Wilhelm II
1917	**Thessaloniki** (replanning post fire)	City of Athens
1917	**Thessaloniki** (garden city settlements)	Greek government
1918	**East Macedonia** (settelements and housing), John Mawson, head of reconstruction	City of Athens
1920	**Athens** (parks and boulevards)	City of Athens
1932	**Loutraki**, Peloponnese, Greece (Edward Prentice Mawson, hotel, casino, bathing beach)	

Index

Picture credits

Section I.—Dovecotes.

Dovecotes for Special Positions.

Dovecotes may be made most attractive features when nicely adapted to special positions, such as turrets, summerhouses and the like, or to fit into the gable ends of buildings.

The accompanying illustration shews a Dovecote

A DOVE COTE ON GARDEN WALL.

with brackets to stride a fruit wall.

On receipt of a photograph or sketch of the proposed position, we shall be very pleased to submit a drawing to intending purchasers shewing a Dovecote suitable for the particular requirements of the case.

The Rampholm Dovecote.

The Rampholm Dovecote is constructed of best quality pine, painted four coats and finished to customers' approved tint, with lead roof and square tapered post, out of 5 ins. x 5 ins. material, and contains eight nests, four on each floor.

Price complete ready for fixing in the ground £4 0 0

The Blakeholm Dovecote

A DOVE COTE

The Blakeholm Dovecote, constructed as above, and with eight nests, is roofed with small oak or elm shingles and provided with strutts at base to allow of fixing to paving, but can also be made with longer post for burying in the ground.

Price complete, painted, £5 0 0

Section 3.—Carriage Gates.

Speaking broadly, entrance gates must, to be effective, be designed to be in keeping with their surroundings, more especially where they form a part of a combined scheme for lodge and entrance. First impressions are nowhere so decisive in their effects as in a garden, and first impressions are obtained from the main entrance. We therefore only give below four representative drawings, and shall be most pleased to submit original designs for any stated opening, with prices, with or without piers, or to carry out the designs of architects, with every possible care as to the correct rendering of detail.

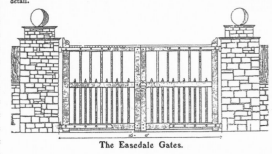

The Easedale Gates.

The Easedale Gates.

Price in pine, 2½ inches thick with 1¼ in. square bars, including wrought-iron hinges, handle and bolt, painted four coats. For 10 ft. opening, £8 15 0
Do. in oak: £10 5 0
Do. in oak with lead capping to top rail as shewn, £11 5 0

The Hawes Gate, 2½ ins. thick, with wrought-iron hinges, and drop handle, balusters in bottom half, and 1¼ in. square bars in deal, for 6 ft. opening, painted four coats and finished to approved tint £9 10 0

Same design but for carriage entrance, 10 feet opening: £11 10 0

The Hawes Gate.

Same design in oak, for 6 feet opening £10 10 0
   „   „   for carriage entrance, 10 feet opening, ... £14 0 0
Paling to Match with curved rail and interspaces filled in with 1½ in. square balusters, total height 5 feet, per yard £1 0 0
  do.   do.   in oak, per lineal yard £1 7 6

For Wrought Iron Gates see Section 12 (Antiques), page 27.

One of the features which contribute to the attractiveness of a garden is the Pergola, which is usually a portion of a walk bordered and canopied over, festooned with flowers, fruit, or greenery, supported on framework of wood, or occasionally supplemented with stone pillars. The framing may be as varied as the gardens themselves, and range from the rough unpeeled Larch posts and heads, to the neatly-squared posts painted or carbolinized, inserted in concrete sockets, with squared bars overhead crossing and recrossing, and perhaps a full substantial moulding running lengthwise along the head of the posts. There are many other ways of diversifying these pleasing features.

We are prepared to submit estimates on learning requirements for Trelliage Porches and Verandahs, suitable for Cottages and small Country Residences.

Rustic Pergola

erected by us near a tennis lawn to provide shade for chairs, tea tables, &c., in conjunction with tennis.

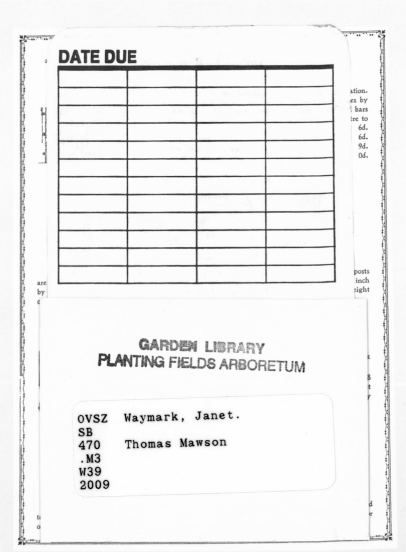